The Complete Idiot's Reference Card

Test Your Own Potential

On a scale of one to ten (ten being highest), evaluate your strengths and weaknesses regarding these entrepreneurial characteristics:

Capacity for work	_____
Goal-oriented	_____
A self-starter	_____
Good judgment	_____
Self-confidence	_____
Honesty	_____
Persistence	_____
A problem-solver	_____
Ability to take a risk	_____
People-oriented	_____
Profit-oriented	_____
Flexibility and adaptability	_____
Accountability	_____
Desire to win	_____
Innovative	_____
Total	_____

The value of this rating depends on the answer you have to one characteristic: honesty. If you haven't been totally honest with yourself in evaluating these factors, you should adjust the results accordingly. It is wiser to evaluate yourself too low than too high.

➤ If your score was between 120 and 150, you have a strong entrepreneurial personality and will probably do very well as the boss of a new business.

➤ If you scored between 100 and 120, you probably have enough of the right stuff to be successful if you make the effort to bolster your skills in the weaker areas.

➤ If you scored between 80 and 100, you probably shouldn't try to shoulder a new business on your own. Look for partners or reliable employees who can strengthen the firm in areas where you are weak.

➤ If you scored less than 80, you'll be happier and more successful as a manager in someone else's company than in a business of your own.

Reprinted with permission of the author, Roger Fritz, from Nobody Gets Rich Working for Somebody Else: An Entrepreneur's Guide. Dr. Fritz is president of Organization Development Consultants in Naperville, Illinois.

alpha books

Business Plan Outline

Executive Summary

Write this section last, so you can give a good 1–2 page overview of the plan as a whole.

Industry Analysis

Assume the banker or investor reading this plan knows nothing about your industry and try to give him a mini-education in this section: what the opportunities are, what's going on in the market, who the big players are, and how they have succeeded.

Market Analysis

Talk specifically about what's happening in your geographic market: what the opportunities are, who the competition is, how you can differentiate yourself from them, and how you will succeed, given market demands and trends.

Business Description

Describe your business: how long it has been in operation, what the legal structure is, who the owners are, what your short-term and long-term goals are, and why you need money now—is it for expansion, marketing, equipment purchase, or debt reduction?

The Competition

Explain how your business is better than the competition and why it will succeed.

Marketing Plan

Explain who your current customers are, who you would like to have as customers, why they would be interested in buying from you, what your pricing strategy is, how you distribute your product, and how you promote your business.

Operations

This section is most important in manufacturing operations, which have many different pieces of equipment and operational processes that need to be described. For service businesses, describe how your business is being run, what the departments are, and how you will be able to expand (by hiring, buying equipment, moving to a new location, outsourcing production, and so on).

Organization

Write a brief paragraph about each of your top managers, detailing their expertise and background. Include an organization chart and describe your plans for adding or subtracting staff members.

Funding Needs

Explain the total amount of money needed, how it will be used (such as for marketing materials, working capital, hiring, equipment purchase), and why that is the right way to spend it.

Financial Statements

This is where you place any past financial information, in the form of income statements and balance sheets, if your business is not a start-up. In addition, include five years of projections: balance sheets, income statements, and a five-year cash flow with monthly projections for the first three years and quarterly projections thereafter.

Appendix

This section should be used for important reference information that need not appear in the body of the plan. For instance, you may want to include a summary of a recent contract you won, a map of planned sites, resumes of key managers, or marketing literature.

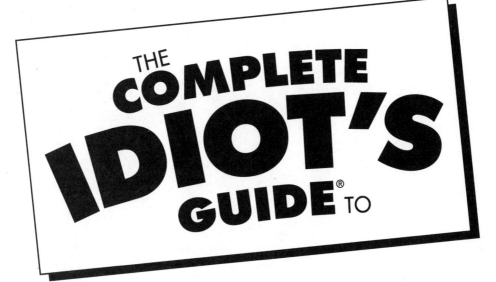

THE COMPLETE IDIOT'S GUIDE® TO

Starting Your Own Business

by Edward Paulson with Marcia Layton

alpha books

A Division of Macmillan General Reference
A Simon & Schuster Macmillan Company
1633 Broadway, New York, NY 10019-6785

Successful business owners and leaders praise the first edition of
***The Complete Idiot's Guide to Starting Your Own Business*:**

"The information in this book isn't just for beginning entrepreneurs. There's great advice for people looking to grow and expand their existing business, too. This book should be on every Microsoft Solution Provider's bookshelf."—Susan J. Hanneld, Executive Director, Association of Microsoft Solution Providers, Houston, TX

"I applied a number of concepts and practices detailed in this fine book to my start-up high-tech business. A must read text for entrepreneurs."—Uday O. Pabrai, Founder, Net Guru Technologies, Oak Brook, IL

"The first day on the job of your new business should be spent reading this one-of-a-kind guide to launching your new venture. Paulson's advice provides practical, relevant strategies to the most important issues facing every small business founder."—Dan McManus, founder and president, McManus Group, Sapulpa, OK

"If you dream about running your own business, don't bother reading this book. But if you are past the dreaming stage and need help making your business happen, it's a great read."—Richard A. Enger, founder and owner, Strata Systems, Atlanta, GA

"Ed Paulson's book does an excellent job of bringing home fundamental financial concepts to the beginner in an easy-to-follow, entertaining format."—Kenneth G. Daemicke, principal, Mulcahy, Pauritsch, Salvador and Co., Ltd., Hinsdale, IL

"This book answers your business questions and is a great resource for anyone who's starting up their dream. The price of the book is saved on what you now won't have to spend on accounting and lawyer advice."—Frank Warner, founder and president, Electronic Script Prompting, Clarendon Hills, IL

"This book is ideal for anyone contemplating starting a business."—Gary M. Cadenhead, PhD, Senior Lecturer in Entrepreneurship, The University of Texas at Austin, Austin, TX

"Anyone starting a business must read this book first. It is a concise, easy-to-understand guide that will save time and money. I recommend it to my business clients."—Geraldine J. Tucker, Attorney and Consultant, Law Office of Geraldine J. Tucker, Austin, TX

"When I graduated from school I believe that I received about 45 minutes on the business aspects of practice. *The Complete Idiot's Guide To Starting Your Own Business* is what is needed and wanted. At the very least, it should be used as a referral to help make those tough early decisions."—Richard C. Gelband, owner and chiropractor, Gelband Chiropractic, Naperville, IL

"I am a business book junky, but I am also fairly selective about what I read. This book was great. It was simple, easy-to-read and right to the point. I only wish I could have read it BEFORE I started my company."—Sam Goodner, president and co-founder, Catapult Systems Corporation, Austin, TX

To my parents, John and Jean Paulson, and my wife Loree, for their continued support of me and my writing.

©1998 Alpha Books

Macmillan Publishing books may be purchased for business or sales promotional use. For information please write: Special Markets Department, Macmillan Publishing USA, 1633 Broadway, New York, NY 10019

International Standard Book Number: 0-02-861979-X
Library of Congress Catalog Card Number: 98-84503

01   00   99   98   4   3

Interpretation of the printing code: the rightmost number of the first series of numbers is the year of the book's printing; the rightmost number of the second series of numbers is the number of the book's printing. For example, a printing code of 98-1 shows that the first printing occurred in 1998.

Printed in the United States of America

Alpha Development Team

Publisher
Kathy Nebenhaus

Editorial Director
Gary M. Krebs

Managing Editor
Bob Shuman

Marketing Brand Manager
Felice Primeau

Senior Editor
Nancy Mikhail

Development Editors
Phil Kitchel
Jennifer Perillo
Amy Zavatto

Editorial Assistant
Maureen Horn

Production Team

Production Editor
Donna Wright

Copy Editor
Kris Simmons

Illustrator
Jody P. Schaeffer

Designer
Glenn Larsen

Cover Designer
Mike Freeland

Photo Editor
Richard H. Fox

Indexer
Chris Barrick

Layout/Proofreading
Angela Calvert
Kim Cofer
Mary Hunt

Contents at a Glance

Contents

4 Preparing Your Business Plan   51

Part 2: Establishing the Framework of Your Business   69

5 Structuring Your Business   71

xi

Foreword

Owning your own business is the epitome of the American dream, the ultimate expression of your professional talents, and the most rewarding work experience you can achieve. It is invigorating, interesting, and may be quite financially rewarding. It can also be scary, challenging, and very complicated.

New entrepreneurs often have no idea how to launch their businesses. Where do you start? How do you work with a bank? Do you need to be on the Internet? What do you need to know about the IRS and employer taxes? What makes a good sales and marketing plan? How can computers help you? These and other crucially important questions are addressed in *The Complete Idiot's Guide to Starting Your Own Business, Second Edition*.

Not everyone succeeds in their own business. As a veteran of business start-ups, Ed Paulson has learned the hard way what it takes to both succeed and fail. In this book, he identifies the unique issues you'll face and shows you how to overcome the challenges. He also provides real stories of how owning a business has both positively and negatively impacted new business owners. His simple and easy-to-read descriptions of complicated business matters will provide you with a comprehensive understanding of the terms, issues, strategies, and challenges associated with creating a successful new business.

As an entrepreneur, I'm familiar with the potential pitfalls of starting a business. The two most negative traits I've seen among unsuccessful business owners are having unrealistic expectations of what it means to own a business and not paying enough attention to customers. Some business owners are so driven by the allure of owning their own business that they ignore the need to raise enough capital, work long hours, or exercise the discipline to control their expenses. Another kind of unsuccessful business owner is so certain of what customers want that they never ask for customer feedback or adjust when the customers don't react as expected. This book will help steer you away from these pitfalls.

On the other hand, the two most common positive traits I've observed among successful business owners is the willingness to work hard and to continually strive to work smart. You *must* be willing to work long hours to get your business off the ground. Every one of your competitors is already ahead of you and will be working hard to stay ahead. However, working long hours isn't enough. You have to work *smarter* than your competition. You have to use your time as efficiently and productively as possible. This requires a well rounded understanding of all the issues impacting your business, so you can prioritize your time, money, and resources appropriately. In this book, Ed shows you how.

As a successful entrepreneur, I can attest to the various benefits associated with having your own business. For me personally, the greatest benefit of owning a business has been the overwhelming sense of personal satisfaction and pride derived from knowing I created something from nothing, something that provides more value to my customers, my employees, and my pocketbook than can be found anywhere else. I only wish I had read this book before starting my first venture. It would have saved me a lot of time and money.

—Peter Squier

Peter J. Squier is founder of Squier Computer Services, Inc. and a co-founder of Productivity Point International, a computer training company with over 100 locations and sales of $200 million. Peter was a Finalist in the Austin, Texas region for the Ernst & Young Entrepreneur of the Year award in 1995 and 1997.

Introduction

You have an idea. You have a vision. You are willing to put your butt on the line to make it happen. Your family is starting to wonder if you have a chemical imbalance in your brain, and the word is out that enthusiasm has entered your life. Okay, this is great, but you don't know where to begin—and you feel like a complete idiot.

Tens of thousands of readers have taken the step you just took. They opened this book, flipped through the pages, and saw enough of value to purchase it and turn it into one of their business tools. I am pleased to welcome you to the pages of this second edition of *The Complete Idiot's Guide to Starting Your Own Business*.

I added a few things to the first book to make it even more valuable to you and your business. But the overall goal of this book remains the same: I want you to succeed!

Within these pages, you'll find the most accurate information on the legal, financial, and operational requirements of starting a business. I added a few new chapters that show you how to use the Internet effectively, how to transact business internationally in a risk-free environment, and how to prepare your production plans. These chapters come from reader feedback, and I thank you for letting me know what needs to be done to keep this book progressively more valuable.

Starting your own business is a lot more complicated than any of us initially realize. It helps to know that you are not alone in your thoughts, desires, fears, and ecstasy. This book was written with the intention of guiding you through the pitfalls and sharing in your successes. Great pains were taken to distill the "mumbo-jumbo" of business down to the basic ingredients that everyone can understand. No critical information was left out.

In this book, I start with you and your motivations. You are the key ingredient in any successful start-up, scary as that might sound. You are your most valuable asset. Who else will work evenings, weekends, and holidays for free? The more you know about you and your motivations, the more likely you are to create a successful business venture.

I have been part of several start-up companies, including a few of my own, and I know there is nothing more exciting than seeing your idea become a thriving reality—and there are few things more painful than letting it die. I learned a lot of lessons along the way, which I hope to pass on to you. You don't have to go through a windshield to learn to wear a seat belt. I've already been through several business "windshields" and the thoughts and ideas in this book can be your seat belt. Take them to heart and apply them where appropriate.

In short, this book not only leads you through the business creation process, but also serves as your mentor as your business comes to life. You will probably keep this book in your desk, near the throne, or on a night stand as a cure for insomnia.

Creation is a uniquely human trait and is not limited to the arts. I had an artist in one of my seminars apologize for her narrow-minded view of business. She thought of art as creative and business as uncreative. After the seminar, she realized that a new business creates job opportunities that didn't exist before. It creates new products and services that perform useful functions. It fulfills dreams for those involved in its success, and each business is a unique reflection of its owner, just like works of art.

You are on the verge of a wonderful roller-coaster ride where you decide the direction of the track and the speed of the cart. Use this book to pick the optimal track layout, and then apply our management philosophy to successfully steer the cart.

I want you to be successful in your new venture. It breaks my heart to talk with entrepreneurs who took the risk, put it all on the line, and lost. If I can talk you out of starting your company in a few chapters, then you really didn't want it badly enough. If you get through the first few chapters and still want to be a business owner, then finish the rest of the book and make your business idea happen! You clearly have strong entrepreneurial tendencies.

If you knew everything that would happen in the future, you probably wouldn't do anything. You will certainly feel more of yourself come to life as your idea unfolds, and if you are *really* lucky, you will never have to worry about financial freedom again. It will be yours in abundance and well deserved. Is that wonderful, or what? All of a sudden, you don't feel like such an idiot, do you?

From one idiot to another, it is a privilege to be invited along with you on your ride. Bon voyage!

How to Use This Book

The book is divided into five parts. The sequence is designed to lead you through the business plan creation and start-up management process step-by-step:

Part 1, "So, You Want to Start a Business," asks you to take a hard look at you, your motivations, and your personal situation. Are you ready to pay the price needed to get your business up and running? Is your family ready? If the answer is still yes, then get into things by comparing short-term gains with long-term wins. Finally, this part includes a business plan outlined with references to a sample business plan included in Appendix A, "The Kwik Chek Auto Evaluation Business Plan."

After finishing Part 1, you either will believe that starting your business is the right thing to do or will realize that you aren't ready yet. Either way is fine, but you will know what awaits you if you decide to take the plunge. You'll also understand the basic components of the business plan, and you will be ready to create your own plan.

Part 2, "Establishing the Framework of Your Business," presents the legal aspects of business formation. This part introduces various legal business structures, such as sole proprietorships, partnerships, and corporations, with special emphasis on corporations. It's kind of dry but critically important. Take the time to read this part because it truly lays the foundation upon which everything else is built. The benefits you get from this section alone will pay for the price of the book.

Part 3, "Marketing Magic and Successful Sales," talks about pricing, advertising, competition, and sales. These four chapters are a lot of fun and provide a welcome relief from the legal stuff in Part 2. I also added a special section dealing with the Internet so that you understand the valuable impact that this technology will have on your business. Living here for awhile is time well spent. Wear shorts and bring the suntan lotion: This topic area can be pretty hot!

Part 4, "Facing Your Financials," or delving into the structured mind of the accountant, presents the essence of financial management. These chapters introduce accounting and financial terminology in an understandable way (a really tough thing to do... trust me!) while making you credible in your presentation to bankers and other financial people. These chapters deal with banks, cash flow management, credit card sales, credit-oriented transactions, and avoiding payment delinquency with your clients. A special chapter was added here to cover the international business that you will receive as a result of using the Internet. Read this chapter and be prepared for the coming international explosion.

Part 5, "Growing Your Business," covers stuff you will need when you are up and running, along with a special chapter on outlining your production plans. When you add people to your organization and begin to move out of the "sink-or-swim" stage, all kinds of things change. Success creates its own set of problems that can also cause your undoing; reading these chapters will prepare you for the typical major crisis points. For sure, read Chapter 17, "Help Wanted: Adding Employees," and Chapter 18, "The Tax Files: Payroll Taxes," before hiring employees.

In addition, I included several appendixes to give you further sources of insight and information. Appendix A contains a complete business plan that I wrote but never used because it didn't meet my personal objectives. It's a real plan that some of you might choose to try. Go ahead! It would be great to see it making someone money. Most importantly, it presents you with a concrete starting point for your plan.

Appendixes B, C, and D offer you further resources to contact, references to read, and a handy glossary of business buzzwords.

Extras

To guide you through the minefields of starting your own business, this book also provides additional tips and bits of information from those who have been there. You'll find words of wisdom, cautions, and helpful tips in these boxes:

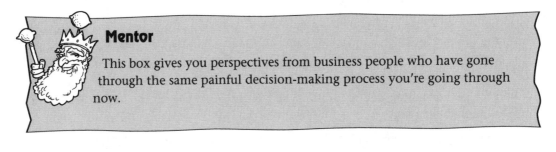

Mentor

This box gives you perspectives from business people who have gone through the same painful decision-making process you're going through now.

Business Tip
This box shows you interesting information, shortcuts, and helpful advice.

Business Buzzword
This sidebar defines technical business terms for you.

Bankruptcy Alert
This box provides warnings to let you know about pitfalls along the way.

Trademarks

Terms suspected of being trademarks or service marks have been appropriately capitalized. Alpha Books cannot attest to the accuracy of this information. Use of a term in this book should not be regarded as affecting the validity of any trademark or service mark.

Acknowledgments

There are numerous people to acknowledge and thank for their contributions to this second edition. Here is a partial list of people who provided vision, comment, inspiration, talent, and information that made this book more than it would have been.

Thank you, Alpha Books and Macmillan, for your success with the *Complete Idiot's* series and for your commitment to this second edition. Thank you, Gary Krebs, for keeping the wheels moving while we feverishly wrote. Thank you, Marcia Layton, for not only enhancing my original manuscript but also becoming a valued business ally in the second edition and beyond. Thank you to Jennifer Perillo for your production talents and insights, the tech editors, and the other members of the production staff for adding the final touches that make this product special.

There is a lifetime of experience and thank-yous that go out to everyone whom I have worked with over the years. Here are several people who contributed to this work in specific ways: Frank Warner for being the incurable entrepreneur that he is; Dick Holmes (alias "Wilson") for general business; Raymond Luckie for accounting; Dave Stanfield for marketing and sales; Jeff Fuller for a banker's perspective; Mark Fern for sports retail; and Jeannie Letteff for restaurant retail. War stories were provided by Jim Cameron, Bill Cartmill, Dave Kalstrom, Jeff Kolling, Jim Herlinger, Ted Keane, Al Shugart, and Dr. An Wang, among others.

How-to-do, and not-do, insight was provided by various people from GenRad, Plantronics, Seagate, NuTech Testing Services, DAVID Systems (DSI ExpressNet), Telenova, IBM, Wang Laboratories, AT&T, and others. If you are not mentioned here, please accept my apologies along with a thank-you for the contribution you know that you made.

My sincere personal appreciation is given to the following people for their assistance in making this second edition a more valuable business tool for its readers: my wife, Loree, for nonstop support and nudging, Dan McManus for being an idea sounding board and reality check, Ken Daemicke for his assistance with the financial chapters, Gerry Tucker for keeping me out of legal hot water, and Cindy Stephens and the folks at Firstar Bank of Naperville, IL, for their assistance with the banking chapter.

A final thank-you goes to you, the reader. Without your ambition and desire to excel, books like this would not be needed. I salute your passion for creation and your desire for something better. You keep me in touch with my own entrepreneurial spirit, and I hope this book returns some of that enthusiasm to you.

Special Thanks to the Technical Reviewer

The Complete Idiot's Guide to Starting Your Own Business, Second Edition was reviewed by an expert who double-checked the accuracy of what you'll learn here, to help us ensure that this book gives you everything you need to know about starting your own business. My special thanks are extended to Terri Lonier.

Terri Lonier is the nation's leading expert on solo entrepreneurs. Her award-winning Working Solo resources—including books, audiotape, Web site (http://www.working-solo.com), monthly e-mail newsletter, and seminars—offer information and inspiration to thousands of solo entrepreneurs worldwide. Working Solo was chosen as the number one book for solo entrepreneurs by *Inc.* magazine.

A successful entrepreneur since 1978, Lonier is an in-demand business speaker on entrepreneurial topics and a frequent media guest. Her work has been featured in *The New York Times, Wall Street Journal, Inc., Fast Company, Business Week*, and other leading business publications as well as on CNBC, CNN/fn, and radio programs nationwide. She was honored as the keynote speaker at the First International Conference of Women in Business in Tokyo.

Part 1
So, You Want to Start a Business

So you think you can be a successful entrepreneur? Well, you can do it. Yes, you read that right; I'm agreeing with you. You can be successful at starting your own business if you take the time up front to do some very important things.

One of those things is choosing the right kind of business to start. Each of us has different skills, interests, and abilities. To give yourself a fighting chance, you need to do some honest self-analysis to determine what kind of business would be best for you. Once you know what kind of business you'd like to start, you need to figure out whether you can make money in this business of yours. You also need to create a plan for starting and running it.

Sounds like a lot of stuff to do, doesn't it? Well, don't worry; this first section is going to help you with all of it.

Why Start Your Own Business?

Bill and his friend were walking through a mall doing some last-minute holiday shopping. In one store, on the second shelf in the back, Bill saw the dual-pronged, slotted trammel-widget-thingy that he had drawn on a cocktail napkin at a company party three years ago. Everyone had agreed that it was a great idea and that Bill should "make it happen."

"I had that idea years ago," said Bill. "I can't believe that somebody is going to make a fortune from my idea. I'll never forgive myself if this thing turns out to make him a million dollars. I should sue him for stealing my idea."

"Why didn't you pursue the idea back when you had it?" asked his friend supportively, but knowing that he was on dangerous ground.

"I had just gotten married and had just received my promotion at work. There was so much going on back then that I never took the time to make it happen. I still have the napkin in my desk drawer at work. Now look at this. Someone is going to make a fortune off my idea. This will never happen to me again. The next idea I have, I'm going to make it happen. After all, I'm in my forties. If not now, then when?"

Have you ever had an experience like Bill's? Did it make you think that you should rush into self-employment as quickly as possible before missing out on other opportunities?

While many people have done just that—rushed to start their own business—I hope that perhaps you'll put off that decision for a short while, until after you've done an analysis of your own situation and goals to determine whether that's really the smartest move. Maybe now is the time for you…or maybe not. Hold off on making any quick decisions one way or another for a few more pages. (Okay, if you can't wait until after you read this book, at least wait until after Chapter 3 "Plan to Win the War.")

Journeys always start at the beginning, which is why we start our discussion with you: your interests, your motivations, and your goals. You must understand your own motivations first in order to decide whether starting your own business will bring you happiness or grief. Believe it or not, not everyone is meant to be an entrepreneur. There are plenty of people who prefer working for someone else. (In fact, some people are better off working for someone else.)

Next, looking at your skills and experience will help you choose what kind of business you should start. And finally, taking into consideration what people want and need will help you decide what kind of business can make money. (I'm making a big assumption here that you *do* want to make lots of money.)

You'll quickly learn that it's extremely easy to start a business. All you have to do is fill out some forms and you're set. However, starting a business that makes money is much more difficult, and you will need help to make decisions that will be both fulfilling and profitable.

What Are Your Motivations?

Just as there is a thin line between love and hate, there is a thin line between masochism and tenacity. If you're having trouble distinguishing between the two, you may want to have a chat with your therapist.

The following sections discuss several of the common situations that lead people to start their own businesses. Think about whether any are similar to your own situation. If you're in the game for the right reasons, you will have one of the most exciting rides of your life. If you're in it for the wrong reasons, you will probably not succeed, and even if you do succeed, it will probably be a hollow victory. Brutal honesty with yourself is the key here as you decide whether this is really for you. Only you know when you are being honest with yourself, and nobody has more to gain from your honesty at this stage than you.

Situational factors such as the amount of money you have, the contacts that you've made, and your expertise in a particular industry are all important to success. But their importance is dwarfed in comparison to the burning desire that you must have to make your business venture succeed. You can always make changes to your business once you start it, but you can't buy burning desire. It has to be there from the start. Otherwise, you're at a severe disadvantage.

If you're considering starting a business because you've had difficulty finding a full-time job that interests you or meets your financial goals, DON'T. Starting a business is not the same thing as creating a job for yourself. Starting a business means that you're ready to give up that regular paycheck, benefits, regular working hours, bureaucracy, clueless coworkers, and policies that make no sense. But I digress….

A business is much more than a job; it's a serious commitment to your customers who will rely on you and to your employees who depend on you to provide their paychecks. Your success or failure doesn't just affect you and your family; many others will feel it, too.

If you're currently employed and thinking about quitting to start a business, don't give up the stability of your day job until you feel confident you'll be able to replace that income in the near future. Starting a business while you're still employed is an excellent way to "test the waters." Once you jump in, you have to be ready to work hard to keep your head above water. Be sure you have the interest and the stamina.

Why Do People Start Their Own Businesses?

Running your own small business is tougher work than anything you have tried before, but it also offers rewards that are generally greater than your current employer can give you. Here is a partial list of common reasons why people decide to start their own businesses:

➤ **Adventure**   They like taking risks.

➤ **Bureaucracy**   They feel it's too hard to accomplish anything in their current job because every decision becomes a political issue.

➤ **Creativity**   They have a great idea for a new product or service that no one is currently offering.

➤ **Competition**   They feel they can do what their current company does but for less money.

➤ **Control**   They want to be their own boss and make their own decisions about their future.

➤ **Earning potential**   They want to be paid for the extra effort they give to their work. They'd rather work more and have the chance to be paid more.

➤ **Flexibility**   They want a schedule that allows them to spend time with their families and work when they want to.

➤ **Fair wages** They feel they aren't paid what they are worth in their current job, and if they worked on their own, they'd make more money.

➤ **Freedom** They want to be able to decide for themselves when, how, and where they complete their work.

Are these valid motivations? Yes. The need to exercise your own judgment, take your own risks, and create something from nothing can be profound. You may want financial independence to provide the freedom to do things with your life that you couldn't do otherwise. You may have an idea that nobody at work supports or thinks is a good idea. If you believe in the idea strongly enough, you have to try it yourself or you will always wonder how it would have turned out.

Mentor

When I (Marcia) decided that I wanted to write business plans for smaller companies in need of financing, I spoke with local businesspeople to see what they thought of the idea. No one liked it. They all had reasons why I wouldn't succeed: "Entrepreneurs don't have money to spend on a business plan," "They can do it themselves by reading a book; why would they hire you?" and so on.

The more people I asked, the more I heard about the lack of business available. On the other hand, I was hearing that government agencies were overloaded with business plan work, suggesting that there really was a need for this kind of assistance. So I started my business anyway.

I started my business simply because the thought of continuing to work for someone else looked a lot like going to prison. I needed to exercise my creative and technical talents in ways that were just not possible in the professional positions I held.

The critics were wrong, or at least, they've been wrong so far. The business is growing at a double-digit pace with more clients signing on each week. The lesson is: If you are convinced your idea will work, you may be right even if no one else agrees.

On the other hand, if everyone you know is telling you that there simply isn't any need for your new product or service and you can find no other evidence to the contrary, hold off starting a company. The point is, pay more attention to what's going on in your market than what skeptics think.

But understand that although you might not report to a supervisor, you will still be working for someone else: your clients and customers. But you will also be working to achieve your own dreams, not those of your employer. You provide the energy, vision, and sustenance that keep the dream alive and strong. You also need determination and dedication to keep going when the going gets tough.

People who start their own businesses, or *entrepreneurs*, are a strange breed. They will give up almost anything to have the right to make their own choices, decisions, opportunities, and mistakes—even when they know that many of those choices and decisions may turn out to be bad ones. Hey, at least they had the power to make them!

> **Business Buzzword**
> An **entrepreneur** is an individual who starts and runs his or her own business, rather than remain an employee of someone else's company.

> **Mentor**
>
> All business owners fantasize about giving up the administrative hassles of running a business from time-to-time. I'll even admit to fantasizing about a mindless job counting screws in a hardware store every once in a while!
>
> A few years ago, when things were on a downturn with my business, I was talking with a fellow entrepreneur. When she asked how things were going, I said, "They are pretty bad right now, and I think some radical changes are due." She asked, "Are you thinking of getting a job?" I smiled and said, "No," to which she replied, "Then things aren't that bad."

When an entrepreneur starts to talk seriously about getting a job working for someone else, you know things must be pretty bad. But business owners who are committed to reaching their goals don't throw in the towel so easily. What often happens at those low points is that entrepreneurs come up with a really creative solution that helps turn things around. The need for money often forces those creative juices to flow!

If you don't feel that level of passion about your venture, then you should reevaluate your plans to become a business owner. If you have doubts about your motivations, then this is probably not your time to take the plunge. Wait until the need to work on your own becomes unbearable; then you know you're ready to start your own business.

Do You Have What It Takes?

Before you start your business, you'll want to be sure that you have a solid foundation in every major aspect of business management, or make friends with good people who do. (Pizza and beer is often a form of entrepreneurial currency.)

In their book, *Do It Right: Essentials for Success*, written and designed by Marcia Rosen of Rosen and Associates LTD and Lucy Rosen of The Business Development Group, the Rosens provide a number of checklists to help you, the potential business owner, learn more about your strengths and weaknesses. But what you'll also find is that the skills and personal characteristics on their list are also traits of successful entrepreneurs. Take a look at the following lists to see how you do. How many of these traits do you already possess?

My work style is:

___ Action-oriented

___ Highly organized

___ Energetic

___ Steady

___ Goal-oriented

___ Decisive

___ Hard-working

___ Determined and persistent

I'd describe myself as:

___ Dependable

___ Sensitive/perceptive

___ A calculated risk-taker

___ Self-motivated

___ Cooperative

___ Outgoing

___ Flexible

___ Resourceful

___ Dynamic

___ Curious

___ Alert to problems and opportunities

I have the following interpersonal skills:

___ Good leader

___ Good in a crisis

___ Intuitive/insightful

___ Supportive of others

___ Good communicator

___ Good boundary-setter

___ Able to compromise

___ Willing to ask for help

These are my practical skills:

___ Smart about money

___ Good problem-solver

___ Street-smart

___ Good troubleshooter

___ Possess sales ability

___ Possess bookkeeping ability

___ Able to juggle many tasks

___ Able to see both the big picture and small details

___ Good writer

___ Good at follow-through

___ Creative/artistic

___ Original thinker

___ Possess research ability

___ Possess computer know-how

___ Strategic thinker

If you find that you have 50 percent or more of the personal characteristics or skills on these lists, you have a solid foundation for becoming a successful entrepreneur. And if you find that you may be lacking in some areas, that doesn't mean you have to give up your dream. It does mean that you have to surround yourself with other people—partners, consultants, or employees—who can help you out in those areas.

Setting—and Reaching—Your Goals

Starting and running a business involves continuous learning. A lot of learning occurs from mistakes that you make along the way and vow never to repeat. Other learning comes from interactions you have with customers, fellow business owners, and friends, who lead you toward success. You set the pace at which you want to learn based on how open you are to new ideas and suggestions you hear from employees, clients, and colleagues. The faster you can adapt, and adopt, what you've learned, the quicker your business will meet your goals.

Some goals that you may set for yourself may involve:

➤ How much money your company will make each year

➤ How much money you'll earn as the owner

➤ How many hours you'll work each week, and how many hours will be spent with your family

➤ What percentage of your time will be spent traveling

➤ The number of customers you'll do business with the first year

➤ How fast your company will grow

➤ The number of employees you'll have on staff

➤ At what age you'll retire to a Caribbean island

As you begin to make decisions about becoming a business owner, you'll want to think about setting goals such as these to help you.

Keep in mind that committing your goals to paper will actually help you reach them. Once your targets are on paper, you can refer to them regularly to track your progress, change them as your company's situation changes, and use them to help keep everyone on your staff focused on what's truly important for your success as a company. Make writing your goals down a top priority.

When setting personal goals, be as specific as possible. Don't say that you want to earn "a decent living." Instead, state that you plan to take home $75,000 your second year in business. The more specific you can be, the easier it is to design a plan to reach those goals.

For example, you can plan several ways to earn that $75,000. You can calculate approximately how many customers you'll need to win, or how many products you'll need to sell, as well as how many employees you'll need to hire.

Business Tip
Set specific goals. With a specific goal as your target, it's often easier to move ahead—you have something concrete that you're working toward. Now you just need to figure out HOW to achieve that goal you've set for your business.

How is this for a great goal? "To reach $200,000 in sales with a profit before tax of 20 percent within 18 months."

So what if you don't make the goal? It depends on how much you are off. If you are over your goal early, pop the champagne and congratulate yourself. If you are at $160,000 in sales with a 25 percent profit before tax, then you still took home some money and you are doing something right. Set your next goal and move on.

If you are at $65,000 in sales and $20,000 in the red, it may be time to reassess your goal, or even consider returning to your day job.

Start with a goal you feel is realistic and work backwards, developing smaller goals along the way that will help you hit your target. Be realistic and optimistic or you can get discouraged if you don't reach your goals. Set goals you can win.

In the following sections, we'll look at specific goals you may set for yourself and your business.

Financial Motivations and Goals

How much money do you *want* to make, and how much money do you *need* to make? Understand that these two amounts are not the same. I've never met anyone who made as much money as they wanted, but most people make as much money as they need. It all comes down to how well they manage the money that they make.

Wealth is a relative term. If you make $100,000 per year and spend $110,000, you are living beyond your means. Most people would consider you poor. However, if you make $65,000 and spend $50,000, then you're saving or investing $15,000 a year. Over the course of just a few years, you would be considered very wealthy.

Business Buzzword
Wealth means consistently having money left over after you pay all your bills.

In short, don't just calculate how much money you want to bring in; also look at what it costs to live your current lifestyle. Calculate how much money you need to cover all your living expenses. You'll also have to account for the expenses associated with your business—federal taxes, state taxes, health insurance, life insurance, tuition assistance programs, vacation time, and so on. (I'll cover these expenses in more detail in Part 4, "Facing Your Financials.")

The total of your minimum living costs and fixed business expenses is the amount you need to earn to live as comfortably as you are living now. You have to make at least this amount of money or one of the following three things must happen:

1. You decrease your expenses.
2. You figure out a way to make more money from your venture.
3. You stay with your current job until your finances are in order.

Look at your finances both on a short-term (12 months) and long-term (2 to 5 years) basis. First, you need to get through the short term to make it to the long term. If you do not have the money to support yourself for at least 12 months (some say 18 to 24 months), then you should hold off starting your venture until you have the needed savings. Or you can look for outside sources to provide the money you need, such as family members, friends, or banks and government agencies. You need to be able to support yourself during those initial lean months when your business probably will not be making enough to pay your rent or your mortgage. So start saving those pennies now.

You should also consider how much money you're willing to invest before you pull the plug on a business that is a cash drain. You may go to Las Vegas determined to stop gambling after you lose $500. Likewise, you should set a limit for how much you're willing to invest in a new business.

Putting your limit in writing up front can help you make the decision to shut your business down if and when the time comes. It's hard to set limits, but doing it up front can save you a lot of time and money.

Most people dream of running their own businesses because they believe that it's the only way they'll become wealthy. For some, this is true. Most of the extremely wealthy members of our society obtained their money by owning a business, either one they started or were given. In many cases, they saw an opportunity to introduce a new product or service to the market and jumped in quickly. Some have succeeded and made millions, even billions. How about Bill Gates of Microsoft, Debbie Fields of Mrs. Fields' cookies, or even Henry Ford?

In their book *The Millionaire Next Door*, authors Thomas Stanley and William Danko suggest that owning a business is one strategy for becoming wealthy. In fact, of the millionaires they studied for their book who were still working, two-thirds of them were self-employed. That figure is well above the national average for self-employment, which is closer to 20 percent.

Not everyone who starts a business becomes wealthy. Statistics suggest that only 20 percent of all new businesses will be around in five years. Generally, when a business fails, the owner doesn't make a lot of money on the deal. The average business owner makes somewhere around $30,000 to $40,000 a year in salary. That may not sound bad to some of you, but just keep in mind the number of hours entrepreneurs have to put in to make that money. It's hard work!

Also look at the amount of money you will invest to get the business up and running. You may have to work for a significant length of time without taking a salary. If you reach that point and still can't afford to pay yourself a reasonable wage, it's time to decide whether this particular business is right for you. Your enthusiasm might be pointed in the wrong direction. Shifting your focus to a new business may be the key that opens your financial door!

Family Motivations and Goals

If you are the type of person who cannot leave your family alone for the evening or weekend without intense feelings of guilt, then you should examine your intentions and your family's needs before you begin a new business venture. Without your family's support, it will be difficult for you to succeed. There will be times when you will need to work at night, on weekends, and on holidays. At these times, you will have to choose between family involvement and business commitments. Your family needs to accept your commitment to your business without being hurt or angry.

Communicate openly with your spouse, children, parents, or friends about what you want to do and what kind of a time and energy commitment it will take. It's a good idea to prepare them in advance for some of the sacrifices that you and they may have to make. And make sure they're willing to make those sacrifices!

If you sense from initial discussions that your family may resent your directing attention away from them and toward a business, think about ways that you can involve them in the company. Instead of thinking that you have to choose between business and family, talk with them about what you can all do together to run a business. Putting your children on the payroll may be a savvy tax strategy to consider. In addition, making your spouse an employee may enable you to pay for your family's health insurance through the company. It's definitely something to look into.

Mentor

I recently saw a friend who has a company that makes metal stamps. He travels around the country selling the copper stamps used for imprinting on wax or a conventional ink stamp pad. It was the Christmas rush, and he had been working a steady 7 a.m. to 11 p.m. day since before Thanksgiving. In fact, his final sale day was Christmas Eve at 11 p.m. His wife was attending the craft shows with him, and the children often came along for the ride. His father had even come over from England to work in the shop making the stamps. In short, the entire family was pulling for the success of the business. He looked vibrant, healthy, and happy. So did his wife.

Imagine how different this scenario would be if the family waited at home grumbling about how their Christmas was being disrupted by dad's obsession.

Many divorces have resulted from the feeling that the business is more important than everything else in the business owner's life. Be sure your family knows that this is not the case. Typically, just telling them won't do it; you have to show them by setting aside time to be with them.

Spend the time to get your family involved from the beginning. Set their expectations properly to best avoid having recurring, ugly scenes later. Your family can become a source of strength if they understand the importance of their support in your and the business' success. Nobody is an island, and you may end up alone snuggling your checkbook if you don't handle your family situation with respect.

What Are Your Spiritual Goals?

Spirituality has more to do with what makes us feel good as human beings than with formal religion. For some of us, a business helps us achieve spiritual goals through the belief that by providing a valued service to our clients, we are improving their lives. Spiritual goals can also be reached by creating an organization to perform social service work, such as a food kitchen or a halfway house. Some entrepreneurs want to create an organization where their employees can realize their full potential.

Mentor

One of my clients is determined to start her own business, but not for any of the reasons we've discussed so far. She has enough money to support herself and has started businesses before, but she now wants to start one to bring new attention to the plight of people in recovery for alcohol or substance abuse. Her belief is that by creating products to better meet the needs of this group, she can draw attention to and help support them, donating the bulk of the profits to related charities and human service agencies. Like many other entrepreneurs, she is dedicated to her business idea; she just happens to be doing it for spiritual reasons.

If you are someone who believes making money is bad, then there is a strong chance you won't make any and your business will fail. If you believe that computer automation is the root of all evil, then you should probably avoid becoming a personal computer dealer. However, if you believe that training people is the most important way to contribute to the quality of their lives, then starting a training business would be a viable option.

In essence, don't neglect the nonbusiness side of your soul when deciding to start your own business. In fact, there are many people who believe that you should look here first.

What Is Your Ultimate Motivation?

Ultimately, it all comes down to you. What do you want and why do you want it? Do you think that running your own business will give you the fulfillment that's been missing in your current job? Are you willing to earn less money for a while as you try to establish your company? How far are you willing to go to make your business work? Are you willing to get up and go to work even when nobody is going to yell at you if you stay home and watch soap operas?

If you like the stability of working 9 to 5, wake up! Owning your own business means that you don't have set hours because you'll be working close to 24 hours a day to get things going. If this paragraph alone is enough to talk you out of pursuing your own business, then send me a thank-you card. You are not ready yet to make that kind of commitment. It doesn't mean that you never will, just that right now is not your time.

On the other hand, if after reading this chapter, you feel that starting your own business is still the right thing to do, then congratulations! If you feel that you were born to be an entrepreneur and are willing to do just about anything to succeed, you have the energy and the drive typical of entrepreneurs. I am privileged to be your tour guide through the maze of planning, legal structuring, and daily management. I hope my insights keep you from bloodying your nose in the same places I did, and I look forward to hearing about your successes.

The Least You Need to Know

> ➤ Understanding your personal goals before you start your own business is critical to later success.

> ➤ Setting a limit on your losses and time investment is a valuable step before you start your own business.

> ➤ Make sure you have enough money saved to support yourself for at least 12 months as you establish your new business.

> ➤ Getting your family's support and acceptance for starting a business is a necessary step, or you might find yourself choosing between the two.

> ➤ Realize that starting your own business means working long hours and believing passionately in the success of your venture—even if no one else does.

Chapter 2

What Kind of Business Should You Start?

In This Chapter

➤ Consider what you like to do

➤ Assess what you are good at

➤ Where are the opportunities?

➤ Can you make money?

"I'm just not sure what I want to do," explained Ann to Sarah, her co-worker, over coffee in the company cafeteria. "I know that I'm bored with what I'm doing here and that I want to start my own business, but what would I do? What would I sell? That's where I get stuck."

"Well, have you thought about what you like to do?" asked Sarah. "I read that book Do What You Love and the Money Will Follow, *which said that if you enjoy the type of work you're doing, you have an excellent chance of being successful."*

"That sounds like a good idea, but when I think about what I enjoy, I'm just not clear on what kind of business that could be," said Ann. "For instance, I really enjoy running. I'm active in the local track club and try and run in the local road races, but how would I make that into a business?"

"What other kinds of things do you like to do?" asked Sarah.

"Well I'm a pretty good seamstress; I like making my own clothes, and I always have fun stitching up the kids' costumes around Halloween. Maybe that's something to look into."

"Running a business that let's you do what you already enjoy makes a lot of sense to me," said Sarah.

There are so many little decisions that need to be made and so many factors to consider before you become a business owner, but if you take it step-by-step you can carefully weigh all your options—and there are a lot of them. Use this chapter to develop a list of possible businesses you might want to start and to begin to find the type of business that's perfect for you.

Have you always wanted to own your own business? There are many people who have had the urge to be on their own since young adulthood. Often this is due to their up-bringing; mom or dad may have been self-employed, serving as entrepreneurial role models. Some of the most successful entrepreneurs started their first business before age 30. Of course, that doesn't mean that their first business did well, just that they started trying to make a go of it early in life. Successful entrepreneurs often start and fail at several businesses before hitting on the one that makes them millionaires.

If you're past the age of 30, don't worry. The extra experience you've gained by working several years may make you more qualified to start your own business than some young whippersnapper. Perhaps you've realized that your job or your career just isn't satisfying anymore, and you want to start fresh with a new idea. Maybe you've thought of a revolutionary product idea you want to introduce to the market.

All of these are valid reasons to start your own business. Now you just have to figure out what kind of business is best for you. There are literally thousands, maybe even millions, of different types of businesses you could start.

You'll find familiar types of businesses, such as franchises for fast-food restaurants, quick oil-change garages, and maid services, all available to you. You'll also see some businesses that have cropped up in response to changes in the way we live and work, such as meal delivery services to help time-starved families, child chauffeur services, and recycled products for our homes and offices. You'll also find some innovative and sometimes bizarre ideas. One that I was rather intrigued by was a dog doo clean-up service. Yes, for a weekly fee, an enterprising business owner will visit your yard and clean up your pet's little leave-behinds!

Business Tip
Skim through magazines such as *Entrepreneur*, *Business Start-Ups*, or *Home Office Computing* to see the range of business ideas that are out there.

Don't feel that you have to come up with a totally new or unique business idea in order to succeed. Most new businesses are similar to existing companies or are even carbon copies. What will make your business successful are the individual talents and experience that you bring to your company.

Developing Your Business Idea

Even though you may have decided that you want to own your own business, it's very possible that you have no idea what type of business to start. There is probably no single answer to this question because it really depends on a number of different things:

➤ Your interests

➤ Your experience

➤ Your abilities

➤ How much money you have to invest

➤ What else you could be doing to make money

You must have a clear picture of what you will sell in order to make money. This can be either a product or a service. In many cases, people stick with what they know; they choose to sell products they are familiar with, such as computers, flowers, or kitchen appliances, or to offer services they are already trained to offer, such as accounting, plumbing, or repairing cars.

The following questionnaire should help you brainstorm some potential businesses to start. Take your time. Jot down your answer to each question in the questionnaire and complete the lists and exercises provided in the next few sections of this chapter. Be honest; these exercises will provide you with insight into what kind of business you will most likely succeed at.

Questions to Ask Yourself in Choosing a Business

1. Based on your education, your current or past jobs, and any special interests and hobbies, what three things do you know the most about? This experience could be the basis for a business.

   _____

   _____

2. What other experiences in your background could you draw upon for a business?

   _____

   _____

3. What do people tell you that you do well? Think about the times you've heard someone say, "You know, you really ought to start a such-and-such; you're so good at that." Maybe they're right. Maybe they would be your first customers.

   _____

   _____

   continues

---

continued

4. What things do you like doing most? Think, for example, about these questions: What do you like to do on your day off?

_____

What kinds of things do you leap out of bed for?

_____

What magazines, books, and newsletters do you enjoy reading?

_____

What headlines catch your eye?

_____

What things did you love doing most when you were a child?

_____

What is it you've always said you were going to do someday?

_____

If this were the last day of your life, what would you say you wished you had done?

_____

5. How much do you want to be involved with people? All the time? Sometimes? From a distance? Not at all? The answers can help you or avoid businesses that have a lot of people contact.

_____

_____

6. How many hours a week are you willing to invest in your business? Do you want a full-time or a part-time business? Be realistic about this. The amount of time you're willing to invest is what separates full-time from part-time and profits from losses.

_____

_____

7. How much money do you need to make? How much money do you want to make? Each week? Each month? Each year? You'll notice that some businesses can charge considerably more than others, so choose a business that will produce the income you want and need.

_____

_____

8. What resources do you have available to you in terms of property, equipment, and know-how? These resources could become the basis of a business. If you look around your home, you may have many untapped resources right under your nose, such as a personal computer, a van, a spare room, an automobile, a camcorder, your kitchen stove, a vacuum sweeper, a backyard, or a sewing machine.

   _____

   _____

9. Do you want to start a business from scratch, or would you prefer a franchise or direct-selling organization such as Amway or Avon that will train you?

   _____

   _____

This information is taken directly from Paul and Sarah Edwards' book, The Best Home Businesses for the 90s, Second Edition, 1994, Jeremy P. Tarcher/Putnam Books, ISBN: 0-87477-784-4, page 20.

Using Your Hobbies and Interests as a Springboard

Taking a long look at how you like to spend your free time is a good place to start in deciding what kind of business is right for you. One of your reasons for starting your own business may be to escape dissatisfaction or boredom with your current job. For this reason alone, make sure that you aren't jumping out of the frying pan and into the fire. Nothing could be worse than quitting a stable job you hate for a more stressful job with longer hours, less pay, and no guarantee that you'll like it any more than the job you just quit.

Make sure that the type of business you start will give you more satisfaction and joy than your current job. By doing this, it is more likely that you'll stay in business because you'll be committed to doing what you love. Hobbies are a good starting point because these are the types of things you choose to do in your free time when you could be doing almost anything.

To begin compiling a list of potential types of businesses you might like to run, use the following form to list all the things you like to do in your spare time. Include formal hobbies, such as drawing or stamp collecting, as well as informal activities, such as reading, running, or cooking.

HOBBIES AND INTERESTS

Apply Your Job Training to Your Own Company

If you've been working the last few years as a dedicated employee somewhere, you've obviously been doing something right to still be on the payroll. During that time, you've been able to improve the quality of your work as you've gained experience. You've probably also developed new skills as a result of training or exposure to different aspects of the company's operations. Maybe you've even been offered jobs at other companies as word has spread about your talents. The more opportunities you've been presented in the last couple of years is a good indication of what kind of demand there may be for your services. For instance, if you've had ten people approach you about working for them on the side, obviously there is a need for your kind of work right now. Although you may have turned down those opportunities, now may be the time to go out on your own and offer others the same services and know-how you've been giving your employer.

That might sound great to some of you, who are thinking, "I can do what I do now, but I won't have to deal with my boss, the jerk. And I can pick and choose what work I take." The reality is that running your own business may mean you're working for a lot of different jerks.

To start planning your business, you first need to determine exactly what you would offer clients. Begin by making a list of your major responsibilities at your current job. Think about what you do on a daily basis and also what big projects you have worked on recently. Are there types of activities you enjoy most? What kinds of things do people ask you to do most often?

JOB RESPONSIBILITIES

In addition to thinking about what you do in your current job, also think back to past jobs you've held, what you did there, and what you enjoyed most about those positions. Add these responsibilities to your list. Make your list as long as possible to be sure you don't overlook any type of work you enjoyed in the past.

What Are Your Strengths?

This question might sound silly at this point, but of all the activities and interests you've listed so far, which ones are you good at? No, really. Which ones do you really excel at? There may be things you like to do in your spare time but that you know could never be the basis of a business, and there may be other interests of which you have an in-depth knowledge that you could apply to a company.

For instance, you might enjoy painting watercolors in your spare time, but you know that in comparing your work to professional artists', people would laugh at your creations. If that's the case, don't try your luck as an artist. However, if you have studied art, spend a lot of time in museums and galleries, and know the local art scene, how about starting an art gallery or establishing a company that specializes in giving tours of local museums and galleries? I know, I know; it's not as simple as that, but you can see my train of thought here.

Gather all of your completed questionnaires and read them through again. What kinds of activities come up repeatedly? Are there some types of things you like doing more than others? Do you see similarities across some of your abilities, skills, and interests? Could they be combined as the basis for a business? This is the process you'll need to go through as you read and re-read the worksheets you've filled out.

Look at what you're good at and what you enjoy, and combine them into a kind of business you could start. It can be a service-related business, based on your past experience as a secretary, medical transcriptionist, or chef. Maybe it's a combination of a hobby you love and your experience volunteering in the community.

If you start a product-related business, what kinds of things can you see yourself selling? Based on your interests and experiences, you can think about selling anything from cars to cosmetics to computers to plants. Make connections between your background and the businesses you might like to run. Keep looking over your lists for new ideas or confirmation that you're on the right track.

Look at what you like, compare it to what you're really good at, and think about related businesses you could run. Here are some simple, yet effective, exercises to go through to determine where you may have the greatest success. (These exercises are adapted from *Job and Career Building*, Chapter 4, "Setting Objectives," Richard Germann and Peter Arnold, 1980, 10 Speed Press, ISBN: 0-89815-048-5.)

1. Take out a piece of paper (yes, you have to write these things down!) and number it from 1 to 15 on the left side of the page. Now, write down a minimum of 10 and a maximum of 15 accomplishments. These events can be from your recent professional past or from your childhood. Typical events might include "Made the varsity basketball team as a freshman," "Raised three children while working full-time," and "Improved sales revenue in my territory over 300 percent in 12 months."

2. Take out 10–15 sheets of paper (depending on how many accomplishments you listed) and write an accomplishment from Step 1 at the top of each sheet and divide the rest of the sheet into two vertical columns. Mark the left column "Successful Skills Applied" and mark the right column "Successful Personal Attributes Applied." You should have a separate sheet completed for each successful project or event you listed in Step 1. Do not worry about listing things more than once. These will be taken into account later in the process.

3. Now, take out two other sheets of paper and rewrite all of the "Successful Skills" on one sheet and the "Success Personal Attributes" on another. Cross out items that are on the lists more than once, and mark the number of times a skill or attribute appeared (on your sheets in Step 2) next to each skill or attribute. Reorganize the lists in decreasing order from most to least frequent. Some items may appear on both the attributes and skills lists; that's okay. At this stage, you should have a pretty good idea of what makes you tick when you are successful.

4. Group the skills and attributes into clusters that describe a general type of work or activity. For example, typing, filing, and detail work may be grouped under administrative skills. Coordinating people and events may be more managerial.

5. Put these clusters into your perceived order of importance from most important to least important.

6. Write a sentence that describes your top skills and attributes so that someone reading it would clearly understand the type of environment where you work best.

There you have it. You should now have a clearer idea of the type of job, work, and business environment in which you stand the best chance of success.

Your Personality and Abilities

In addition to your interests and experiences, your personality and abilities also play an important role in determining what kind of business is best for you.

Take a look at the list of activities in Table 2.1, and circle the ones that you like to do. Focusing on what you're good at can lead you toward a certain type of business.

Table 2.1 Your Skills and Abilities

Information-Oriented	People-Oriented	Thing-Oriented
Working with words	Advising	Cleaning
Working with numbers	Caring	Making
Analyzing	Communicating	Organizing
Compiling	Helping	Repairing
Creating	Informing	Working with animals
Evaluating	Organizing	Working with food
Finding	Negotiating	Working with plants
Keyboarding	Performing	Working with tools
Organizing	Persuading	
Synthesizing	Planning events	
	Teaching	

This information is taken directly from Paul and Sarah Edwards' book, The Best Home Businesses for the 90s, Second Edition, 1994, Jeremy P. Tarcher/Putnam Books, ISBN: 0-87477-784-4, page 21.

Bankruptcy Alert
Not everyone is a potential entrepreneur. Some like stability, routine, and a regular paycheck from someone else. If this is you, you'll be unhappy in the always-changing, stressful life of a business owner. If you're really not excited by working long hours and relying on customers, rather than an employer, for your rent and food money, maybe you should put this book aside for a while.

What Are the Results Telling You?

The questionnaire, exercises, and forms in this chapter are designed to help you find the business that's right for you. Look at each of the forms you've completed and find the commonalities. What types of activities keep coming up over and over? Can you envision certain kinds of businesses that you would like to start? Are there others you now know are of absolutely no interest to you? Keep coming up with new ideas and refining them according to some other factors I go over in a minute.

What Does the Market Need Now and in the Future?

Up until this point, you've been focused solely on what you like to do, what kind of work experience you've had, and what types of products or services you could offer clients. Now you need to consider whether there is demand for what you have to offer in the way of products and services. This is a crucial consideration because it really doesn't matter what you are good at if no one is willing to pay you for it. I might have the best recipe for chocolate-covered grasshoppers, but if there are only a handful of people in my town who would consider eating them, there really isn't a business opportunity here.

It may be easiest to start this process by looking at recent trends in the market to give you some ideas for where you should focus your attention. To figure that out, you need to do some research. This doesn't have to be the typical, tedious, lengthy process you may be used to; it can be done in short spurts over time.

Researching Opportunities

The best way to learn about what people and businesses need is to turn to the media. Newspapers, magazines, reports, Web sites, and radio and television stations reflect all our interests and concerns. By studying what kinds of things they've been writing about or talking about, you learn a great deal about products and services that everyone needs.

The best way to undertake this research is to read the following:

Business Tip
Pick up a copy of *American Demographics*, whose sole purpose is to monitor trends as a result of changes in the population.

➤ National and trade business magazines.

➤ Local newspapers (and watch local news programs).

➤ Publications about subjects you're interested in.

➤ National news and business publications.

➤ Perform a search on the Internet for related materials and Web sites.

Keep an eye and ear open for topics that everyone seems to be interested in or that everyone is talking about. Collectible stuffed animals, such as Beanie Babies, are all the rage now, as well as electronic pets. The Internet is always in the news as a new means of communicating, gathering information, and marketing. And remember how the O.J. Simpson trial occupied our lives? Are there related products or services you can imagine that would tie into events such as these? That's how you have to start thinking.

If you already know what you want to sell but don't know whether people will pay you for it, narrow the focus of your research to similar businesses in your area. Study them, read all the recent articles about them in your local library's clipping files, and talk to the owners about how their business is going.

In your conversations with business owners and people you know, ask them what they would be willing to pay for the product or service you intend to sell. Keep track of what price they tell you is reasonable. After several such conversations, you should have a pretty good idea of what people want and what they'd be willing to pay.

Business Tip
If you find that local companies are unwilling to share their secrets, call a similar business owners in another town or state. Because you're unlikely to be a competitor, they may be willing to talk with you about what they've done that has worked...and not worked. The online world may also provide insight by logging into forums, discussion groups and chats with business owners who can provide advice based on their experiences.

Your Employer Could Be Your First Customer

One of the first questions to ask yourself is, do you currently do something for an employer that other individuals or businesses may also need? You've probably heard about the new trend toward *outsourcing*, which is pushing companies to keep their full-time staff small and pay others to handle short-term projects or work unrelated to the company's main business. Essentially, instead of hiring more full-time workers, companies are relying more and more on short-term workers with a certain talent or skill. Outsourcing may provide opportunities for you to secure some new clients.

Business Buzzword
Outsourcing is corporate-speak for hiring outside consultants, freelancers, or companies to provide services that in the past have been provided by employees.

What outsourcing can mean for you is the chance to continue doing what you do for your employer, but as an outside consultant, *independent contractor,* or

Business Buzzword
A **freelancer** is an individual who works for several different companies at once, helping out on specific projects. Freelancers are like consultants and are paid a set rate for their services but receive no benefits, sick pay, or vacation allowance.

Independent contractor is another expression that the IRS uses for freelancer. It means that the company you're working for is not your employer. You have the freedom to decide when, where, and how you get the work done. You pay your own taxes and benefits, but you can also deduct work-related expenses. To be sure that the IRS agrees that you are an independent contractor, request a copy of their guidelines from your local IRS office.

Bankruptcy Alert
If your client begins requiring you to work certain hours and to complete your work in a certain way, you're being treated more like an employee than a freelancer or independent contractor, and your tax status may be affected. Be careful.

freelancer. When companies lay off workers, typically they don't eliminate the work that person was doing; they just shift the burden to someone else. That can work in the short term, but after a while, employees get overburdened and downright irritable at having to do everyone else's work in addition to their own.

A potential solution for many companies is to hire people on a per-project basis when the workload is too great or to turn over responsibility for a particular type of activity to an outside company that specializes in that area. Larger corporations started this trend several years ago as they sought ways to cut costs by cutting back on the number of employees on the payroll. Eastman Kodak, for instance, turned over responsibility for maintaining corporate computers to an outside company that specialized in computers. Kodak wanted to focus its attention on its own products, not on keeping everyone's computers running properly.

To determine whether your current employer might consider paying you to do what you do now as an independent contractor, freelancer, or consultant, consider your boss's point of view. What are the advantages for your employer?

➤ As an independent contractor, you do not have to be paid benefits or have taxes taken out of your pay.

➤ In some cases, you may be able to work on individual projects and be paid a flat fee for that work, rather than an hourly wage, potentially saving the company money.

➤ You don't need an office or work space at the company. Equipment such as a computer, telephone, copier, and fax machine are not provided.

If you have a good relationship with your boss and your employer and you believe that there is a way for you to continue to do work as a business owner, it might make sense to suggest that your employer become a client. I suggest having this discussion with your boss when you are sure that you want to leave and are ready to start your business. If your employer becomes angry that you want to leave, you may find yourself on your own faster than you expected. Don't bet the farm on winning your employer as your first client, but go after the opportunity when you're ready to start your business.

Think of your former employer as a potential client, just like anyone else who has a need for your product or service. Don't just assume that your boss will want to hire you as a freelancer. (He or she may not.)

Will You Make Money?

Before jumping in with both feet, wouldn't it be nice if you could get a better idea of whether your business will succeed? Yes, I've heard that fortune tellers can be helpful, but how about some basic financial analyses? Don't worry; you don't have to be an accountant to do this stuff.

Start-Up Dollars and Your Business Choice

Enthusiasm, skill, and guts will take you far, but combining these traits with cash will get you much closer to the brass ring. The reality is that *service businesses* (those that offer services such as accounting, consulting, or massage) generally cost less to start than *product businesses* (those that offer products, such as computers, clothes, or widgets). You could start a dog-walking company on little money as long as you keep your expenses on a short leash. (Sorry; the pun was too good to resist.) Seriously, though, leashes, collars, a phone line, and business cards are all you need to get into your own dog-walking business.

On the other hand, starting a product business often requires major machinery and equipment, office space, employees, and more. Maybe a lot more. Each of these items translates into more dollars and more delay before sales start rolling in.

Due to this fact of life, many companies start as service businesses and move on to include products as their cash and sales situation improves. For example, a computer programmer can start by offering software consulting (a service) and eventually develop and sell her own software programs (a product). Starting on a small budget doesn't mean you necessarily have to stay small, but it does help to keep expenses down when sales are lower.

Business Buzzword
A product-based business is a company that makes money by selling products that are either developed and manufactured by the company or purchased by the company for resales. IBM, Nike, and Wal-Mart are examples of product-based businesses.

Service-based businesses are companies that make money by selling services, rather than products, provided by employees or contractors. Examples included doctors, consultants, house cleaners, and dog walkers.

How Much Can You Invest?

You don't have to have millions of dollars to start a business—far from it. Many people start small, often on a part-time basis, spreading their money between living expenses and business start-up costs. Other business owners get loans for thousands and thousands of dollars. For example, some fast-food franchises cost more than $100,000 just to open.

Bankruptcy Alert
When calculating how much money you need to start your business, you must include the cost of your living expenses during the startup phase. Don't assume you can live on bread and water until the business hits. You will start to resent the business if you find yourself lacking a decent meal several nights in a row. This can cloud your judgment and significantly dampen your enthusiasm.

You have to decide for yourself how much money you are willing and able to set aside to start your business. It may be less than a thousand dollars, or it may be much more. Everyone's situation is different. Just be aware that the type or size of business you start may be somewhat limited by the amount of money you have available. Don't expect to start a restaurant with just a couple thousand dollars, for example; it's highly unlikely that you could afford to pay for everything you need. Even if you were able to squeak by the first month, you may be jeopardizing your future by not having enough money to fall back on.

It All Comes Down to Numbers

Only by estimating how much money you can make, and how much it will cost to run your business, will you know whether you should continue to pursue your dream. If there is no money to be made by starting the business, then you should drop the idea. Although there are probably several reasons why you want to start your own business, the first and foremost must be that you expect to make money at it.

What's Your Potential?

Let's compare the long-term earning potential of product versus service businesses. Although a service business is less expensive to start, it is also harder to grow into a larger company. Why? Simple. Every night when your employees go home, your company stops earning money. The time your employees spend on customer work is how you make money. When they're sleeping, they're not billing your customers. Your company's growth is limited by the number of hours you and your employees can bill in a day.

A product business, on the other hand, can make money as long as it has products on hand. You can sell 20 products on Monday and 500 on Tuesday and work your equipment extra hard Tuesday night to manufacture more products to sell on Wednesday. While you sleep, your equipment is still churning out more products.

Also, services are usually sold and provided by a set group of people (your employees). Products, on the other hand, can be sold through several different channels, such as retail stores, mail order catalogs, and telemarketing.

Starting small, such as with a service orientation, can help to reduce your start-up expenses. Later you can add products to your company's mix, when you have the money available to support it. But when you're first starting out, you need to be sure you have enough money to start-up and sustain your company for at least a year.

To estimate the total start-up costs of your company, determine how much money you need to start the business and how much money you need to pay yourself during that time to cover your basic living expenses. For example, if the business requires $50,000 to start and you need $48,000 to cover your personal living expenses until the company is on its feet, then the initial investment required is $98,000, not $50,000.

Don't scale your living expenses to the bone when you estimate these costs because, if for some reason, sales are slower to appear than anticipated, you don't want to be out of business just as things start to pick up. If no additional money is available, then the initial $98,000 could be lost just as the company is getting off the ground. Once you've already received one loan to get the company started, it is even tougher to go back to your investors and ask for just a little more to keep you going. Make sure you can cover your living expenses for several months, and give yourself some leeway.

Use the following figure to estimate your start-up costs.

Startup Costs

Equipment to be purchased	$_____
Office rental	$_____
Inventory	$_____
Renovations	$_____
Supplies	$_____
Marketing	$_____
Utilities	$_____
Other: _____	$_____
_____	$_____
_____	$_____
_____	$_____
_____	$_____
Total	$_____

Living Expenses

Rent or mortgage	$_____
Food	$_____
Car payment	$_____
Utilities	$_____
Insurance	$_____
School tuition	$_____
Credit card	$_____
Other: _____	$_____
_____	$_____
_____	$_____
_____	$_____
_____	$_____
Total	$_____ per month
	= $_____ for 6 months
Total start-up cost plus 6-month living expenses	$_____

Business Tip
Assume you need to cover at least six months of living expenses before the company becomes profitable. It may take 18 to 24 months, but use 6 months as an absolute minimum.

Business Buzzword
Opportunity cost is the profit that you could have gained by pursuing another investment instead of the one you currently have. For example, if you go out on a date with one person, you lose the potentially good time you could have had with someone else during that time. Sound familiar? That is opportunity cost.

It is either your money or your investor's money that funds the business. It will definitely be your time, and time is also worth money. Professional investors require a formal business plan before they will invest. Even if you don't need outside financing because you have the cash to invest yourself, be as serious about evaluating the opportunity as an investor would be. (Check out Chapter 4, "Preparing Your Business Plan," to learn more about creating a business plan.) Make sure that this is an investment you believe is going to pay off for you.

What else could you be doing with your money? How could it be spent if not working to start your business? All those other ways that you could have spent your money is what the financial pros call the *opportunity cost* of starting your business. Investors frequently look at situations in terms of opportunity cost: What other investment options are they giving up by investing their money here, rather than there? If the return from your business idea is lower than their next-best option, then they will not give you the money.

How Much Do You Give Up and When Do You Make It Back?

There are worse fates than having a business fail miserably. One of them is having it fail gradually so that it slowly bleeds your reserve funds and energy. It never really takes off, but it never really is bad enough to close the doors. Beware because the steady drip-drip-drip of cash leaving the company on a monthly basis will keep you around while draining your finances. When this happens, you find yourself digging into your personal savings each month to keep the company afloat, all the time believing that it will turn around. The problem is that both you and the company may now go bankrupt.

For this reason, I suggest that you set some guidelines for when you will evaluate your company's performance. These milestones should include desired, or even required, levels of personal income and time investment required to keep the business running. If you exceed these goals, then you and your business are successful. If you are below those goals, then you need to make some goal adjustments or business management adjustments. At that time, you can choose to either recommit to the venture or decide that it's time to call the idea a bad one, and move on by either closing, selling, or restructuring the business to meet your desired goals.

Get your family involved in this goal-setting process. It is important that they know the sacrifices on their part are only in place for a set period of time, after which things will be reevaluated. If the business does well, you'll all benefit, but if it never takes off, your family can take comfort in knowing you'll shut it down after a certain period of time and try something else. Believe me when I say that your family is afraid for you and for themselves if the business goes under.

The hardest question to answer is, "How long do I keep investing in the company before I can expect a profit?" This is a tough question, but you can expect to lose some money for at least 18 to 24 months, and you should be making a decent living at between 36 and 48 months. (These are simply rules of thumb based on discussions with other business owners and do not represent scientific findings.)

When Do You Break Even?

One way to get a rough idea of whether your business can make any money is to do a *break-even analysis*. In a nutshell, a break-even analysis tells you how much you have to make in dollars or products sold to cover all your costs. Obviously, your goal is to do much better than that, but start first with ensuring you can at least pay for the products or services to be produced.

Business Buzzword
A **break-even analysis** is a calculation of how much money you need to make to cover your basic costs of doing business. Above that, you're profitable.

A break-even analysis takes into consideration three pieces of information:

➤ The average price of what you sell, which can be for products or services. Just estimate how much your typical sale will be.

➤ The average cost of what you sell, or how much it costs to produce your typical sale.

➤ Your total fixed costs per year, which are your total expenses for the year that you have to pay no matter how much you sell. This includes things such as rent, your phone bill, insurance, tax, employee salaries, and utilities. (See Chapter 11, "Making Sure That You're Making It," for a more detailed discussion of fixed expenses.)

Your break-even price in dollars is calculated by dividing

Fixed costs/(1 – average cost of products/average price of products)

The average cost of producing your products can be calculated by adding all of your expenses associated with manufacturing, such as raw material costs, labor costs, and waste and dividing it by the number of products produced. That's your average. Some individual units may have cost more than the next one to produce, but over time the cost evens out.

Similarly, the average price of your product can be determined by adding your anticipated sales for the next year and dividing by the total number of units you expect to sell. While you may make more per product when you sell through some channels, calculating the average takes those differences into account.

For example, if I have annual fixed costs of $30,000 and sell software programs that are priced at an average of $100 and cost me $20, my break-even in dollars is $37,500:

$$\$30,000/(1 - 20/100) = \$30,000/.8 = \$37,500$$

This means that I have to have sales of $37,500 a year just for my business to break even. To calculate the number of software programs I have to sell, I just divide $37,500 by the price of the program, which is $100:

$$\$37,500/100 = 37.5 \text{ or } 38 \text{ units}$$

These numbers by themselves may mean nothing to you, but if you put in some estimates of your average sales price, cost, and total fixed costs, you see what you can expect. Once you figure out the break-even in dollars and units, think about whether those figures seem high, low, or reasonable.

For those of you starting a service business who think there's no way to figure out an average sale price, here are some pointers. Keep in mind that calculating your break-even point isn't supposed to be exact at the moment. You're just trying to get a rough idea of whether you can ever sell enough of your product or service to pay all your expenses and make some money.

Business Tip
When you perform a break-even analysis, be sure to divide the average cost by the average price first, before subtracting the number from 1. (Remember that old math rule about doing the work within the parentheses first, and that division should be done before subtraction, and so on, to get the right answer.)

If you're not selling a product, there are other ways of estimating your break-even point. If you are thinking of becoming a consultant, for instance, you determine your hourly rate and divide your fixed costs by your hourly rate. That tells you the minimum number of hours you need to bill each month to break even. If you come up with 10 or 11 hours a week, or 40 a month, you're doing well. The average number of hours that a new consultant bills weekly is around 14; this number should get up to around 24–30 hours a week once the company gets up and going. If you're having trouble choosing an hourly rate, call some of your competitors and ask what their rate is; that is a guide for what local clients are willing to pay.

Even if you are selling a product and you can't figure out the average price, just take the prices of all or most of your products and calculate an average. If you own a restaurant, you can estimate the average meal price by taking the average price of an appetizer and adding it to the average entree price and drink price. Taking that number, which could run anywhere from $5.00 at McDonald's to over $50 at an upscale eatery, and dividing your costs by that number tells you how many people you need to feed each month. Does it look feasible given the number of hours you'll be open? These are the types of questions you're trying to answer with this exercise.

If you come up with a number that is much higher than you think you could ever achieve, your business may have serious problems. Are there ways you can reduce your fixed costs, such as by setting up a home-based office or not hiring employees right away? Those are the kinds of decisions you need to make to create a successful business. However, if your break-even appears well within reason in terms of sales, look again at your numbers to be sure you haven't forgotten to take something into consideration.

One Last Look at All Your Options

Now that you've done some initial research into the kind of business you want to have and what it might cost to make it a reality, step back and consider what else you could do with your time, energy, and money over the next few years. If you weren't starting a business, what would you do? Would you stay with your current employer? Find a new job? Chuck it all and move to the Caribbean to rent snorkels on the beach? These are all valid options that you need to reevaluate before committing all your resources to starting a business.

Starting a business is exciting, exhausting, and expensive (the three Es). If, at this point, you're questioning whether you're ready to take the plunge, consider some of these options to hold you over until you're ready:

➤ Ask for a transfer to another division of your current employer to learn some parts of the business that you know nothing about.

➤ Apply for a job at another company.

➤ Sign up for some training or course work to teach you the skills you need to get a different kind of job.

The same is true if you start a business and it doesn't succeed immediately; you always have other options:

➤ You can shut down the business and get a job working for someone else again.

➤ You can apply for a loan to invest more in the business to help it grow faster.

➤ You can look for a partner who has business skills you've discovered you don't have.

The list goes on and on, but the point is that you always have options. Make sure that starting a business is your best option, and if so, go for it!

The Least You Need to Know

➤ You can increase your odds of starting a successful business by taking your personal interests, experience, qualifications, and financial resources into account.

➤ Just because someone else is making tons of money with a particular type of business does not mean that you should do the same thing.

➤ The best business for you combines your interests, abilities, and experience with a market need.

➤ The amount of money you have to invest in a new business may be a limiting factor in the kind you can afford to start.

➤ If no one is interested in buying the products or services you want to sell, you have no business.

➤ Financial tools such as break-even analyses can help you determine whether your business has potential.

➤ Service businesses cost less to start than product businesses but are harder to grow into large companies.

Chapter 3

Plan to Win the War

In This Chapter

➤ The difference between strategy and tactics

➤ Creating your own business strategy

➤ Ensuring that your personal goals further your company goals

➤ Taking action to achieve goals

"Why the special staff meeting?" asked Jake, the sales manager. "Not sure," was the reply from his colleague, who was responsible for production.

The company had started out as a small beverage manufacturer; it now sold millions of dollars a year in fruit drink products. It had recently introduced two new lines of frozen fast foods. The response to the new products had been tepid at first, but was slowly improving.

The company's real moneymaker, the main beverage product line, was doing well and supporting the new ventures, but Jake had reservations about how long it could last without the new frozen food lines carrying their respective part of the profits (which was just starting to happen). It seemed a good time to maintain the status quo, but the company president (who was also the founder) liked new projects. Jake didn't think the company could stand another product introduction so soon after the frozen food lines' near fiasco.

"Thanks for coming," said the president. "Now that I have more free time, I have been experimenting with new methods of food preparation. I think the American people will pay for fresh, vegetable-based foods that taste good and are easy to prepare. As a result, I want to introduce three new, fresh vegetable side dish lines that will open up new markets for the company and take us into new retail outlets. I expect the full support of management in taking these products to market."

Jake mustered up his courage and asked, "Sir, don't you think we should wait a little while before moving into new markets? Our frozen foods line is just now being accepted, and I have a concern that diffusing our efforts with fresh vegetable lines may be too much for us now. Why don't you take some time and perfect the recipes and give our distribution channel a chance to settle down?"

As the president and founder, what would you do? Would you make Jake sell rice noodles for not supporting your plan? Would you listen to him and take his advice? Would you thank him for his input and do what you want anyway? How you respond to questions like these will determine how your company grows, and whether it grows in the right direction. How do you determine what the proper response should be?

In this chapter, we'll talk about the importance of *strategic* and *tactical* planning when starting a new business. You are the leader, and you need to set a course your company will follow.

The topic of strategy is presented early in this book to help you set short-term goals, while also filling a strategic role that leads to success in the future. Success is always a balance between today's activities and tomorrow's promise. When you get into the daily fire-fighting mode, it is easy to get pulled off course. Set the course now and use your initial business plan (discussed in the next chapter) as a compass reading of where you are today.

Comparing Strategic and Tactical Actions

Don't let the terminology scare you. Strategic and tactical planning are a part of everyday life, though you may not think of every decision you make as strategic or tactical. For instance, have you ever said:

"She won the battle, but lost the war."

"Don't throw out the baby with the bathwater."

"He can't see the forest for the trees."

Each of these quotes refers to a short-term event or situation and its effect on the overall results of something else. Each quote suggests that by focusing too much on the short term (the battle), or on what's right in front of us, we lose sight of the bigger picture (the war). This is the essence of strategic and tactical planning.

A strategic plan is made up of many tactics, or short-term actions, that together help you reach your goal. For example, winning the battle may have been a tactical success, but if it contributed to losing the war, then it was a strategic mistake. Introducing a new advertising program is a tactic you might use to increase sales, but if your products aren't manufactured yet, you'll wind up with irritated customers who may not want to buy from you even when the products arrive. That would be a strategic mistake. Your efforts to bring in immediate sales caused more harm than good because your company simply wasn't ready to handle the sales.

Business Buzzword
A **strategy** is a careful plan or method; the art of devising or employing plans toward a goal. **Tactics** are small-scale actions that serve a larger purpose, such as a strategy.

Every decision you make in your company either moves you closer to or further away from reaching a strategic goal. It is the responsibility of the company's management (you) to determine the strategic direction for the company and to ensure that all employees know what to do to achieve those corporate strategic goals.

Taking the time to create an overall strategy is time well spent because it provides a road map for future decisions.

Short- and Long-Term Planning

Nothing happens in the long term without short-term actions that move you toward your desired outcome. Short-term actions cannot help achieve any particular goal if no goals have been set or no plan has been developed. You have to know where you're going before you can figure out a route to get there, right?

Taking the time to determine your own goals and your company's long-term mission and objectives will guide your daily actions. Without this framework, you and your employees may be busy, but the business will not move forward because everyone is pulling in separate directions. Making sure everyone knows and understands the goals and objectives of the company will make life a lot easier—for you and your employees. Defining the company's goals will minimize employee frustration because they will know what they're working toward. You can minimize confusion by identifying and eliminating activities that don't directly support the goals of the company.

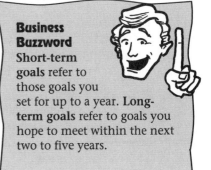

Business Buzzword
Short-term goals refer to those goals you set for up to a year. **Long-term goals** refer to goals you hope to meet within the next two to five years.

It all starts with you. Take the time to learn more about yourself, your personal motivations, and your long-term goals, to ensure that you take the company in the proper direction. For example, if you like the idea of working alone from a home office, make sure that you're not setting your business up to grow to a point where you have to hire employees or get an office outside your home. If your business starts to grow in a direction or at a speed that makes you uncomfortable, you may start to resent the business and eventually unravel what is otherwise a good thing. You can avoid this by simply deciding up front what kind of business you want to have, both short term and long term. Once you decide, you can move ahead to make it happen.

You Are a Key Part of the Strategy

Businesses, like people, develop *momentum.* Once they get moving in a particular direction, it is difficult to reorient the people and procedures to a new way of thinking and doing business. Businesses also develop *inertia,* or resistance to change. The larger the organization, the longer it takes for change to occur, even with total support from top management. This means that your business may be nimble when there are only a few employees, but you can expect it to become harder to turn around as it grows in size.

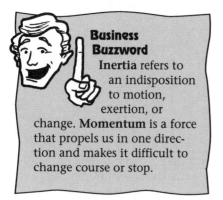

Business Buzzword

Inertia refers to an indisposition to motion, exertion, or change. **Momentum** is a force that propels us in one direction and makes it difficult to change course or stop.

Beware. You, the owner, also have momentum and inertia that may take you and your business in directions you may not have intended. The rallying cry "We can do anything!" may be true, but on limited resources, you can get yourself and the company into a lot of trouble. Be careful not to try to do too much too quickly. Like the food and beverage company example at the beginning of this chapter, you have to pick your battles and fight them well, or your company can become spread so thin that it loses its focus and competitive advantage. The essential value of strategic planning and goal setting is that it

1. Keeps your own personal inclination on track with the business goals, and

2. Provides you with the freedom to go with your instincts while giving everyone else in the company a framework for decisions

Synchronize Your Goals with Company Goals

Here's an interesting question: Do you work for the company or does the company work for you? After all, you pay the bills, you sign the checks. You provide the overall direction and determine whether someone has performed effectively. You do the hiring and firing. Shouldn't the company dance to your tune? Yes and no.

A part of your job is to ensure the company's survival. If the company goes under, so does your dream of independence and all of your hard work. There go the paychecks for all of your employees. Away go the services you provide your clients that they have come to depend upon. So who works for whom? Do you work for the company and its clients or does the company work for you? In the final analysis, it's really a balancing act and your customers are the ultimate bosses.

Take it from Tuco in the movie *The Good, The Bad and The Ugly*, "There are two types of people in this world, my friend. Those with the gun and those who dig." The one with the gun sets the overall direction, and the one who digs gets the job done on a day-to-day basis. The one with the gun is the leader and probably has more of a *start-up temperament*. The workers have more of a *maintenance temperament*.

If you are the type of person who enjoys the start-up phase of business, then the daily routine of running the business will probably bore you to tears after a while. Interestingly, some entrepreneurs, unconsciously, create change within the organization just to feed their need for the excitement of solving real-time problems. Others come up with endless ideas for new products and services, new markets to go into, new distribution channels to conquer. Anything to bring back the excitement of a new venture. Unfortunately, change and new directions may not be what your young, or even mature, company needs. With the limited resources associated with smaller companies, small doses of change are the best prescription unless market forces mandate a higher level of change.

Business Buzzword
Someone with a **start-up temperament** thrives on new and exciting challenges and projects. Someone with a **maintenance temperament** enjoys keeping established systems running like a well-oiled machine.

If you are a person who dislikes change, who prefers routine, you will go to extremes, once again unconsciously, to avoid disrupting the status quo. This is also not the best situation, because business life is never static, no matter how much you may want it to be, and treating it as such is a guaranteed death knell. Ignoring opportunities for expansion or product improvements that everyone is clamoring for is very dangerous.

A blending of the two types of temperaments is required for success, and the first step is knowing where you sit on the mayhem-to-routine continuum. Surround yourself with people who have different temperaments than the one you have. If you have a maintenance temperament, make sure you have start-up people around to keep you from becoming static. If you have a start-up temperament, make sure you have maintenance temperament people around to keep you from creating chaos and driving everyone crazy. In both cases, creating balance in your organization will help keep the business from going under.

Know that you, the boss, set the course for the organization. You set the strategic direction for the company. The more aware you are of your own strengths and weaknesses, the more likely you will be to steer the company in its best direction, instead of the one most in accord with your personality. Look for the ideal where the company's goals and your goals are in sync and have the best of both worlds.

You should now understand why chapters 1 and 2 dealt with you and your goals. The homework that you did in those chapters will help you make sure that your business is one that you want to work with and one that provides you with the stimulation you need. If it doesn't, you might find you and your company are not working toward a common goal.

For example, let's say you decide to start an Italian restaurant because you love to create new pasta dishes. Let's also assume that people start coming to the restaurant because they love your pasta recipes.

As more people come to the restaurant, you will be required to keep making the same old pasta recipes day after day because that is what your customers want. If you get bored with this repetition, you might decide to modify the existing recipes a little to see if your customers like them. Notice that you are now feeding your own need for variety at the expense of the customer's need for consistently good food that can be relied upon.

If you love the creation of new recipes and not the cooking of the existing recipes, you have a potential problem.

Solution: Plan to hire someone to do the daily cooking while you go off creating new dishes that are introduced in a way that complements the existing business flow. This is best done gradually: If you get the hots for Chinese food and force that inclination on your restaurant, your customers might get confused by a Chinese/Italian menu and take their business elsewhere.

Changing the focus of your business, no matter what products and services you're offering, can jeopardize your relationships with your customers and put your business at risk. There is a big difference between adapting to meet customer demands and reengineering your whole business. Making minor adjustments for the sake of your customers is good and may help increase business; transitioning your business away from its primary mission, however, is dangerous.

For example, adding binding to your list of services available at your copy shop makes sense if customers have been requesting it. Adding massage services, on the other hand, doesn't.

Make sure that you spend your time on areas that complement the strategic direction of the company as defined in your initial plan. If you must try other things, do it in a way that does not interfere with daily business operation.

Grow Beyond Your Own Capabilities

With success comes a new challenge: What do you do when your own limitations are holding your company back? Beyond getting the venture off the ground, this is often the biggest challenge that small business owners face. In order to grow, they have to learn how to delegate work that they normally handled themselves.

Once you have developed enough business to exceed your own personal capacity, you'll face some tough decisions. Do you now need to turn over your favorite accounts and routine activities to somebody else? You may find effective delegation difficult at first. But the business will eventually stagnate if you just can't let go.

Employees can become frustrated if they think you don't trust them. And your clients can become frustrated because they are no longer getting the level of service they expect from your company simply because you are too busy to respond to their needs in a timely manner. You can become frustrated because you are paying your employees to work for you so that you can improve the quality of your life—here you are working 60 hours per week when they only work 40 to 50. What are you paying them for, anyway?

This is a common situation and one that has strangled more than one small company. The need for more people is a sign that you are doing something right. Trusting your employees enough to delegate responsibility to them, while continuing to keep a close eye on the important things, can make or break your company.

Plan from the beginning to grow beyond your own abilities, or know that you will always need to live within the resources you alone provide. Plan to grow not only in the day-to-day *logistics* (paperwork), but also in the strategic areas.

Adding people to your company in either an employee or partnership capacity (see Chapter 5, "Structuring Your Business") opens up new opportunities that were previously not available due to your limited expertise. That's right! You can't do everything, even though you think you can. Let go of the things that do not make the best use of your time and give them to people who want to do them well. Spend your time doing what you do well, and use your team to balance the other areas.

You need to determine those skills that you brought to your clients which caused them to repeatedly use your company. Quite often, you might find that your style of customer interaction or methods of design are the things that made your company successful in the past. If so, make sure that you maintain control of these high-visibility items while delegating the others that cannot substantially affect your clients' satisfaction level.

On the other side of that coin, don't give away everything you like to do, or you could find yourself in a job you would never have taken with another company at

Business Tip
As a first stab at delegation, you might consider using an outside consultant who is a professional in the area needed. (For example, if the company books are getting too complicated to manage, you might hire a professional accountant to do it for you.) You free up your time while still ensuring a high-quality output. You also make time to generate more revenue by getting rid of responsibility for activities that don't directly create sales. The consultant approach may cost a little more, but it may also be a low-risk way to experiment with delegation of work.

Business Buzzword
Logistics are those activities that make the daily routine effective. You will probably need clerical help, once you become successful, to hand off the daily routine paperwork so that you can have time for other activities.

any price. It is still your company, and you have the expertise that made it successful. Apply that expertise as appropriate, add other people as applicable, and delegate the items that make minimal use of your specific talents. In this way, you lay the groundwork for yourself, your employees, your client relationships, and the company to grow beyond your limitations.

Your Mission: Defining Your Mission Statement

If this next section turns you on, check out *The Essence of Small Business* by Colin Barrow. Before you can even begin creating your business plan, which outlines how you will run your business on a daily basis, you must identify the strategic direction of the business you're about to create. You need to define the overall company direction in a *mission statement*. This simple statement covers, in just a few sentences, the reason for your company's existence. It provides the overall umbrella under which all other goals and actions fall. It says what your company does and who it does it for.

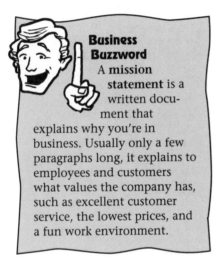

Business Buzzword
A **mission statement** is a written document that explains why you're in business. Usually only a few paragraphs long, it explains to employees and customers what values the company has, such as excellent customer service, the lowest prices, and a fun work environment.

A typical mission statement for a clothing retailer, for example, might be the following:

> "To provide trendy, natural-fiber clothing to health-conscious women between 18 and 35 years old, at reasonable prices in an environment where buying is fun."

Notice that the mission statement is brief and to the point, determining the overall direction of the company. It also sets limits. If a vendor tempts you with a hot men's clothing line, you can see that men's clothing would clearly be in violation of the mission statement. Either the company's prescribed mission statement needs to be changed or the idea to add men's clothing needs to be dropped so that the company can stay focused on its core mission.

When you create your company's mission statement, consider the following:

➤ What do you plan to do? For example, "We will sell second-hand office equipment."

➤ Who do you plan to do it for? For example, "We will focus on price-sensitive customers in the local geographic area."

➤ What best ensures success? For example, "We will target sale prices of products to be at 60 percent of new retail price for comparable products."

You can embellish these simple objectives with more specific points that add more details to the mission statement frame. Additional items might include the following:

➤ The time frame within which it will be done, such as within the next 18 months or the next five years.

➤ How your company will deal with changes in the marketplace (such as technology advancement, new competition)—for example, by investing in new equipment or hiring more staff.

➤ The *benefits* (not the *features)* of your product or service, which will persuade customers to buy from you (such as free delivery within 24 hours of purchase). By focusing on benefits, rather than features, you will concentrate on the true value of your product to the customer.

➤ How following the mission statement will contribute to the company's short- and long-term success, such as by keeping the company focused on a high-growth market or keeping expenses down.

It may take you days to write these simple sentences. But it is these sentences that define everything else that occurs within the company, so defining these statements is time well spent.

After defining your company's mission statement, you can now define the company's overall *objectives,* or *goals.* These are projects that comply with the mission statement and have specific time frames and measurable results. A typical objective may be to "add three new products to the line over the next 12 months."

You can then break these goals down into individual *tasks* that you assign to individuals for completion within specified time frames. These tasks all contribute to the completion of a particular objective. A task in our scenario may be "review the new product lines for 15 potential vendors within the next six months."

Tasks give rise to *action plans* that literally define who is doing what on which day. For example, "Visit XYZ Dress Company on Tuesday from 1 to 3 p.m.," would be a typical action item that helps complete a particular task. Completing the task moves the company closer to achieving its objectives and continues to support its mission.

> **Business Buzzword**
> **Features** are the different characteristics of a product or service. For example, the features of a drill bit may include its size, length, and the type of material it is made of. **Benefits** are what the customer gains by using your product or service. One benefit of the drill bit is that it makes holes of a specific size.

> **Business Buzzword**
> **Action plans** are the detailed activities you do to help the company achieve its goals. These include meetings, proposals, visits, or creations you make. **Tasks** are individual assignments given to people to help the company reach its objective. Each task is broken down into action plans. **Objectives** are large projects that affect your company and involve several people. Objectives help the company grow and become more successful. They are usually rather involved and may take several months to reach.

Action plans, tasks, and objectives are related to each other in the same way that tactics and strategies are. Action plans make up tasks, which make up objectives, just as tactics are components of a strategic plan. Different words, same idea. The following figure shows how they all stack up.

All actions ultimately support the mission statement by achieving short-term and strategic (long-term) goals.

Mission Statement

Strategic Goals

Short-Term Goals

Action Plans

Once you've got your business up and running, you should periodically take a look at the specific actions you are performing (say, within the last week) and then read your mission statement. Do your actions support that mission statement and further its overall intent? If so, congratulate yourself on your focus. If not, then you should evaluate how you spend your time. Have you gotten yourself into areas that do not correspond with your initial intentions? Does your initial mission statement need modification, or does how you spend your day need modification?

Aim For Tomorrow's Goals—Today

So here is the challenge (like you needed another one at this point): Keep one eye on the long-term opportunity while taking care of today. This is where focusing on your goals is so incredibly valuable. The daily "fires" that erupt can look critically important when, in fact, they are irrelevant to the long-term objective. Actually, some of those fires can be left alone to burn themselves out while you focus on those objectives that lead to your desired strategic goal.

Hopefully, at this point, you are starting to understand the difference between strategic and tactical planning. Do things today that make tomorrow's goals a reality.

Action Without Direction

Ever said this? "I was busy all day, but when I walked out the door, I didn't really remember what I did or feel like I accomplished anything."

This is a classic action-without-direction statement. You may have dealt with many small issues that appeared important at the time but which overall did not contribute to achieving your objectives.

If you find yourself in a high-stress, high-activity, and low-sense-of-accomplishment mode, time-management techniques are available to help keep you on track. The essence of most techniques is simply teaching yourself to focus on the important things and to allow the less critical things to take a back seat. You can also hand off tasks to a person (if you are at that stage) who can take care of them for you. Prioritizing the most important tasks helps ensure that you'll spend time on those activities that will make a difference, and you will move closer to achieving your goals. Ask around for recommendations on an effective time-management class and carve out the time to take it.

One technique that I use is to assign a priority (A = high, B = medium, C = low) to each item and then assign a payoff (1 = high, 2 = medium, 3 = low) to the same item. The priority sets how important the completion of this item is to the company. The payoff sets how much I expect to enjoy the item as it is being completed. I will likely do the high-payoff items first, because those are the ones I like to do.

If an item is a high-payoff, high-priority item, then it will probably get done. If it is high-priority, low-payoff, we have a potential problem since I really won't want to do this very important item. I either buckle down and just do it, or try to find someone who will. Low-priority, high-payoff items are time-wasters that you like to do—beware of these, too.

Personal Payoff

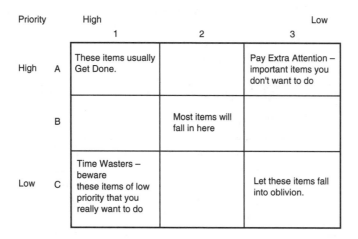

Tracking tasks and time best ensures that you spend your time on the items that need your attention. Not managing your time may make you feel like a feather blowing in the wind with no obvious direction or purpose.

You'll Never Have All the Information You Need

Evaluating a lot but doing nothing is "*analysis paralysis*." In this mode, you never know enough to make a decision or take any action and, consequently, nothing gets done. You keep trying to gather more information before you make a decision. If you find yourself having meetings to schedule your next meeting, you are in real trouble. Take your staff out for a meeting and say good-bye, because this is a surefire way to kill any start-up company.

Business Buzzword

Analysis paralysis is a state of being in which you continually evaluate, reassess, and analyze your business concept without making any headway whatsoever. Instead of taking action, you are paralyzed with inaction.

Best guess is making a decision based on the information you have available right now as to the right step to take. When starting a new business, rarely do you know everything there is to know about being successful. So you learn along the way by making your best guess when faced with a difficult decision about what to do.

Bankruptcy Alert

Don't create a task, objective, or goal without a time frame attached or you will never accomplish the actions needed to make it happen. Train yourself to look for items without time frames like a hawk looks for a field mouse. They are the items that will drag down your financial and energy reserves.

You'll never have all the information you need; so in many cases, you have to just make a *"best guess"* and proceed. At first, this will be extremely nerve-racking, but once you see that one bad decision won't make or break your company, you'll become better at moving ahead.

You have to do something, or nothing will get done. Don't be too afraid to make a mistake, or you will get too bogged down trying to make a perfect decision and you will accomplish nothing. You can analyze a problem to death, and if this happens often enough, it will kill your business and dreams along with it while stifling those around you in the process.

Setting Deadlines for Your Goals

Remember from the figure earlier in the chapter that the mission statement is at the top of the stack, but it translates into specific actions that make the company's mission become a reality. Deadlines and time-frame commitments drive action. If you do not have a time frame attached to an action, objective, or task, you will probably never achieve it. If your objective or task is important enough to track as a project, then it is important enough to have a time frame attached.

Risk and Reward Go Together

"If it sounds too good to be true, it probably is." Few people would argue with the wisdom of this statement, and we want to take a few moments to investigate why we know this to be so. We all know that few valuable things come without risk. If someone offers you something of value with no risk, you immediately get suspicious, or you question whether it has any value at all.

Know that you will be making risky decisions as you move your business along. The risk is created from not knowing what will happen as a result of the decision you made yesterday or the one you're making today. You will never know everything there is to know about a decision before you make it. Some people say that if we knew everything, we wouldn't do anything, because the eventual outcomes are rarely what we expect them to be. Accept the fact that you will need to make risky decisions with incomplete information, and do everything you can to minimize the uncertainties.

As time goes on, the unknowns often become known and you can reevaluate your decisions.

Managing your business in a constant state of high risk creates a high-stress environment that can eventually undermine morale, enthusiasm, and customer service. Be prepared to take risks, but choose your risks properly to ensure that you use your company resources to their best advantage.

From Small Tactical Wins to Major Strategic Victories

Many of your projects and objectives may take months to complete. The middle of a project often looks like the inside of a tunnel with darkness behind and in front of you. At times like this, like the middle chapters of a long book, you simply need to keep moving forward until the light at the end appears. (Hopefully, you're not feeling that way about this book.)

Keep yourself going by creating a set of "small wins." These are the interim milestones you use to pat yourself on the back for a job well done. For example, I may treat myself to an expensive sundae when I hit specific milestones, such as making a certain number of sales calls. On occasion, I will throw an unexpected office party for my staff to let them know I appreciate their accomplishing a particularly important project.

Add up enough small wins and the strategic objective is met, which is what you ultimately want to happen. There is nothing like winning, and the small-wins technique leads to the big wins that really count.

> ### Mentor
>
> Lee Iacocca was once asked what he did to become successful. "I waited 62 years," was his response. This funny statement belies the underlying philosophy that he later expressed when asked how to become successful. "Get an education, learn as much as you can about your field, and for God's sake, do something!"

The Least You Need to Know

➤ You have to learn to manage yourself before you can effectively manage the rest of your business.

➤ Plan short-term tactics in support of your long-term strategies.

➤ Your goals and those of the company should be in sync, or trouble may later arise.

➤ Thinking is good, but taking action is what makes things happen. In some situations, you'll just have to go with your gut instinct.

➤ Give all action items a time frame for completion or drop them from your list. Nothing happens on its own without a pending completion date.

➤ Managing means getting things done through others. Even one-person businesses need to manage their clients and suppliers.

➤ Understand risk and the impact it has on you and your business.

Chapter 4

Preparing Your Business Plan

In This Chapter

➤ Why write a business plan?

➤ How to find the information you need for your business plan

➤ Identifying the contents of a business plan

➤ How to use your plan

➤ What to do if your plan is not financially feasible

"If I could just raise $100,000, I know the business would be successful," says Dave to his friend, Allan. "Everyone is so dependent on being able to send documents via facsimile machines that I'm sure a business that sets up public fax machines would do amazingly well. I just need the money to buy all the systems."

"Where would you install these fax machines?" asked Allan. "Most companies already own their own, so why would they use a public one?"

"Think of all the traveling sales and business people who are trying to do business while making sales calls and attending business meetings in several cities. If I put these fax machines where they are likely to be, such as in hotels, convention centers and public buildings, like court houses and libraries, I can make a fortune," explained Dave.

Hating to sound skeptical, Allan pointed out that "Most hotels provide fax services through the concierge, or even in the rooms themselves, so I doubt that hotels would allow you to set up a competing machine in their lobby. And government facilities have to go out to bid in situations where money is being made, don't they? What about the new portable fax machines and printers, too, Dave? Can't sales reps set them up in their cars? Where are you getting this information?"

"I did a little research in the library as I was preparing my business plan, but I hadn't heard any of this before," said Dave. "I guess I'll have to adjust the financial projections in my business plan."

"That's great that you're preparing a business plan, Dave," said Allan, "but don't rush to send it out to investors before you figure out whether there really is money to be made here. Don't just adjust your numbers, really look into it. I'd hate to have you waste a lot of time and money on a business idea that's just not going to fly."

The most important part of writing a business plan is not the finished document you'll use to pursue investors or to manage your growing firm, the most important part is the process of researching, analyzing, and evaluating the business opportunity you're considering. Carefully evaluating a business idea or opportunity helps you to identify all the potential weaknesses and problem areas before you're in the trenches, struggling to make a go of it. In addition to showing you how to write a plan, this chapter will show you how to use a business plan as a tool to assess, manage, and sell your business idea.

A good business plan cannot guarantee success, but you can bet that not having one increases your chances of failing. If you don't know where you're going, you probably won't ever get there.

Although everyone knows that a business plan is a good idea, I have to be honest and tell you that not many businesses actually have one. According to an AT&T survey, only 42 percent of all businesses have a written business plan. Maybe this explains why only 20 percent of all new businesses will be around after 5 years! Do you want to risk being part of the 80 percent that won't be around? I didn't think so. This chapter shows you how to put together a business plan that works.

Business Plan Basics

Most people plan more extensively for a vacation than they do for a new business. Big mistake! Don't quit your day job until you research the type of business you want to start and feel confident that you can succeed. Unless you are pretty sure that over time you can earn a better salary with your own business than you can if you stay at your current job, why risk what you have? However, if you take the time to plan all the steps involved in starting and running your new business, you are on your way to success.

In previous chapters, you learned the importance of understanding your motivations for starting your own business, the need to evaluate the soundness of your business idea, and the importance of planning a strategic direction for your company to ensure that you reach your goals. Now you have to turn all that initial thinking into a written report, called a *business plan*, which clearly explains just what you intend to do and how you intend to do it. You can do this; it only takes a little discipline, research, and clear thinking to put your ideas into a typical business plan format.

A business plan is a document about 40 to 50 pages long that outlines your plans and intentions for running your business. It serves as your guidebook for managing your business as it grows, as well as a reference manual for your management team.

Some sections of the plan can remain confidential (such as financial information, new technology overviews, or client data); you won't share them with outsiders. However, you should assume that most of the plan will become public because you'll be sharing it with many different audiences. Those less-sensitive sections might include information about your personnel, existing products, and services, industry analyses, and any other company background information that normally appears in marketing literature.

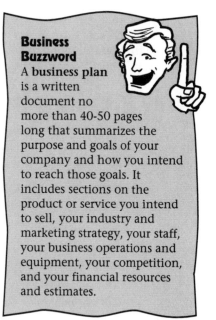

Business Buzzword
A **business plan** is a written document no more than 40-50 pages long that summarizes the purpose and goals of your company and how you intend to reach those goals. It includes sections on the product or service you intend to sell, your industry and marketing strategy, your staff, your business operations and equipment, your competition, and your financial resources and estimates.

The Kwik Chek Business Plan

Almost anything is easier to do when you have a picture of how it's supposed to look when it's done. It's kind of like trying to assemble a model or toy without the picture of what it's supposed to look like all put together. It's one thing to read about how a business plan is created and something completely different to see or read an actual plan.

For this reason, I included an actual business plan in Appendix A, "The Kwik Chek Auto Evaluation Business Plan." This plan is one I wrote for a used car evaluation service business I called Kwik Chek. When I wrote this business plan many years ago, I did it so that I could find out whether the idea would fly or whether I should go back to the drawing board. My original intent was to franchise the business nationwide, and I created the plan to meet that goal.

The Kwik Chek business concept didn't work for me because I wanted to be an absentee owner and franchise the concept rather than be an owner-operator. Fortunately, by going through the process of writing the business plan, I could see that this business wasn't going to help me achieve my goals. The idea still seems sound, it's just not right for me.

Should you decide to pursue the idea using this business plan, good luck! If you succeed with the idea, please let me know; send me a dozen free car inspection certificates, and buy me dinner some time when you're passing through Austin.

You might want to take this opportunity to read through the Kwik Chek plan because I frequently refer to it throughout this chapter. The Kwik Chek plan gives you concrete examples of how a plan can help you start and manage your business better. Although the format I used in preparing the Kwik Chek plan is not the only one that works, it provides a starting place and a guide for you to follow when you start to write your own plan. You thought you were going to be able to get away with just reading business plans, didn't you? Wrong! You'll be writing yours soon enough.

Why Prepare a Business Plan?

Although you might have heard that you only need a business plan if you are trying to get financing to start a company, this is not true. Besides using a business plan to secure funding, there are several other reasons to write one:

➤ Putting your goals and ideas down on paper helps to organize your thinking.

➤ Writing down your plans and goals demonstrates your commitment to your business, which impresses potential investors, suppliers, and employees.

➤ Once you have your plan down on paper, you have a guide to achieving your goals that you can refer to regularly.

➤ Not only do you have a guide that helps keep you on track, it also ensures that all your employees understand where you plan to take the business.

➤ Your plan helps focus your organization on its mission, reducing the chance that the business becomes sidetracked by other less important activities.

Let's face it: Others do not believe in your idea as you do. Part of the reason is that they probably don't know as much about your business, your product, and your plans as you do. For everyone else to believe in your idea, they need to see what you intend to do. There will probably be many different people who want to see your business plan, each for different reasons, including some of the following:

➤ Banks and other funding sources will use your plan to determine whether you are capable of starting and running the business.

➤ The Small Business Administration (SBA) will review your plan to make sure it will be profitable so that you won't have any problem repaying their guaranteed loan (if you opt to apply for one).

➤ Your board of directors or management team will want to review your plan to understand the future direction of the company.

➤ Employees will want to see sections of the business plan to understand whether the company has long-term career opportunities for them.

➤ Strategic partners or joint venture participants will want to read your plan to determine whether your overall direction is in alignment with their plans and their mission.

Be Honest

If you want to show your business plan to potential investors, include the assumptions you made when writing the plan, potential risks and rewards, and important milestones to ensure that the investors understand the whole picture. Making your situation appear too "rosy" will make investors skeptical, but making it appear too risky might scare them off. By simply being honest about what you see as the strengths and weaknesses of your situation, you allow investors to make up their own minds based on as much information as you have.

Being up front with potential investors helps you avoid problems down the road if things don't go as well as you planned. Given the right opportunity, you can lead professional investors into a minefield, as long as you first tell them that there is a minefield. Investors bring resources to the table that can keep you from getting into big trouble if and when it arises. However, if they feel you misrepresented your company and the potential rewards they can expect, you might seriously damage your working relationship.

Business Tip
Don't worry about hitting your business projections exactly; experienced investors know that things can go "off plan" as a project unfolds and that these figures are your best guess. They simply want to minimize the likelihood of losing their investment due to mistakes or poor management on your part. The business plan provides a framework for working out the details of your relationship with investors.

Researching Your Plan

God bless libraries and the librarians who run them. Virtually all the information you ever need to research your business idea is out there. You just have to know where to look for it.

Before you can begin to write your business plan, you must first learn more about your business: the market you're working in, the types of products or services

Business Tip
Talk nicely (and softly) to your librarian; he might be willing to do a lot of your research for you.

you're offering, and the needs of your customers. (Check out Chapter 2, "What Kind of Business Should You Start?," for more about developing your business idea.) Although you might have years of experience in the type of business that you want to start (perhaps you've been working in your family's printing shop for decades), investors want to feel confident that your instincts are correct.

To show them that your ideas are on target, you have to give them proof in the form of reliable published articles, reports, and other statistics. Saying that you know the market for printing is growing exponentially each year is nice, but being able to back up that statement with a report from the Department of Commerce that says essentially the same thing gives you a lot more credibility—and that's what you need at this point. To accomplish this, all you need to do is turn to reliable experts, such as publications, reports, and market gurus. All are available by phone, fax, Internet, or at the library.

With the growth of the Internet, it is likely that you can find all the information you ever need in cyberspace. If you're gifted at Net searches (and equipped with a computer), you might be able to avoid trouping off to the library. However, I still find that trained librarians are often able to point me in just the right direction.

Some of the most useful databases available to help you in learning more about an industry, a company, or a group of target customers include:

➤ Lexis/Nexis

➤ ProQuest

➤ Dow Jones

The following are some helpful Web sites you can turn to for assistance:

➤ http://www.fuld.com   A competitive intelligence resource

➤ http://www.thomasregister.com   The Thomas Register

➤ http://www.dnb.com   Dun and Bradstreet

Business Tip
Subscribe to industry-specific publications and trade groups. They offer support and research that might not be available to the general public. Find a Federal Repository, frequently located at a local university, that contains all the latest government document information. You already paid for the research with your tax dollars, so you might as well use it. A listing of documents is also available from the Government Printing Office. Call 202-512-0000.

If you're lucky, you might find that more information exists than you could ever use in your business plan. Chances are good that somebody, somewhere has compiled exactly the information you want. The challenge becomes finding it. Once you find it, you also might need help getting it in the form you want. (I know a guy who studies the sex life of fire ants. Go figure!) The point: Somebody, somewhere, is working to find an answer to your questions.

Public and university libraries contain a gold mine of information. General information is available from books, and more up-to-date information is found in magazines, newspapers, and industry newsletters. Using the *Reader's Guide to Periodicals* or the online search services in the library, you can get your hands on articles that relate exactly to what you're interested in. I talk more about the online services available to you for your research in Chapter 10, "Cybermarket: Starting an Internet-Based Business."

It is unlikely that you'll find all the information you need in a single article. You might need to piece together information from several sources to get a complete picture of the market or industry you're considering entering.

Using the Kwik Chek used car evaluation business plan as an example, assume that you need to know the number of used cars in service today, along with the expected growth in used-car ownership over the next five years. In one article, you might find the percentage of households in the U.S. that own used cars, and another article might contain the growth rate expected, by household, in ownership of used cars over the next five years.

Census data can tell you the total number of households in the U.S., and with some simple math, you can calculate the number of used cars and the expected increase over the next five years. You now have the total available market information needed to estimate market size and potential sales revenues. For example, the market demand evaluation data found in the Scarborough Report (see the "Market Analysis" section of the Kwik Chek Plan) shows that 14 percent of car buyers in Austin, Texas plan to buy used cars.

Business Tip
To check out the latest data from the Census, visit the Web site at http://www.census.gov.

Getting Help

You are not alone when you prepare your plan, even though it might feel that way. Organizations out there have a vested interest in helping you succeed at starting your own business. These include the local Chamber of Commerce, entrepreneurial associations, and the Federal government. That's right! Here are a few resources that can help:

➤ The Small Business Administration (SBA) works with a group of retired executives called SCORE (Service Corps of Retired Executives) to help you create a business plan and acquire funding. These are people who have already been where you plan to go; they can help you assemble the plan. Better yet, their services are free! Simply contact your local SBA office (see Appendix B, "Resources") and ask for the phone number of the local SCORE office.

➤ Small Business Development Centers (SBDCs), which are collaborative programs developed by the SBA and local colleges and universities, also provide free counseling help to people starting a business. There are more than 750 SBDC locations across the country to assist you. You can find a local office by calling 202-205-6766.

➤ Women and minority-owned companies can also turn to Minority Business Development Centers (MBDCs) for low-cost assistance. Centers across the U.S. help minority and women-owned companies write a business plan, develop a marketing campaign, and pursue government contracts for hourly rates typically under $20. See Appendix B for more contact information.

The Pieces of Your Plan

Effective business planning is a lot like assembling a jigsaw puzzle. All these stray pieces need to be put together in a logical order for the puzzle to work. As you become more familiar with the pieces, the proper fit reveals itself, and there is only one way to assemble the puzzle that makes any sense.

The more complicated the puzzle, the longer it takes to put it together. Most people start with the border and work their way to the center. Establishing this reference point helps identify where the other pieces should fall and simplifies puzzle assembly.

The puzzle analogy carries over directly to business plan preparation. You need to arrange the various pieces of business information you've collected and organize it so that it tells a story. Once you've developed an outline of the major pieces of information about the business you want to communicate, you can start to write, fitting all the bits of information together.

The business plan is essentially a document that is broken into chapters. Each chapter deals with an important part of the way you manage the business. Your business plan should contain the following basic elements:

I. Table of Contents

II. Executive Summary

III. Market and Industry Analysis

IV. Business Description

V. The Competition

VI. Marketing Strategy

VII. Operations Plan

VIII. The Management Team

IX. Funding Needs

X. Appendixes or Supplementary Materials

Take a look at each of these sections in detail.

Business Tip
You will learn more about your business idea, as a result of the planning process, than you ever thought possible. Treat it as a learning experience, and watch where it takes you.

Business Tip
One of my early sales managers described an effective sales presentation in this way: First, tell them what you are going to tell them (Executive Summary), tell them what you want to tell them (the detail sections), then tell them what you told them (Summary and Conclusions). A business plan is ultimately a sales document that explains your business idea in a similar way.

Table of Contents

The Table of Contents is not a major element of your business plan, but it helps show the reader what information they will find in the coming pages. Because tables of contents are generally found in well-organized documents, you can make a good impression by including one at the front of your plan.

Executive Summary

Although this section is the first in the business plan, it is much easier if you write it after you write all the other sections. Write up one paragraph to describe each section of the plan. Finish the Executive Summary by listing the amount of money required, the projected return on investment, and the major advantages your company will have over the competition.

The Executive Summary should be one to two pages long and is often the only section a potential investor will read. Based on those few paragraphs, he or she will decide whether to continue to read the rest of the plan. If the investor doesn't proceed to read your plan, you've just lost a potential investor. For this reason, your summary needs to catch and hold the reader's attention.

Take a look at the Executive Summary provided in the sample plan in Appendix A. It is short and concise and describes the Kwik Chek concept and the amount of investment required for the business to make a profit, explains the potential market penetration, and includes a brief explanation of why and how it will be a successful business.

Bankruptcy Alert
Make sure that "Company Confidential Information" is marked on every page of the plan (in the header or footer), including the Executive Summary. This alerts readers that the information should not be shared with outsiders.

Market and Industry Analysis

The Market and Industry Analysis section presents information describing the market need for your product or service. This is where you detail all the information you gathered regarding the size of your market, the number of potential customers for your product or service, and the growth rate for your market or for the industry as a whole (which usually means worldwide). This section not only relies heavily on the results of your research, but also on your ability to compile the information into a simple, concise, and easy-to-read format. See Chapter 7, "Masterful Marketing," for details regarding creating market estimates.

You must make a number of assumptions when completing your market analysis. For example, the percentage of available customers that you expect will pay for your product or service, called *potential market penetration*, is a key estimate in determining the amount

Market penetration is a measure of the percentage of total customers that have bought from you. If there are 1 million people in your market and 500,000 have bought your product, you have captured 50 percent of the market.

Potential market penetration is your estimate of how much of the total market you can capture over time.

Your **potential sales revenue** is the dollar value of sales you would achieve if everyone who is a potential customer bought from you.

of money you will make if every potential customer bought from you (your *potential sales revenue).*

You can come up with some decent projections of *potential market penetration* through information from other companies who did what you plan to do or from "guesstimates" from people experienced in the field. No one expects you to know exactly how many sales you will make during the first year, or even the first two years, but you can provide fairly accurate estimates by making some educated assumptions.

Looking at the Market Analysis section in the Kwik Chek plan, you notice immediately how I used facts and figures to support my belief that there was a market opportunity. These facts were summarized from all the information I gathered when I researched my business concept.

Business Description

The Business Description part of the plan explains your product or service idea and how it meets the needs of your market. Describe exactly what it is you will be selling and why people, or businesses, will buy it. How is it different from similar items already on the market? If it is a revolutionary concept, explain why the world needs this new breakthrough.

For instance, is it a new kind of car, a tasty new type of cookie, or a better house-cleaning service? Explain what the product or service does for the user—what the benefits are and why customers will buy it. If there are similar products or services already on the market, briefly compare them to what you are offering and explain how yours is better. If your new product or service is unlike anything currently available, convince the reader that it is needed.

Take a look at the idea described in the Kwik Chek plan in the Description section. For this business concept, you see a real-world scenario that explains how the Kwik Chek service will benefit a customer. It provides a clear description of all the areas of the car that the service will check, the average amount of time it will take to perform the service, and how the service will be performed (the Kwik Chek van comes to the customer). It also explains the benefits to the customer; this is the difference between Kwik Chek and the competition.

In this section, you'll also want to briefly touch on how your company has been organized, such as whether it has been structured as a corporation, partnership or sole proprietorship, whether any stock has been issued, and who invested any money to start it and how much. If you intend to use your plan for financing, these questions will come up immediately as you start to talk with investors, so you may as well take care of some of the questions right away.

The Competition

Who are the established companies already selling products and services similar to yours? How will they react to your company? Depending upon your idea and how long your product or service has been available, your competition might consist of other new and aggressive companies just like yours or established companies from whom you intend to take business. Anyone who believes that they have no competition is in for a rude awakening, even if he has a totally revolutionary product. Remember the introduction of the fax machine just a few short years ago? The fax machine replaced services that already existed, such as overnight mail and TELEX.

There is no reason to be afraid of competition. In fact, if you pretend that you have none or suggest that that's the case, no one will take you seriously. Accept that you have competitors and take every opportunity to learn from them. What are they doing right, and what can you do better? It is okay to mimic things your competition does well and to learn from their mistakes as long as you don't infringe on any trademarks or copyrights they may have in place. Generally this means that you can copy certain ways of doing business, such as offering free delivery with your service or guaranteeing your work, but not their advertising or designs. I tell you more about dealing with the competition in Chapter 9, "Beating the Competition."

Bankruptcy Alert
We all think our business ideas are unique, but the customer might think it's like dozens of others. Rely more on the market data you've collected rather than your opinion about whether there is a similar idea already in existence.

In this section, it's a good idea to provide a list of the other major players in the marketplace to show that you know exactly who your competition is. You should also indicate your impression of their strengths, weaknesses, and overall success in the market. By learning about your competition, the reader of your plan can better understand how you will succeed: either by going after a market opportunity that no existing competitor is addressing or by doing what everyone else is doing, but with a different twist.

The competition for the Kwik Chek concept is defined in the plan in the Market Analysis and the Competition sections. There is a clear description of what each competitor offers the customer, the price of their service, and additional information about each business, which gives investors an honest picture of how your idea stands up to the businesses already out there making money.

Marketing Strategy

If nobody buys your product or service, you're out of business. Period! Nothing ends a business faster than no customers. In this section of your business plan, you need to explain to the reader what you intend to do to get customers.

As part of your marketing strategy, you should describe how you intend to let the public know that you're in business, such as through a number of marketing methods that I cover. You should also explain your sales approach, such as selling by direct sales representatives, with a mail-order catalog, or through a retail storefront. You'll find a detailed discussion of all the different ways you can market your business later in the book, but start to think about how you'll describe your plans to the reader of your business plan.

In the Kwik Chek plan, I outlined the major approaches I will take for getting word to my target audience about the benefits of the Kwik Chek service. Notice that to effectively bring in customers, several methods are used to increase public awareness of Kwik Chek.

Operations Plan

This section describes operational procedures, manufacturing equipment, the level of production required, locations, international arrangements, licensing arrangements, and any other aspects related to providing the product or service defined in the idea section.

For those of you who are starting service businesses, this section might be short because service providers (such as management consultants, accountants, and attorneys) sell their time and experience. They don't use big machines to crank out words of wisdom, so production capacity is less of an issue. Assumptions should still explain how many hours per month you expect to spend on client-related work that you'll be paid for.

Check out the Operations Plan and the assumptions outlined in the financial statements in the Kwik Chek plan for one way to address operational issues for a service business.

The Management Team

One of the most important elements of your business plan is the section telling the reader why you and your partners are the most qualified group to start and run this business. Investors want to feel confident that you have experience in the type of business you're starting and that other members of your management team complement your skills. That means that if you hate numbers and love marketing, it is smart to hire someone who loves numbers so that he or she can handle the financial and accounting aspects of the business.

Assuming that you intend to grow, you also want to describe the types of people you'll need to hire in the first year. You don't need a particular person in mind for each position to be filled; you just have to know that you need someone to do a certain job. If you end up with more than five people on your staff in the first year, draw up a simple organizational chart to explain what each person is responsible for and who they report to. (Of course, if you are president, secretary, and janitor all rolled into one, skip the chart.)

In this section, you need to briefly describe the backgrounds and experience of your management team to show the reader that you know what you're doing. If you have an associate with 25 years of experience in the business who's going to be working with you, be sure to mention it; it makes your company much more credible.

Define each of the major jobs that will be held by the people who will be working with you. If you have three people who'll be working for you at the start, describe what their titles are, what their responsibilities will be, and why they are qualified to have the jobs. You're going to put their resumes in the Appendix at the back of the plan (in case anyone wants to read the specifics), but also write a paragraph or two about each person in this section (nothing too lengthy).

If you have advisors or consultants who have been working with you and giving you advice, mention them if they are fairly well-known or if they have a lot of experience. If you've set up a board of directors, briefly mention the members of your board. The point of mentioning other people here is to show the reader that you're not trying to do everything yourself and that you recognize you don't know everything and rely on professionals in those instances. Many business owners think they know everything and don't need advice from other people. These are usually the ones who don't last very long.

The Management Team section in the Kwik Chek plan describes a very small management team consisting of two people. One person will provide the marketing and technical expertise for the company; the other person will be the bookkeeper and office manager of the company.

Funding Needs

Now, it's down to the bottom line. Everything else up to this point was presented as the foundation for the financial analysis. This section spells out the actual investment required and when and how the business will make enough money to pay it back. You define the amount of initial investment and how much you will need in the future based on certain sales and operations projections. The investors really want to know how much money will be invested, how much they can expect to make, and the time frame in which they'll make it. Everything else is simply a teaser to whet their appetite for the financial feast that follows. You should also include a break-even analysis that covers the volume required to push the company from a deficit to a profitable operation.

Business Buzzword
The **break-even point** is the point where you are making just enough money to cover your expenses. You are living at a subsistence level, with just enough money to pay the rent and put food on the table, but nothing extra for movies and popcorn.

You should include an *income statement*, *balance sheet*, and *cash flow analysis* that projects the first three years of operations. (You'll learn more about preparing these forms in Chapter 11, "Making Sure That You're Making It.") This is sometimes called a pro-forma income statement. A *pro-forma balance sheet* for the next three years is also a necessary component. Pro-forma just means that the numbers are projections, or estimates, of future sales and expenses.

Your income statement summarizes how much money you made and how much money you spent for a specified period of time, which is typically one year. It allows you to look at the big picture of how much money you expect to make.

Use a balance sheet to determine the value of what you own (your assets) and what you owe (your liabilities) at a particular point in time, usually the last day of the year. Bankers are interested in this statement because it gives them an idea of what your business is worth and whether you can pay off your loan by selling all your assets.

> **Business Buzzword**
>
> The **income statement** reflects all income and expenses for a particular period of time (usually a year). The **balance sheet** shows your total assets and liabilities. The **cash flow analysis** shows exactly how much you received and how much you spent on a monthly basis. A **pro-forma balance sheet** estimates your future sales and expenses.

Now for the clincher: Estimate and show your actual cash needs for the first 12 months, broken out by month, and then for years 2 and 3 on an annual basis. The key here is figuring out exactly when you will receive payment for your sales, keeping in mind that if you do not receive payment when you sell your product (as you do in a fast-food restaurant), you will always be waiting for some customers to pay their bills. There is sometimes a time lag between when you make a sale and when you get paid that you have to account for. Putting together a cash flow statement ensures that you are always ahead of your expenses so you won't run out of cash to pay your bills. (Generally, that's called bankruptcy.)

The initial capital required to start the business, the funding sources, and how it will be spent is summarized in the "Funds Needed and Their Uses" section.

Appendixes or Supplementary Materials

Most of the work that goes into building a house doesn't show, such as the foundation and the walls. However, without these "invisible" ingredients, the house wouldn't stand up on its own. The appendixes and supplementary materials are similar in that you refer to them often throughout the plan, but they appear as detailed references at the end. Included are the charts, graphs, extrapolations, resumes, and literature pieces needed to convince the investor that you have done your homework.

Size Doesn't Matter

In business plans, as in many important aspects of life, it's not what you have, but how you use it. A small plan that clearly and concisely addresses all the major points of interest will be better received than a lengthy one that drones on about irrelevant information for pages and pages. You don't get bonus points for the weight of your plan.

Busy people, which includes most investors, won't take the time to read a plan that is much longer than 40 or 50 pages. They also won't figure out what you're talking about if you haven't been crystal clear. You need to do the work for them; spell out your information in plain English. Lead your readers through the plan, step-by-step, explaining your idea and how you intend to make money doing it. Present the information succinctly to that end, and keep the following in mind:

➤ Don't present an opinion as fact without any supporting information. Investors want to hear facts, not your personal beliefs.

➤ Don't present droves of information. Just because you walked ten miles through the snow doesn't mean someone else has to. Take the time to make the important points easily understood.

➤ Create a financial section to organize the detailed financial charts and tables and other supporting information.

➤ Summarize the implications associated with the information presented. Don't just present facts and figures without explaining why investors should care. (Investors can easily miss the point if left to draw their own conclusions.)

➤ Don't present conflicting information. (Analysts will eat you alive if you present inconsistent information.)

➤ Don't trivialize the competition. (They are already there. Where are you?)

➤ Don't use obsolete data while analyzing a rapidly changing marketplace. (You might not have a choice if new information isn't available, but avoid this mistake if possible.)

➤ Don't lose focus midstream and meander your way to the end without direction. (This might work at parties, but not with business plans. Stay on target.)

➤ Don't use a lot of technical jargon; keep it simple.

➤ Don't assume that customers will buy simply because it's your idea. (Get real! Your ego will not sell product!) It is price, quality, availability, and competitive positioning that will close the deal. Concentrate on these areas and leave your ego at home.

➤ Don't assume that everyone who said he would work with you will actually work with you when the chips are down. As a former IBM employee was told when he went out on his own looking for business as a consultant, "Oh, you no longer work for IBM? Sorry."

➤ Typos, spelling errors, and grammatical gaffes are inexcusable. Hire a professional proofreader if you need to, but be sure your plan is polished and error-free before you give it to anyone important to read.

➤ You never get a second chance to make a first impression; make sure your plan looks just as professional on the outside as it does inside. This means printing it on bond paper, creating a nice cover, and binding it or placing it in a nice presentation package.

Keep the Plan Alive!

Congratulations! You've finished your business plan. Take your family out to dinner at a nice restaurant and gloat on your recent triumph. Enjoy the moment while you can because you now have to make it work according to your estimates.

Business Buzzword
Performance to plan is a comparison of how well you thought you'd do (financially and otherwise) and how well you actually did.

Business Tip
The sales targets you set now can be used later to evaluate how well you're doing. Make sure you are willing to live up to your projections and that you can make them a reality. Otherwise, the targets are useless.

Don't throw away the business plan now that it's done or leave it on the shelf to accumulate dust. It is a working document that outlines your best guess on how to create a successful business. In a lot of ways, it becomes a friend who reminds you of what was important to you when you were just starting out. Use it as a barometer for determining your performance as compared to estimates (sometimes called *performance to plan*). Know that your investors will be checking your performance against the business plan on a regular basis because that is the set of specifications against which they made their investment. A well-executed business plan provides milestones for determining whether your initial estimates and assumptions were accurate, which allows for midcourse corrections if needed.

Many companies evaluate their performance on a quarterly basis, although reviewing your progress more frequently is a smart idea. You can't re-read your plan too frequently.

It's also a good idea to allocate time at the end of each year to track your performance to date and to budget for the next year. This exercise allows you to make corrections in anticipation for the upcoming year and minimizes the likelihood that mistakes from the prior year are carried over to the next. Use it wisely as a reference point to obtain the best return on your initially invested time and money.

If Your Plan Isn't Up to Par

What a drag! You perform the entire analysis to discover the idea does not hold financial water. Now what? Be thankful! You have just saved yourself from a nasty experience.

If you find that the business just won't work, then your original assumptions were not valid. If you had pursued the venture based on those assumptions, you would be either personally bankrupt after investing all your hard-earned savings or apologizing to your angry investors. Take heart! A negative outcome on this round does not negate the entire venture. You can now consider a different, potentially more successful approach.

Take a look at your approach to the business to see if modifying it can provide a better, and more profitable, strategy:

➤ Is the problem with the idea itself or simply how it is presented?

➤ Are you the right person to shepherd the idea to success, or should you be looking for others to round out other critical positions? Should you look at merging your talents with another more established firm?

➤ Do you need more money to buy you additional time to achieve the needed market recognition?

➤ Should you initially offer a product or service that is more readily acceptable and then convert your customers over to your new product or service line once they are already familiar with you and your company?

➤ Are your sales estimates too low? What could you do to increase the sales faster, and what would be the additional cost?

➤ Are there things you can do to minimize the level of perceived risk?

Keep your chin up and remember: Creating a successful business plan is a lot like solving a mystery. You have many stray facts that need to fit properly before the venture makes sense on all levels. Take the time to learn the facts.

Using Business Planning Software

Automation is a wonderful thing for performing routine tasks such as extensive number crunching and the creation of standard text. Almost all business plans contain the same basic information, and the overall structure is fairly well defined. For this reason, you might find that business planning software can help you start writing your plan. A number of business-planning software packages on the market are designed to ask you questions to fill in the blanks. Your responses are then entered into the appropriate plan sections, and the plan contents are automatically created.

That is the good news. The bad news is that no automated business planning computer software can add your personality and style to the plan, and your personality is crucial to

Business Tip
Two of the more popular business planning applications you can pick up at your local computer store are Biz Plan Builder ($129) and MultiMedia MBA ($99.95). For more information on Biz Plan Builder, call 800-346-5426; for MultiMedia MBA, call 800-228-5609.

the success of your venture. In addition, nobody can predict all of the special situations that apply to your business idea. As a result, some topics won't be addressed and unnecessary topics might be included. Also, investors don't always like to see the "plan-in-a-can" format that results from using one of these packages.

Computers perform routine tasks in a highly efficient manner, but they have zero capability to create something new. The creative aspects of the plan are in your hands. Using an automated business planning software package is worth a try because it forces you to organize your thoughts and gives you a place to start. If you are really lucky, it creates a plan that is adequate for your needs. To make sure, run the plan past a colleague or "friendly" investor for preliminary feedback. I talk about the basic use of this software and other business software in Chapter 20, "Get Automated."

The Least You Need to Know

➤ The process of creating a business plan is probably more important than the end product. The learning and decision-making that occurs as part of the journey is invaluable.

➤ Use your business plan as a sales document to convince someone to give you money.

➤ Your business plan is also a valuable management tool that can help you make decisions for your business.

➤ Going through the process of writing a business plan helps you determine if the business is worth starting. You might find that your original idea can't make money.

➤ A business plan is a requirement in today's business climate, and if you cooperate with the process instead of fighting it, you learn a lot about your proposed business idea and yourself.

Part 2
Establishing the Framework of Your Business

Now that you have an idea for what you want to accomplish with your business, you need to make some decisions about the legal structure of your business. Some people start a business and never incorporate. Others incorporate first thing. Still others simply hang out a sign and start selling stuff. People starting partnerships write up some sort of agreement, whether they file the paperwork to that effect or not.

An entire chapter deals with the special issues related to corporations. The reason that people approach the process of incorporating very differently is that there are a lot of things to consider. From taxes, to liability, to taxes, to raising money, to taxes... there are many things to think about. In this section, you can figure out what kind of business structure might be best for you, and you will receive some tips on setting up a corporation, if that is what you choose to do.

Chapter 5

Structuring Your Business

In This Chapter

➤ The difference between sole proprietorships, partnerships, and corporations

➤ The legal implications of each type of business structure

➤ How taxes affect each kind of business

➤ The type of business structure that is right for you

Bill shouted, "What do you mean I could lose everything I own? I didn't even know Ted bought that equipment for the company."

"The problem is that you never incorporated as you planned, and the law treats the two of you as a partnership," replied the attorney. "Under the law, you are responsible for the company obligations whether you agreed to them or not."

"No way," shouted Bill. "I'm not going to pay. Let them go after Ted first."

"The equipment company will first go after the business and then you and Ted at the same time. As far as the law is concerned, you and Ted are both equally liable for paying off the debt. Sorry, but you have no choice. Next time, pick your partners more carefully and consider incorporating to avoid this situation again."

Bill didn't like it, but he accepted what he heard as the truth. How could his life savings and a thriving company take a dive so quickly based on the irresponsible actions of one person? What could he have done differently? How could he have known?

Just as one house style does not meet the living requirements of all families, no single business structure meets everyone's business needs. Depending on your current situation and future business aspirations, one business structure might meet those needs better than another. Take the time to determine where you want the company to go using the information provided in Chapter 3, "Plan to Win the War." This long-term perspective suggests the best structure for your specific situation. In this chapter, I review the different structures and discuss the pros and cons of each one.

You should use this chapter as a general starting point. Understand the information presented and then apply it to your situation. This is your homework portion of the process. You should then run your assessment by the proper legal and accounting professionals to ensure that you are set up properly for your particular situation. Try to avoid the temptation to "go it alone" at this stage, because an error regarding your company's structure can have serious strategic consequences later on.

What Are the Various Business Structures?

The three basic business organizational structures are *sole proprietorships*, *partnerships*, and *corporations*. Under each category are subclasses that apply to specific situations.

A *sole proprietorship* is the most common and easiest type of business to create. Anyone who performs any services of any kind, such as a gardener, caterer, or even baby-sitter, is by default a sole proprietor unless he or she specifically sets it up otherwise. A small company with only one employee is often kept as a sole proprietorship, but there are no restrictions on how big a sole proprietorship can become. It depends exclusively on the desires of the owner, or *proprietor*. The majority of small businesses in the U.S. are sole proprietorships.

Business Buzzword

In a **sole proprietorship**, you are personally responsible for all the business's obligations, such as debt, even though the business might have a different name from you. Essentially, you and the business are one and the same.

A *partnership* is formed whenever two or more people decide to enter a for-profit business venture. Typically, each partner owns a portion of the company's profits and debts, which can be set up in a written agreement between you and the other partners. You do not need to file any special paperwork to form a partnership, but you should make sure you and your partners sign an agreement to minimize misunderstandings regarding each person's rights and liabilities. If you do not have an agreement signed by all parties, then any partnership-related disputes are handled under statutes based on the Uniform Partnership Act (UPA) used in most states.

A partnership agreement states the terms and conditions of the partnership. However, the UPA defines generally accepted standards on items not covered in the agreement. It is essentially a "gap filler." Any law library has detailed information on the UPA, but the best way to avoid UPA issues is to work with a complete partnership agreement from the beginning.

Most larger bookstores carry books that cover creating partnerships for your particular state. These books are inexpensive and helpful in making sure that you and your partners dot the right i's and cross the right t's. Once you have done the grunt work, I suggest that you present it to an attorney to make sure all of the proper legal lingo is included and that everyone's interests are protected.

For many people, forming a corporation is a sign of how serious you are about your business because it is more involved and more expensive to set up a corporation than to set up a sole proprietorship or partnership.

When you form a *corporation*, you actually establish a separate organization—separate and distinct from you personally. Some of you may ask why that's such a big deal; what's the advantage? The advantage is that if the corporation is sued, you are not personally responsible for any damages that might be awarded (unless, of course, you are also named in the suit). Paperwork and record-keeping is also more involved with a corporation, which is why some people decide it's not worth the hassles. There are other ways besides incorporating to protect yourself personally from liability.

Corporations are legal entities created through the states where the business is incorporated. A corporation is created by owners who purchase shares in the corporation. The percentage of ownership is based on the number of shares owned compared to the total number of shares sold.

Many corporations are formed in the state of Delaware because of its unrestrictive incorporation laws. Delaware was one of the early states to allow you to incorporate while conducting business and keeping headquarters in another state. Most other states now allow the same procedure.

It is important to understand that the various business structures have their own sets of tax-related problems and benefits, which are outlined throughout this chapter and in the next chapter that deals with detailed corporation considerations.

> **Business Buzzword**
> In a **partnership**, you and one or more people form a business marriage legally linking your debts and assets from the start. Any partner can make a commitment for the business, which also commits the other partners. Unless there is a specific agreement to the contrary, each partner owns an equal portion of the company's profits, assets, and debts.

> **Business Buzzword**
> A **corporation** is a separate legal entity created through the state where the business is incorporated. A corporation has owners who purchase shares in the corporation. A properly organized corporation bears all legal and fiscal liability, shielding shareholders (owners) from personal risk (unless they are also sued personally or they guarantee corporate obligations).

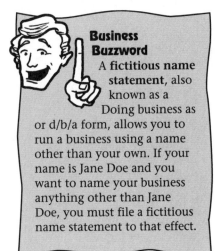

Just remember that the best business structure is the one that provides the required level of legal protection and enough flexibility to address future financial needs. This is a tricky balancing act that requires attention on your part.

Select the business structure that is right for you based on where you are today and where you want to wind up down the road. Consider the advantages and disadvantages of each business structure before making a decision. There is a great online resource for California businesses which is located at http://www.sba.gov/SCORE/ca/bus_type.html. This information is specifically pertinent to California, while providing an excellent overview of the pro's and con's associated with the various business structures. You might want to check it out even if you don't live in California.

Sole Proprietorship: Going It Alone

Judy woke up this morning and decided to begin selling those little wooden dolls she makes and gives away every Christmas. She just became the head of a sole proprietorship.

Once you begin providing products or services with the intention of making money from these activities, you become a sole proprietor. Your business expenses are deductible, all income is taxable, and you assume the liabilities of the business. (More on the tax implications later.)

Notice that Judy did not have to create a separate name to start her business. She simply started her business and began selling her product, using her own name. This is why the sole proprietorship is such a popular business structure.

Business Buzzword
A **fictitious name statement**, also known as a Doing business as or d/b/a form, allows you to run a business using a name other than your own. If your name is Jane Doe and you want to name your business anything other than Jane Doe, you must file a fictitious name statement to that effect.

However, if Judy wants to call her business "Dolls and Such," she must file a Doing business as d/b/a form with the local authorities, usually the county clerk's office in the area where she plans to do business. The d/b/a filing is sometimes called a *fictitious name statement*. If no one else is using the name she chooses, after filing her d/b/a form, Judy can transact business as Dolls and Such. Filing the d/b/a gives her legal rights to the name within the jurisdiction of the governing body, which is typically the county. If someone else later uses the name within the county, Judy can ask the courts to order that person to cease operations under the name she legally owns. The other business is then forced to rename itself.

A sole proprietorship is easy and inexpensive to create, and all profits go directly to the owner. The major disadvantage is that all legal and financial obligations incurred by the company are also passed directly to the owner. That means that if the company is sued for any reason, such as if a child eats one of Judy's dolls and is hospitalized, Judy is personally responsible for answering that lawsuit. Judy could lose everything she personally owns if the business-related lawsuit is lost and the damages are high. For this liability reason alone, many people choose to change their structure from a sole proprietorship to a corporation.

Being a sole proprietorship does not limit whether you have employees, although many sole proprietorships are one-person businesses. You can hire employees as a sole proprietorship, but you, as the owner, become the target for any claims made against the business as a result of any of the actions of your employees. You must apply for an employer identification number (EIN) as a corporation does since this is the IRS' tracking mechanism for employers. (See Chapter 18, "The Tax Files: Payroll Taxes," for details on obtaining an EIN.)

The flexibility associated with being the only owner is often attractive enough to keep people in business as a sole proprietorship, even after the company grows large in revenues.

Partnerships: A Business Marriage

Partnership is a wonderful term that evokes warm, comforting feelings. Who wouldn't want a partner to share the good and bad times in a business? Well, if you have ever been in a bad relationship, you know the damage it can do to your psychological and financial well-being. You should treat business partnerships with the same amount of respect.

When two or more people form a partnership, they are essentially married, from a business standpoint. Either party can obligate the other via the business, and everything the business and the partners own individually is on the line. In essence, a partnership is like a sole proprietorship owned by several people. All liability is passed to the partners.

A special partnership type, called a *limited partnership*, provides certain partners with a maximum financial liability equal to their investment. To maintain this limited financial liability status, these partners, called *limited partners*, cannot participate in the daily operation of the business. The *general partner* is responsible for the day-to-day management of the business. Limited partners invest in the company and rely on the general partner to run the business.

Special laws govern the operation of a limited partnership, and if they are not precisely followed, the courts might hold that the partnership was general, not

Business Buzzword
In a limited partnership, some partners (called **limited partners**) invest money but do not participate in the daily operation of the business. They are liable only for the amount of money that they each have invested. A **general partner** is responsible for the daily operations of the business.

limited. The formerly limited partner might find himself as liable as a general partner for business-related debts. Be aware that you must complete and file special paperwork with the state to form a limited partnership.

Corporations: Share the Wealth

Creating a corporation is like creating a new business life. A corporation is a separate and distinct business entity that is responsible for itself. Upon formation, the corporation issues shares of stock to *shareholders*, the owners. The shareholders exchange money, goods, or expertise to receive their shares of stock.

A *board of directors*, elected by the shareholders, manages the corporation. This board then appoints *officers* of the corporation to handle the day-to-day affairs of the company. In essence, the board members represent the interests of the shareholders in the company operations. In many small corporations depending on the state in which the business is incorporated, the business owner may be the primary, or only, shareholder and only board member. This same person is listed as the president, secretary, and treasurer of the corporation.

The corporation pays taxes on its annual profits and passes the profits to the shareholders in the form of *dividends*. The board of directors determines the amount of the dividends.

Business Buzzword

In a corporation, **shareholders**, or **stockholders**, own a percentage of the business, expressed in terms of the number of shares of stock they own in relation to the total number of shares issued. The corporation is managed by employees who take their overall direction from a board of directors. Annual profits are passed on to shareholders in the form of dividends, although annual dividend payments are not mandatory. The amount of the dividends is determined by the board of directors.

The major benefits associated with a corporate business form is that the corporation is liable for its own financial and civil liabilities. The shareholders risk only the amount of money they have invested in their respective shares of stock.

Using the earlier Dolls and Such example, assume that the business is a corporation with $500,000 in its bank account. If someone were to win a judgment against Dolls and Such for $1 million, the company would probably go out of business and only $500,000 would change hands. The person who won the legal judgment against the corporation would have no immediate legal basis for getting money from the shareholders personally.

However, this is not the case with a partnership or sole proprietorship. As a partner or sole proprietor, your personal finances are put squarely at risk in this scenario, and you could lose a lifetime of work. You might end up owing an additional $500,000 to the judgment holder if that situation ever came to pass.

Another major corporate benefit involves raising money for the business by selling shares in the corporation. Once the buyer and seller agree to a price per share of stock, the buyer simply purchases the number of shares needed to equal the amount of money needed. For instance, assume you need to raise $100,000. If you find a buyer who is willing to pay you $4 per share, then you sell them 25,000 shares of stock to receive the $100,000. Life is rarely this simple, but this example outlines the basic benefit associated with corporation finances.

To further illustrate the point, assume you still need $100,000 but don't know anyone with that kind of money on hand. Instead of selling 25,000 shares at $4 each to one person, you could sell 2,500 shares to 10 different investors for $4 each and still get the money you need. You now have ten shareholders instead of one, but you got the money you needed. Corporations are the route to take if you eventually plan to sell a large amount of stock to a number of different people.

Public or Private?

There is a difference between a publicly held and privately held corporation. Publicly held corporations are traded on the various public stock exchanges, such as the New York Stock Exchange, American Stock Exchange, and NASDAQ. The shareholders are typically large numbers of people who never come in direct contact with each other. They trust the board of directors to manage their investments for them.

Privately held, or *close*, corporations are more common. The shares are held by a few people, often family members, who also sit on the board and participate as officers of the corporation. The shares are also not offered to the general public.

Unless you are planning to create a very large business, you will probably create a privately held corporation with you and a few others as the only shareholders. It is generally easier to form a small or close corporation in the state where the principal shareholders reside and work. Because state tax laws vary, be sure to check with an accountant before making this decision.

If the number of shareholders exceeds 35, you must comply with the *Securities and Exchange Commission (SEC)* regulations for publicly offered companies, or choose to form a limited liability company (LLC)—more on this topic later—that permits more than 35 shareholders. You will definitely need legal and

Business Buzzword
A close corporation, or privately held corporation, is owned by a small number of shareholders, often only one. In this case, the corporation may be viewed as an extension of the individual. You must still act as a corporation with separate checking accounts, loans, and finances.

Business Buzzword
The **Securities and Exchange Commission** (SEC) regulates public offerings of company securities. The SEC mandates strict guidelines for the dissemination and content of company financial information to help assure investors that the information they receive on public companies is reliable and reasonably comprehensive.

accounting services. There has been some talk of increasing the 35 shareholder limit to 75 shareholders, but nothing had occurred in this regard at the time of this writing.

When a company "goes public," it offers to sell shares in the company to the general public. This is a common way for the founding members of a company to make oodles of money from the large numbers of stock shares they received during the start-up stages. The founders often buy or receive this stock at the outset for a nominal price, sometimes pennies per share. When the company goes public, the shares might sell for dollars per share. You don't need to be a CPA to figure out that several hundred thousand shares sold at a public offering can add up to a lot of profit. This opportunity alone keeps many people actively working for start-up companies, along with their associated risks, instead of working for larger, more stable companies.

Subchapter S Corporations: A Little Bit of Protection

Suppose you want the legal protection provided by a corporation but want the income to pass directly to you that so you can declare it on your personal income tax statement. You can thank the IRS and Congress because they created the *subchapter S corporation* for just this purpose.

In a subchapter S or S corporation, instead of the corporation paying taxes on its income, the business income is passed to the shareholders, who then declare the income on their personal income tax statements. Subchapter S corporations retain all the legal protection provided by a standard C corporation (any corporation that is not an S corporation).

Business Buzzword
A **subchapter S** or **S corporation** is a type of corporation with few shareholders. All profits are passed directly to the owners and taxed as income which avoids double taxation.

Why opt for the S instead of C corporation? If you are personally in a lower tax bracket than the corporation, then passing the business income to you decreases the overall taxes paid. In addition, if the corporation loses money, you can use that loss to offset personal income earned from other investments you may have. However, if you don't plan properly or if the company does better than you expected, you can find yourself with a huge tax bill at the end of the year.

If you think the S corporation is right for you, check with an accountant and an attorney before taking the plunge. A little prevention goes a long way to avoid unforeseen problems down the road. Notice that the decision is heavily based on how much revenue you anticipate the company will generate. This is why the strategic planning aspects of business are so critically important.

You first incorporate as you would any corporation, and then file IRS Form 2553 to establish your S corporation tax status.

Limited Liability Company (LLC)

How would you like the advantages of a corporation or partnership without some of the restrictions regarding shareholders? That's what a new form of business organization, called a *limited liability company (LLC)*, can provide.

Limited liability companies are now authorized in most states, and the remaining states are expected to approve a similar structure soon. The reason for their new popularity is that LLCs provide business owners with personal liability protection, just as corporations and partnerships do, and still provide tax profits at the individual level only, as subchapter S corporations do.

What sets LLCs apart from the popular S corporations is that LLCs do not have the same restrictions regarding shareholders. S corporations limit the number of shareholders to 35 and require that they be U.S. citizens; foreigners, domestic corporations, and co-owners of partnerships may not participate. LLCs, on the other hand, have no limits on the number of shareholders and do not place restrictions on the makeup or citizenship of shareholders. In addition, LLCs can have more than one *class (kind)* of stock and can own stock in another corporation. An LLC allows you to avoid double taxation as seen with a standard C corporation but provides most of the legal options regarding liability protection and stock sales that a C corporation has. For most small business owners, setting up an LLC may be overkill.

Because of these advantages, some people expect that LLCs will exceed subchapter S corporations, regular C corporations, partnerships, and limited partnerships as the preferred organizational structure. Others feel that the added complexity associated with setting up an LLC will diminish their popularity. Only history will know the outcome.

Because conversion to an LLC from another type of business structure can be costly, LLCs are generally recommended more for start-ups instead of established businesses.

Business Buzzword
A limited liability company (LLC) is a new type of business structure available in almost every state that has many of the advantages of a partnership or subchapter S corporation but fewer of the disadvantages.

Business Buzzword
Corporations can sell different **classes of stock**, such as preferred stock or common stock, at different prices. The various classes differ in when and under what circumstances dividends are paid.

Business Tip
Liability issues can also be addressed through insurance, so while limited liability is one reason to choose a corporate form of organization, check with knowlegable advisors before making a final decision.

One concern about LLCs, however, is that there is no unified set of tax laws because individual states created their own laws regarding LLCs, which were then copied by other states. The IRS has yet to provide a general set of national tax laws for LLCs. Check with your secretary of state to find out more about the laws governing LLCs in your state. If you are not careful, you might set up your LLC only to find out that the IRS will treat your company as a partnership for tax purposes.

Professional Corporations

Business Buzzword

A **professional corporation** is a special corporation sometimes used by lawyers, doctors, and accountants.

A special corporation structure addresses the needs of professionals who share a practice, such as lawyers, doctors, and accountants. The *professional corporation*, as it was initially called, provided special tax-related benefits to the participants. Many of the benefits have been reduced since 1981, however, and the growth in the number of professional corporations has declined. If you are a licensed professional who falls into this special category, check with your accountant to determine whether a professional corporation provides you any special benefits. Professional corporations use the letters P.C. after the company name to indicate the kind of corporation.

Franchises: Paying for Their Experience

Although a *franchise* is not technically a business structure, it is a way to start a business using the experience and training provided by an existing company. You are familiar with franchises if you have ever eaten at a McDonald's or had coffee at a Starbucks.

The franchise process works in the following manner:

Business Buzzword

A **franchise** is a company that has created a successful business operation and concept and offers to sell the rights to the operation and idea on a limited geographic or market basis. The buyer of the franchise rights is called the **franchisee**.

1. You decide you want to be in business.

2. You look around for business areas that interest you.

3. You find a franchisor who has developed a good business concept with a successful track record in helping people start similar operations.

4. You purchase the franchise rights to their procedures and name recognition in exchange for an up-front fee and a recurring annual percentage of your income.

5. After a few years, you start to resent paying the fee to the franchisor and begin looking for ways to sever the link.

(Step 5 might not always happen, but I have heard about it from enough successful franchisees that you may as well expecting that reaction eventually.)

You benefit from the franchise relationship because it removes a lot of the risky trial and error associated with starting a new business. A successful franchisor, such as McDonald's, knows precisely how to run your business so that you have the best chance for success. That expertise is not free, but it might save you from going under while you work your way up the learning curve.

The three basic franchise flavors are *distributor*, *chain-style*, and *manufacturing*.

The *distributor franchise* is typically used with automobile dealerships where the franchisee (the dealer) is licensed to sell the franchisor's products. The franchisee is given some type of exclusive marketing arrangement for a specific geographic or market segment. The franchisee's main role is to sell the company's products, rather than become involved in manufacturing or other functions. A good example of a distributor franchise is Ford Motor Company.

The *chain-style franchise* is used with fast-food establishments. The franchisee (the local owner) is licensed and required to prepare the food in accordance with the franchisor's standards. The local store is often required to purchase all supplies from the franchisor, maintain quality standards, and (often) hit specific sales volume targets. McDonald's is a famous example of a chain-style franchise.

In a *manufacturing franchise*, the franchisee is licensed to create a product in accordance with the franchisor's specifications. The franchise then resells the product at a wholesale price to the distribution channel. Coca-Cola is an example of a product sold through a manufacturing franchise.

A franchise arrangement allows you to start your own business with strong expertise behind you. This improves your likelihood of success and might decrease the amount of up-front cash required because many franchisors assist with the initial funding. However, it might increase the up-front total investment required (cash and loans) because you are buying a share of a proven business franchise concept. Unless you are dead set on "doing it your own way," you should consider the purchasing of a franchised operation as a business option.

When you purchase a franchise, you need to set up a company just the same as if you start it from scratch.

Business Buzzword
In a **distributor franchise**, the franchisee (the dealer) is licensed to sell the franchisor's products. In a **chain-style franchise**, the franchisee (the local owner) is licensed and required to prepare the food in accordance with the franchisor's standards. In a **manufacturing franchise**, the franchisee is licensed to create a product in accordance with the franchisor's specifications.

Business Tip
Every January, *Entrepreneur* magazine does an issue on top franchises. Check it out!

You still need to evaluate which form of doing business is best for your situation: sole proprietorship, partnership, or corporation. Look to your franchisor for guidance regarding these fundamental decisions. If your franchisor does not offer assistance in these areas, you might reconsider whether the organization is the right horse to which you should attach your cart. Where will the franchisor be when difficult questions arise?

State to State

As if life wasn't complicated enough, you now want to operate your business with offices in several states. The good news is that this is possible. If the majority of your business comes from your home base in one state, you can avoid the multistate headache. The bad news is that, if this is not the case, you need to perform some filings and registrations to qualify in each state where you do business.

Some firms specialize in setting up companies that need to operate in several states at once. Contact a law firm and get a referral to one of these firms or simply contract the law firm to perform the needed paperwork for you.

Business Tip
The Company Corporation in Wilmington, Delaware, offers online corporate registration via CompuServe and other online services. The $49 base fee it quotes might not cover all the costs you have to pay, but entrepreneurs all over the country have found this to be one reasonable way to incorporate. Call 302-575-0440.

You can do all the legwork yourself; however, this approach might become a black hole for time and effort. You are probably better off farming it out to those who do it for a living. This is particularly important when considering a name for your organization because the name must be available in all states of interest. (Read Chapter 6, "The Implications of Corporations," for more information about names.) If you insist on doing it yourself, contact the secretary of state in each state of interest for filing guidelines and fees.

Don't forget that once you set up offices in separate states, you should begin tracking sales tax for these states along with the percent of corporate revenue derived from operations in these states. The tax collectors in each state want their "fair" piece of your profit pie, and if you don't track it carefully from the beginning, you might spend December through March of each year unraveling your finances so that you can accurately pay your business and sales taxes in each state.

When to Use a Lawyer

When should you use a lawyer? I think the best answer to this question is "before you need one." By this I mean that prevention is the best cure for legal problems. If your business agreements are created and documented in a responsible way with all parties equally involved in the discussions, you can minimize the likelihood of future legal action.

Lawyers will tell you that much of their income is generated in repairing the damage done by people who attempt to economize on legal fees up front and develop contracts and agreements on their own—only to find out that the document they developed doesn't accomplish its objective.

If you have the money (or even if you think you don't), have an attorney draw up the necessary filing documents for you. If money is a real concern, take your best shot at completing legal documents on your own and then run them past an attorney for review.

You can purchase prewritten articles of incorporation, stock certificates, and corporation bylaws from the same companies that supply your attorney. Ask an attorney where he or she gets corporation documents, and you might be able to save yourself hundreds of dollars. Of course, you do inherit the hassle of putting the things together properly.

As always, if any agreement covers a large amount of money and binds you in critical ways, you should consult an attorney before negotiating and signing it. A few hundred dollars up front can save thousands of dollars and hundreds of hours later.

> **Business Tip**
> Numerous computer software packages can automatically generate a wide variety of legal documents for you, from a bill of sale to articles of incorporation. Most packages even modify the documents to suit the state in which you do business. They usually cost under $100 and pay for themselves with one use. Check out *PC World*, *MacWorld*, NOLO Press, or *PC* magazine for an assessment of the software.

Here are a few things to consider when selecting a lawyer:

1. Talk to colleagues first to obtain a lawyer from a positive referral.

2. Don't assume that the lawyer has the expertise you need. Ask about their experience with companies of your type and size.

3. Write a list of questions before meeting with the lawyer so that you don't forget anything or become rattled and lose your focus.

4. Check with your local SCORE office to see if they have a group of lawyers that provide SCORE assistance. Once again, just because SCORE recommends a lawyer doesn't mean that this lawyer is right for you.

5. Make sure that your lawyer is familiar with the laws of the state(s) in which you plan to conduct business.

Special Opportunities for Women and Minorities

Governmental organizations, along with most large businesses, have implemented programs that provide special opportunities for minority-owned businesses. The definition of a minority is inconsistent between agencies, so investigate your eligibility as a minority business enterprise. These types of organizations are also known as Historically Underutilized Businesses (HUB), Disadvantaged Business Enterprises (DBE), or Woman Business Enterprises (WBE).

These procurement programs are designed to ensure that a certain percentage of government-issued contracts go to special business types. You are more likely to get a government request for a proposal if you are listed as a DBE or WBE. Getting the name of your business on a procurement list opens doors that you otherwise have to discover on your own. This doesn't guarantee that you get the business, but at least you get a shot at it. Contact the government procurement office, General Services Commission, or Corporate Purchasing to get more information.

Dealing with the Tax Man

Taxes never go away. All you can do is try to minimize their negative impact on your profits. The impact of taxes on your choice of organizational structure is worth a brief discussion. I present only general concepts here about income taxes; talk to your accountant about your specific situation. Remember, there are many other taxes your business will have to pay. You need to learn about all of them in your area—city, county, state, sales, franchise, and so on.

The company income will pass directly to you as owner or major stockholder (of any type of business structure except for the C corporation). You then declare it on your personal tax return. In corporations, all salary expenses (including the owner's salary) are deducted from the company's revenues prior to determining how much tax must be paid. You then pay personal income tax only on your salary, just as you do for any company.

Self-employed individuals really feel the bite of FICA (Social Security) and Medicare taxes because they pay both the employee's share and the employer's share of these taxes.

In a corporation, however, dividends paid to shareholders are taxed twice; they are paid out of company income after the corporate taxes have been paid. The dividends are then paid to the shareholders who pay tax on the dividends because it is part of their personal income. This is called *double taxation*, and it can get expensive.

Sometimes, corporations come up with creative ways to avoid or minimize the financial bite taken out of their shareholder's dividends as a result of double taxation. Some people get so focused on avoiding paying taxes that they lose track of their primary concern: running a successful and profitable business that fulfills their personal and financial goals. We all hate giving Uncle Sam a nickel, but avoid the temptation to fiddle with your tax planning to the point that you lose focus on your business.

Individuals and corporations do not pay taxes at the same rate. You will find that the break points between tax levels differ. Depending on your situation and the company's income levels, you might be better off leaving the money in the company and paying corporate taxes instead of paying yourself a large salary and paying personal income tax. Check out Table 5.1 for the relative rates for personal and corporate taxes.

Table 5.1 Personal and Corporate Taxable Income Rates

Single		Married Filing Jointly		Corporate	
Income	*Tax Rate*	*Income*	*Tax Rate*	*Income*	*Tax Rate*
$0–24,650	15%	$0–41,200	15%	$0–50,000	15%
$24,650–59,750	28%	$41,200–99,600	28%	$50,000–75,000	25%
$59,750–124,650	31%	$99,600–151,750	31%	$75,000–100,000	34%
$124,650–271,650	36%	$151,750–271,050	36%	$100,000–335,000	39%
$271,050+	39.6%	$271,050	39.6%	$335,000–10M	34%

Single people should look at this table and smile. Check out the corporate tax benefit offered to single people who earn between $24,650 and $50,000. The personal tax rate is 28 percent, but the corporation's is 15 percent. That 13 percent (28 percent minus 15 percent) can be left in the corporation for business use at a lower tax rate than what a sole proprietor must pay.

Remember that if you pay the money left over in the corporation to yourself as a salary bonus at the end of the year, you have to pay the company's portion of the payroll tax (7.62 percent) and you then pay 28 percent in personal income tax instead of the corporate rate of 15 percent if you just leave it in the company. This means that a total of 35.62 percent of each corporate revenue dollar paid to you in salary goes to taxes before it ends up in your pocket. On the other hand, if you need the money to pay your personal bills, you have to pay yourself and take the tax bite.

> **Business Tip**
> Your company must pay FICA (Social Security), unemployment, and Medicare taxes for each employee over and above the standard salary. This currently amounts to around 7.62 percent. The employee also pays these taxes. See Chapter 18 for more information on taxes.

Notice that a C corporation allows you the option of leaving the money in the corporation or paying yourself in the form of a bonus or dividend. An S corporation takes this decision out of your hands and makes you treat the left-over corporate profits as personal income, without having to apply the payroll taxes.

The Least You Need to Know

➤ Select the business structure based on your expected strategic goals. Each form has its own benefits; you want to choose the one best suited to your needs.

➤ Sole proprietorships, partnerships, and corporations are not the same. Choose your business structure based on operational considerations, not tax considerations.

➤ Corporations provide the highest level of legal protection but can subject income to double taxation.

➤ Don't be afraid to investigate franchising; you can profit from other people's experiences.

➤ Taxes are a part of life for any business. Recognize that you have to learn about them or find competent help.

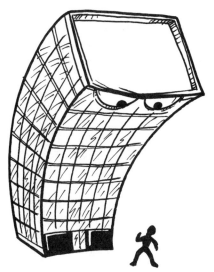

The Implications of Corporations

In This Chapter

➤ How to set up a corporation

➤ Naming your company

➤ Setting up a board of directors

➤ An overview of articles of incorporation and bylaws

There was a sense of destiny in the air as Susan made her way to her office. She said good morning to her assistant and anxiously looked for the folder that contained the artist's renderings of their company logo. She liked the name. Her husband chose it from the final list of contenders. He beamed when she told him that they would use it. It was fun to see him enjoy participating with her in the dream she had wanted for years. It surely made life at home easier.

The artist's renderings were beautiful. The colors were just what she wanted and the name and logo were clear enough that anyone who saw them would understand what her company had to offer. It cost around $4,000 for the public relations firm to create the name and renderings. The company was now ready to go.

At that moment Walter, the company attorney, walked into the room. He was holding a piece of paper in his hand and had a somber look on his face: even for Walter. He handed Susan the piece of paper and waited. The letter was from the secretary of state's office. It said that the name they chose was already in use by another company within the state and that their request for the name reservation was denied.

Susan's mind did a few somersaults and then landed. They were back to square one and $4,000 poorer than before they started. Why did they rush to have that logo created? Couldn't they have waited to hear back from the secretary of state? Susan's mind was racing. "I guess it's back to the drawing board again," she sighed. "But this time, let's send several potential names to the state for approval, rather than just one. I certainly don't want to waste any more time or money on choosing a name."

Business Tip
Unlike sole proprietorships, which typically involve just one piece of paper filed with the county clerk's office, a corporation is formed at the state level by the secretary of state.

Creating a corporation is like creating a new business life. The corporation has the ability to make commitments, incur debt, hire employees, flourish (if successful), and go out of business (if not). You are the principle avenue through which this entity is created, and the responsibility for performing the proper legal steps involved with the corporation's birth is in your hands.

Corporations are created under guidelines established by the state where the corporation will reside. Each state has its own regulations that govern the creation and operation of a corporation. The secretary of state's office defines these guidelines and is your contact point for initial information. In this chapter, I give you a general overview of the process.

Creating a Corporation

First, determine who is going to be a shareholder in the corporation. How many shareholders will there be? Almost always, you need a minimum of one shareholder or officer of the corporation before the state allows you to incorporate. Some states require a minimum of two officers. You are asked for the names of the president, treasurer, and secretary. These can all be you. Just like the general store owner in a small town, you might have to wear several hats in your corporation.

Next, determine the states where you intend to do business. Many states allow you to incorporate in that particular state but have your main offices and operations in another state. (Delaware is one state that permits this situation.)

The major benefits for "long-distance incorporation" are usually tax-related. If a state does not have a corporate income tax, or has a small one, it is financially advantageous to incorporate there; but you still have to pay the applicable business state income taxes for the states where you actually run your business. Therefore, depending on your state regulations, it may or may not make sense to do an out-of-state incorporation.

Beware of taxes presenting themselves under a different name. For example, Texas has no state income tax, but does levy a "franchise fee" that is really the equivalent of a tax. (By the way, the fee applies to businesses, even if they are not franchises). It surely feels like a tax when you write the check to pay it. Check with corporations in your state of interest to confirm the flies in the corporate ointment.

The corporation filing fees you have to pay to the state to set up your corporation vary widely, from as low as $40 to as high as $900 or more. (California, where else? Ouch!) Unless becoming a national company immediately is important to you, you are probably better off keeping the process simple and incorporating only in your home state. Start-up life is complicated enough without adding more complexity than is necessary.

If you dream of going national quickly, however, see Chapter 5 about doing business in more than one state and plan early for the complexities.

Your corporation must have a name that serves both a legal and marketing use. The name must comply with the state's legal requirements and should also convey something about your offerings to your customers. Naming details are covered in the following section "What's in a Name?"

Finally, you must file *articles of incorporation* with the state. The articles outline the basic characteristics of the business and become the legal framework within which the corporation must operate. The business's purpose, planned duration of existence, and capital structure, such as how many shares of stock have been issued and who owns what, are defined in the articles. (You'll learn more about articles of incorporation later in this chapter.) Once you file the articles and the fees are paid, you are incorporated!

Congratulations! You have just given birth to a business with a life and identity all its own. The secretary of state will send you the official "birth announcement." Establishing a trusty board of directors is a natural next step. Later in the chapter, I show you how to do just that.

Bankruptcy Alert
Check the laws of your home state carefully. If you incorporate in another state, your state might charge stiff taxes to out-of-state corporations, negating a lot of the tax advantages of incorporating elsewhere. If you do business in more than one state, you might have to file tax returns and pay taxes in all of them. You must also track and pay applicable sales taxes for the states where you have sales or operations offices.

Business Buzzword
Articles of incorporation establish the structure and stock ownership of the corporation. The articles are filed with the secretary of state. The state will probably issue a certificate of incorporation along with a **state charter number** (the official number assigned to your corporation, like a Social Security number). This is your official record of incorporation.

Bylaws are the rules and operating policies of the corporation that the shareholders approve and that the corporation must follow.

What's in a Name?

Just as a child must have a name, so must a corporation. However, unlike children, who can share names such as Lisa, Tom, and Mary, every corporation must have a unique name easily distinguished from other businesses in the state where you incorporate.

The reason for such strict rules about similar names is to avoid confusion. For example, if a company called Art Treasures, Inc. is already doing business in Miami, Florida, it has all the legal rights to that name. You probably would not be permitted to incorporate as Art Treasures, Inc. in another part of Florida because it would cause too much confusion. This protects you, the other corporation, and consumers who purchase from these companies. Once your company is successful, you don't want another company benefiting from your company's success and reputation. Here are some additional things to consider when choosing a name for your business:

➤ To be most effective, the company's name should tell prospective customers something about the types of products or services you offer, either by including the product name as part of the company name, as in Toys R Us, or by suggesting the benefits of buying from the company, as in Wall to Wall Sound.

➤ Avoid making the company name too complicated or obscure. Cute can work to your advantage, but if your company's name is too cute and nobody understands the joke, nobody will use your services. Make it straightforward but distinctive.

➤ The official corporation's name must indicate that it is a corporation by including the word "corporation," "company," "incorporated," or "limited." The secretary of state's office can help you with this.

➤ Make it a name your company can grow with—not too narrow.

Public relations firms and advertising agencies often assist companies in finding a name that works for their situations. You might want to get a bid from a company that specializes in naming. After all, you usually keep your name for life.

Business Tip
You can use brainstorming software, such as IdeaFisher, to come up with potential names. Check at any software retailer to either purchase or order a copy.

Your company will carry its name for many years, and you will spend a tremendous amount of time and money promoting it. Your customer "mind share," or way of thinking about your company, will revolve around the name. Treat it as gold because it is! Jealously guard your company name, just as you would guard your own. See Chapter 7, "Masterful Marketing," for a detailed discussion of mind share and its impact on a business.

Once you find the name you want to use, you must reserve it with the state for a period of time (usually two to six months) by filing a *fictitious name form* with the secretary of state office. There is a nominal fee for reserving the name.

The office performs a name search and tells you whether the name you want to use is still available or some other company is already using it. I suggest giving the secretary of state several names to check at once so that you don't have to keep going back to the drawing board if your top choice is already in use. You must incorporate within the two-to-six-month window or the name is forfeited.

If you want to incorporate in several states, the same name must be available in each state. Finding that one free name in all the target states can be a frustrating and expensive procedure. Don't commission a designer for your corporate name and logo until you have the name reserved, or you might be throwing money away. Nothing is more complicated than explaining to a client the reason behind having two names.

Mentor

My company started out as a sole proprietorship, but I decided to incorporate a few years ago. When I tried to incorporate under the sole proprietorship name, I learned that the name was already taken by a business in another city. We now have two operational names: one for the local community, Applied Concepts, and one for outside the local area, Technology and Communications, Inc. We retained the local name due to its local recognition, but the headaches associated with having two business names should not be ignored. When you pick a name, make sure it is available from the start to prevent customer confusion.

Laying Down the Law: Articles of Incorporation and Bylaws

How do you establish the articles of incorporation and the bylaws for your company? These two documents spell out the overall intent of your corporation. You file the articles of incorporation with the state as part of the corporation formation procedure. The board of directors creates the bylaws and determines the company operating procedures.

Articles of Incorporation: The Basic Ingredients

The articles of incorporation need not be lengthy. They just need to be accurate and to provide the state with the necessary information for incorporation. Most of the articles are easily created. Try this basic structure as a starting place. In the following articles, type the bold sentences and fill in the italic requests.

➤ Article One: The Company Name

The name of the corporation is *(enter your company name)*.

➤ Article Two: The Period of Duration

The period of the company duration is *(enter the number of years your company will be in existence, which is usually assumed to be PERPETUAL)*.

➤ Article Three: The Company Purpose

The purpose of the company is to *(enter the basic reasons why the company exists; most people simply use FOR ANY LEGAL PURPOSE)*.

' You can also be a little more specific and mention the types of products or services the corporation will be selling. However, if you ever decide to change the purpose of the corporation, you might have to alter or amend your articles of incorporation. For this reason, it is best to be somewhat general.

➤ Article Four: The Capital Structure

The total number of shares that the company is authorized to issue is *(enter the number of shares)* **at a par value of** *(enter the par value of each share)* **dollars each**.

For example, you can assume that the company is authorized to issue 100,000 shares at a par value of $.01 each. (Don't confuse *authorized shares* with *issued shares*. Issued shares are actually in the hands of a shareholder. Authorized shares are shares that can be sold by the company but need not be.)

You can even authorize and issue different classes of stock, but this is certainly overkill for the vast majority of businesses at your current stage of development. Get big and profitable enough to make worrying about multiple stock classes important, and then hire some financial wizards to help you put it together.

Keep this section simple unless you have specific reasons for creating a more complicated capital structure, and be sure to verify your capital structure with your accountant and lawyer before finalizing your articles. You need to file amended articles of incorporation if you ever decide to change your capital structure. In addition, if you sell shares and then change your capital structure, you need to convert the old shares to new ones.

Business Buzzword

The total number of shares of stock the corporation is permitted to issue is known as the number of **authorized shares**. For instance, if 1,000 shares of stock are authorized at the start of the corporation, only a total of 1,000 shares can ever be sold to shareholders—no more than that. **Issued shares** are the number of shares that are actually issued.

➤ Article Five: Initial Capitalization

Most business transactions are not considered binding, or final, until money has changed hands. For this reason, your corporation might require some form of *consideration* to officially start.

The corporation will not commence business until it has received for the issuance of its shares consideration of the value of *(enter the desired amount of money or valued services amount; usually not less than $1,000).*

Notice that this initial capitalization must be paid for by corporate stock and that stock currently has a par value of whatever you set in your articles of incorporation. For example, assume that you invest $10,000 in your corporation and that your articles of incorporation authorize 100,000 shares at a $1-each par value. This means that the corporation must issue 10,000 shares of $1 par value stock, or 10 percent of authorized shares, to you in exchange for the initial capital investment. Check with your particular state's authorities to determine if a minimum percentage must be issued to validate the corporation existence.

➤ Article Six: Address and Registered Agent

The address of the corporation's *registered office* is *(enter the address)* **and the name of its registered agent at such address is** *(enter your name or the name of the person who is the primary contact for all company-related business including legal matters).*

The address must be a street address, not a P.O. box.

➤ Article Seven: Board of Directors Information

The number of directors is *(enter the number of directors, typically 1 to 3),* **and their names and addresses are** *(enter the names and addresses of each board member).*

Bankruptcy Alert
Don't issue all authorized shares of stock to yourself when you first start and capitalize your company or you might limit how you work with and sell shares of stock later.

Business Buzzword
Consideration is a legal term for "something of value." That something could be money or the right to do something. Many contracts are not valid until some form of consideration has changed hands; in some cases, that consideration can be as little as $1 to make the transaction official.

Bankruptcy Alert
If you do not handle all financial transfers between you and the corporation as you do those with either a standard investor or employee, then you might place your corporation status and protections in jeopardy. You would document a loan made to or received from a third party, and you must do the same between you and the corporation.

Business Buzzword
The **registered agent** is the official person to contact for all legal matters. The registered agent may or may not be located at the official corporate address, also called the **registered office**. In some states, the registered agent must be an attorney, and in others, you can serve as the registered agent.

Business Buzzword
An **advisory board** counsels and guides the senior management of a company, much as a board of directors does. However, an advisory board has no financial stake in the company and assumes no liability for the corporation's actions.

Some corporations have a *board of directors* consisting of only one or two people, such as the owner and the owner's spouse, but then also establish an *advisory board* to give business advice and guidance. An advisory board works in the same way as a board of directors in counseling the president, helping identify new opportunities, and giving feedback on the direction of the company.

The difference is that the members of the advisory board have no financial interest in the company; they are not shareholders, and they assume no liability for the corporation's actions. In some cases, you might find that successful business people are more likely to agree to serve on an advisory board than on a board of directors because they don't want to be held liable for the consequences of the corporation's actions.

➤ Article Eight: Name of the Incorporator

The name and address of the incorporator is *(enter your name, assuming that you are the person forming the corporation).*

This can be a third party with no interest in the company at all who is simply completing the paperwork for you, such as an attorney.

The incorporator must sign the articles in front of a notary public. Then, you file the articles, or a copy of them, with the state.

Bylaws: The Basic Ingredients

Your corporation now exists. What is it going to do and how will it conduct itself on a daily basis? The bylaws should explain. They are the internal rules that govern employees' and officers' actions when the directors are not there to supervise. Violation of the corporation bylaws is usually treated as a grievous offense and can be grounds for dismissal in most companies.

Of course, when you're both the president and the board of directors, you can fire yourself whenever you want. If you have outside shareholders—investors other than you and a spouse or close family member—be aware that they can use a violation of the bylaws as a reason to bring in someone else to run the company if they hold a majority of the shares. If you own the majority of your corporation's shares, they probably can't fire you, but they can still cause problems for you. The moral of the story: Set up bylaws that you should have no problem living by.

The first board of directors meeting is used to adopt the corporate bylaws. The bylaws can cover any areas of conduct deemed necessary and generally include company policy in areas such as

➤ When and where shareholder meetings are held

➤ When and how the board is formed

➤ How frequently meetings are held

➤ Voting rights of shareholders and directors

➤ Procedures for hiring and dismissing company officers and a description of their duties

➤ The overall handling of stock shares and dividends

➤ Usage of the corporate seal

➤ Internal approval procedures for legally committing the company

➤ Definition of the company fiscal year, which is frequently the calendar year for simplicity's sake

➤ References to the articles of incorporation as needed and procedures for amending the bylaws

The bylaws contain a lot of information that helps to maintain consistency in company policy in the midst of the daily pressures. Make sure that the bylaws reflect the business and spiritual integrity of the organization; then stick with what you have or change the bylaws to better reflect your mission.

Bylaws and Articles "in a Can"

Most bylaws and articles of incorporation include standard language with only minor changes for specific company-related information. For this reason, many people decide to write their own using a computer program with the standard format for incorporating, which they then edit for their own situation. Software packages such as It's Legal by Parson Technologies give you the standard language for under $50. Many software catalogs and computer retailers carry these programs.

Business Tip
Pull out your bylaws every 6 to 12 months to remind you of the direction in which you initially intended to steer the company. Daily pressures can take you off track, and this review will help you to keep company operations consistent over the long term.

Business Tip
If you choose to use software to create your articles, be sure to verify your capital structure with a financial adviser before finalizing them. The software simply works with the information you provide and does not verify its accuracy. If the information you type is incorrect, your articles of incorporation will be flawed.

Business Tip
Now that you are incorporated with the state, you can issue stock and stamp official corporate documents with your corporate seal. There are companies across the country that specialize in creating these corporation kits for a fee. Do you need to have the kit? Not if you do not plan to sell shares to anyone other than yourself. Is it a good idea to have one? I think so, and the expense is usually under $100. One such company is Liberty Legal, located in Houston, Texas. Contact 800-392-3720.

Although you might be tempted to save a few hundred dollars by using "canned" software to form your corporation, be aware that you could create serious problems for yourself down the line. You should always consider having significant documents (such as contracts and official paperwork) reviewed by your attorney to make sure you establish your legal structure the way you intend. Changing them later requires filing the changes with the state, which costs money and time.

Establishing a Board of Directors

It has been said that human beings are reasonable in that we can always justify and rationalize our desires and actions. This is a dangerous trait when you run your own business. It is often helpful to have someone to report to, or you'll find reasons to take the company into business areas where no company has gone before—or where no company should go.

This is a wonderful reason for creating a board of directors. A board of directors is a group of people who are not involved with the daily operation of the business but who have a vested interest in keeping the company on track. Board members usually serve for one year, but three-year terms are not uncommon.

If you plan to keep your company small, you can act as your own board. This certainly keeps arguments between the board and upper management to a minimum. If you plan to grow past the "mom-and-pop" stage, you should consider a board of directors consisting of advisors from the business community.

Directors are required to act with the best interests of the corporation and its shareholders in mind. As long as they act with integrity and make decisions that any "reasonable" person would make given the same information, they are generally protected from potential lawsuits or claims as a result of their decisions. This is the *business judgment rule* designed to protect directors from claims derived from frivolous lawsuits filed by irate shareholders who may have lost money on their investments.

For example, if a board of directors decides to stop selling a particular product because it is losing money for the company and a customer becomes upset at that decision, the customer can still sue the corporation, but the members of the board of directors cannot be sued unless the customer can prove the decision was a poor one for the company.

With an advisory board, the members are still expected to act in the company's best interests and to recommend actions that further the corporation's goals, but the issue of liability doesn't come up. That's because an advisory board is much less formal than a board of directors and because the advisory board members generally receive no compensation for giving advice. In most cases, no formal, written relationship exists between the advisory board members and the corporation. As a sign of your appreciation for their time and guidance, you should probably buy them dinner once in a while, but you don't have to give them shares of stock or big payments.

Directors generally serve on a board for indirect benefits, such as business contacts, prestige, and other related rewards. Typically, board members receive payment of travel expenses for attending meetings, as well as nominal payment for serving on the board. Board members are frequently majority stockholders in the corporation, which ensures that board decisions are made on behalf of the shareholders and not simply to serve the company officers. When you own all of the shares of stock, this is not such a big deal. As you involve more shareholders, the board becomes more important. In fact, most large investors want a seat on the board to have a vote in company direction and operation.

A diverse board is better than one comprising people from the same industry or background; people with varied backgrounds bring different perspectives and contacts to the company. Board members who own shares will act in a more responsible manner because they have a direct interest in the company's success. Adding board members with financial, legal, managerial, and political experience can assist the company greatly when fast decisions must be made. This higher level of expertise shortens the information-gathering phase because the experts are often right there in the room.

Business Buzzword
The **business judgment rule** protects members of corporate boards of directors from lawsuits filed by shareholders, customers, or others if the decision that caused the lawsuit was made in the best interests of the corporation.

It is a good idea to have the director stock ownership phased in over a period of time based upon participation and overall company performance. This means that board members receive a small number of shares on joining the board, which are increased over time, based on how well the company does and how much time the board members spend on company business. Setting up a stock ownership plan that takes effect over several years takes more time up front but ensures that the directors are motivated to make your company, and you, succeed.

Finally, make sure that all board members agree to disclose any potential conflict of interest situations that may arise. Most organizations require that all board members sign a disclosure form up front, either stating that there are no known conflicts of interest or explaining potential conflicts. Nothing breeds contempt and distrust faster than finding out that one of your confidants is cavorting with a competitor without your knowledge.

The Right to Vote

Voting rights in a corporation can get pretty complicated. In a small corporation, the topic is a little less complicated but is still important if you plan to create a board of directors to help you steer your company. If you aren't careful, you can have a board of directors that steers you right out of the company. Read on and learn the pros and cons of corporation voting rights and the creation of a board of directors.

Shareholder Voting Rights

Who gets to vote on the operation of the business? Everyone may feel that they have a say, but only specific people, shareholders and board members, get to actually vote on the company's direction.

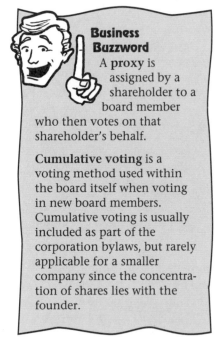

Business Buzzword

A proxy is assigned by a shareholder to a board member who then votes on that shareholder's behalf.

Cumulative voting is a voting method used within the board itself when voting in new board members. Cumulative voting is usually included as part of the corporation bylaws, but rarely applicable for a smaller company since the concentration of shares lies with the founder.

In general, shareholders hold a single vote for each share of stock that is owned. Because it is not feasible for a shareholder to be involved in daily business decisions, shareholder voting rights are typically applied to topics that affect the entire corporation, such as changing the articles of incorporation, amending the bylaws, approving mergers or the purchase of another company, and dissolving the corporation and selling most or all of the company assets. Shareholders also vote on who will be on the board of directors, although the first board is created by the company management.

Shareholders also indirectly vote at the board level through the use of a *proxy*, which allows the designated board member to vote on that shareholder's behalf when choosing new board members using a process called *cumulative voting*. Cumulative voting is not covered here in detail because it usually does not apply to a small corporation, but you should learn how it works once your company gets big enough that additional board members are selected. Remember that board members vote on what you can do with regard to daily operation of the company.

Board Member Voting Rights

Decisions regarding the daily operation of the company are made at the board level. The board of directors votes on items such as the addition or removal of corporation officers (such as you), officer salaries (such as yours), dividend payment decisions, product lines, addition and removal of services, labor negotiations, issuance of shares or bonds, and other related operational activities. This voting occurs on a one-vote-per-board-member basis and is not dependent on the number of shares held by each board member.

Board member voting presents some interesting situations that you should be aware of. For example, assume that the board gets mad at you and decides to get back at you for reasons that have nothing to do with business. If the majority of the board votes to remove you as president of the company, they can do this even against your wishes. Would you normally expect this to happen from the trusted people you put on your board? Certainly not, or you never would have put them on your board in the first place. Could this happen in a close corporation where the other board members are also family members who might have a personal ax to grind? Unfortunately, yes.

Is the addition of a board of directors still a good thing? In general, I think the answer is yes if you want your company to grow. You can protect yourself from becoming personally liable for all company debts and then being voted out of company management by the board of the company you founded. Change the bylaws to require that the president and CEO of the company (that is, you) cannot be removed from office without a shareholder vote. Because you hold the majority of the shares, you cannot be voted out of office by the board members who are almost always minority shareholders, unless you also vote yourself out.

Shareholder Proxy

Any fundamental changes to a corporation must be approved by a shareholder vote, as outlined earlier. This voting is either done through a *direct shareholder vote*, where each shareholder shows up and casts his or her vote (rarely done), or through a *proxy statement*, in which the shareholder authorizes a board member with a proxy endorsement to vote on that shareholder's behalf (the usual method).

It is common for board members in large corporations to solicit proxy authorizations from shareholders so that they can concentrate voting authority under their specific director seat's authority. In most smaller corporations, the president is the default recipient of the shareholder proxy.

A quorum of shares (over 50 percent of issued shares) must be represented for the vote on resolutions to have validity. Of the quorum voters present, over 50 percent of the vote on a resolution decides whether it passes. Some states allow for nonquorum stockholder meetings to decide on resolutions if 100 percent of those present vote in the same way.

Business Buzzword
In a **direct shareholder vote**, each shareholder shows up and casts his or her vote. More commonly, a shareholder votes through a **proxy statement**, in which he or she authorizes a board member with a proxy endorsement to vote on his or her behalf.

Handling the Vote

In a small corporation that you founded, here are a few things that are unique compared to larger corporations:

1. You are the majority shareholder, and as such, you will be asked and required to personally guarantee all major company debts. If the company goes under, the banks want to be able to come after you to recover their money.

2. Major issues are presented to the shareholders who vote on the items either directly at a shareholder meeting or through a proxy, which is generally given to the president.

3. You create your initial board of directors. The typical term for a board member is one year, from annual stockholder meeting to annual stockholder meeting. Subsequent board members are elected by the existing board through cumulative voting, which is a nonissue as long as you hold the vast majority of the shares and the number of board seats is small.

4. Operational issues are decided by the board on a one-member, one-vote basis. The majority of board member votes wins, even if it represents the minority of shares.

5. I recommend changing your bylaws to state that the president and CEO who is also a major shareholder can only be voted out of office by a shareholder vote.

Business Buzzword
Vesting period is often applied to stock option plans and refers to the timeframe over which a person obtains the right to purchase their shares. Three to five year vesting periods are not uncommon with a specific percentage of total shares vested each year.

6. Set up some form of long-term stock sharing and acquisition policy with your board members so that they have a vested interest in seeing the company succeed. For example, allocate 1 to 2 percent of stock for each board member who vests over a five-year period with the requirement that the person be on the board for at least two years before he or she can vest any of the stock.

7. Make sure that you keep track of board meetings and annual shareholder meetings by taking minutes at the meetings. Some software packages on the market provide a standardized method of creating minutes.

Now you're well on your way to incorporating. The process should now be clearer to you than before so that whether you hire an attorney to prepare the documents or you do them yourself, you are familiar with what's involved.

The Least You Need to Know

➤ Each state has its own regulations regarding incorporating. Contact the secretary of state's office in your state's capital.

➤ The incorporation process is fairly simple and inexpensive in most states, costing between $300 and $1500 depending on the state. Only one shareholder is usually required to incorporate.

➤ Choosing the right name is crucial. Start with the name, verify its availability in the states where you'll be doing business, and reserve it until you finish the articles of incorporation.

➤ A board of directors will greatly assist your progress in developing the mega-company you envision. Look for board members from the start and choose wisely.

➤ Change your bylaws to preclude the possibility of you being voted out of your own company.

➤ Do your homework before you incorporate. It is often difficult and costly to change mistakes.

➤ Time your date of incorporation so that it includes the bulk of the tax year, or you could end up filing a tax return for a corporation that was only in operation for a few days within the tax year.

Part 3
Marketing Magic and Successful Sales

Now that your business is set up and you filed all the necessary paperwork, you need to get some customers. Customers will make or break you because customers bring in money. In this section, you'll learn how to use marketing to get customers and keep them. You'll also discover the basics of selling, along with how your competitors can help you succeed. Finally, I take a look at the Internet and how you can expect to use it positively in your business.

If you thought that marketing and selling were the same thing, you're in the majority, but actually, they're not. In this section, you'll learn what the difference is, why you should care, and how marketing and sales are the key to your success.

Chapter 7

Masterful Marketing

In This Chapter

➤ The difference between sales and marketing

➤ Target marketing and demographics

➤ Pricing strategies

➤ Promotional methods

➤ Distribution considerations

Jamie, the marketing consultant, brought the company executives into the room to report her findings. The company had seen a drop in its sales, yet it was spending more money on marketing and sales activities. The president felt that they were doing something fundamentally wrong. She had always believed that the harder you pushed something, the more it moved. For the first time in her company history, the harder she pushed by spending more money and energy, the less she got back.

"Okay. Let's start at the beginning. It appears that you have a loyal customer base and that they all come from four general industry groups. Would you agree with that?" asked Jamie. The president nodded.

"Then why are you spending all of this time and money selling into new market areas when you still have room for growth in your target areas?"

"We cannot depend on the same old customers for our livelihood. What if something happens to one of them? Then where are we?" the president inquired defiantly.

"Good point," said Jamie, "That would be true if your current customers and their respective market segments had minimal sales growth opportunity, but it appears that you are in the enviable position of having a firm market presence in a growing industry. You should first concentrate on taking care of business in your strong areas before moving into areas where you are unknown. Let me show you how a target marketing campaign to companies in your strong market segments can improve sales, decrease personnel requirements, and decrease cost. Interested?"

"What do you think?" said the smiling, yet doubtful, president.

How do you make sure your product or service is targeted to the people who can use it most? This chapter introduces you to the basic concepts of marketing and provides a background for the next chapter.

Despite the fact that most people use the words *sales* and *marketing* interchangeably, the two activities really are different.

Marketing consists of strategies to identify your customers, figure out what they need, determine what to charge them, tell them that you have what they need, and then sell it to them efficiently. In MBA programs, those are also called the "4 Ps" of marketing: product, pricing, promotion, and place of sale, which is also called distribution. If you want to get technical, they should really be called the "3 Ps and 1 D" of marketing, but let's not get nitpicky.

It is marketing's responsibility to identify the most likely customers, design the best product or service offering, set the product or service's price range, and choose the overall advertising message and presentation content most likely to get customers to buy. Specific marketing activities include market research, product or service development, analysis of pricing levels, creation of marketing materials and sales aids, advertising, public relations, and sales support.

Sales efforts work best when the salesperson addresses the customers most likely to buy, with a product they are most likely to use, for a price that is within their budget, with a presentation that delivers the right message in an easily understood format.

Sales activities include contacting customers, making presentations, and getting the orders, among other things. The most effective marketing tells your salesperson the company

Business Buzzword

Marketing involves selecting the right product, pricing strategy, promotional programs, and distribution outlets for your particular audience, or market.

Sales is part of marketing and involves all the steps you take to get the customer to buy your product or service. It can be done in person by salespeople meeting the customer or by telephone, direct mail, or advertising that prompts the customer to place an order for your product.

type (industry or size) and contact person title most likely to buy from your company, which products they'll probably use, a viable pricing strategy, and why the customer would use your company's products or services over a competitor's.

Effective marketing and sales campaigns require that you get close to your customers and understand their buying habits. You might not get it right the first time, but careful planning makes sure that your darts hit the board and experience leads you to the bull's-eye.

Who Is Your Market?

We human beings like to believe that we are all different and that we are each unique, and on some basic level, we are. However, in other areas, we fall into certain groups that think, act, buy, and react alike. We're not all lemmings who jump off a cliff at once, but we do have certain characteristics that bind us as a group. These characteristics are often called *demographics* and include such things as age, income level, educational level, and marital status.

Breaking down your target customers by demographic characteristics is called *market segmentation*. When marketing people discuss the *demographic profile* of their ideal customer, they are looking for the common characteristics associated with their most likely customer.

A bank, for example, might segment its customers by age because people's banking needs change during different phases of their lives. People over the age of 50 are more likely to be interested in retirement-related products than 18-year-olds, and 18-year-olds are more likely to be interested in college loan details than 30-something couples who want to buy a home with a bank mortgage. Market segmentation helps the bank to group similar customers together and develop products that they will be interested in.

Compiling information on potential customers is the challenge for market research companies. They gather information through mail and phone surveys and personal interviews to determine people's buying habits. As a business owner, you can then buy and use this information to develop effective marketing programs to sell to these potential buyers.

Business Buzzword

Demographics are a set of objective characteristics (including age, number of children, marital status, education level, job title, and others) that describe a group of people.

A **demographic profile** refers to a specific set of demographic characteristics that sales and marketing people use to target likely sales prospects.

An **ideal customer profile** is a demographic description of the type of customer most likely to benefit from your product or service.

Market segmentation refers to dividing the total available market (everyone who may ever buy the product) into smaller groups, or segments, by specific attributes such as age, sex, location, interests, industry, or other pertinent criteria.

Anyone can buy marketing surveys (unless the survey was paid for by a specific company for its use only). Check with your local library first to see if they subscribe to any of these reports. Typically, the library purchases a wide variety of these reports and makes them available to the public. Look for a federal repository, which is a library that carries a lot of federal reports and documents. These reports were created with your tax dollars and are freely available to anyone who wants to read them. Ask the librarian for assistance, but keep your voice down.

This type of information may be available for free from other sources, too. The federal government compiles information about the age, household size, and financial status of all Americans in the form of a national census every ten years (the last census was completed in 1990) and makes it available at most libraries. The census contains substantial information about the American public and breaks the country into areas called Standard Metropolitan Statistical Areas (SMSAs).

Target Marketing: Picking Your Customer

If you sell beef products, it wouldn't make sense to invest time and money displaying your products at a vegetarian convention. Obviously, people who don't eat meat aren't the best sales prospects for a meat product.

Identifying your customer is an important part of the marketing process. If you don't know who will buy your product and why, you have no idea who to contact and how to present your wares. When you don't know who your likely customers are, the result is a *scattergun marketing* approach, in which you blanket the market with a general message and hope that someone sees it and calls. This is not a very effective approach because it is costly and time-consuming and results in few sales.

Target marketing, on the other hand, focuses your financial and personnel resources on the people most likely to purchase what you offer. Suppose a particular geographic area has 100,000 potential customers for your products or services. A direct mail piece sent to this group at $1 each would cost $100,000. From this mailer, you might get a 2 percent response (which is a typical response rate). This means that 2,000 people want more information from you. Of those people, assume 10 percent of those people, or 200, actually buy your product or service. For a $100,000 investment, you sold your company's goods to 200 people. A little statistics and customer characteristics analyses will probably show that these 200 people have similarities that propel them into a specific market segment (which I discussed earlier).

Although promotional methods such as direct mail are discussed later, I should point out that you just spent $500 per customer to get each sale. Now, if you're selling a $10,000 item, you've done well, but if you're selling a $20 item, you've lost big bucks.

To develop a target marketing approach, you first need to define which markets contain your best potential customers. This means that you need to know something about what you're selling and who needs it most.

For example, you might find that your market segment is mostly women between 25 and 45 years of age, or that they are mostly college educated or work in specific industries. You can also use certain circumstances as market segmentation criteria; for example, people moving to a new location usually need new telephone equipment. To contact people most likely to purchase a telephone system, your first step might be identifying people who are moving or planning to move shortly.

Target marketing does not waste time, money, and effort approaching people who are not good prospects. As a result, you get much better results from your marketing efforts. The types of results you get vary widely from situation to situation, but you will always find target marketing a more manageable and efficient marketing effort than the scattergun approach.

Name Your Price

Price is an interesting phenomenon in our capitalist society. It often represents more than just the amount of money that is paid for a product. Price is often viewed as a status symbol or a measure of worth over and above the amount that changes hands; the most expensive suit wins. Pricing a product too low can make it appear inferior and can make people avoid it, even though it's of comparable quality to more expensive models.

Ultimately, the customer pays a price that is consistent with his perceived value of the offering. If the name on the product is perceived by the customer as having high value (such as designer clothing), then the customer might be willing to pay a high price to wear those designer duds.

Other pricing strategies are cost-based and market-based. You can calculate cost-based prices by determining the

Bankruptcy Alert
Do not ever let your ego dictate price for your products. I have seen several companies with a substantial jump on the market fall flat due to the faulty belief that people would pay more for their product simply because it was new or different or because its name was on it! Price your products according to more than what you want people to pay.

> **Business Buzzword**
> **Perceived value** is the overall value that the customer places on a particular product or service. This includes much more than price; it considers features such as delivery lead time, quality of salesmanship, service, style, and other less tangible items. With a perceived-value pricing strategy, you set a price for your product or service by determining what people are willing to pay yet making sure that you can still cover all your costs.

costs of producing a product or delivering a service and then adding a profit margin. This means that you'd better accurately know your costs or this can really "cost" you the farm. You might think that you're doing great, only to find out that your costs were wrong and you are selling for less than your overall costs.

You determine market-based prices by studying what similar products or services cost and asking a similar price.

You need a lot of information about your product costs, your competitors' pricing, and how customers decide what and when to buy to accurately and comfortably fix pricing for your offerings. Here are some basic rules that might help you determine the best price for your service or products:

➤ Don't ever price the product below your cost. You need to make a profit on virtually every sale to stay in business. Some people think that if they sell huge amounts, they'll come out okay in the end. Wrong! You can't lose a nickel on each unit and expect to make up the profit in volume.

➤ If you have a new company or a new product, you generally cannot match price with an established company with a similar offering. This is because the other company is already known and trusted and is a less risky choice for the customer. For the same price, its offering is considered a better purchase.

➤ You generally have to price lower than the established competition until you get a foothold in the market (unless your offering is perceived by the customer as unique and more valuable because it cannot be found anywhere else).

➤ You can generally sell intangibles such as better service, deliverability, and location for up to 20 percent over a competitor's price. Over that point, the customer will probably treat your offering as too expensive for his or her perceived value.

➤ Don't always price your offering on a cost-plus-profit-margin basis. Although this approach is easy to compute, it usually leaves money on the customer's table that you could have otherwise put in your company bank account. Market-based pricing is generally more complicated but best ensures the most profit on each sale. In other words, if you do a better job producing the product and lowering your costs, market-based pricing (which remains constant due to market forces) gives higher dollar profits, whereas cost-based pricing cut your sales price and ultimately, your profit. (By the way, if you understood this last sentence, you are getting this important topic under your belt. If not, keep working at it until you do.)

➤ Quantity discounts are an effective way to encourage your customers to purchase more of your product at a given time. However, watch the discount amounts, or you might find yourself selling a lot for a minimal profit.

Obviously, you can set your prices wherever you want, but your best price means more sales for you because you will have figured out what your customers believe is a fair price for your goods. In return, they buy more. Knowing what your competitors' profit margin is can help you adjust your own pricing strategy.

You must answer several key questions when determining a pricing strategy:

1. What are your competitors offering your potential customers in terms of their basic product or service price and the price of any add-on services?

2. How much does it cost you to supply the product or service desired by the customer (including those additional intangibles just discussed)?

3. What additional features do you offer your customers that your competitors do not and are these features worth more money?

The costs associated with a product vary, depending upon where it is in the product life cycle. The next section provides a brief overview of a new product's typical life cycle. You can use this model as a guide in determining your pricing, distribution, and marketing message strategies.

Business Buzzword
When your price is calculated using the cost to the company plus whatever profit margin is reasonable for your industry, you are using **cost plus profit pricing**. A widget that costs $1 to produce with a desired 50 percent profit margin would sell for $1+ (1×5) = $1.50. You're simply adding on your desired profit percentage to your costs.

When you price offerings at a level set by what everyone else is charging, rather than by costs, you are using **market-based pricing**. With this strategy, you can generally make more money assuming your competition is charging reasonable rates and you can keep your costs down.

Business Tip
Profit margins for a company are available, sorted by Standard Industrial Code (SIC), from the Dun & Bradstreet report, Robert Morris Associates' Annual Statement Studies, or the annual report of publicly traded, established companies. Most publicly traded companies will send you a copy of their annual report if you call their investor relations department.

> ### Mentor
>
> I have a friend who prides himself on his hourly consulting rate of $300. When I asked him how many hours he bills a month, he said three, on average. This means that he makes $900 per month from his consulting work. Another colleague, on the other hand, bills at $110 per hour and works 30 to 50 hours per month on average, which equates to $3,300 to $5,500 per month of income. Who is better off? It depends on each person's needs, but if the intent is to make money, then the lower billing rate is the way to go.

The Life Cycle

Every product or service goes through a *life cycle* from its introduction until the time it is discontinued or taken off the market. The life cycle usually refers to products, but services go through a similar evolution. The life cycle is divided into four basic stages:

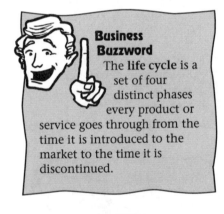

Business Buzzword

The **life cycle** is a set of four distinct phases every product or service goes through from the time it is introduced to the market to the time it is discontinued.

Business Buzzword

When so many competitors enter the market that everyone has to keep dropping their prices to win sales, **price erosion** lowers the market price and profit margins.

Stage 1: Market development (a.k.a. embryonic) The product or service is new to the market, having recently been introduced. Sales are slow at this stage and customers take longer to make a purchase decision due to their lack of familiarity with the product. Only potential customers who have shown a willingness to experiment with new products or services are good prospects at this stage. That group of experimenters is often referred to as *early adopters* because they are the first to try something new.

Stage 2: Market growth Sales are increasing steadily and there is a general awareness of the product or service. Competition usually starts to show up at this point.

Stage 3: Maturity Overall demand starts to level off as customers purchase the offering as a routine part of doing business. Customers have a high degree of familiarity with the offering. *Price erosion* can happen at this point due to intense competition from what is now an established market for the product or service.

Stage 4: Market decline Customer demand for the product or service starts to decline due to improved variations of the product by other companies, new technology, or other market forces that make the product inferior or obsolete.

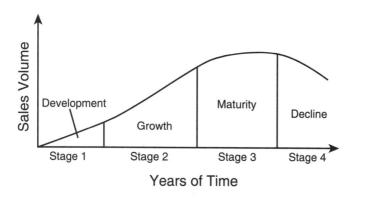

Product/service life cycle.

Although most products or services go through a life cycle in a matter of years or a decade, fad products such as novelty gifts (the mood ring or pet rock) might experience an entire life cycle in a very short period of time (such as a single Christmas buying season). Durable goods, such as microwaves, might have an extended life cycle caused by the level of technological sophistication and a high level of consumer acceptance.

Notice that the perceived value of your offering changes over the life cycle. In the early days, when customers are just learning about what you are selling, only a small segment takes a chance by making a purchase.

In the growth stage, with demand for your offering increasing, you might be in the driver's seat. This means you can charge a premium price because you have something everyone wants.

By the time you enter the maturity stage, you probably encounter competitors who have developed similar products, forcing you to compete on price and service. For example, the personal computer industry is in the maturity stage of its development. Notice the rapid price erosion combined with improved performance that this industry has experienced. This is typical of an industry in the maturity stage of the life cycle.

The product life-cycle concept affects your pricing strategy. Once you determine where your product or service offerings fall on the product life cycle, you can make a better choice about your long-term strategy. The price you set for your rates as a new consultant, for example, is different from that of an experienced, nationally known consultant.

Use the three different strategies—cost, market, and perceived value pricing—to choose the price level that will generate the most sales. Then make sure that your price is consistent with your life-cycle position.

Your Marketing Message and Positioning

I regularly play racquetball with two guys in their 60s, and they whip me every time. As if getting beaten isn't bad enough, at the end of the game, I'm totally exhausted, and they're only slightly winded! One time, I finally put aside my pride and asked about the secret to their racquetball success. They replied, "It isn't the speed with which you hit the ball as much as your position when you hit it."

Business Buzzword

Creating a positive image in the minds of potential and existing customers is called **market positioning**. The purpose of market positioning is to have potential customers perceive your product or service in a particular way that makes them more likely to want to buy from you.

Positioning is everything in sports and in business. I don't mean the geographic location of your company, necessarily, but the way your company is perceived by your customers.

Take a moment and think about the hundreds of marketing-related messages that bombard you on a daily basis. How do you sift through the irrelevant ones and focus on the ones of importance to you? It depends on the way the product is presented and whether it communicates a message of interest to you. The marketing message, the essence of your positioning goal, is the key to customer perception.

The message should be simple, easy to remember, and easy to understand. The only way you can effectively position your company or your product in your customer's mind is to understand his or her thinking and lifestyle. You must know your competition's marketing approach and

1. Make sure that your company is seen as different from the others, or

2. Make customers more comfortable with your totally new company or product by making it look a lot like your competition, which adds validity to your company by association

Here are some examples of typical positioning statements:

➤ Lower price with superior quality.

➤ More convenient and better-stocked store shelves.

➤ More fun at a lower price.

➤ Earn your college tuition in exchange for several years of training.

The range of positioning statements is infinite and limited only by your creativity. Your marketing message clearly and simply conveys the positioning benefit perception you want your customers to understand. Spend a lot of time thinking about this and try out several variations on colleagues. The marketing message will appear in almost everything you produce and will create the perception your salespeople work with during the sales process. If your message is off, you are in trouble because your customers won't even think of you when they need exactly the products or services you provide!

Stay Consistent

Change may be a natural part of life, but it generally causes confusion when dealing with marketing messages and positioning. It takes months (or years) to create a solid market positioning in a customer's mind, and you should not tamper with it in a careless way. Confusion is a dangerous thing when dealing with customers.

Decide on the positioning and stay with it unless you are absolutely sure it doesn't work. You can tamper somewhat with the message as long as all the adjustments convey the same positioning benefits to your customers.

If you know someone who changes careers on a regular basis, you know how hard it is to discuss this person's professional capabilities. She may be brilliant, but if she cannot explain her qualifications in a simple way that means something to the listener, she remains an enigma. Enigmas are interesting at cocktail parties but rarely get hired for important projects.

The same is true of your offerings. Keep the positioning consistent, and make sure your marketing message accurately conveys the customer benefits associated with the positioning. You will get tired of using the same message well before your customers will. In fact, just as you get bored with it and want to change it is when the customers start taking notice.

Bankruptcy Alert
Because potential customers must see your message numerous times before taking action to buy from you, don't change your message too quickly or too frequently. If you do, customers get confused about who your company is and why they should do business with you. On average, people have to see your message seven times before they recognize they need to buy what you're offering.

Promoting Your Company and Products

Getting the public's attention is crucial to marketing success. The following sections describe some ways you can bring attention to your company's offerings (some are even free).

Publicity Is Free

Newspapers, magazines, TV, and radio shows are always hungry for fresh stories. You wouldn't believe what a large percentage of those stories are provided by companies looking for a mention. The key is looking for something that your company is doing that will interest the media. If you can find that, you might have the basis for a story about your company. That is free advertising with credibility attached because it comes from a third-party, objective source. This free advertising is called *publicity*.

Business Buzzword
Mention of your company or offering in newspaper or magazine articles, television, or radio shows is called **publicity**. There is no cost for this coverage, other than the fees you might want to pay a professional public relations firm to assist you.

Media includes reporters, journalists, editors at publications, and assignment editors or news directors at television and radio stations.

Getting publicity is a wonderful opportunity, but it takes work. You have to train yourself to continually watch for chances to turn daily occurrences into something people want to read or hear about. Once you find a situation where your company is a potential source of information for a reporter or editor, the first step is making contact with the media to let them know. It will probably not happen on the first try, but just as with any type of advertising, repetition works. It might take several contacts before the editors and reporters recognize your company or personal name and think of how to use it as a story.

Some public relations (PR) firms specialize in making the desired media contacts for you. Many PR firms in your area already know the editors, which often makes it easier for them to persuade an editor to profile your business or to quote you. Although it costs you money to hire a PR firm, its services will probably help improve sales for your company. Look at the fee as a marketing investment that yields results in the form of sales. If money is tight (and it usually is, isn't it?), then get to know the editors yourself. You can work on them to run your story.

Business Tip

For more information on securing publicity for your company, take a look at one or more of the following:

Do-It-Yourself Publicity by David Ramacitti

Getting Publicity: The Very Best Book for Your Small Business by Tana Fletcher and Julia Rockler

The Public Relations Writer's Handbook by Merry Aronson and Don Spetner

Any story you propose to the media needs a "hook" or interesting angle. Stories such as "Local entrepreneur sells mom's cake recipe for lots of dough" or "Austin-based business closes a large baking deal" are both newsworthy pieces that could result in free publicity. Okay, okay, these aren't the best headlines in the world, but you get the picture.

To get started, create a written announcement (officially called a press release) and contact the business editor at the publication, radio, or TV station where you want to be featured. The press release must contain your company contact person's name, address, phone, and fax. The release title must convey the essence of the release and the release itself should be one page long (two pages maximum, unless you are better established). Make sure that you cover the 5 Ws of journalism in the release: who, what, when, where, and why. Your company should be prominently mentioned, and the first paragraph should be short and to the point. Make sure you write in the "inverted pyramid" style, in which the main message is delivered in the first paragraph and the other paragraphs simply add details.

Good PR

Publicity is just one aspect of a complete program for dealing with the media and your customers. Here are a few tips to help you start creating a public relations program:

➤ Start studying the local media to learn about the types of stories they regularly cover. This gives you an idea of what might be of interest.

➤ Ask around for sample press releases written and sent out by other companies and compare them to yours. Watch to see what stories actually appear in the press.

➤ Keep a running list of items that might have significance to the local public.

➤ Outline possible story ideas when you think of them, even if they are only a few sentences long. These moments of inspiration are often fleeting and lost if not promptly recorded.

Working with the media is fun, but it can also be a mixed blessing. The advantage of media exposure is that everyone hears about you for free, but the disadvantage is that you have no control over what information the media decides to use. If you want to ensure control over where and when a particular message appears in the press, try advertising.

Although companies are usually paranoid about how their company will be portrayed in a news story, the truth is that bad publicity may not be so bad. Attorney Jim "The Hammer" Shapiro, known for his obnoxious television advertising campaign, has been interviewed numerous times regarding his "in your face" marketing program. The publicity surrounding his annoying commercials has actually boosted his visibility.

Of course, in times of crisis, there is no avoiding some bad press. The Tylenol scare years ago could have closed the doors of its manufacturer. But because company executives responded immediately to scares of product tampering, worked closely with the media, and took its products off the market to prevent potential injury to customers, the company is still in business and Tylenol is selling well.

Community Events

You and your company are unique, and there are tons of opportunities for getting your name and offerings into the public eye. I have already discussed publicity, and here are some ways of contributing to the community that get your name out there in plain view:

➤ Sponsor a local sports team such as little league, softball, or soccer. Every uniform will have your company name on it.

➤ Speak at the Rotary club, Chamber of Commerce, and other community-oriented organizations. Make sure your company name is on all the literature handed out at the function.

➤ Keep your eyes open for cooperative events such as donating food for people participating at a civic function or donating cups and water for a 5K race. Why not sponsor the race? Give away some of your products or services in conjunction with a local radio or television station.

➤ Finally, trade shows are a way to display your offerings (but often at a substantial cost). See if you can share space with another company to offset the substantial investment involved with many trade shows.

Be aware that working locally might not help your company's sales if most of your customers are located in other cities, such as with mail order businesses. Local promotion does help you when working with the local business community and when hiring new personnel.

Mentor

In the early '80s, I developed a novelty gift product that I sold nationwide. I put together a press release that included the product's box, a press release, and a black-and-white photo of the product. We got exposure in dozens of newspapers, magazines, and national television coverage. I was ecstatic until the following month. I was sued by more than 14 people whom I had never met or had contact with in my life. They had seen the various media coverage and decided that I had stolen their product and were intent on getting their proper justice.

In no way, shape, or form had I known of any of their products prior to this point, and I certainly had not stolen anyone's idea. The legal hassles associated with this fiasco eventually put the company under because we simply weren't capitalized to handle the unexpected legal expenses that amounted to tens of thousands of dollars.

All About Advertising

Advertising is good for increasing awareness of your company and its offerings. Unless you're in retail, don't expect to close many sales directly from your advertising. The point of advertising is to firmly plant your marketing message into the consumer's mind so that they think about you when they look for what you offer. Advertising also gets the company in front of a wide variety of people in a timely manner.

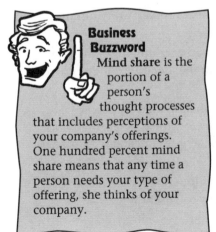

Business Buzzword

Mind share is the portion of a person's thought processes that includes perceptions of your company's offerings. One hundred percent mind share means that any time a person needs your type of offering, she thinks of your company.

Marketers (or marketeers) call this *mind share*. This is the part of a person's thought process occupied by perceptions associated with your specific company. The greater the mind share, the more likely people are to contact you when they are looking for what you offer. If you have no mind share, then they won't even know to call. You develop mind share by using advertising, publicity, promotion, and personal experience with your company.

Pushing and Pulling

Advertising is useful for creating a *pull marketing strategy*, which means that the customers "pull" your product through the distribution channel by asking for it. A pull strategy is expensive because it requires massive marketing to your potential customers to alert them to your product's availability.

At the other extreme is the *push marketing strategy*, which requires you to convince distributors to carry and promote your product, hoping that customers purchase it. A push strategy might show faster results but depends on the activities of the specific distributor. Some companies begin with a pull strategy, then they are lucky enough to build visibility through customer demand. This often raises distributor's interest level, and it transforms into a push strategy.

Keep the following points in mind when you consider advertising:

Business Buzzword
A **pull marketing strategy** convinces your potential customers to request your offering through their suppliers. In essence, the end user pulls your offering through the distribution channel by putting pressure on suppliers to carry it in their inventory. A **push marketing strategy** sells your product to distributors, who then promote it to their customers. A pull strategy is driven by customers. A push strategy is driven by distributors.

➤ Many companies provide money to distributors for cooperative advertising. If you mention their products in specific ways in your ads, they pay for a portion of the ad. Include enough suppliers and the entire ad can be paid for by the suppliers. Contact each of your suppliers for their specific restrictions.

➤ Yellow Page advertising is a must for any business trying to reach the general public, such as a restaurant. The phone book comes out only once a year, so you should plan in advance to be included. Check with colleagues about their success with the various ad types and sizes; take the plunge and hope for the best.

➤ Placing an ad just one time in a paper or on TV or radio is generally useless. You need to repeat your ad on a regular basis to get the best results, so plan for six to ten insertions, or don't waste your money.

➤ Advertising firms specialize in making companies like yours succeed with advertising. They also have an art department that can design an ad for you.

➤ Contact each publication, radio, and TV station you are interested in advertising with and ask them to send you a media kit. The kit includes demographic information about the people who read each publication, listen to specific radio programs, and watch individual TV shows. Typical information includes age, sex, education, and marital status. This information lets you determine whether the people who will see or hear the ad are the ones most likely to buy from you.

➤ Ask each media supplier if they have ever run ads like yours before and what type of responses they received. This might help you determine if it makes sense to invest in advertising there.

Infomercials are currently popular as a means of marketing products (such as the Victoria Jackson line of cosmetics) and services (such as the Psychic Friends Network) and must be effective, based on the rapid increase in the number of infomercials currently on television. There's a lot of money riding on the success of some of these infomercials; some cost hundreds of thousands of dollars to produce, and they are generally beyond the financial reach of the conventional entrepreneur. This doesn't mean that this avenue should not be pursued, but only that the start-up costs should not be ignored. Producing a half-hour or hour-long commercial is extremely expensive, and on top of that, add the cost of buying the TV time.

Business Buzzword
Media kits are prepared by the advertising departments of newspapers, magazines, and television and radio stations as a means of encouraging companies to buy ads. These kits typically contain demographic information about their audience, a rate card, and an editorial calendar for publications, which tells readers what to expect in upcoming issues.

There are a number of new advertising tools now available via the Internet, including banner ads, site ads, and search engine listings. For people using the Internet regularly, this can be a great way to get their attention. To explore how to use the Internet as one of your marketing tools, check out Chapter 10, "Cybermarket: Using the Internet."

Advertising can be a useful tool when used properly, but it can also drain massive amounts of cash from your company with minimal financial return. Make sure that wherever your ads appear, they are seen or heard by serious potential customers for your company's product or service offerings. It is also wise to pay for professional help when producing ads. There's no sense paying for ad time or space only to run an ineffective, poorly designed advertisement.

Your Selling Approach

How does your customer buy your product? That is the question. Is it better to pay commissions to independent sales representatives, sell products at wholesale rates, or to simply sell it to your customers with a direct sales force?

Using Distribution Channels

Business Buzzword
The **distribution channel** is how your product or service gets from your facilities into the hands of customers. Different ways of distributing your product include direct sales, employees who sell your offerings, retail stores, mail order, network marketing through independent representatives, and independent sales or manufacturers representatives.

The *distribution channel* has a profound impact on your contact with the customer, the profit margin available, and the lead time for delivery.

The distribution channels you use to get your product or service into the hands of customers affect the markup and profit margin you can expect. Markup and profit margin are related but definitely different; be sure you understand each before pricing your products.

Markup is added to the cost of a product, whereas *profit margin* is a calculation of what percent of a product's price is profit; the difference is the product's cost. Because there are many businesses involved in the process of getting a product from the manufacturer to you, there are also many different markups added at every step of the way.

A product typically starts at the manufacturer who actually produces the product. The manufacturer adds a markup to the cost of producing the product and sells it to a distributor. The distributor is responsible for getting the product to a wholesaler, who may sell within a particular city or region. Each adds another markup for their own businesses to make money. Retailers, who are the only members of the distribution channel to have direct contact with customers, also add a markup. From the manufacturer to the retailer, there could be several markups along the way, resulting in a retail price that is passed along to the customer.

Industry standards dictate what kind of profit margin and markup are reasonable, and these standards are useful as a guideline in setting your own pricing guidelines. Many clothing department stores have at least a 100 percent markup, meaning they sell their clothing for double their cost. Advertising and marketing agencies, on the other hand, might mark up their services from 10 to 20 percent, and commercial suppliers might have markups of only 5 to 10 percent. It all depends on the industry. You can often find out these markups by simply calling distributors in a non-competing geography and asking about their pricing structures. Often, they will tell you everything that you need to know as long as they are convinced that their information won't be used against them in their own territory. Getting them to open up is a matter of personal taste and style and often involves free food.

Business Buzzword
Markup is the percentage increase you add to the cost of a product or service to come up with the price you charge customers. A 100 percent markup means that a shirt costing you $10.00 costs customers $20.00. You calculate markup by adding ($10.00 × 100 percent) to the original price. One hundred percent % is also expressed as 1. So ($10×1) + $10 =$20.

Profit margin is the amount of profit you make on a sale, expressed as a percent of the product's price. Using the previous shirt example, the profit margin on each shirt can be calculated by subtracting the cost of the shirt from the purchase price and then dividing by the purchase price: ($20 – 10)/20 = 10/20 = .50 = 50 percent profit margin. The amount of profit margin depends on the markup of each product; the higher the markup, the higher the profit margin.

Business Tip

Why start from scratch? Why not look at how your competitors sell their offerings to get some ideas about what has been tried before and what has worked well for existing companies? Do they have retail storefronts, or do they sell through a distribution channel to many retail outlets? What distributors already carry your competitors' products? Ask the retailers; they will tell you who they buy from and their alternate sources.

Bankruptcy Alert

By law, you have to ship a prepaid order in 30 days or offer a refund to a customer who doesn't want to wait any longer. Although it might improve your cash situation to produce according to how many orders you receive, make sure you can deliver in 30 days or less.

The best part of using third parties, such as independent distributors or sales representatives, is that they are out selling your products while your employees stay focused on internal company activities, such as marketing and creating new products. A few minutes spent evaluating the positive and negative aspects of the various distribution channels should help you in deciding your course of action. Read more about sales and the use of sales representatives in Chapter 8, "Without Sales, Nothing Happens."

Mail Order and Direct Mail

Do you want to take on the opportunities and headaches associated with mail order? With a mail order system, you get the order along with its payment and then you are responsible for getting the product into the hands of the customer. You have 30 days from the time you receive the order to the time you have to ship it, which gives you plenty of time in many cases to produce or acquire needed products, instead of stockpiling a huge inventory.

A big down side is that customers can cancel the orders after you ship them. Credit-card fraud is also a real problem with mail-order sales, which means that you might never get paid for the order. Accepting credit cards is crucial for mail-order sales, or you risk having even worse collection problems if you rely solely on checks for payment. Many companies wait until a check clears before shipping the product to the customer as one way to combat bad checks.

Because there are huge up-front costs required to create and mail a catalog, companies have to be confident they will receive enough orders to at least pay for production and mailing of the catalog. With response rates in the 0.5 to 3 percent range, you must have a high profit margin on the products sold to cover the initial investment.

The Least You Need to Know

➤ Marketing lays the groundwork by communicating why customers should buy your service or your product. Sales closes the deal and brings in the money.

➤ Price is not the only buying criteria; customers look at the total value and benefits of your offering.

➤ Create a simple, yet clear, marketing message that describes your company's market positioning and stick with it.

➤ Advertising and promotion are important to positioning your company in the marketplace. A company or product's position affects how people perceive it.

➤ The distribution channel that you decide is the best way to get your products in the hands of customers will have a significant impact on how quickly sales occur.

Lemonade 5¢

Chapter 8

Without Sales, Nothing Happens

In This Chapter

➤ What are sales?

➤ Standard sales procedures

➤ Evaluating direct and distribution sales

➤ Selling services

"So what happened?" asked the board member who provided the initial funding for the company.

"The sales just didn't come in as expected," said the president, a professional engineer and former operations manager. "We've been through three sets of salespeople and can't seem to find a good group. They all seem to just want more money and don't bring in the bacon."

"Have you ever been with them on a sales call?" asked the board member.

"Not really," replied the president. "I have been working with our technical people to make sure the product can do what we promised. Selling is what I have sales managers for. Why pay them if I have to do everything myself?" He knew he was on shaky ground.

"Let's make sure I understand. We have a product and a production facility that works perfectly due to your involvement, but we have nobody who wants to buy what we build. Is that correct?" Heads nodded around the room. "What is wrong with this picture and what are your plans to correct it?"

Picture a salesperson. What do you see? A fast-talking nonlistener who is always looking at your pocketbook? A slick dresser who continually promises to do things in "your own best interest" but who is obviously only interested in selling you something—anything—whether you need it or not?

When you go into a retail store to find a particular item, do you ask the salesperson for help or tell her that you are "just browsing" when she offers to assist? If you are like most people who do not use her help, it may be because you have had bad experiences with salespeople before and prefer not to have something you don't need forced on you.

Of course, these are the horror stories, the examples of poor salespeople who do their employers and their customers no good whatsoever, but understanding the sales process and what it takes to succeed at selling is important in running a business. Whether you will be selling for your company directly or just be overseeing the sales department, this chapter can help.

I call sales the money funnel because no cash comes into the company unless someone has sold your product or service to a customer and you have the customer's money. Selling is an integral part of doing business. To succeed, you must give it the attention and respect you give to other areas of the business such as operations, marketing, and finance. This doesn't mean that you must do the selling yourself, however. If you lack the interest or the ability to sell successfully, find someone who can.

No matter how you feel about sales, there is one undeniable fact: Without sales, you are without a business. Period.

Manipulating and Selling: Not the Same Thing

Most of us have had someone convince us to buy something we later realized was not in our best interest. We felt manipulated by the whole process and by the salesperson involved.

Manipulation has nothing to do with sales! If you manipulate someone to buy your offering and they don't want it, they will resent you, your company, and its offerings for a long time. That single sale could cost you a fortune in future revenues, not only from that one customer who will never buy from you again but also from everyone he tells about his negative buying experience with you.

Sales is the process of matching your products or services with a customer who truly needs them. You are helping the customer solve a problem by providing a service or a product that will make her life easier. It could be as simple as selling a pair of shoes for a special party or as complicated as setting up an international experiment on the space shuttle. If the customer has a need for your offering and you provide a credible product or service that meets her needs, within her budget, then she will buy! It is just that simple. If she doesn't, there is either something wrong with your offering, how it is being presented to the customer, or who it was presented to.

Manipulative selling might earn you a fast buck, but it also eliminates the chance for a future sale to that customer. Professional selling is the action of solving a customer's problems through your company's offerings. It is service-based instead of manipulation-based.

Many new salespeople have shifted from average performers who just do their jobs to outstanding performers who like what they do by simply making this conceptual shift. The difference between these two approaches is trying to sell something to a customer without caring whether she needs it (manipulation-based) versus determining first whether the customer has a need that your product or service can meet (service-based).

If it turns out that the customer has a need for what you're offering, the sales process begins. Obviously, more satisfied customers result from professional selling than from manipulative types of selling. You don't need to be a business guru to understand that satisfied people buy more and tell their friends to buy from you. This is good.

True business and selling success usually comes from a lot of smaller successful clients instead of a single "killing." The huge deals make good press and media headlines but really don't reflect the reality of day-to-day business success.

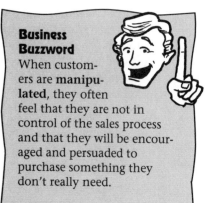

Business Buzzword
When customers are **manipulated**, they often feel that they are not in control of the sales process and that they will be encouraged and persuaded to purchase something they don't really need.

Getting Close to Closing the Sale

The sales process takes place in a number of stages. Look at the way you buy anything. You go through your own set of questions and stages before actually forking over your money. You might evaluate the available information, read about the product in magazine or newspaper articles, ask knowledgeable friends for their opinions, flip a coin, call your mom for her advice, and eventually decide on a purchase.

Professional selling involves numerous small events and exchanges of information that must occur before the sale can happen. At each step along the way, the salesperson makes small requests for customer action or *closes*, which eventually leads to a sale. For example, asking to meet with someone face-to-face is a small close in that you are asking the customer to take an

Business Buzzword
A **close** (pronounced cloze) is a request by a salesperson for a specific action on the customer's part. Asking for the order is the ultimate close, but smaller closes occur at each stage of the selling process to gradually move the customer toward committing to the purchase.

action that leads in the direction of the sale. If the customer agrees, you are one step nearer to getting him to make a purchase. Asking the customer to provide you with detailed information about his needs is another small close because you are asking the customer to take steps toward buying your product or your service. Once the customer is satisfied that buying your product or service is the right decision, he or she commits to a purchase.

People expect to be asked reasonable questions that help them solve their problem, and they also expect you to ask for the purchase. If you don't ask for the order, you can't blame them if they don't give it to you.

Mentor

I was coaching a new salesperson on a sales call where we had just demonstrated a new telephone system to an interested prospect. Everything went well and the customer was clearly ready to purchase, but the new salesperson was so interested in the "dazzling" nature of his presentation that he missed all of the prospect's buying signs. The salesperson eventually ran out of things to say and things fell quiet to a point that the silence became a little painful. I asked the customer if there was anything that he wanted to ask us, and he looked straight at the salesperson and said, "Aren't you going to ask me to buy?" He did and got the order.

Everyone Has to Sell, but Not Everyone Closes

It is important to ask for the order at the right time in the sales process, or the salesperson can alienate the customer. Nothing is more irritating to a customer than to be continually asked to buy something before she is ready. Eventually the salesperson's lack of sensitivity gets in the customer's way of making a rational decision. At this point, the customer might leave simply because it is too much of a hassle to buy from the salesperson.

Everyone in your organization should support the sales process by providing information, support, service, and guidance when requested by the customer. When it is time for the final order to be placed, the salesperson takes care of writing up the sale. Everyone in a company needs to be part of the selling process, but only a few really need to close; beware of the difference.

Aggressive selling is closing when it is inappropriate to close and is rarely effective because it turns off the customer. Professional selling is closing when it is necessary to move the customer forward to a new sales stage, and the customer is comfortable moving ahead to the next stage. The moral of the story: Don't rush customers into making a decision, or you might lose them forever.

Is Your Offering a Special or Commodity Item?

Your company's approach to selling is largely determined by your market positioning and message. (This was covered in Chapter 7, "Masterful Marketing.") Offerings with plenty of competition, where the products and services are pretty much the same, require that features and benefits such as price, delivery, warranty, and stability be emphasized to set your company apart. Specialty products and services, such as high-technology electronics or tailored clothing, require a higher level of personalized service and credibility as part of the sales process because each product is so different from the others on the market.

Where does your product fit? *Commodities* rely more on the distribution channel to effectively get products in the hands of customers, as well as established customers who use your product on a regular basis. There is little or no difference between commodity products, which include milk, white envelopes, and lead pencils.

Specialty products require a higher level of technical and sales sophistication because the product's competitive advantage must be explained well. The salesperson has to know about the benefits of the competitors' products and services and how they compare to his own company's offerings in order to sell the customer on why his is better.

Is Your Customer Qualified?

All the sweet talking, wining, dining, and fancy brochures in the world will not close a sale from an *unqualified prospect* (someone who is not able to buy). I have seen more new, and even experienced, salespeople invest valuable time on prospective customers that were really never qualified to purchase in the first place. Here is a list of five criteria you can use to determine whether you are dealing with a *qualified customer*.

A qualified customer is someone who is interested in buying from you and has the means to do so. If you don't know the answers to these five key questions, you haven't qualified the potential customer. Get the answers, or you might waste a tremendous amount of time and energy on a prospect who cannot buy from you.

1. **Does your customer need what you have to offer?** If your customers don't need what you offer, then you can't blame them for not buying it. Would you buy something you didn't need just to make the salesperson happy? No way, and they won't either!

   Make sure you really understand their needs and that they understand what you have to offer.

Business Buzzword

An **unqualified prospect** is an individual who says that he needs your product or service but who has not yet confirmed that he is able to make the purchase decision. To be sure you are dealing with someone who can buy from you, work through the five qualification criteria.

Your challenge is to accurately identify your potential customers' needs and make sure your marketing message addresses them. If you determine you cannot meet their needs, get out of their way.

You might even want to help the customers find an alternate source if your offerings are not what they need. Doing this makes the potential customers feel good about your company because you are truly doing something that has no immediate reward for you (because you know they aren't going to buy from you right now). In the long run, your willingness to help find a better source might pay off with the customers coming back to buy from you later because you've demonstrated that you really have their needs at heart.

2. **Are you working with the decision maker?** Ultimately, a single person will authorize the purchase of your offering. If you are not dealing with the person in charge of the budget, who can say "yes" and sign on the dotted line, then you are only dealing with someone who has the authority to say "no" to the sale or at best can only influence the outcome.

   Instead of wasting time and energy convincing someone who is not authorized to make a decision to buy from you, first determine who the decision maker is. This might require that you meet with nondecision makers until you find the right person. You then work to meet with that person. Meeting with anyone else but the decision maker doesn't get you any closer to making the sale.

3. **Is there money budgeted for this purchase?** If there is no money available to pay for a purchase, there is no potential for a sale. It is perfectly okay to ask whether money is already in the budget for this purchase. You might find that the money is coming out of next year's budget and that the sale is on hold until the next fiscal year starts. You might also find that there is no money currently budgeted for this project, which should set off warning bells in your head. You might discover that your customer needs to spend the budgeted money by the end of this fiscal year, which provides an added incentive on his part to move the sale forward. This is called a *pending event*.

Business Buzzword
A **pending event** is something expected to happen in the future that affects when a decision is made.

4. **Is there a pending event?** A pending event is something expected to happen in the future that affects when a decision is made. Typical pending events include ending fiscal years (when budgeted money needs to be spent or lost), management orders, moving offices, and mergers. If there is no pending event, the customer can, and might, take forever to make a decision. Why should they force the decision when a decision is not necessary? If there is no critical deadline, you might spend a lot of time trying to convince an unmotivated customer to buy.

5. **Is your customer politically open to using your offering?** Sometimes you can have everything in place, the deal looks like it can't help but close, and then it falls apart. It is almost as though an unknown power stepped in and killed the deal. That is probably just what happened. Many companies have divisions and subsidiaries they are supposed to buy from, and if it is discovered they are planning to buy from another company, someone might try to kill the deal. Why would a company buy from you if they have a subsidiary that offers the same product at a comparable price? They won't! Not because the product isn't right. Not because you did a poor job of selling. Simply because they have a company policy that says all purchases must first be made from an internal business partner. Period.

Try to find out about these barriers to your sales early and save yourself a lot of frustration and anguish later. You can do this by researching all the divisions of a large company to determine whether there are groups providing the same service or the same product that you are. It might also be useful to know who the company is currently buying from to determine whether you'll be able to win business away from them.

Mentor

As a new salesperson, I was working on selling some test equipment systems to a major automaker. The contact people were always happy to meet with me and arranged the meetings for around 11:30 in the morning. Several other people would show up for lunch on my nickel. After several such fruitless meetings, I asked my boss what I could do to move the sale forward. He congratulated me on seeing that something was wrong and explained. "These guys only buy test equipment from Vendor A (a competitor). They have a game going to see how many times they can get a free lunch out of a salesperson before he realizes that there is no possibility of a sale."

The Nine Stages of Selling

Baking bread can be a frustrating and exhilarating experience at the same time. It is an art form, and anyone who has failed in the bread-baking process can verify this. You must follow specific steps in precisely the right order and at precisely the right time. Reordering the sequence or trying to rush the process invariably leads to a poor-tasting loaf.

The sales process is similar; a sale will go through specific stages before the deal is either lost or won. Performing these steps out of sequence usually leads to poor results, and skipping a step usually leads to disappointment. Plan your sales strategy to include moving the customer from one stage to another, with small closes along the way, rather than rush them forward to the final close. I walk you through these stages and explain what occurs and what you should accomplish.

The Suspect Stage

At this stage, you have heard from a friend of a friend that perhaps Company A needs your products or services. Suppose you provide business consulting services. This is the first stage in the process, and it usually occurs as a result of your marketing efforts, such as a direct mail letter, advertisement, or phone call.

When you don't know much about Company A, but you think they might need your services, they are considered a suspect or a lead. There really is no close at this stage other than to make contact with a person on the staff at Company A to verify he has a need for your services.

The Prospect Stage

If you make contact with a representative of Company A and learn they do indeed need the services you provide, you have just received confirmation and can move Company A to the next stage as a prospect. In the first stage, you just suspected that Company A had a need, and now after receiving confirmation, you know for a fact that they have a need. They are now a prospective customer.

Confirmation from a prospect can come in the form of a response to your direct-mail campaign, a request for additional information, or a phone call made by your salesperson. The close for this stage is to have Company A agree to an in-depth discussion about their business needs. Not your needs, but their needs! This discussion can occur in person or over the phone depending on geography and industry.

The Entree Stage

In the entree stage, you have your first major interaction with the prospect. This contact is often made in person. For technical sales in particular, personal contact is usually required to explain complex products and features.

This stage enables you to learn more about the prospect's need for your services and lay the groundwork for the next stage. Here you qualify Company A regarding money, time frame, and the decision-making process. Your close for this stage is to have the prospect detail for you exactly what they intend to buy: how many, for what purpose, when, at what price, and so on. The more you know about their plans and needs, the better the job you can do in convincing them that you are the best choice for this project.

The Discovery Stage

In some cases, there is no need for a discovery stage because the prospect has already indicated their needs to you and has requested a specific proposal or quote from you. When this happens, you can proceed to Stage 5.

When you are dealing with larger companies, you might find you have to speak and meet with several people before being ready to send a proposal. Often, this is because many layers of management need to give their "okay" to whatever business you might be trying to win. This might mean many presentations, meetings, or visits just to be sure you've spoken with everyone involved in deciding which vendor company the prospect should use. When you're meeting with numerous people, you have to repeat the process of learning each person's needs and concerns.

If you haven't already collected this kind of information in Stage 3, determine the prospect's situation, what they think may be the best way to improve the situation, the kind of budget they have, how quickly they want the work done, and the most important factors they use in picking a supplier. Armed with this information, you can write a proposal that shows you truly understand their situation and that you can provide a solution that's also in their budget.

The Proposal Stage

Once the prospect's needs are defined and the overall sales criteria are established, it is time for you to present your best solution: your proposal. This can be in the form of a formal written document or bid, or you can simply tell the prospect that the shoes cost $75. In either case, you now explain to the prospect that you recommend a specific solution to improving his situation, and the cost is such-and-such.

For a large dollar sale, this stage might involve a formal presentation to a committee of people. Make sure that you don't have food stains on your shirt or blouse.

Initial Trial Close Stage

In the initial trial close stage, you ask the prospect for his reaction to your proposal, and whether he plans to buy from you. Don't take "no" as final at this stage. "No" might only suggest that you missed something or that the prospect needs time to consider your proposal. Ask for some feedback on your proposal and just listen to what the prospect tells you. You might be surprised by what you hear. Adjust your proposal accordingly and resubmit. Feedback at this stage is your friend if they don't accept your proposal as you presented it.

The Budget Stage

Many large purchases must go through an approval process at the prospect's company, which can take anywhere from a few hours to a few months, depending on the company and the offerings involved. This stage is often nerve-wracking and requires patience. Unfortunately, all you can do is maintain regular contact with the prospect to ensure that nothing stops the positive momentum toward the sale.

For a small purchase, this stage can be as simple as running a credit card through the machine and getting an approval code.

The Close Stage

The close stage is when you ask for the order and either get it, find out what is missing, or simply lose the deal to another company. All prior closing stages lead to this point. If you read the situation properly and had valid information, you stand an excellent chance of winning the sale. This is an exciting and scary time for both you and your customer, particularly when the sale involves a large amount of money.

Many salespeople are very skilled at getting prospects to this stage but then lose a sale because they simply don't ask for it. Few prospects ask you if they can sign a contract on the spot or issue a purchase order unless specifically asked by the salesperson. Don't leave the prospect hanging at this stage; just ask for the sale.

If you get a "no" or a "maybe," return to the discovery stage to find out if you missed some crucial bit of information or if the prospect's needs have changed. Then go through the rest of the stages again.

Business Tip
Start tracking and forecasting your sales as soon as you receive an inquiry from a potential customer. Monitor the prospect's progression through each of the sales stages so that you can better gauge when the actual sales transaction may occur. This gives you a consistent way of forecasting sales and predicting cash inflow.

The Post-Sale Stage

You've made the sale and the deal is closed. Everyone should be happy, right? Check back with the decision maker to make sure things are going okay. Make sure the customer is still happy with his choice and isn't having doubts or misgivings. This is an often overlooked and critically important stage to building long-term customer satisfaction.

It is much less expensive to keep an existing customer than to find a new one. Your most valuable assets are your repeat customers. Guard them jealously. To ensure that they continue to be repeat customers, check back with them after each sale to confirm they are pleased with their purchase. Show your customers that you have their best interests at heart and weren't just after the sale.

A Commodity Sale Versus a Complex Sale

The sales process varies somewhat, depending on whether you are selling a CD player at a department store, a fancy house on a lake, or a $500,000 computer system. Although the timing of each stage might differ, the sequence must be followed or the sale process gets disrupted.

For example, the department store sale stages are something like this: The customer walks up and asks for assistance. This handles Stages 1 through 3. You ask what she is looking for and how much she wants to spend. There are Stages 4 and 5. You find a unit that you think matches her needs and ask whether she wants to buy; end Stage 6. Her credit card is processed, and she signs the receipt and walks out the door with her CD player (Stages 7 and 8). Asking her how she likes the CD player the next time she comes into the store covers Stage 9.

The sales process becomes more complex when working with high dollar items or services, but the stages of the sale are the same. Trying to charge a consumer's credit card for a CD player before she has agreed on a unit would definitely not work in this scenario. Why do you think that placing Stages 7 and 8 before the other stages would work when selling a $500,000 computer system?

Map out your sales cycle and expected stages to set realistic expectations about what is needed at each stage of the sales process and the time frames involved in moving a prospect from Stage 1 to Stage 8.

Your Sales Channels

Salespeople are important people in your organization. Just as important, in many cases, are the people who support the sales team such as the customer service personnel. You might want to have a few salespeople responsible for finding new customers but also have a number of support people who are solely responsible for serving and selling to existing customers.

These two tasks, finding new customers and supporting existing customers, require different skills. The support person has a relatively routine job that revolves around meeting delivery deadlines and keeping account information up-to-date, but the new business salesperson must create opportunities on a daily basis.

Running an efficient and productive sales team requires focused attention, enthusiasm, and commitment. But you don't have to do it all by yourself. Hire the help you need to keep sales coming in.

There are a couple of different options for how your sales staff can reach new customers. You can use independent distributors to expand distribution of your product quickly through its own sales channels, or you can build a direct sales force that deals directly with customers. Both approaches have pluses and minuses.

Distributors as Sales Agents

Using *distributors* or independent representatives removes you and your sales force from direct customer contact. The advantage is that you now have a sales force of hundreds or thousands selling your product or service. A disadvantage is that it is more difficult to get customer feedback because you have a barrier between your company and the customer.

It is critical to get customer feedback so you can accurately determine whether you should be developing new products or services. Can you trust the distributor or rep to make that assessment for you? In most cases, the answer is no, so you have to decide

Business Buzzword

A **distributor** is a company that purchases products from you at a reduced rate and then sells those products to its own customers. Distributors are commonly used in commodity industries. Money is made on the difference between the sale price to the customer and the cost of the materials as purchased from your company.

A **manufacturer's representative** is a person or company who sells your products on your behalf. Reps do not purchase the products; they only sell them to their existing customer base. They make their money on the agreed-upon commissions earned from successful sales.

Bankruptcy Alert

You do lose control when you use distributors or reps to perform the sales function for your company. Major problems can erupt when distributors make commitments or promises on your behalf. Be sure that you define up front each party's responsibilities to avoid such situations.

whether the additional sales from using this independent organization is worth giving up direct contact with customers. You might have to add personnel to your staff to acquire the information you would otherwise have obtained from your sales force.

Using distributors usually means you need to hire fewer salespeople to cover a comparable geographic area or market, allowing you to keep your costs down. However, you need to interview and qualify distributors as carefully as you would a full-time salesperson because that distributor is going to represent your company. Make sure you are comfortable with that.

Should You Use Your Own Sales Force?

When is it time to set up your own direct sales force instead of selling through distributors? That is a good question and one each company must make based on its own set of circumstances.

Here are a few things to consider when making the choice:

1. The overhead associated with an internal sales force is substantially higher than with distributors. Those overhead costs eat into your profits every month, whether the sales are there to support that overhead or not.

2. You gain more control over your customer relations when you sell direct. This provides you with better management information for decision-making.

3. Selling direct does not take advantage of established customer relationships your distributors may already have in place. Your direct sales force must generate its own contacts and relationships, and that can take a longer time to develop, delaying sales in the process.

4. Sales for highly technical products and services are often handled better by an internal sales force you can train fully and who is less likely to make promises your company can't keep.

5. Some companies start out selling direct on a smaller scale until they determine the proper sales strategy for their offering. They then approach larger distributors about introducing their products or services through the distributor's sales channels.

You have more control and flexibility with an internal sales force, but you also have higher expenses. You need to examine your marketing strategy to decide which approach makes more sense for you right now.

Selling Services Instead of Products

Services provide an interesting sales situation. The customer is buying something of value, but when the project is completed, she might not have anything tangible to show for it. For example, the result of your service contract with a customer might appear in the form of a new organization structure, better-trained staff, a new logo design, or a piece of software. These items clearly contribute to the company's success, but they are less obvious to the customer.

You have to keep in mind that services solve people's problems through your expertise and experience. Because the customer doesn't walk away with a tangible product, he must walk away with the belief that he benefited from using your service. Benefit-oriented selling is an important part of any sale, but it is critical when selling services such as consulting or training.

Clearly defining the *scope of work* from the beginning is critical to success when selling services instead of products. Because the customer might not have something tangible at the end of a project, it is important to clearly define at what point the project is complete. More than one company has been left holding the bag when they submit an invoice that the customer feels is too high or should not be paid at all because the customer doesn't feel he got his money's worth. The company providing the service may have done everything they were asked to do, but if the customer thought he was getting something else, it becomes difficult to get paid.

> **Business Buzzword**
> The agreement on exactly what services will be provided to a customer is the **scope of work**. For instance, the scope of a project might be writing a press release or painting a building. Mailing all the press releases or painting the business owner's house is beyond the scope of work, meaning that those activities were not included as part of the agreement and would have to be paid for separately.

To avoid such situations, the best policy is to get it in writing. In your proposal to your potential customer, state clearly what you are offering to do for them and at what price. Make the desired outcome as specific as possible, preferably through the delivery of a final report. If there is nothing tangible you can provide to signify the completion of a contract, such as with service contracts and warranties, set a specific time period during which your services are offered. After that period is up, your services stop.

Always avoid vague, ambiguous statements such as "We will edit the new corporate brochure until the customer is happy with it." This one is a time bomb just waiting to explode. What happens after you've done 25 versions of the customer's brochure and he just can't make up his mind? Is your work done or do you have to continue to edit and re-edit until the customer is satisfied? If you state exactly how many rewrites you provide as part of the agreement, the answer is probably no—you don't have to keep working forever—but with vague statements, you will probably never get paid.

Business Buzzword

Milestones are important target dates or goals that help you track how well you're performing against your long-term business goals. Milestones can indicate that a specific percentage of a project has been completed, once a certain step has been taken, or it can provide evidence that the project is completed.

Instead, use carefully chosen and specific wording, such as the wording I used for a sales brochure design proposal: "We will provide an initial concept design followed by a professionally created first draft and then a second final version of the brochure that includes any requested customer changes from the first draft." Establish *milestones*—that is, measurable targets or events that demonstrate you have provided the service and reached your objective.

Advance payments (retainers) or down payments are always good, but they are particularly valuable with contracts for service. People have convenient memories, and a little cash on the line always seems to keep the memory of both parties active and on track. It's also an excellent sales qualifier. Any prospect who is unwilling to pay a percentage of the total project cost is not someone you want to do business with. A charge of 25 percent is the suggested minimum, and 35 to 50 percent is not out of the question. Submit invoices regularly (determined in agreement with your customer) if you are billing on an hourly basis so you receive regular payments for your work.

The Least You Need to Know

➤ Sales are necessary for a company to survive. If you are not highly sales-motivated, then you should hire someone who is.

➤ Selling is a process, not an end in itself.

➤ Closing and selling are not the same thing.

➤ Don't waste time on a prospect who doesn't have decision-making authority.

➤ Every sale must go through nine specific stages before the customer is willing to make a commitment.

➤ Selling direct or through external sales representatives fills different needs and requires different approaches.

Beating the Competition

In This Chapter

➤ How to evaluate your competitors

➤ When the competition poses a real threat

➤ Scoping out the competition

➤ How to defend yourself against competitive pressure

My boss sat back in his chair and reflected for a moment. His eyes brightened, and he smiled as he moved forward in his chair.

"I was on a plane going to Minneapolis," he said, "and two guys behind me were talking about a large sale they were working on. When one guy said the name of the company and the contact's name, I realized that it was one of my customers. He then outlined the entire sale situation, including the dollars involved, the basic technical requirements, the time frame within which a decision would be made, and who would make the decision. In short, he told me everything I needed to know to steal the sale."

"What did you do?" I asked, knowing that my boss liked inquisitive people, because it really was a good sales story.

"I called the customer immediately after arriving at the airport and told him that I had heard he was looking for some equipment and that I had what he needed at a price that just happened to be 5 percent cheaper than the bid provided by the guy on the plane," he replied. "I closed the deal that afternoon before the other guy even had a chance to claim his luggage."

This is a paraphrasing of a true story (except the luggage part). There is always some competitor out there who will take your lunch away, and you might not even know how it happened! This chapter shows you how to meet—and beat—the competition.

Is the Competition Real?

It is easy to overreact when dealing with the competition. You might treat your competitors as insignificant (watch your ego on this one) or as a major threat (watch your paranoia on this one). Both of these approaches are inappropriate unless you know something about the competitor. You need an honest understanding of your competition's strengths and weaknesses before deciding how you should respond.

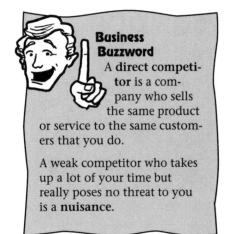

Business Buzzword

A direct competitor is a company who sells the same product or service to the same customers that you do.

A weak competitor who takes up a lot of your time but really poses no threat to you is a **nuisance**.

In general, *direct competitors* (companies who sell the same product or services to the same customers as you) pose either *strategic* or *tactical threats* to your business. A strategic threat can affect you negatively down the road but might only make itself a minor nuisance at the present time. A tactical threat takes money out of your pocket today when your customers go to your competitor instead of you to spend their money.

A strategic threat can easily become a tactical pain in the butt if you don't pay attention to it and take the proper actions to protect yourself. A tactical threat, if large enough, can cause major problems for you. This is especially true when you have a small customer base that provides most of your sales. If your competition takes one customer, which they will definitely try to do, they can hurt you both today and down the road when others wonder what is so special about them that they took a major account away from you.

When you start your business, you are in the enviable position of having no major competitor take you seriously. This provides you with a tremendous amount of freedom because nobody will be aiming to eliminate you in sales situations. You know that you are doing okay when competitors start to know your name and change their marketing strategy to go after you. That's good news and bad news at once.

Because you are just starting out, you should be collecting as much information about the companies in your particular market segment as possible. People might not yet view you as a competitor and might be more open with their information. Sit down with the information and imagine the picture that your prospective customers have in their minds about each of your competitors. This is generally created by your competitors' marketing message and positioning. (See Chapter 7, "Masterful Marketing," for more on this topic.)

How does your offering compare to the competitors'? If you were a customer looking at the two companies, would you see them as direct competitors or as two companies in separate market segments? Does this perception come from the fact that they offer different products or services or that their marketing message presents it differently?

From this approach, you can get a first cut on who to treat as a competitor.

Accumulating Competitive Information

The Central Intelligence Agency calls it information; I call it the essence of competitive action. No matter what you call it, information is the key to making informed and appropriate competitive decisions.

Information is everywhere, and all you need to do is keep looking for it, collate it, and finally, put it into some semblance of organization and order. It is amazing how fragments of information can give you an excellent overall picture of a competitor.

> **Mentor**
>
> I had the dubious honor of serving our country as a nuclear weapons electronics technician. As part of this military honor, I received a top secret security clearance. As part of the indoctrination, I was told to keep my mouth shut and my ears open at all times and to report any shred of information to a specific party. When I asked a central intelligence person the value of this procedure, he told me that each little piece of information by itself is meaningless, but when it is combined with dozens of others from different sources, a pattern and picture begins to emerge that clearly identifies specific tendencies. You should gather information about your competition in much the same way.

Where do you start looking for competitive information? How about the Yellow Pages? Who is listed in the category you would choose for yourself? Are they also listed in another category? If so, why? How many companies are listed there? How do they position themselves in the ad? Is it a display ad or simply a small-column ad? Grab last year's Yellow Pages and compare it to this year's. Has the number of competitors increased or decreased? Did some of the advertisers advance to a display ad? Did their positioning change from last year to this year? Look at how much insight you can obtain about your market by simply looking at the Yellow Pages.

Scour the newspapers and trade publications for advertising, articles, and quotes from any of your potential competitors. Ask your friends to do the same. They might find something that you missed. Start a folder for each of the competitors (they really deserve at least a manila folder, don't they?). Your local library might also keep files on local companies that you can scan for free. Every time you find a piece of information, write it down if you heard it, or photocopy it if you found it in print. Date and place the information in

Business Tip
Useful sources for competitive information include the following: Yellow Pages, newspapers and magazines, your customers and your competitors' customers, annual reports, social gatherings and networking functions, sales brochures, and Web sites, to name a few.

Business Tip
One of the biggest clipping services is Luce Press Clippings. They can be reached at 800-528-8226. Bigger is better in this case because they scan a wider selection of publications on a regular basis.

that folder. I promise that you won't exactly remember it later, and the mind has a convenient way of changing its perception of reality over time.

Ask your customers what they know about your competition; how do they like dealing with them? What do they like? Dislike? What is their satisfaction level? Why don't they use you for the same products and services in which they are using your competition? Notice this discussion opens another level of communication with your customers, which is always a good idea.

Ask customers for pricing information when you have either lost or won a bid; they just might give it to you. Note that if they give you this information, they will probably share it with your competition in the same way. I have actually had clients give me a complete competitor's bid with all references to the company deleted. In this way, the information appears generic in nature and does not reveal the source, yet provides valuable insight into the competitor's overall offering. Guard this customer confidence like a diamond! It is a tribute to your client-vendor relationship when a customer opens up in this way, and you should treat it with the high degree of respect it deserves.

Review the company's own sales literature such as brochures and catalogs. Check out its Web site. It might tell you more about the people, sites, plans, products, services, policies, warranties, and pricing than you can get anywhere else. By the way, they will also check out your Web site, so don't put information there unless you want it found.

Some companies specialize in accumulating information about companies for a fee. These *clipping services* review a set number of publications for information regarding certain companies. You tell them which companies you want them to watch for and which newspapers or magazines you want them to read. They generally photocopy an article that appears and send it to you on a regular (usually weekly) basis. This service is not free, but it might pay for itself in the valuable information on your competitors you may have overlooked.

Finally, you can call your competitors and ask for information. A lot of times, they will send it to you. Don't use a fake personal or company name. If you misrepresent yourself, you are toying with *industrial espionage*, which is really scary. Penalties for fraud and misrepresentation can be severe and can seriously damage your business and your credibility. Just give them your name, number, and address and hope that you're talking to someone who doesn't know who you are. Don't volunteer information unless asked. This approach is probably a safe bet when you first start out and will become more difficult as your success builds along with your reputation. With public companies, just call the investor relations department and ask for a copy of the company's annual report.

Opened ears, focused attention, closed mouths, and organized details are the secrets to accumulating competitor information. It's a job that requires constant diligence and doesn't take much time once you begin.

Comparing Yourself to Them

Okay, so you've played super-sleuth and acquired a wealth of information about your competition. Put down your pipe, Sherlock; it's time to get into the trenches and start analyzing the information you've collected. How do you compare to the competition from your customer's perspective? When you find the answer to this question, you are on your way to determining your own position in the marketplace.

Here's an exercise that will help you find some answers. Take out a pad of paper or create a spreadsheet to automate the easy calculations that follow:

➤ Divide your sheet of paper or spreadsheet into four columns: A, B, C, and D.

➤ In Column A, write down the top ten criteria your customers probably use in deciding who to buy from. Characteristics can include technical competency, service, phone support, convenience, credit terms, years in business, depth of offering, price, and so on.

➤ In Column B, place a number that corresponds to the amount of importance you believe a customer places on this particular item, based on your experience. Make 1 stand for most unimportant and 10 stand for a must-have. Although these are your opinions, they are still worthwhile to note. Your chart should look something like the following figure:

		Your Company		Competitor #1	
Ⓐ Characteristics	Ⓑ Importance (1-10)	Ⓒ Effect (1-10)	Ⓓ Result (B x C)	Ⓔ Effect (1-10)	Ⓕ Result (B x E)
Years in Business	4	3	12	6	24
Credit Terms	7	8	56	8	56
Hours of Operation	7	8	56	8	56
Depth of Offering	6	6	36	8	48
Prior Experience with Company	8	5	40	6	48
Certification	5	8	40	6	30
Ideal	**370**	**Totals**	**240**		**262**
		Sale Price	**$75**		**$95**

In this example, Competitor #1 has a superior market position compared to your company, as indicated by the higher total (262). This higher total helps to justify the higher product price.

143

➤ Create individual columns for each of your competitors and your company. These columns will contain a number between 1 and 10 that gives your *subjective assessment* of how well each company meets customers' needs. (See Effect Columns C and E in the example.)

➤ Create another column for your company and each of your competitors. For each company and each of your competitors, multiply the subjective assessment column's number (Column C and E) by the importance number (Column B) and insert the result in each column you've just created.

➤ At the bottom of each column, total all the numbers in the column for your company and each competitor. This final number provides a relative weighting assessment of how each competitor compares against the others and your company.

How does the number in your last column compare with those of your competitors? Is your number higher or lower? The same? How does your price compare with the others when compared against the summary numbers, such as in Columns D and F in the example?

In general, you want your number here to be high because it indicates how close you are to ideal for your customers. Ideal is calculated by totaling the importance column and multiplying by 10—the perfect score for each item. For example, the sum of the importance column in the previous table equals 37, which multiplied by 10 equals 370 points for the ideal.

Divide your rating (such as 240) by the ideal (such as 370) to see how close you are from a percentage standpoint (240/370 = 65 percent). What is the proper percentage level? This is a relative setting and one that is highly dependent upon your business and customer type. In general, you should strive to be in the upper 25 percent or have a percentage rating of 75 percent or higher, which would give you a C in high school.

Numbers are okay, but I think in pictures, so I plot price and Total Relative Weighting Importance Factor against each other for my company and my competitors (see the following chart). Just follow the horizontal line until you get to the proper weighting factor and then follow that until you intersect with the proper price horizontal line. Put a dot there and label the dot. Repeat this process for your company and all others. You can now visually see where you are compared to the competition. If you really want to be thorough, you can also plot the ideal weighting against a realistic ideal price to see how you compare to it.

Notice from the example that the competitor charges a higher price and also provides a higher weighting factor, which probably justifies their charging a higher price. If you keep your products and services the same and then offer a discount price, you will continue to move down along a vertical line because you are decreasing pricing and keeping the weighting the same. Keep this up, and you will be busy and out of business.

Total Relative Weighting Importance Factor

The results of your relative weighting assessment.

```
Sale Price
$100 ┬  △ The
     │     Death
     │     Knoll        ┌────────────────────┐
     │                  │  Competitor #1 ●    │
 $80 ┼                  │                     │   Most successful
     │                  │                     │   businesses operate
     │                  │        ●            │   within this box
 $60 ┼                  │   Your Company      │
     │                  │                     │
     │                  └────────────────────┘
 $40 ┼
     │                       Busy and probably
     │                         losing money
 $20 ┼  △ Cheesy Discount Store      △
     │
     └──┬────┬────┬────┬────┬────┬──────────►
        50  100  150  200  250  300
     Low Value                  High Value
       Area   Importance Factor   Area
```

On the other hand, decreasing services and keeping the price the same also eventually rings the death knoll for your business because people will eventually stop buying from you. Graphically, you move to the left along a horizontal line when you keep price the same and decrease services, which decreases your weighting.

Where to beef up services? Where you get the best weighting factor return for the dollars spent? Offering longer hours of operation or better credit terms increases your weighting factors on two items of high importance, whereas spending money on certification provides a lower weighting factor return.

Okay, enough of all this graphing and other technical stuff. Will you make decisions strictly by this weighting analysis and chart? Probably not. Will the results from this analysis provide you with a structured way of analyzing your competition so that you can make informed decisions? Absolutely yes. This is a good reality check and one worth performing on a regular basis, when you're not checking out your competitors.

You should now have a pretty good idea of how you stack up against your competition. You might be less expensive than they are, but you don't offer the extra services that they do. You can deal with this lack of services by either adding services (and potentially raising your prices) or emphasizing in your marketing program that customers will get a bargain when dealing with your company.

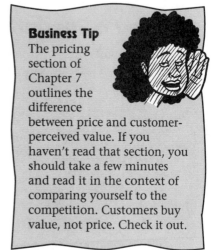

Business Tip
The pricing section of Chapter 7 outlines the difference between price and customer-perceived value. If you haven't read that section, you should take a few minutes and read it in the context of comparing yourself to the competition. Customers buy value, not price. Check it out.

On the other hand, if your price is too low and you have a higher total value, you might want to consider raising the price on your offering. Why leave money on the table if you don't have to?

The Price Wars

Here is the best of all worlds: Your competition decides to gain customers by dropping their price. This often starts a *price war* where all companies try to keep their customers by matching or lowering their prices even more. This is a dangerous cycle that usually winds up with suppliers hurt, the customer confused and dissatisfied, and substantially lower profit margins all around. The airline and computer industries go through this cycle on a regular basis. It tears the entire industry apart and takes years (if ever) to recover lost finances, and there's really no reason for it.

Business Buzzword
When all competitors compete based on price and keep undercutting their competitors to get sales, they are engaged in a **price war**. As each company lowers its own price, others drop their prices to compete, resulting in profit margins in the industry as a whole falling to critically low levels.

There is a way to beat this cycle if it happens to your industry, but it takes amazing courage and fast reflexes. Instead of lowering your price, keep the price where it is. Beef up your extra services and sell the increased quality that you can provide for the higher price. Any experienced corporate business person knows you have to make a reasonable profit margin to stay in business. Instead of automatically dropping price as a reflex reaction, try this approach first, but continue to monitor your sales carefully. If you can't keep sales up, then you might just have to join the fray and hope that you survive.

Are You a Specialty Store or a Superstore?

Are the other folks in your industry large companies with deep pockets and a wide selection of offerings (*superstores* such as Wal-Mart)? Are they smaller companies that provide a specialized, niche offering that a few people use (*specialty stores* such as Candles Are Us)? It's important that you understand where you want to fit in the continuum between the two types of businesses. Note that these terms apply equally well to service or product businesses. You could be a full-service health club or a specialty massage practitioner.

Business Buzzword
Superstores are large companies with deep pockets and a wide selection of offerings. **Specialty stores** are smaller companies that provide a specialized, niche offering that few people use.

If you're trying to be a superstore but don't have the money to provide the required variety and volume of products needed, you will probably go out of business. The financial demands of making a business of this size work will affect your ability to maintain appropriate inventory or personnel expertise levels. Once your "shelves" appear naked or you don't provide a proper service level, customers take their business elsewhere.

If you are a smaller business that tries to cater to everyone's needs, you will probably fail—not because you lack skills or ability but because your customers will expect more than you can offer. In addition, your smaller quantity of purchases will keep your costs, and prices, higher. The superstore firms will clobber you on price alone.

It is interesting that the superstores are wary of the specialty stores eroding their business in key areas. A specialty store can provide a much higher level of personalized service to customers than a superstore can ever hope to provide. The specialty store can also charge a little more for the service because the customer perceives it as having more value. In this way, the specialty store keeps margins high and expenses low, which is always a good way to run a business. However, you need to know your customers and offer the specialty items that they need.

In technical areas, a specialty store may be one that customizes computer equipment or software for the customer while also selling the software. The company makes money on both the software product and the service. The customer wins because she knows that her purchase will be handled in a low-risk, professional manner. Customers will pay for the service, especially if they have been burned by the cheap or large department store route.

In retail, a specialty store might be one that deals only in candles and related items. The customer might be able to find a cheaper candle in a superstore, but could he find "just the right one?" Probably not, and that is the benefit of a specialty store. People expect to pay more for the added selection and service. Value is what sells; don't shortchange yourself on that count, but don't gouge your customers either.

> **Business Tip**
> Suppliers often lower prices to purchasers who buy in big volume. They'd rather deal with selling huge quantities to the big store and will charge you more because it's inconvenient to deal with a little store. The cost of providing a product is smaller when sold in larger quantities. This volume buying allows major corporations to get great prices on products and services that you can't match.

A typical service-oriented superstore is one of the "big" accounting firms that provide a wide array of accounting and consulting services. The local tax preparation service would be the industry's specialty store because they do taxes, and only taxes, and may or may not charge a premium for the specialization.

Trying to be a superstore when you should be a specialty store is surefire trouble, as is the reverse. If you don't have the broad range of products or services to qualify as a superstore in your industry, stick with serving a small niche as a specialty store. You'll probably make more money by establishing a reputation as a specialist in a particular area, rather than a generalist who tries to do everything.

Market Makers and Followers

Market makers are those companies with the financial backing and marketing know-how to create whole new business opportunities. Some examples of current market makers include larger companies such as Microsoft, MCI, and General Foods. They have the deep pockets required to pay for the process of educating consumers about a new product or service. The gradual increase in customer awareness required to create new market opportunities is both expensive and time-consuming. Larger corporations can afford to be the leader in creating whole new markets because they have other business areas that subsidize the new venture, but you don't have to be a leader to succeed in a new market.

Business Buzzword
Market makers are those companies with the financial backing and marketing know-how to create whole new business opportunities.

Even if you have a product that is unique and innovative, you still might have a difficult time convincing the public to buy it. Be prepared. Generating enough interest in your product (or service) to result in sales might not be worth your effort unless you have an established distribution channel—that is, unless you have a way to get it out quickly to the people who want to buy it.

Getting your product into a distributor's hands might be one of the most difficult challenges you'll face, especially if you have a kind of food to sell. Competition for retail "shelf space" at grocery and convenience stores is brutal, and most grocery stores charge the manufacturer for the privilege of being able to sell their products there. Sounds unbelievable, doesn't it? The grocery stores know that they are the key to reaching your potential customers, and they have thousands of products to choose from, so why not ask for a fee to showcase your product? If you offer a service, distribution is less of an issue because there are fewer ways that you can provide your service to your customers; you either perform the service yourself, such as hairstyling or copywriting, or you have sales representatives making contacts for you, lining up new customers. Web site designers faced this "new" service problem a few years ago but have now become a highly sought-after service.

It is always cheaper, and less risky, to piggyback your offering on something that is already accepted and trusted in the market. Instead of creating a new market or introducing a totally new kind of product that no one has ever seen before, let the big folks spend their money doing it. Let them increase understanding and awareness of this new market opportunity. Then you can jump in later with your own product and benefit from all the money they've spent marketing to the public. This is called a *free rider* in MBA-ese, and free is always good.

When you are starting out, try first to be a market follower. You can become a leader later when you have the big bank account and the market acceptance needed to steer the market ship. Microsoft started out as a market follower by riding on IBM's coattails. Now when Bill Gates sneezes, people think that a new market for tissue has been created.

Using Market Segmentation to Your Advantage

Within every market and industry are smaller pockets of opportunity called *market niches*. Larger companies don't waste their time trying to meet the needs of a small portion of the market, but you might want to. Niches can be very profitable if you have the right offering.

These market niches are often like a vacuum in that once you make your product available, everything you produce will get sucked into the niche, too. You can also easily establish a strong reputation that will make it difficult for larger competitors to compete with. Too cool! Even though niches might have fewer potential customers, they are often easier to sell to.

By the way, a hot unique product in a hungry niche market means you can charge more for your offering and increase profit margins. Get a good mental picture of what this means and watch the smile grow on your face.

Business Buzzword
A **market niche** is a smaller segment of a bigger market that is more specialized. For example, attorneys that specialize in construction industry accidents are pursuing a niche within the larger legal profession. Or vegetarian restaurants are another type of business targeting that segment of the population that doesn't eat meat. Each use a niche strategy.

Cooperation Versus Competition

The Chinese have a saying that goes something like this: Who knows you better than your enemies. This also applies to business competitors.

It is not uncommon to find that you and your competitors, or even your noncompetitors, have more in common than it initially appears. They might address a particular market niche much more effectively than you and vice versa. Combined, you might offer something that is truly more powerful than each of your individual strengths. You can cooperatively market your offerings. You can share mailing and administrative costs and aid each other in new product development activities.

Suppose that you are a corporate bookkeeping service that doesn't prepare taxes. It makes sense for you to align yourself or partner in some way with a tax preparation service. The benefit is that your customers perceive you as providing a higher level of service: bookkeeping and tax preparations. You send them tax leads and they send you bookkeeping leads. Everyone is a happy family as long as both parties play by the agreed-upon rules and don't start moving into the other alliance member's sandbox.

There is a potential down side to all of this cooperation. You will probably have to share sensitive company information such as your customer list with them to a much larger degree than you otherwise do with a competitor. You need to weigh the pros and cons of doing this, but if the benefits of the alliance outweigh the risks, you should go for it. One way to consider partnering opportunities is a defense against the strong-arm tactics of the superstores that might try and muscle in on your territory. Working with other related companies, you make it more difficult for the superstore to win customers.

The Least You Need to Know

➤ Competition will always exist, but that's not necessarily bad. Comparing your products and services to those of your competitors helps you stay on top of what customers want.

➤ Watching your competitors provides insight into what's going on in your market and what they believe customers want. This information can help you better plan for the future.

➤ Customers purchase value, not price. Just because your competitors drop their prices doesn't mean that you have to. A price war can often present an opportunity, depending on your particular market segment and product offering.

➤ You might find that working with your competitors against other common foes is a better strategy than trying to "go it alone" against everyone.

Chapter 10

Cybermarket: Using the Internet

"How did you come up with these copyright forms so quickly?" asked Howard.

"Simple," said James, one of Howard's employees. "I went out on the Internet, did a search on Lycos, accessed the government's Web site and downloaded the file. It all took about 10 minutes."

I couldn't even walk to the library in 10 minutes, thought Howard. To have the form in my hand and never even leave the office is pretty cool. Howard all of a sudden got a little depressed. Here he was, the owner of a successful small business, only in his mid-40s, and already feeling like an antique.

"Heck. You could learn how to do this, boss. You just need to get over your fear of the initial logons. And, by the way, you are paying for the connection and the logon is in your name, so why not use it?"

Howard took a deep breath and looked at James. He took to the Internet so naturally, it was a little disconcerting. But, on the other hand, perhaps other people James' age also took to the Internet so easily.

"I hear that some companies actually allow their customers to retrieve information and even place orders over the Internet. Is that true?" asked Howard.

James lit up like a Christmas tree. "You bet," he said. "I just ordered a new stereo from some guys in California and regularly check out our competition's Web sites to see what they are offering to their customers."

Now Howard was interested. The Internet had just moved from being a cool toy to a business tool. If his competition was already doing it, he had better check it out or risk being lost in the cyber-dust.

"Could you help us get set up to provide information to our customers? Do you think that they are also using the Internet? How long will it take and what do you think it will cost?"

"I've been working on this at home, on my own time, just because I like it. Let me loose on our Web site during work time, and I will have a demo for you within a week. How about them apples?" responded a very pumped up James.

Well, thought Howard, you spend money to make money. Let's see how this works out. "You're on, James. Let's meet later so you can fill me in on how the process works."

At this point in the book, you might feel like you have a ton of different balls to juggle, and if any fall, you might suffer a business black eye. Well, you're right about that.

As if you haven't had enough, I am now going to introduce you to the Internet and the opportunities presented by this marvelous technological revolution.

Why should I care, you might be asking. Well, here's why. There's a whole world out there that might be able to use your products or services. Getting hold of these possible prospects who may live on the other side of the U.S. or on the other side of the world might seem like a daunting task. It just doesn't have to be that complicated any more. You have a natural connection in the Internet.

Your prospects and competition are probably already using the Internet to research personal and business matters. If they aren't, they will be soon.

The Internet is an integral part of modern life, both personal and business, and will definitely become more important going into the next millennium. You should already be thinking about ways to take advantage of this shift, and this chapter moves you in that direction.

Advantages of the Internet

To take advantage of the Internet, you first have to change your thinking. Electronics, which is the mechanism of the Internet, operates at high speeds (almost at the speed of light). Although traveling from New York to Los Angeles is a trip of several thousand miles and several hours by plane, an electron travels that distance in a small fraction of a second. Japan is only a little farther.

As a result, time and distance, as we know it on a daily basis, do not have the same meaning with the Internet. You can connect to a computer in Switzerland just as quickly, for all practical purposes, as you can connect to a computer in Chicago or in New Zealand. Many of the barriers that separate two Internet-connected systems have been removed so that all users and computers share a common technological language through which communication and business can flow.

If you think that doing business in Australia is expensive due to the long-distance charges, you need to shift your thinking. For an Internet user in Sydney, a computer system in New York is only a local Australian phone call away. The Internet provides the connection between Sydney and New York, and it usually does it for a flat fee, independent of how many hours the connection is used.

Get the picture? Where before you had to let people in Sydney know that your company existed—which meant getting a Sydney mailing list, preparing a direct mail piece, mailing the piece, and following up with a phone call—you can now allow Sydney residents to see your information over the Internet at minimal cost to both you and them. Not only can someone in Sydney see your site, but he or she can also place an order for products. Are you ready to handle that order? Check out Chapter 16, "Doing Business Internationally," for information about handling international business situations.

I once heard Steve Jobs, the founder of Apple Computer, on a radio talk show about the Internet. He commented that one of the most fascinating aspects of the Internet is that a small company can look just as large as IBM on the Internet. Nobody is physically visiting the company's building. They are only seeing what you put on the Internet. Do a good job on your company's Internet presentation, and you can play with the big guys. He also mentioned that the Internet and its associated technology represents a major step in the direction of a universal language that is spoken around the world.

Mentor

I recently taught a group of Russian networking technology professionals on the operation of Windows NT, a computer program. They couldn't speak any English, but they understood the icons and menu selections, even when presented in English. Think about this. We couldn't say hello to each other without a translator, but when we worked with the Internet, we could discuss things in broken, technology-based English terms and via images and icons.

Is there a technological challenge associated with making this leap into the Internet? Yes. Can you jump these hurdles? The answer once again is yes, and you can do it yourself or hire someone to do it for you. In either event, you must address this important business tool or be left in the electronic dust.

Can you expect to make money directly off of your Web site and other Internet-related activities? Probably not in the short term. You should think of your Internet activities such as a Web site or electronic mail as the modern day equivalent or a business card. Have you ever made money directly from your business card? Probably not. Is transacting business easier because of your business card? Absolutely.

Once your clients get trained to use your Web site for information and mail, you can then present them with the electronic commerce features that allow you to process orders online.

Mentor

I have successfully kept my employee headcount to a minimum through effective use of the Internet and outsourcing. Providing product information about our courseware is a routine task, and many of our clients need this information after business hours since they teach classes during the day. We set up a Web site at http://www.course-store.com that allows our clients to obtain class outlines, pricing, development strategies and other pertinent information. When they want to place an order, they call an 800 telephone number, and send a fax order form that they obtained from the Web site. A fulfillment center in Nevada then processes the order.

Setting Up on the Internet

Several components compose an Internet site. This section presents some of the major terms that you will encounter and shows you how you can use Internet technology in your own business. This section is not designed to make you a technical geek. It does, however, give you an overview of the language and technology of the Internet so that you can fully appreciate the business opportunities it presents.

To make the connection you will need a computer, modem, Internet connection software, and an agreement with a company that provides a local telephone number for Internet access. This process used to be pretty complicated and now is about as simple as software installation. Don't be scared off by the technology. My mother and father use the Internet. You can, too.

Web Words

Think of the World Wide Web (WWW) as a huge network of interconnected computers. If you draw lines between all of these computers, you have something that looks like a spider web. Picture the WWW as a interconnected, or internetworked, group of computers.

These computers are connected for all types of Internet-related services. I am going to concentrate on the components that you control, create, or purchase for use by your company on a daily basis.

Your home computer that is accessing information from the WWW primarily deals with computers that host, or act as the home computer, for a Web site. A Web site is an electronic location on the WWW where a company stores and displays the information that it wants seen by others.

Like an individual's street address, all Web sites have addresses, known as *domain names*. For example, if you type an address such as *http://www.course-store.com* (my company's address), your computer looks for the WWW location with a domain name of *coursestore.com*. (The HTTP tells the computer to transport what it finds there to your computer using the *Hypertext Transfer Protocol* (HTTP), which means that the underlying text information is translated and displayed using the *Hypertext Markup Language* (HTML).

> **Business Buzzword**
> A **domain name** is a unique name given to your Internet location that is used by people who want to view your Internet site. Most business domain names end with .com.
>
> **Hypertext Markup Language** (HTML) is the language used by Internet Web sites.
>
> **Hypertext Transfer Protocol** (HTTP) is the mechanism by which HTML information is transferred from one point to another over the Internet.

If all of this seems like a lot of jargon, just think of it this way: Your computer uses the www.course-store.com address to find the computer on the Internet. The HTTP tells the two systems how to transfer the information and the HTML allows the underlying information to be displayed as intended by the person who created the received document.

Here is the really cool and magical part. Every computer in the world that uses a *browser* (a software tool used to surf the Internet) can read a file stored in HTML format on a Web site location. Every computer connected to the Internet has some form of browser associated with it. This means that anyone who has access to the Internet can access your Web site and perform any number of standardized operations—such as reading site information, placing orders, providing feedback to the site designers, and paying for purchased products.

Finding an Internet Service Provider

All this talk about Web sites is good, but how do you even get onto the Internet in the first place? Well, you can set up your own Internet access by purchasing a computer, setting up the network connections, spending weeks in training classes, and losing hairs off your head. If you are into that kind of "challenge," then have at it and call me from your asylum room on visiting days.

An easier way is to rely on an *Internet service provider* (ISP). Your ISP is the company that connects you to the Internet through a dial-up telephone number that is accessed by your computer's modem

Business Buzzword
Your **Internet service provider** (ISP) is the company with which you contract so that you can get your connection to the Internet. This company provides you with a local phone number and a browser that you should use for the connection. The service is usually billed for a flat monthly fee.

There are numerous ISPs, and you probably have local ones that provide specials for your local area. A few of the national ISPs include FlashNet, AT&T WorldNet, and SpryNet.

Other vendors that provide their own private networks along with Internet access include America Online (AOL), CompuServe (CIS), and Microsoft Network (MSN). With these services, you can send mail and messages to other users who are members of the same network, use custom services that are only available to that network's members, access the Internet, and also send and receive electronic mail to other Internet users.

Let the ISP worry about the latest and greatest methods of connecting to the Internet. You just worry about connecting to your ISP, letting your customers know about your e-mail and Web site addresses (more on that later), and keeping your Web site up to date.

How do you choose an ISP? This choice really depends on your specific situation, but here are a few rules to get you started:

➤ Choose a provider that charges a flat connection fee per month, independent of the number of connected hours. (The flat monthly fee is usually in the $15 to $29 range.)

➤ Make sure that the ISP has 24-hour, 7-days-a-week access.

➤ Make sure that there is a customer service line that you can call when you need help.

➤ If you travel and want to retrieve your electronic mail messages while on the road, or even in another country, then make sure that your ISP has local access numbers in the cities that you visit the most. If it does not have these local access numbers, then you inherit the toll telephone charge back to your home city so that you can access the network.

➤ Make sure that your ISP provides enough hard disk space for you to store your anticipated electronic mail messages.

➤ Check to see if the ISP for your electronic mail service also provides Web site hosting services. You can often get the two features in a single package for a discount rate.

➤ Get the name of a few customers who already use the ISP's services, and find out how often they receive a busy signal when trying to connect. The answer should be "rarely" or "never" or you should look somewhere else.

Naming Your Domain

The domain name is the address that people go to when they want to find your company. Your domain name is how Internet people learn to recognize you. For example, Microsoft uses www.microsoft.com, which makes sense and is easy to remember.

Mentor

When we first tried to find a domain name for my company, Technology and Communications, Inc., we struck out because all the names related to the company name were already taken by other companies. Surprising? Not really, when you consider that a domain name must be unique on the entire Internet. We finally tried course-store.com and found that it was available, so we took it.

When you have your own unique domain name, you must also have a unique IP (Internet Protocol) address. Your ISP will handle all of this for you.

Your IP address is obtained from the InterNic, an organization that manages the Internet. Your Internet service provider handles this registration for you. Just know that you need to find an ISP and a domain that is not taken to set up a domain name and Web site location.

You can have a domain name that is related to another vendor, such as jones-inc.worldnet.att.net, which means that your Web site is hosted by AT&T on its WorldNet service. This is the simplest way to establish a Web site—even though the name looks complicated— but it has its drawbacks. Suppose that you promote your AT&T-associated Web site for months, and all your customers are accustomed to visiting this site

Business Tip
It is a good idea to take the time and incur the added expense associated with owning your own domain name that is independent of your provider. This way, you can change providers without having to notify all your Internet customers of the name change.

when they need information or want to place an order. Now also suppose that you decide to change to another network provider, such as MCI or SPRINT. You will probably have to change your domain name because it is associated with AT&T and you no longer use their services. This means that every time that you change Internet Web site hosting providers, you have to give your customers a new Web address. This is not a good idea.

Business Tip
Internet domain names are a hot commodity. You should think of a name that you like, that is catchy, and that accurately depicts your company and register it right away (through the InterNic at www.internic. net). You need an assigned IP address before you can register the domain name, so get that number from your Web site host provider first.

I set up my company's domain name to be separate from any Web site hosting provider. I can change providers without having to change my domain name or retrain my customers. This might seem like a small point, but it can be incredibly important if you want to change Web site providers, so I highly recommend that you set up a domain name that is independent of the underlying provider and tell your customers to use this site.

Once you establish an Internet-based electronic mail account with your ISP, talk with your ISP about registering a non-ISP specific domain name that is hosted by your ISP. In this way, you can minimize your headaches, use the same ISP for both your electronic mail and Web site hosting, and write one check for both services.

Browsing the Internet

Assume that you sign up with an ISP. You perform your setup as directed and now you want to access the Internet. Here's where the fun starts. (By the way, make sure that you allocate plenty of time for your first trip onto the Internet because a number of people go on and don't come back for hours on their first visit. It is easy to do, even for non-geeks, so be forewarned.)

Business Buzzword
A **browser** is a software tool that runs on your computer and interacts with the Web site documents. The browser reads the HTML codes embedded in the Web site documents, translates them, and then displays the page on your screen. Two popular browsers are Microsoft Internet Explorer and Netscape Navigator.

Your ISP provided you with a *browser*, which is a software tool used to cruise, surf, or browse your way from one Internet site to another and also send and receive electronic mail. Just as you browse a book by flipping the pages, you can browse the Internet by flipping from one site to another. The major difference is that pages in a book are all in your hand, but the separate Web sites might be on opposite ends of the globe.

The browser's job is to connect you to various sites, relay the proper commands to translate the HTML code, and then display the HTML information on your computer screen in a way that matches the document creator's intention.

There are many browser variations, but the two major contenders for your browser space are Netscape Navigator and Microsoft Internet Explorer. Both companies partner with ISPs to get their browsers on your desktop, and each provides all kinds of different financial deals to get you into their technology. Why? Simply because the larger the number of installed browsers, the more marketing and political clout that particular vendor has with the Internet community.

In either case, you win. Both are good products and certainly can serve your needs at this stage of the game unless you specifically plan to be an ISP or more sophisticated Internet design or consulting firm.

I suggest that you simply use the browser provided by your ISP and be happy that it works. Once your site is up and running, leave well enough alone until you are forced to upgrade to the next generation of browsers, which will happen around every 9 to 18 months.

Sending and Receiving E-Mail

Ever lost a letter in the mail? Ever told a client in the morning that you already mailed an item only to know that you really planned to mail it later that day? After all, the mail goes out at the end of the day anyway and you gained an extra day while not disappointing the client. Well, those days are gone with electronic mail, or *e-mail*.

E-mail allows you to send messages and files instantly from one e-mail address to another. Your clients can now say, "Why not e-mail it to me, and I'll review it in a few minutes?" and this can really happen. Is it great? You bet. You can save on postage and you know that your mail is delivered independent of the weather.

Your ISP usually provides you with an electronic mail address that you can then give to clients. You use this account for sending and receiving mail. Mail is a built-in function of most ISP browser/mail signup combinations.

Once again, beware of connecting yourself with a single vendor. If you tell all of your clients to send e-mail to a CompuServe account, for example, and then you change to a standard Internet mail account, you have to retrain your customers to send mail to the new address. For this reason, many companies tie their e-mail accounts to their domain names, which, if kept independent of the provider's name, allows you to move from one network to another without retraining your customers.

Business Buzzword
E-mail (electronic mail) is a method of delivering mail between people with access to a message network such as the Internet. It allows you to send a message and even attach files, such as an Excel document, that is instantaneously sent across the room or around the world.

Creating Your Web Site

Just look at you now—with your new ISP connection, your hot e-mail address, and your own personal Web site location. Oops! There isn't any information on your Web site! When people access the Internet through their ISP and connect to your Web site, they get a blank screen or an exciting message such as "site under construction." Somehow, this leaves something to be desired.

You fix this situation by creating *Web site content,* which is displayed when someone accesses your site with a browser. Content is actually a bunch of HTML-coded pages that display in a specific way when the browser downloads and translates the information.

HTML code is pretty cryptic and early Web site designers had to live with HTML to make any kind of attractive site. HTML is still around, but the software world has made it easier for normal people like you and me to create content by developing automated content-creation tools such as Microsoft FrontPage, Corel WebMaster Suite, DeltaPoint QuickSite, Adobe PageMill, ClarisWorks Internet Edition, Cold Fusion, and Netscape Navigator Gold. These tools work similarly to any Windows graphic design utility, but the final output is an HTML file that can be placed on a Web site for viewing with a browser.

These content creation tools are not for the computer novice, but they are also not so complicated that you need three college degrees and a pocket protector to create an attractive and functional Web site. Some people pay to have the initial site created and use it as a training experience for a standard employee.

All of this Web site technology is pretty impressive. Wait until I talk about links. A *link* is a section of your HTML page that refers to another Internet location, such as another Web site. For example, assume that your company sells widgets for the XYZ Widget company and that your Web site refers to the BANGO product also produced by XYZ Widget. Your Web site can include a link to the www.xyzwidget.com Web site location for additional information about the BANGO product. Your site is referring, or linking, the browser to the other Web site that you don't control. You are now taking advantage of XYZ Widget's Web site development effort by automatically sending your users to its site when they click the link. (Oh, by the way, your site may be in New Jersey and the BANGO information may be on a site in Tokyo. It is all automatic to the person viewing the information and clicking the link.)

> **Business Buzzword**
> Your **Web site content** is the text and visuals that are displayed on your Web site. Typical content includes company history, company logo, mail and phone addresses, products and services offered, and sales or marketing contact information.

> **Business Buzzword**
> A **link** is a section of a displayed Web page. When clicked by the user, the link connects the user to the Internet site associated (or linked) with the clicked selection. Think of the Web site like a magazine, and a Web page like a page in that magazine. Links jump you between sites and pages.

Links can also refer to various locations in your own Web site, which is common when your site becomes longer than a few pages. In fact, the majority of your links refer to other pages within your own site. Links are easily created, tested, and managed using the technology built into the content-creation software packages mentioned earlier.

Here are a few words of caution regarding Web site creation strategies:

➤ Don't ever forget that the site is a sales tool first and not someplace to show "cool" stuff that does not contribute to your sales and advertising goals.

➤ Snazzy design is important, but not as important as providing the information that your clients want.

➤ Make your site easy to follow and user friendly.

➤ Keep the site information current and display the date that you last modified the page contents.

➤ Ask around for sites that people like, and model your initial site after what already works.

➤ Graphics (visual images) download slowly from the Internet, so keep the number and size of graphics on your site to a minimum.

➤ Make sure that the content-creation software you use does not lock you into a specific browser type that excludes all others. As a result, people might not be able to view or use your site. For example, make sure that the content you create will at least work with both Microsoft Internet Explorer and Netscape Navigator.

➤ Anything you put on your site can also be viewed by your competition. Don't put it out there unless you want it found.

What if you don't feel up to writing and designing your own Web site? Luckily, Web site design services are popping up all over the place. Some are good, and some just don't get it. Make sure that you work with someone who understands that the site is first a business and sales tool and secondly a cool technology play toy.

For around $1,000, you should be able to get a decent site design that is functional. The monthly hosting of the site by a service provider should run between $15 and $50, depending on the level of advanced services required and the size of the site.

This section was designed to introduce you to the processes involved in creating your own Web site.

Bankruptcy Alert

I have seen some cool, trendy sites that just did not get used. Why, you might ask. Simple. It took a lot of large graphic files to make them look flashy, and graphics take forever to download. In addition, they allowed content to suffer in favor of form. Even though the sites were flashy, they weren't very useful. Remember to make your site a useful business service tool for your customers.

The process is not that difficult, and it can really be a lot of fun. Once your site is set up, you are sure that your customers are receiving your sales and marketing information in the way that you want.

Helping People Find You on the Net

Once you've got a beautiful, informative site, how can you ensure that surfers will find your page among the hundreds of thousands of sites out there? Luckily, *search services* help Web readers find the sites related to subjects that interest them.

The most popular search services are Yahoo! (http://www.yahoo.com), Lycos (http://www.lycos.com), Excite (http://www.excite.com), and several others. You can go to one of these sites, type the subject you are interested in (business or parenting or stamps, for example), and you are given a list of links to sites that meet your criteria.

How do the search services collect all those lists? They use *search engines* to scan the Internet for new sites and determine the content of those sites.

You want to make sure that search engines can appropriately categorize your site. You can do this by learning a lot about the *hidden metafields* that are used by search engines to categorize your site. (A hidden metafield is information that is part of your content but is not visible on your site.) If you do not use metafields properly, you can create a great site and nobody will know that it exists.

Java: Advanced Business on the Web

At this point, you are fully Internet functional. Your Web site is providing information about your company and offerings. You receive e-mail at your villa in Spain while researching that next big service offering. You connect to the Internet from pool side while sipping Merlot and research the upcoming industrial trend that will bring you your next million. Okay—enough fantasy Netting, and down to business.

Once you are functional, you might still want to advance to another level of efficiency. What if you can make your site adapt its presentation to whomever is accessing it? For example, if certain viewers present a name and password, they get access to special areas of the site. Maybe their standard logon name is the passkey to special chat areas on your site. In short, you can program your site to behave one way with one user and another way with a second user.

The good news is that the possibilities associated with this capability are endless. The bad news is that it requires that you program your own custom applications that interact with the site and the user.

Web site interaction is where Java steps in. Java is more than just an opportunity for creating coffee puns. It is a sophisticated programming language that allows users to perform special functions with your site: place orders, track their order status, and even see your site in another language.

Are you going to do this programming yourself? Probably not. Java is a complicated language; you want to contract your Java site enhancements to consultants who understand that technology.

Your computer automated systems can really start to pay dividends for you. I have a friend who is in the tropical fish business. He wants to allow customers to place orders for his fish over the Internet. To place the order, his customers must know about the stock on hand. He already has a database that contains information about his fish, including their life span, environmental conditions, a picture of the fish, and the quantity he has on hand. He plans to make that information available on his Web site so that users can click a button and determine how many and what kind they want to order.

Are you starting to see how all this automation can save you time, money, and personnel costs? It would cost my friend one or two staff personnel to answer these questions and take the orders. By the time this project is complete, however, his customers will be able to place orders any time and have a current listing of all his stock. He will be able to confirm orders by e-mail, meaning that he doesn't even have a postage charge for mailing back the order confirmation. This is only the beginning of the Internet commerce game.

The Least You Need to Know

➤ The Internet is a computer-based public communication network with connections that spans countries.

➤ Web sites can be easily created using content-creation software.

➤ Make sure your Web site is clean, clear, and up to date. Remember, it is a sales and marketing tool for your business.

➤ You might ultimately need Java to customize your Web site for sales and inventory operations.

➤ Plan to eventually (within 24 to 36 months) integrate your Web site with your operations database so that you can obtain highest automation efficiencies.

Part 4
Facing Your Financials

I know that you're tempted to skip right over this part because it has that ugly word on it—financial. Yes, I know that financial stuff can be boring and confusing if not explained well. But have no fear; this part isn't that bad. More importantly, if you skip it, you can lose a lot of money, which is really bad.

There are many different ways to figure out if you're succeeding in business, and the most fundamental one is to look at your financial situation. Are you making money with all your hard work? Unless you read this part, you won't know how to do that, will you? So stick with me and I'll help you through it. If you have to put it down every once in a while to take a breather, I'll understand, but make sure you come back! Finally, make sure that you at least skim the international chapter. The information contained in that chapter might open a whole new world for you.

Chapter 11

Making Sure That You're Making It

In This Chapter

➤ Why you need to understand accounting procedures

➤ Basic accounting principles

➤ An overview of balance sheets and income statements

➤ An introduction to ratio analysis

➤ Cash flow analyses

➤ When to use a CPA

Jake, who lived in Tulsa, was in Chicago for a business seminar and was excited about seeing his friend Dan. They worked on cars together in high school and now owned their own auto repair businesses. It was great to talk about business; they shared the same problems and could be honest with each other because they were not competitors. Dan's business was in its fifth year of operation. Jake started his about two years ago and was clearly not making it. Things were tough, and this seminar was his last shot at turning things around before he had to "bag it" and get a "real job."

"I don't understand," said Dan. "You're a great mechanic and you love working with people. What's wrong with your business that you aren't making ends meet?"

Jake looked out the window and back at Dan. "Good question. I'm busy as all get-out and often have to turn business away, but at the end of the year, my accountant tells me I don't have enough money to pay myself what I need. Something's wrong, and if it doesn't get fixed soon, I go back to work for the dealership."

"What is your percentage profit margin?" was Dan's initial question. "And how does your pricing compare with the competition in town?"

"I have the lowest prices around," said Jake proudly. "I dropped our prices 20 percent last year, and that was when things really cut loose. We're doing more work than ever, and my sales are twice what they were last year. I even had to add space to my garage to handle the new business."

Dan smiled and then looked Jake squarely in the eye. "High sales and profits do not always go hand-in-hand. If you can't keep your profit margins where they need to be, you're in trouble. What's your percentage profit margin?"

"I don't know," replied Jake. "I let my accountant take care of all that financial stuff for me. I do cars; he does numbers. I just tell him what I want our prices to be and he takes it from there. That's what I pay him for."

"So he makes your financial decisions? What does he know about the car business? Does he care if you don't make money? You really don't review your financial statements more than once a year? I have a bad feeling that you're a great mechanic who never made the transition to being a business manager. Let's get a copy of your financial statements and compare them to mine. I bet we can get an idea of where things are going wrong," said Dan warmly. "Your business means too much to you to let it go under due to bad pricing and financial decisions."

Jake nodded with a somber look on his face, silently hoping that Dan would buy lunch. He started to realize that managing the business like a hobby instead of a business might have hurt his dream of independence. This time, he would stay awake during the seminar's financial analysis segment.

Like Dan, most business owners treat accounting as a necessary evil. I understand completely because I did the same thing. Because I did not treat the accounting aspects of managing my company seriously, I made a few financial decisions based on bad information, much to my regret. I now believe in the value of accurate accounting, and I encourage you to learn from my mistakes.

This chapter won't make an accountant or bookkeeper out of you, but it will introduce you to accounting terms and methods. You'll also learn enough to manage an accountant in a way that is valuable to your own business situation. Remember that your accountant works for you, not the other way around. Get him involved early so that he understands your needs.

Accounting 101

Communication is a wonderful thing—when it works. Hazy communication can lead to confusion and hard feelings. Communication takes on a new importance when it's about money. Money is a basic necessity of life, and most people treat threats to their money as threats to their person. How do you communicate about money when you run a business?

This question introduces the purpose of the highly structured world of *accounting*—to provide business managers and others with the information they need to manage a business or evaluate their investments. Accounting is how business keeps score, and, just like keeping score in baseball, there are numerous rules and procedures to accurately reflect the results of the actions on the field.

You need to accumulate information that is timely, reliable, and useful, and you don't want to take valuable time away from making money. Fortunately, accounting principles and policies can make accounting for your business easier. Several software packages are now on the market that make accounting a much simpler task than ever before. We talk about them in more detail later in the chapter.

The following sections provide some basic accounting concepts so you can understand the considerations involved in setting up and maintaining your accounting systems. Time spent planning and developing good procedures can save you countless hours of frustration down the road.

Business Tip
If you are publishing financial information for use outside the company, you need to consider an additional set of special accounting rules (called *GAAP*, or *Generally Accepted Accounting Principles*) when you prepare your financial statements. For managing a business, however, you only need to make sure your accounting system makes sense.

Accounting Periods

Accounting periods are periods of time, such as months, quarters, or years, that allow a company's financial reports to be compared from one time frame to another. It's a good idea to review your company's performance on a regular basis so you can become aware of potential problems, such as running out of cash or lower sales figures, before it's too late.

Accounting periods also provide a basis for comparing company performance from one period to the next, from quarter to quarter or from year to year. Additionally, to file your tax returns, you have to determine in what month you want your year to end so you can report your profit or loss for that year.

For starters, you need to determine when your company will evaluate its financial performance. Most companies, small and large, look at their basic financial statements at least quarterly (every three months) to measure their progress towards long-term goals, and most managers review their financial statements on a

Business Buzzword
Accounting periods are periods of time, such as months, quarters, or years, that allow a company's financial reports to be compared from one time frame to another.

A year in a company's history is called a **fiscal year**.

When the company's financial reporting period is the same as the calendar year, which extends from January 1st to December 31st, it is called a **calendar fiscal year**.

daily or weekly basis. It's always good to know where your sales are coming from and how your money is being spent.

The next question is, "When does your company's financial year begin and end?" A year in a company's history is a *fiscal year*. Unless there is some reason to do otherwise (as recommended by your accountant), keep your fiscal year the same as the calendar year, from January 1st to December 31st. This means your quarters will end on March 31, June 30, September 30, and December 31.

Of course, you need to consider whether the IRS has any relevant rules before you can comfortably select a fiscal year end. The good news is that you can always change your fiscal year after you have been in business for a while, so you shouldn't worry too much about this selection. Start out with a standard calendar year and change it later if needed.

Sales and Costs

Assume that your client pays you today for work you intend to perform in 60 days. First off, kiss this customer and keep him happy; this type of client is rare, indeed. Second, take a look at whether you should declare that payment as *earned income*. (In other words,

Business Buzzword

Income is the general term for money received from selling a product or service to a customer. Any money paid to you before the product or service is fully given to the customer is **unearned income**. If the customer can cancel his or her contract and get the money back, you have not truly earned it.

On the other hand, money you have received for work performed or for products provided is known as **earned income**. You've done everything the customer requested, according to some formal or informal agreement, and you can consider the money yours.

can you spend the money today knowing you won't have to give it back, or should you wait?)

In the *accrual* accounting world (don't worry, I define accrual soon), when you receive payment from a customer for work that hasn't been completed yet, for accounting purposes, you need to show that payment as *unearned income* until the work is done. When the earning process is complete, the accrual basis of accounting reports that transaction as *income*.

If the customer can cancel his order, then the money really hasn't been earned yet, has it? You are essentially holding the money for him until you complete the work. In short, if you haven't finished earning the money by meeting all the terms of your contract with the customer, you shouldn't consider the revenue from those sales as truly yours.

If you have a non-cancelable contract along with a non-refundable advance, then the money you received is yours. At that point, you can include it as revenue.

If you use the cash basis of accounting (described in the next section), you don't need to know the difference between collections and earned income. In the cash-based accounting world, everything you receive from sales is considered income when it is collected, and you don't make any special accounting entries to show when it is earned.

I usually recognize the sales revenue at the time of invoice generation unless the dollars involved are so large that they can make a material difference to my company's financial well-being.

Which Accounting Method Is Right for You?

Here's a fundamental accounting question: When do you actually incur an expense? Is it when you use the product or service, or when you pay for the product or service? The answer is different, depending on whether you use the *cash basis* or *accrual basis* of accounting. These are two approaches to accounting, and you need to know which one is more appropriate for your business.

The *cash basis* of accounting recognizes sales and expenses when money is actually received or spent. The *accrual basis* of accounting focuses on the earning process and matches sales revenue to the period when the earning process is completed. The accrual basis also matches expenses incurred to generate those sales to the period in which the income is reported.

If your business has inventory, the IRS says you must use the accrual basis of accounting, so that decision is made for you. However, if you run a service business, especially if you are a small business, you might find that keeping your books on the cash basis is much simpler.

Here's an example to illustrate the differences between the two methods.

Assume you run a small consulting firm, and you have only one project right now. Last month, you spent $400 on supplies and office expenses, paid your staff $1,000, and billed your client $2,500 for the project. This month, your client pays the bill (and the check clears the bank!). Under the cash basis of accounting, you show a loss of $1,400 last month because you paid for the supplies and salaries then, and you show a profit of $2,500 this month because you collected the payment now. Under the accrual basis, you match the expenses incurred last month with the revenue earned last month and show a profit of $1,100 ($2,500 in revenue less $1,400 in expenses). Note, however, that this does not necessarily mean you have $1,100 in the bank.

> **Business Buzzword**
> The **cash basis** of accounting recognizes sales and expenses when cash is actually received or spent. The **accrual basis** focuses on the earning process and matches sales revenue to the period when the earning process is completed.

If you have a fairly simple business, with expenses incurred close to the time sales revenues are collected, the cash basis of accounting might give you information that is accurate and timely enough to let you run your business. However, most larger businesses use the accrual basis of accounting, for some or all of the following reasons:

➤ They have inventories, so the IRS makes them use accrual accounting.

➤ There are long lags between the time expenses are incurred and the time sales revenues are collected, and the business managers feel that cash basis accounting gives them a distorted picture of operations.

➤ The business sells a small number of large items, and showing earnings based on collections results in dramatic swings in reported performance from month to month, even though the underlying operations might not be fluctuating nearly as much.

Bankruptcy Alert
Don't track part of your business on cash basis and part on accrual. This can get very confusing when reading financial statements. And it is guaranteed to make your banker question the validity of the rest of the numbers.

➤ The business has more than one owner, and the owners want a clear picture of the earnings of the business, not just the cash collections. (Cash basis accounting gets particularly messy when partners split up.)

➤ Their accountant talked them into it. (Accountants believe the accrual basis of accounting provides better information on the results of business operations, even though an accrual-basis system might be more complicated or costly to maintain.)

The Cash Basis Accounting Method

How do you track money owed to you when you're using the cash basis of accounting? Very simply, you complete work for customers and you bill them. In some businesses, you receive payment right away, such as if you are running a restaurant; customers pay after they eat. You keep track of who owes what by having waiters and waitresses use order slips. At the end of the night, you total the amount on all the order slips collected and match them with the amount of money in your cash register. You then deposit most of that money in your bank account and keep some in the register to use as change the next day.

If you run almost any other kind of business, however, you probably have to wait to receive payment. You might bill a customer on the first of the month and have to wait 30 days until the check arrives. To keep track of who owes what, create a file of all the invoices sent to customers. As customers pay, you deposit their checks in the bank and take their invoice copies out of the file. You can always check to see whose invoice is outstanding by looking in your file. Once more than 30 days has passed, you want to give the customer a call and find out if there is a problem. (See Chapter 15, "Collections: When Customers Don't Pay," for more on collections.)

The Accrual Accounting Method

Accrual accounting imposes an additional accounting step; now you have to use the accounting system to track when a customer is billed as well as when the collection comes in, and you might be making accounting entries at times when no cash has changed hands.

Furthermore, accrual accounting might report handsome profits while you have no cash in the bank to pay suppliers—because your customers haven't paid you yet. When managing any business, large or small, remember that cash is king, and track your bank balances and expectations about cash flows using the techniques discussed later in this chapter. Many businesses have shared the sad experience of running out of cash before all the bills have been paid; try not to join them!

Accrual accounting might also impose tax complications. No one likes paying taxes on reported income before the cash from those sales has been collected, but that can be the way accrual accounting works. Your accountant or tax advisor can give you suggestions on techniques to minimize this source of pain.

Table 11.1 summarizes the advantages and disadvantages of cash basis and accrual basis accounting.

Table 11.1 Cash versus Accrual Accounting

Cash Basis	Accrual Basis
Advantages	
Relatively simple to use.	Provides a conceptually more correct picture of the results of your business operations.
Understandable to anyone who has balanced a checkbook.	Consistent with the way bigger companies report their financial results.
Reports income when you have the cash to pay the taxes.	Accepted by the IRS if your business has inventory.
	Simplifies accounting during change in ownership.
	Makes reporting to outsiders more comprehensible (bankers, potential investors, and so on) because they are used to accrual-basis statements.
Disadvantages	
Can distort the results of operations, possibly leading to bad business decisions.	Can be costly and time consuming.

continues

Table 11.1 Continued

Cash Basis	Accrual Basis
Not acceptable to the IRS if your business has inventory.	Might not match reported income and cash availability.
Not comparable to the way bigger companies report their financial results.	Requires some thought to understand the accrual accounting concepts.
Complicates accounting during changes in ownership.	
Can make your company's financial condition appear worse than it is if you offer credit terms to your customers.	

Understanding Financial Statements

Settle down in a comfortable chair and make a pot of coffee; it's time to learn the language of accounting. It's not nearly as fun as the language of love, but stick with me. Even if you intend to use an accountant to manage your records, you still need to understand basic financial terms so you can make reasonable financial decisions on your own.

Understanding financial statements isn't difficult. Yes, even you can pick it up. Effectively using financial statements along with a valid sales forecast gives you a preview of good and bad times before they hit, so you can take proactive measures if necessary.

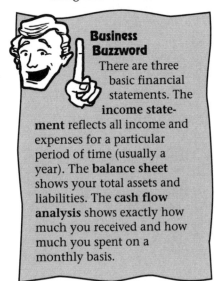

Business Buzzword
There are three basic financial statements. The **income statement** reflects all income and expenses for a particular period of time (usually a year). The **balance sheet** shows your total assets and liabilities. The **cash flow analysis** shows exactly how much you received and how much you spent on a monthly basis.

This section introduces you to financial statements and explains their basic purpose. There are three basic financial statements: the *income statement*, *balance sheet*, and *cash flow analysis*. The income statement shows you the amount of money brought in and spent during a specific accounting period, which is usually a year. The balance sheet shows you how much you own and how much you owe at a particular point in time, which is usually calculated at the end of a fiscal quarter and on the last day of the year. The cash flow analysis shows exactly how much you actually received in revenue and how much you spent on a monthly basis. You really need to watch your cash flow statement carefully. Your cash flow statement keeps you informed about how much money you have in your bank account to pay all your bills.

A Chart of Accounts

One of the procedures accountants use to make record-keeping easier and more understandable is summarizing transactions so that similar transactions are grouped together. This is done by using a *chart of accounts*, which lists all the possible categories of transactions and organizes them to make producing financial statements easier. Accounts that summarize the assets and liabilities of the company are grouped together to form the balance sheet. Accounts that summarize the sales and expenses of the company are grouped together to form the income statement. Those statements, taken together, describe the total financial condition and results of operations for the company.

It is critically important to set up these accounts so that they are not only useful for tax purposes but also so that you can get the financial management information (reports) you need to make effective financial decisions.

For example, tax accounting only requires that you know the amount of revenue received and the total costs associated with earning that revenue. Management accounting tracks the revenues and costs associated with products or business areas, so that management can determine which business activities are profitable, and which are losers. The specifics of setting up these management accounting categories is dependent upon your particular business, but the importance of setting these management accounts up early in the process applies to all businesses.

If you are using the accrual basis of accounting, you also need a financial statement that details cash flow activity, which is likely to be different from the activity shown on the income statement. Cash-basis companies might not need as elaborate an analysis to generate a good understanding of their cash flows, but they should still be aware that lags between billing and collection can adversely affect their cash position. Depending on the size of the business and the complexity of the collections, a cash-basis company might need to develop a full-fledged cash flow analysis report, too.

Business Buzzword
A chart of accounts is a list of all the categories used by a business to organize its financial expenditures and sales.

The Income Statement

Your *income statement* (or *profit and loss statement* or *P and L*) tells you whether your business is profitable. The income statement totals the amount of *revenue* and then subtracts the expenses associated with making that revenue. The result is the *pretax profit*.

Income statements show you how much you sold and how much it cost you to create those sales during a particular period of time. Most businesses prepare year-end income statements so they can see how they did during the year. You can also prepare income statements for any period, such as quarterly or the year-to-date.

Expenses fall into two categories: *cost of sales* expenses and *operating* expenses. Cost of sales expenses (also called the cost of goods sold, or COGS) are those directly related to producing your product or providing your service. These generally include the cost of raw materials, the cost of labor to run the machine that produced the widget you sold, and other expenses required to obtain or create the product or service.

Business Buzzword

Your **gross profit** is the amount of money left after you cover the cost of sales: Gross Profit = Revenue – Cost of Sales. Out of gross profit, you pay your operating expenses.

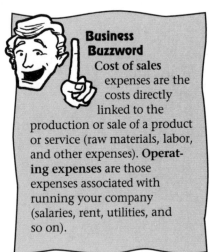

Business Buzzword

Cost of sales expenses are the costs directly linked to the production or sale of a product or service (raw materials, labor, and other expenses). **Operating expenses** are those expenses associated with running your company (salaries, rent, utilities, and so on).

For example, suppose you sold a coffee mug for $5.00 and it cost you $3.00 to purchase it. The cost of sales is $3.00, which is what you paid for the mug. The *gross profit* calculation associated with this single mug's sale is Revenue – Cost of Sales = Gross Profit, or $5.00 – $3.00 = $2.00 Gross Profit. Because the costs of producing your product change depending on how much you manufacture at a time, cost of sales are called *variable expenses*. Just as things usually cost less when you buy them in bulk, producing a product in large quantities works the same way. The more you produce, generally the lower the cost per product and the higher the gross profit.

Operating expenses are those expenses associated with running your business. You still have some amount of these expenses regardless of how much you sell in a month. These include your salary, your rent payment, the cost of the electricity in your office, insurance, administrative salaries, commissions, and other similar costs of operating the company. Operating expenses are paid out of the gross profit. Notice that operating expenses include commissions that vary with the sales level, so they are not strictly "fixed" expenses.

Now that I've given you an overview of what the income statement provides for you, take a look at one.

Remember the earlier coverage of accrual and cash-based accounting? Look at the following income statement and notice how the relationship between expenses and revenues is directly linked to profit calculations. Unless the two are synchronized, there is no way to accurately determine if you made money during the time period you're examining.

A typical income statement.

A Simplified Income Statement
Jackson Surveying—Income Statement
Period Ending December 31, 20XX

Income Statement

Item	Dollar Amount	Description of Its Income Statement Function
Sales	$250,000	All revenues
Cost of Sales (variable costs)	$95,000	Variable costs associated with the revenues
Gross Profit (Gross Margin)	$155,000	Sales - Cost of Sales
Operating (Fixed) Expenses:		All nonvariable expenses:
Salaries	$65,000	Usually administrative and executive salaries
Rent	$18,000	What you pay to keep your doors open
Marketing and Sales	$55,000	What it costs you to sell your offering
Total Other Expenses	$138,000	Total of All Other Expenses
Pre-Tax Profit	$17,000	Gross Profit - Total Other Expenses
Federal/State Taxes	$5,950	Taxes due on the Pre-Tax Profit
Net Income	$11,050	Pre-Tax Profit - Federal and State Taxes

The Balance Sheet

Whereas an income statement reflects the flow of money in and out of a company during a specific time frame (as videotape records events over a period of time), the *balance sheet* shows the amount of company assets and liabilities at a particular point in time (a snapshot of how things are at a particular moment). The balance sheet is based on a fundamental equation of accounting: Assets = Liabilities + Owner's Equity.

Assets are those items of value the company owns, such as cash in the checking account, accounts receivable, equipment, and property. The value of an asset is based on its initial purchase price minus any applicable *depreciation* (the accounting-tracked decrease in value that occurs as an asset ages).

Bankruptcy Alert

When you are analyzing the depreciation of an asset, don't confuse book value with market value. For example, your ten-year-old car might have $0 book value. Does that mean that the car is no longer worth anything? Not necessarily. The car probably has some market value in that someone would be willing to pay you something for it. The market might think that an asset has value even after it is fully depreciated.

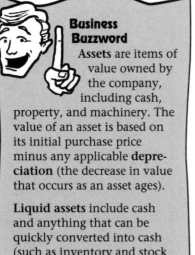

Business Buzzword

Assets are items of value owned by the company, including cash, property, and machinery. The value of an asset is based on its initial purchase price minus any applicable **depreciation** (the decrease in value that occurs as an asset ages).

Liquid assets include cash and anything that can be quickly converted into cash (such as inventory and stock and bonds). **Fixed assets** are those that are difficult to convert quickly, such as buildings or machinery.

The **book value** of an asset is its purchase price less the total amount of depreciation that has already been applied to the asset.

The **market value** of an asset is what someone would pay for the asset, even though it may have been partially or fully depreciated.

Business Buzzword

Liabilities are amounts that you owe, including loans, credit cards, and taxes. **Short-term liabilities** (those due within 12 months) are also called **accounts payable**.

For example, cash is an asset. You obtain the cash either from selling stock, obtaining a loan, or selling your services or products. Cash is money you can spend on the spot. It is called a *liquid asset*; you can use it immediately to pay off a debt or to purchase items. Other common liquid assets include accounts receivable and inventory. Liquid assets are part of current assets and represent those assets that you expect to be converted into cash within a year.

Fixed assets have a longer life and are more difficult to convert into cash quickly. Typical fixed assets include buildings, machinery, and land. The net book value of an asset is based on its initial purchase price less any depreciation. Different fixed assets have different depreciation terms, or depreciable lives. Check with an accountant to determine the proper depreciable life of a given item.

Liabilities are amounts that you owe. Typical liabilities include accounts payable, which reflects amounts owed to suppliers, loans, credit cards, taxes, and other people or organizations to whom you owe money. Short-term liabilities, which are paid back within 12 months, are also called current liabilities. Long-term liabilities include the portions of mortgages and equipment loans that are not due in the next year.

Owner's equity is what is left over when the liabilities are subtracted from the assets. Take what you have, subtract what you owe, and you are left with owner's equity. This is the number that you want to maximize because it can reflect the book value of your company. The initial investment of your company stock and retained earnings are added together to calculate owner's equity.

The amount of *net income* (see the sample income statement earlier in this chapter) determined at the end of the year is added to an equity account named *retained earnings*. You add the current year's net income to the prior year's retained earnings to calculate the company's retained earnings at the end of the period in question. Ideally, retained earnings become cash used by the company to promote further growth.

Table 11.2 is an example of how to organize your accounts in preparation for making your balance sheet.

Table 11.2 Typical Balance Sheet Accounts

Assets	Description
Cash	Bank accounts, petty cash, investments.
Accounts Receivable	What other companies owe you on a credit basis, to be paid within 30 days.
Inventory	Raw materials, finished goods, product being built, retail merchandise, training manuals, and so on.
Fixed Assets	Land, buildings, machinery, office equipment, depreciation expense.

Liabilities	Description
Short-term (current) liabilities	Must be paid in less than 12 months. Includes accounts payable to suppliers, unpaid wages, taxes, credit card debt, short-term loans, and long-term notes with less than 12 months left on their term.
Long-term liabilities	Due over a period that is longer than 12 months. Includes mortgages, equipment loans, bank loans, and other long-term financial obligations.
Equity	Assets – Liabilities = Equity
Capital Stock	Owned by shareholders. Includes common stock and preferred stock.
Retained Earnings	Current and cumulative year's net profits or losses as accumulated from prior and current year income statements.

So here you are with accounts and numbers. Now look at the following figure to see how to put them together to create a balance sheet.

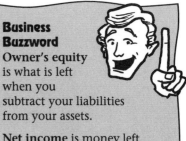

Business Buzzword
Owner's equity is what is left when you subtract your liabilities from your assets.

Net income is money left over after all company expenses have been paid out of revenues.

This typical balance sheet shows the format for organizing all your balance sheet accounts.

A Simplified Balance Statement Jackson Surveying—Balance Sheet Period Ending December 31, 20XX	
Current Assets	
Cash in Bank	$15,000
Accounts Receivable	$25,000
Inventory	$18,000
Other Current Assets	$7,000
Total Current Assets	$65,000
Fixed Assets	
Land and Building	$250,000
Machinery	$75,000
Office Equipment	$35,000
Accumulated Depreciation	($25,000)
Total Fixed Assets	$335,000
Total Assets	**$400,000**
Current Liabilities	
Credit Cards	$3,000
Wages Payable	$9,500
Taxes Payable	$3,000
Line of Credit	$5,500
Accounts Payable	$4,500
Total Current Liabilities	$25,500
Long-Term Liabilities	
Mortgage Loan	$185,000
Machinery Loan	$55,000
Equipment Loan	$30,000
Total Long-Term Liabilities	$270,000
Total Liabilities	**$295,500**
Owner's Equity	
Common Stock	$45,000
Retained Earnings	$59,500
Total Owner's Equity	$104,500
Total Liabilities and Equity	**$400,000**

As your company grows, the numbers on your assets and liabilities and equity line will grow larger and larger. This is due to purchasing new equipment, increasing your accounts receivable because of higher sales, or improving your cash situation. Companies just starting out will have a small number on their assets and liabilities and equity line.

Owner's equity, your company's net worth, is calculated by subtracting the liabilities from the assets. This means that as your assets (what you own) increase and your liabilities (what you owe) decrease, your equity increases. This makes logical sense, and the balance sheet puts it into a form where it can be precisely calculated. Realize, however, that your owner's equity usually does not reflect your company's market value. Setting the market value for an ongoing company is usually a complicated matter and heavily industry-dependent.

Although your balance sheet might not change drastically from week to week, it's a good idea to regularly review whether you are taking on more debt or increasing the equity of the company. Most financial software packages can easily provide you with a balance sheet and income statement whenever you want to look at it.

Cash Flow Analysis

A *cash flow analysis* can be your most important financial statement because it tells you whether you have enough cash to pay your bills. Although tracking your assets and liabilities is important over the long term, when you're just starting out, the key challenge is keeping the money coming in.

A cash flow analysis, or cash flow statement, looks a lot like an income statement (see the following figure). The major difference is that your income statement focuses on earnings from operations, whereas the cash flow analysis also reflects investments, borrowings, repayments of loans, and other balance sheet changes. Cash flow from operations might also be significantly different from reported earnings, especially if you are using the accrual basis of accounting.

The reason you need both an income statement and a cash flow analysis is that you might have a really good month of sales and then a really bad month of sales. So bad, in fact, that you have to get a loan to cover your expenses. By watching your cash flow analysis, you can see in advance when you will start to run out of cash during that month. However, because an income statement based on an accrual basis of accounting records when obligations are made, not when the cash is either spent or received, the good months and bad months often even themselves out. You wouldn't know by looking at your income statement that August almost put you out of business due to lack of available cash, but your monthly cash flow analysis would alert you to potential problems before they become real problems. You should now see that you must use all three financial statements to get an accurate picture of your company's financial condition.

It is also a good idea to become good friends with your receivable aging report. This is the report that tells you who still owes you money and how far past due they are with their payments. If you offer net 30-day terms, and you see most of your clients paying in 45 to 60 days, then you are providing them with additional credit for the extra 15 to 30 days. In essence, you are taking out a loan to cover for their delayed payment. If that is okay with you, then you are more generous than most small business owners I know. Get your collections in order, and you might find your need for cash decrease accordingly. See Chapter 15 for actions you can take if they don't pay.

	January	February	March	April	May	June
Revenues						
Product Sales	$1,200	$1,620	$2,187	$2,952	$3,986	$5,381
Services	$300	$405	$547	$738	$996	$1,345
Net Revenues	**$1,500**	**$2,025**	**$2,734**	**$3,691**	**$4,982**	**$6,726**
Cost of Sales						
Product Cost	$300	$405	$547	$738	$996	$1,345
Services Cost	$45	$61	$82	$111	$149	$202
Total Cost of Sales	**$345**	**$466**	**$629**	**$849**	**$1,146**	**$1,547**
Gross Margin	**$1,155**	**$1,559**	**$2,105**	**$2,842**	**$3,836**	**$5,179**
Overhead Expenses						
Salaries	$3,500	$3,500	$3,500	$3,500	$3,500	$3,500
Payroll Taxes and Benefits	$700	$700	$700	$700	$700	$700
Advertising and Promotion	$300	$300	$300	$300	$300	$300
Depreciation	$150	$150	$150	$150	$150	$150
Supplies and Postage	$100	$100	$100	$100	$100	$100
Professional Fees	$175	$175	$175	$175	$175	$175
Printing	$200	$200	$200	$200	$200	$200
Telephone	$250	$250	$250	$250	$250	$250
Equipment Rental and Repair	$50	$50	$50	$50	$50	$50
Travel	$650	$650	$650	$650	$650	$650
Miscellaneous	$225	$225	$225	$225	$225	$225
Office Space	$900	$900	$900	$900	$900	$900
Total Overhead Expenses	**$7,200**	**$7,200**	**$7,200**	**$7,200**	**$7,200**	**$7,200**
Net Income (Loss) Before Tax	**($6,045)**	**($5,641)**	**($5,095)**	**($4,358)**	**($3,364)**	**($2,021)**
Provisions for Income Tax						
Federal Income Tax	$ -	$ -	$ -	$ -	$ -	$ -	$
State Income Tax	$ -	$ -	$ -	$ -	$ -	$ -	$
Total Tax Provisions	$ -	$ -	$ -	$ -	$ -	$ -	$
Net Income (loss)	**($6,045)**	**($5,641)**	**($5,095)**	**($4,358)**	**($3,364)**	**($2,021)**

Note: Tax deductions not included to simplify analysis.

July	August	September	October	November	December	2000
$6,995	$9,094	$11,822	$15,368	$19,979	$25,972	$106,556
$1,749	$2,273	$2,955	$3,842	$4,995	$6,493	$26,639
$8,744	**$11,367**	**$14,777**	**$19,210**	**$24,973**	**$32,465**	**$133,195**
$1,749	$2,273	$2,955	$3,842	$4,995	$6,493	$26,639
$262	$341	$443	$576	$749	$974	$3,996
$2,011	**$2,614**	**$3,399**	**$4,418**	**$5,744**	**$7,467**	**$30,635**
$6,733	**$8,753**	**$11,378**	**$14,792**	**$19,229**	**$24,998**	**$102,560**
$3,500	$3,500	$3,500	$3,500	$3,500	$3,500	$42,000
$700	$700	$700	$700	$700	$700	$8,400
$300	$300	$300	$300	$300	$300	$3,600
$150	$150	$150	$150	$150	$150	$1,800
$100	$100	$100	$100	$100	$100	$1,200
$175	$175	$175	$175	$175	$175	$2,100
$200	$200	$200	$200	$200	$200	$2,400
$250	$250	$250	$250	$250	$250	$3,000
$50	$50	$50	$50	$50	$50	$600
$650	$650	$650	$650	$650	$650	$7,800
$225	$225	$225	$225	$225	$225	$2,700
$900	$900	$900	$900	$900	$900	$10,800
$7,200	**$7,200**	**$7,200**	**$7,200**	**$7,200**	**$7,200**	**$86,400**
($467)	**$1,553**	**$4,178**	**$7,592**	**$12,029**	**$17,798**	**$16,160**
$ -	$ -	$ -	$ -	$ -	$ -	$0
$ -	$ -	$ -	$ -	$ -	$ -	$0
$ -	$ -	$ -	$ -	$ -	$ -	$0
($467)	**$1,553**	**$4,178**	**$7,592**	**$12,029**	**$17,798**	**$16,160**

A typical cash flow analysis.

Using Financial Statements

You now have tons of information neatly arranged in little columns. So what? How do you use it to your financial and management benefit? Try the following suggestions on for size:

➤ Use last year's cash flow analysis as a guide to estimating what your sales and expenses will be this year, month by month. Use it as a goal-setting tool to help improve your company's financial situation month by month.

➤ Use your income statement to estimate year-end totals for sales and expenses so you can compare where you are today to where you expect to be by the end of the year. Are you ahead of where you thought you would be sales-wise? Are your expenses growing faster than you had originally planned? Watching and comparing these numbers will help manage your business's financial situation better.

➤ The same goes for your balance sheet. Do you intend to pay off some of those start-up loans this year? Will you be buying a new building for your business? Create a projected balance sheet for the coming year: Estimate what your balance sheet will look like once you pay off those debts during the year or after you buy your building.

Bankruptcy Alert
Make sure that your accountant doesn't lock you into a proprietary accounting system that requires you to use his or her services. Otherwise, you might have to re-create all the bookkeeping entries made to date if you change accountants.

Be sure you trust whomever you choose to track your financial information. No matter what you do, don't hand over signature authority to someone else. You should be the only one able to write checks for your company.

To CPA or Not to CPA

Face it: You probably don't want to be an accountant or bookkeeper. You could go out and buy one of those green eyeshades and a pocket protector, but you still have to spend your evenings and weekends putting the numbers into the computer and paying bills. It is more fun to be out there working with customers, isn't it? It should be, if you're trying to start a business. Is it in your best interest to spend time doing accounting and tax returns when you could be helping to make sales for the company? Probably not.

If you don't know the financially accepted practices for your industry or business, consider consulting a professional who has the necessary experience to help you set up efficient systems. Once good accounting systems are established, keeping the records becomes a clerical task that can be delegated to an adequately trained employee or performed by an outsider if you aren't interested in keeping the books yourself.

Divide the accounting world into three basic regions: *bookkeeping*, *tax accounting*, and *managerial accounting*.

Bookkeeping involves accurately tracking where your money is coming from and where it is going, getting the numbers into the right accounts with the proper values. You can hire a bookkeeper to manage your record-keeping or invest in a computer program to do much the same thing. Bookkeepers are not necessarily accountants, although they do help organize all your information for use by your accountant.

Tax accounting is a type of accounting concerned solely with how much money you have to pay in taxes, so you can keep as much of your profits from Uncle Sam as possible. Tax accountants can help you take steps to minimize your tax bill.

Managerial accountants help you use your financial information to make business decisions. Generally, these accountants are on staff at a company and are responsible for record-keeping and reporting.

Although you want to stay closely involved with monitoring your financial statements, you can certainly hire a tax accountant or bookkeeper to help in those areas. Tax returns are becoming more complex, requiring a dedicated effort to take the best advantage of legal deductions. An accountant, even a CPA (certified public accountant), generally pays for herself in this area.

A CPA is an accountant who has passed certain experience and testing requirements as set by your state *board of accountancy*. Investors use an independent accountant, who is usually a CPA, to provide credibility to the accuracy of your business financial statements. The CPA audits your financial condition, giving an extra level of assurance to potential investors and shareholders that the numbers represented are substantially accurate.

Bookkeeping is time-consuming, tedious, and relatively inexpensive to turn over to a third party. You should ask your accountant if she wants to do both your bookkeeping and your tax planning. Accountants sometimes price a package deal including tax-return preparation when they do your bookkeeping because their tax preparation software might extract numbers they've been tracking for you that apply to your tax return.

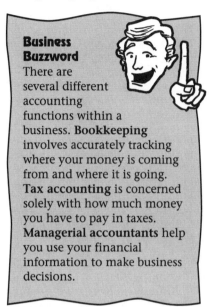

Business Buzzword
There are several different accounting functions within a business. **Bookkeeping** involves accurately tracking where your money is coming from and where it is going. **Tax accounting** is concerned solely with how much money you have to pay in taxes. **Managerial accountants** help you use your financial information to make business decisions.

Bankruptcy Alert
Make sure that your accountant actually spends some time analyzing your numbers before preparing the return. If she prepares the return based on erroneous numbers, you inherit the consequences, which can have a large financial impact on your taxes. Skimping on the tax return preparation to save a few hundred dollars in preparation fees is probably not a good idea.

You might want to act as your own accountant in the early days to save money, but if you're not good with numbers, find someone to handle this for you right away. Otherwise, you can do the company financial records a lot of damage that you'll have to pay to correct later.

Mentor

A number of CPAs I have met tend to be very conservative with respect to declaring expenses. Because of this, your CPA can cost you money on those gray areas that are a judgment call. He or she should advise you of the laws and then go along with your decision as long as nothing unethical or illegal is involved.

Business Tip
The current crop of accounting software packages makes bookkeeping pretty easy. You might want to try it yourself just so you understand what is involved and then rely on the software to keep your accounts up to date. Programs such as QuickBooks, DacEasy, or M.Y.O.B make the basic bookkeeping process easier. They all sell for under $200 and come with a payroll module.

Consider these suggestions for your starting point in dealing with accounting professionals:

➤ Automate from the beginning. Get a computer and a software package that helps track your sales and expenses. Back up your data regularly.

➤ Use an accountant, not necessarily a CPA, for your tax return. This certainly pays for itself.

➤ Farm out the bookkeeping aspects if at all possible. Talk to your accountant, and you might get the bookkeeping and tax return as part of an inexpensive package deal.

➤ Graduate to a CPA when you need to work with external financial companies that require the independent assurance that a CPA provides. The CPA does not necessarily need to perform your bookkeeping to be able to perform an accounting assurance evaluation. They simply enclose a disclaimer stating that the financial statements were prepared from records provided by you, the client.

The Least You Need to Know

➤ Accounting is the tool used to determine the financial health of your business. It is a necessary and integral part of your business and you should pay close attention to it from the start.

➤ Financial statements include an income statement, cash flow analysis, and balance sheet.

➤ Accrual and cash basis accounting provide different profit and loss information for the same accounting period.

➤ Bookkeeping is basically clerical in nature; financial accounting involves analyzing financial performance and comparing current results with prior accounting periods.

➤ When in doubt, get an accountant. You might not need a CPA right away.

➤ Automate from the beginning and make sure that your software package can handle growth in areas such as receivable tracking, inventory, and accrual accounting.

Banking on Your Business

"These guys have absolutely no vision," said Bill. "This is a great idea, and all I need is $25,000. That's nothing to a bank their size, but NO-O-O! They want all of this supporting documentation before they will even consider the loan. Why do I bother with banks in the first place?"

"They have money, and you need money. Isn't that right?" asked Bill's father.

"Sure, but why make it so complicated? It makes me want to pull my account and take my business to another bank that appreciates a good deal," said Bill. "I know this business. They have no idea what they're throwing away."

"That might be the key to your problem," his father said quietly. "If they don't understand the opportunity, can you blame them for not seeing its value? After all, whose job is it to convince them to give you money? Theirs or yours?"

This might seem obvious, but at some point in your company's life you will have to work with a bank. The relationship might be as simple as a checking account or might be complicated. One thing is for certain: Your relationship with the bank is easier if you understand how bankers think.

This chapter introduces you to the banker mentality along with an overview of the services you can reasonably expect from a bank.

I wish someone had told me this stuff when I started my business. Read, learn, understand, and move past any preconceived notions you might have about banks.

What Does a Bank Bring to the Table?

In a word: money! As your company grows, its need for cash also grows. Banks are storage houses for money, which is the one element most lacking in a new company. To get an idea of what it is like to be a banker, think about the last time you lent someone money and they were slow in paying you back. How does it feel to be a banker? Are you going to be more cautious the next time you lend someone money? Keep that feeling in mind when you talk to your banker, and you will have a much better understanding of her side of the desk.

Where does a bank fit into a new business's life? In the beginning, you will most likely have to turn to sources other than a bank for business financing. When you are just starting out, the bank has no experience with you, and your company has little to no financial track record. On what basis is the bank going to lend you money? Your good intentions? Your smile?

Initially, expect the bank to provide checking services and accept wire transfers, federal tax deposits, and credit card deposits, along with other standard banking services. Over time, the bank will see your record of frequent deposits and a growing bank account, thus documenting solid growth and financial performance. Then, the bank will be more willing to risk loaning your company money. When you want a line of credit or a loan secured by a business asset of some type, you need to work with a bank.

Banks exist to serve customers, but as the old joke says, "The only way you can get a loan is to prove you don't need it." Consequently, many start-up companies have difficulty getting a loan from a bank—even if they have the best idea in the world. This is where your personal credit becomes very important (more about this later).

You have to deal with banks anyway, loan or not, for your business checking account, payroll tax deposits, credit card processing, and other administrative details. It's a good idea to start now to develop a good relationship with your bank—and with the loan officers at your branch. Why? Well, one of these days your business will be well-established and a banker who understands your company can be a great resource in supporting your profitable growth.

Start now, long before you are asking for money, to lay the groundwork that will convince your banker that you are a solid customer and a good business risk. Besides, bankers see a lot of different businesses, and you might be able to get some good business advice from your banker at the best price: free!

Why don't banks lend to companies just starting out? The banks have to be convinced that they will get their money back, with interest, when it is supposed to be repaid. Start-up companies are notoriously bad about paying loans back on time, if at all, and after the turmoil in the banking industry with the savings and loan crisis of the mid-80s, loan officers tend to shy away from risky situations. Yes, they might be missing a golden opportunity to support your business in the early stages, but they also miss the opportunity to lose the money they loan you if your company doesn't work out the way you hope.

Don't take it personally, but recognize it as part of the business environment you're not likely to change and build your strategies accordingly. If you need financing to start your business, you probably need to get it from investors or nonbank sources (which are discussed more in Chapter 13, "Cash Is King").

After you establish a track record in business, how do you deal with a bank? The next few sections boil down the lessons it took me several years and a lot of rejection to learn. I hope these lessons make it easier for you.

The Loan Officer Is Your Friend

Whom would you rather give money to—someone who treats you with contempt and antagonism every time you meet or someone who appears to appreciate you for what you have to offer? Would you give money for a risky venture to someone you barely know or someone you have known for awhile and trust? The answer to these questions is simple, and my point is probably already made. Meet the loan officer responsible for your account when you first open the account—before you need money. Keep him updated on your progress and help him become more familiar with your company. You'll find that bringing him into the loop early will make him an ally when you need to ask for a loan. Don't wait until you're desperate for money to bring him up to speed on your activities.

Make sure that this first meeting goes well—no matter what! Appear to know what you're doing, even if you're feeling doubtful. The doubts will pass, but the initial impression on the loan officer will stay.

Business Tip
It's a good idea to get to know several loan officers at your branch, so if your main contact leaves, you don't have to start from scratch getting to know someone else. These days, people don't stay at one job very long, so it's likely that by the time you're ready to apply for a loan, your original loan officer will be working somewhere else. It is also a good idea to get to know your loan officer's boss. Positive strokes to a boss even works for bankers.

Look and act like the president of your own company, someone who deserves as much money as you want! This meeting doesn't have to be lengthy, but you must leave a positive impression so the loan officer will remember you when you need to borrow money.

Don't underestimate the value that this loan officer brings to your business. As with any bureaucracy, it is really good to know someone inside who can steer you through the maze and support your cause when needed.

Banks Will Give You Money Only When You Don't Need It

Banks make money by lending it to individuals and businesses. The loan officer's obligation to the bank is to make loans to the businesses that are most likely to pay them back.

The lending policies of nationally regulated banks are monitored by the state's Office of the Comptroller of Currency, or OCC. (You can recognize a national bank by the word "national" or letters "NA" in its name.) The loan officer of a national bank must walk the line between pursuing the best business opportunity for the bank and complying with regulatory agencies such as the OCC. Private banks, on the other hand, have more discretion about their lending policies.

From a bank's perspective, lending money to a small business provides risks and advantages that are different from those associated with a large company. Take a look at some of these risks and advantages.

Business Tip
When you request a loan for an amount greater than the loan officer's lending authority (which can be as little as $15,000 or as much as $100,000, depending on the bank), the loan officer must get approval from her supervisor or from a loan committee that makes decisions regarding larger loans.

The smaller business loans have a higher risk associated with them because the business is usually newer and might have fewer assets to be used as collateral. This increases the interest rate the small business must pay, which increases the revenue banks receive. Small businesses are also attractive as loan customers because funds from a loan can usually be covered by money from company checking and savings accounts at the bank. Because small businesses are likely to keep their money in one bank, banks are becoming more willing to lend them money.

Larger companies have large lending needs that require extra attention from the bank (401K plans, lock box, and so on). These lending services generate fee income for the bank, but the loans are priced at a lower interest rate because the larger customers are in a better negotiating position. However, larger businesses rarely have all their money in one or two accounts; it's invested in several other places.

To get them to provide you and your company with money, you must sell them on your company, your ideas and on you, or this money may go to other, less risk ventures. Be prepared to present a case to your banker on why you should get the loan.

In addition, it is generally safer for a bank to invest money in several ways, rather than all in one basket. Several small business loans spread the risk over several businesses so that even if one business owner starts to have trouble repaying his loan, the whole bank is not threatened.

The primary reason banks have conservative lending policies is that loan defaults are expensive. They can only provide loans that are an acceptable risk in the eyes of their depositors and the regulatory agencies to whom they report. They are not in the business of providing high-risk, high-profit, potential venture capital loans.

As a small business owner, you must create a personal and business track record in advance that will qualify your company for a loan when you need it. Here's what you can do:

> ➤ Keep your personal and business financial situation healthy by using standard accounting practices and watching your cash flow.

> ➤ Try to get a small line of credit early on to get your credit established with the bank. A business line of credit is usually increased when you pay it off on a regular basis.

Calling your loan officer and saying, "I need the money tomorrow" is a red flag that something is out of control with the company and its management. A panic situation raises questions about your managerial ability. Plan ahead to make sure that you can get a bank to lend you money when you really do need it.

You can also expect to personally guarantee any loans given to your company by a bank. Every bank that I have ever worked with has wanted the same thing, and the first time that you sign the papers giving the bank the right to go after your personal stuff should the business loan go into default, you can feel your skin crawl a little. It just comes with the territory and you should not take it personally. On the other hand, more

Business Tip
Banks often use tax returns as the basis for determining a business's and individual's financial (and consequently loan) status. Keep both your company and personal returns in order to improve your loan chances with the bank.

Business Tip
To give you an idea of how much a default costs a bank, consider a company with a $10,000 loan that defaults. The bank has lost the $10,000 plus the interest on the loan, which is generally 2 to 3 percent in profit to the bank. To make up that loss, the bank has to lend an additional $333,333 just to get its money back. A $333,333 loan would generate close to $10,000 in interest income in a year.

than one business owner has worked those extra hours with the image of his banker sitting in the other room monitoring loan payment status.

I know of a bank in Illinois that waives this personal guarantee ritual when the company officers and owners each individually own less than 20 percent of the company. There is your out for having to personally guarantee each business loan: Simply give away 81 percent of your company ownership.

If you didn't take that as a joke, you are taking this stuff way too seriously. Make a lot of money first and then look at getting around the personal guarantee by selling ownership.

Bank Loans That You Can Get

Now you understand the world of finance from the bankers' perspective. How does this translate into your ability to get money when you need it? Here are some loan options for you to consider.

An *unsecured line of credit* can be given on a personal basis to the company officers. This is essentially a personal loan to officers (based on the personal credit history of the individuals), who then loan it to the company. This loan is not given directly to the company because the company has not proven it could pay the loan back. The officers arrange reasonable repayment terms with the company. If you are the officer of a corporation, make sure the loan conditions, such as the interest rate and the term of the loan, are similar to those you would see in normal business transactions.

A *secured line of credit* is the next best option. In this scenario, the bank loans the company money to purchase an asset, such as new equipment or a new building. The asset is then used to secure the loan until the company pays it back, just like a house secures a mortgage, which is simply another kind of loan. In this case, the company typically must provide at least 20 percent of the purchase amount. (A $50,000 purchase requires $10,000 invested by the company and $40,000 by the bank.) If the loan can't be repaid, the assets are sold to recover the bank's investment. Liquid assets, such as a certificate of deposit, a receivable note, or inventory are the most desirable and easiest to loan against because they are the easiest to sell if the company defaults on the loan. Next best are fixed assets such as equipment and computers.

Business Tip
The value of assets is usually discounted when used as security for a loan. As my banker says, "We are in the business of lending money, not selling items to recover debt."

Notes, or loans, secured by larger assets such as major equipment and property are considered long-term and can have a 36- to 60-month repayment period.

You might also be able to get *short-term loans* (under a year) by using receivables or inventory as your collateral. This type of loan is really a line of credit with special provisions. You provide a summary to the bank showing that your company has a certain level of liquid assets—accounts receivables from customers, inventory, or CDs—that can be used as security on the loan. The bank will only loan 70 to

80 percent of the value of the assets, which is recalculated each month. The danger is that if your assets decline from one month to the next, you might have to shell out some additional money.

That is the strict letter of the relationship. Now, here is what usually happens in reality. You talk to your banker and show a historical record of receivables, inventory, and receivables aging. From the amounts and aging, you and your banker agree on a reasonable amount of liquid asset value and the bank opens a line of credit for that amount. The 70 to 80 percent rule still applies, and my experience has been that this keeping of the loan no more than the agreed-upon 80 percent value is handled on the honor system. My banker only asked for my receivables value at the one-year anniversary but reserved the right to investigate them monthly if desired. Your banker will probably only exercise this right if she believes that the note or the company is in jeopardy.

For example, assume that you secured your line of credit last month with $50,000 in receivables, giving you $35,000 in credit (70 percent of $50,000). If your receivables drop to $40,000 the next month, your collateral is worth only $28,000 (70 percent of $40,000). The $7,000 difference between the $35,000 and the $28,000 value of your assets must be paid to the bank immediately to meet the terms of the original loan agreement. This can be a tough check to write if you haven't planned for it. Will you get caught if you try to stretch the situation? Probably not. Is it worth the risk? I think not because if you are caught, you are in violation of a banking agreement, which can torpedo any prospects you have in keeping that banker on your side.

> **Bankruptcy Alert**
> When calculating the value of your inventory, bankers use 50 percent of the retail price as the value. They don't consider the inventory worth the full price you paid for it because the bank must sell it for less if you go out of business.

Sell Your Banker on Your Company

People naturally avoid risk, and bankers make risk avoidance an art form. There is only one issue ever discussed with a loan officer: How will the bank get the money back if the loan defaults? Where will the money come from? A new company has no established source of cash. The entire business is assumed very risky. The only thing the loan officer has to refer to is the business plan.

Your bank wants to be sure you've thought through all aspects of your business and believe it can work. If you don't believe in it, why should they? Can you imagine giving $50,000 to someone who is wishy-washy about where they plan to go, how they'll get there, when they'll arrive, and how they'll pay you back? I can't! I've done that and been burned. Your business plan is your opportunity to explain what you want to do and how you intend to succeed.

The bank is going to expect something from you before it gives credit. First, you must do your homework and prepare a comprehensive business plan with realistic sales and expense projections. Next, you must provide personal financial statements to give the bank an idea of your own financial situation, separate from the company. Any person with 20 percent or more ownership in the venture is required to personally guarantee the debt, meaning that they agree to repay it if the company defaults. Period. Later you will have more negotiating room, but early on, this is the norm.

Your challenge is to convince your bank that you are credit worthy. As a new business owner, your personal credit history along with a well thought out business plan are the best cards that you can play. My banker told me that the loans I received in my second year of business were based on my personal credibility, personal asset value, and the strength of my business plan. So far, so good!

Banks will evaluate you based on the five Cs of lending:

➤ **Character.** What are you like? Confident? Ethical? Self-assured? This is treated as a very important consideration when first starting out. Make the initial meetings count!

➤ **Capacity or cash flow.** Can you repay the debt? Do you have the cash flow to support the monthly, or periodic, payments required?

➤ **Collateral.** What can the bank take if the loan defaults? Make it clear that you don't intend to default but that the bank is covered should the worst happen.

➤ **Condition.** What is the general economic condition of the area and what is the intended use for the money?

➤ **Capital.** What is the company's net worth or equity?

Banks make their money by lending money, and they are always looking for solid loan prospects. If you have a clean financial report, both personal and business, and a company with a solid, proven, financial record, you can get money from your bank. Notice that you must perform to a certain level before your bank will consider loaning you money, and only for minimum risk opportunities. You would treat anyone with money as a friend, and that should apply to your banker also.

Commercial Checking Accounts: A Different Animal

Balance your commercial checking account just as you do your personal checkbook—but do it more often! Your company writes checks and makes deposits as you do in your personal checking account, but the rules are slightly different. You can shop around and find a better deal on fees and transaction costs on business checking accounts, but make sure the rules and requirements fit your needs. Don't overlook the important factors of convenience and security; after all, you hope to be taking a lot of money to the bank, so make sure the bank you select is accessible and safe.

Keep the following in mind when you set up a commercial checking account for your company:

➤ You are charged for your commercial account based on the number of transactions and the average account balance.

➤ You can expect to pay around $.10 for each check that you deposit, along with a transaction fee for the deposit. (Can you believe it? Only a bank would bill you for giving them money!) At some banks, the rate billed for each check varies according to whether it is local, in state, out of state, or from your cousin Vinnie!

➤ You are also billed for each check you write.

➤ You receive a statement from the bank that outlines the charges billed to your checking account for those transactions. This statement is in addition to the basic checking statement listing all the checks and deposits that have cleared. The formal term for this is an *analysis statement*.

➤ Banks charge transaction fees for each deposit you make and check you write, but they also give you an *earning credit* on the money in your account, which you can use to pay for those transaction fees. By keeping enough in your account to offset transaction fees, you save some money.

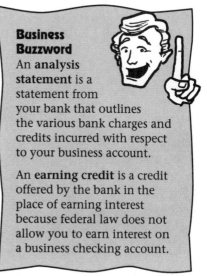

Business Buzzword
An **analysis statement** is a statement from your bank that outlines the various bank charges and credits incurred with respect to your business account.

An **earning credit** is a credit offered by the bank in the place of earning interest because federal law does not allow you to earn interest on a business checking account.

You should shop around to get the best checking account for your company, based on whether you expect to have a lot of transactions or just a few and whether you can maintain the minimum balance to avoid additional charges.

Enter the Small Business Administration (SBA)

When nobody else will help, the Small Business Administration (SBA) comes to the rescue. Maybe. It used to be difficult to get an SBA loan, but the SBA has changed and might be able to help if the loan amount is under $100,000. What used to generate a one-inch folder of paperwork is now down to a two-page application as part of the LowDoc loan program. This is good news, but you should understand the process to see how the SBA can help you in the early days.

Bankruptcy Alert

The SBA requires that you keep thorough records. All funds disbursed must be accounted for by the bank and the borrower. The record-keeping load is substantial, so be ready for it.

Business Tip

Think of the bank as the initial approval gate keeper. The SBA only considers giving you a guarantee if three banks have already rejected you for traditional financing. You must go to banks first to get rejected and then to the SBA, which relies a lot on the bank's assessment of your situation.

The SBA doesn't give you money. A bank actually issues the check. The SBA just guarantees the bank that the loan will be repaid and charges you a 2 percent fee for the insurance policy. A guarantee from the SBA that the loan will be repaid makes the loan very attractive to a bank.

Why would the SBA loan you money when a bank won't? Because the federal government thinks that small business must flourish for the domestic economy to grow, and its guarantee is the SBA's way of putting its money where its mouth is. The SBA lets the bank do the legwork and then either approves the guarantee or not.

Not all banks are SBA lenders, and you should check with the bank before starting the process. Some banks are in a position where the SBA will always approve a loan guarantee request from these banks. Call the local SBA office for information regarding these banks.

Don't assume that you need an SBA guarantee to get a loan. Fill out a loan application at the bank of your choice, which will require your personal financial information and a business plan. Should your loan not meet the bank criteria for lending (the five5 Cs), the bank can then turn to the SBA for a loan guarantee. If the SBA approves, the loan is funded from the bank with a guarantee provided by the SBA. The bank approves the loan if the SBA provides an 80 to 90 percent repayment guarantee. Quite often, banks would rather give you the loan themselves instead of involving the SBA because it makes working with the loan more complicated for the bank.

There are several different SBA loan types, and they change on a regular basis. Contact your local SBA office and sit through one of their introductory talks (around one hour long). It provides a solid basis for understanding the procedure and how to work with a bank to obtain a loan. Preferred SBA vendors do a lot of business with the SBA, so get a listing of them and work with one of the preferred banks from the beginning.

Big Banks, Small Banks

Which is better—a small bank with easy access to the lending managers or a big bank with deeper pockets and higher approval levels? The answer: It depends.

All banks have lending guidelines, but the internal policies are more flexible with a small bank. The officers are more likely to bend the rules in a small bank than in a big one. With a small bank, you get to know the officers better and quicker, but the loan amount that can be approved might be smaller. This means that you should check out the bank's philosophy of operation and verify that they actually do what their marketing literature says that they do. Ask for a few references of companies in your size range and then call these references and ask them questions.

Start with the banks where you already have a relationship. If the big banks give you grief, go to a smaller one. You might look like a large fish in a small pond, so beware that the pond might not be deep enough as you grow.

Average small business loan amounts are in the $25,000 to $50,000 range, which is well within the reach of any bank. Be aware that because it takes just as much paperwork to process a $25,000 loan as a $250,000 loan, most banks prefer to process the larger amount, where they earn more interest on the loan.

The Least You Need to Know

➤ You will almost certainly need the assistance of a bank as your business succeeds and your cash requirements increase, so get to know the officers of your bank now.

➤ Your personal credit history and business plan are your best selling points when trying to get money in the early stages.

➤ The five Cs determine your credit worthiness. Make sure that you have effectively addressed all of them to increase your chances of success.

➤ The SBA requires the same amount of preparation for a loan guarantee as a bank does. Apply for a loan at a bank first, and if you are turned down, the SBA might be able to help get it approved by guaranteeing repayment for you.

Cash Is King

In This Chapter

➤ The value of cash in your organization

➤ Turning receivables into cash

➤ How success can hurt your business

➤ Using credit to your advantage

➤ Selling stock to raise cash

Laurie stared in disbelief at her conference room table. She had heard of this happening to other companies; she couldn't believe it happened to hers.

"We're out of money," she said. "I can make payroll, but I don't have enough left over to pay our suppliers."

"That's impossible," said Philip, the VP of Sales and Marketing. "We just had three of our best months this quarter. In fact, our current revenues are triple that of last year at this time, and our income statement clearly shows a profit for this quarter. What gives?"

"The earnings are right, but we haven't collected on those large sales over the past few months. And remember, we've had to pay our workers and suppliers even though we haven't yet been paid by our customers. It'll be great when all those sales are collected, but if we keep growing as we have been, we're likely to need even more cash."

"So, are you trying to tell me that our marketing success has put the company in jeopardy?" cried Philip.

"Not at all," said Laurie. "We simply did not plan for the rapid increase and came up short with our lines of credit and other ways of getting cash into our bank account. It was mine and Jerry's responsibility to plan for this, and we got caught with our pants down. We need to tell our vendors our dilemma. I think honesty is the best policy. Let's just hope they will let us stall our payments. We can't let it happen again!"

Everyone nodded their heads at the seriousness of the situation. They had been so happy about being successful that they had forgotten that cash is king.

Keeping the cash flowing into your business is key to growth and expansion, not to mention paying your bills in a timely manner. This chapter will help you develop strategies for keeping the money flowing into your business so that you don't run into the same trouble Laurie's company did.

When You're Out of Money, You're Out of Business (Usually)

Love may make the world go 'round, but it's cash that keeps a business going. Try to keep an employee around when you cannot pay him, and you will understand that cash is the business equivalent of air. Lose your employees, the good ones, and you have substantially hurt your business. Once they're gone, they're usually gone for good.

Take a look at your vendors. How long will they keep providing you with the materials you need if you cannot pay your bills? About as long as a snowball would last in a west Texas desert. Once again, you cannot blame them for putting a stop to your credit line. Guess who is paying her employees out of her own pocket because she gave you credit and you can't pay? Your vendor! She has to cover her own behind just like you do. (See Chapter 14, "Taking Charge: Credit Card Sales," for more insights regarding providing credit to risky customers.)

Now, what about you? What happens if you cannot pay yourself? How long will you keep the business alive and pay your employees when you are not being paid? A few months, maybe, but when it becomes a way of life, you will be seriously tempted to pull the plug and "get a real job," not because you don't love what you do, but simply because that's what an organism does when its air supply is taken away.

A cash problem hurts your employees, your vendors, and you personally. Lack of cash might cause your usually professional employees to become disgruntled, might cause the quality of your product to decline, and might lead to your own loss of enthusiasm. The result is that your customers will be affected, and they probably won't like it. Their opinion of your company might drop as employees become more snippy over the phone or in person. Unfortunately, customers don't really care why the quality has declined; they just recognize that it has, and they might decide to take their business elsewhere if it continues.

All this because you forgot that cash is king! Income is great. Equipment is wonderful. Receivables are heartwarming. Inventory gives you something to count on boring weekends and at the end of the year. But cash is what makes it all work on a daily basis.

How Success Can Kill Your Business

How good can it get? Here you are with a 300 percent increase in sales over the last six months. Your people are flying high, and you just can't seem to do anything wrong. As a matter of fact, the projects coming your way are larger than you ever thought you would have, and it looks like you'll get them all! Your initial dreams have come true, and you're on the verge of becoming unbearable to everyone around you. Don't worry. Life is about to humble you, unless you have taken the proper steps to deal with the growth.

Have you ever met someone who told you that he was so successful, he went out of business? If not, you should look for such a person and buy him dinner (or a drink, depending on how he dealt with the loss). Just as you don't need to go through a windshield to learn that seatbelts are a good thing, you don't need to go out of business to learn the dangers of rapid growth.

Picture this scenario: You used to provide $10,000 per month in services and all your customers paid cash on delivery or by credit card. When you completed the sale, you got the cash. Everyone was happy. Then customers began asking for credit terms. After all, your competitor offered them credit, and they have consistently used your company instead. It wasn't such a big deal, and they were stable. Why not offer them credit? So you did.

Take a look at what happened when you agreed to accept credit terms instead of cash. You took the cash you would have received this month and told the customer that they could pay you next month, at the earliest. However, you still need to pay your employees and vendors at the end of this month. Where is that money going to come from? Unless your company has a lot of cash on hand (and wouldn't we all like that situation?), it will have to come from you. When the customer pays, you will simply pay yourself back and all is fine. Sort of....

Now let's be really successful and bump your monthly sales to $30,000. Wonderful! Who is going to provide the cash needed to cover the month-end bills? You? Do you have the $30,000 on hand to lend the company? Even if you do have the cash at $30,000, you might not when sales hit $50,000 or $100,000.

My point is this: Someday you will no longer be able to personally provide this kind of cash advance to the company. Uh-oh! There go your employees and all those wonderful vendor relationships. When they leave, they place everything that made you successful in jeopardy. In short, the whopping success that you enjoyed has just put you precariously close to being out of business. Isn't it amazing how a few short (or very long) weeks can turn your business on its ear? That is exactly what will happen if you don't take steps to avoid a cash crunch.

I'm not trying to talk you out of making your business as wildly successful as you can imagine. I'm just trying to convince you to open your eyes to the fact that success can destroy all that you have built if you don't also deal with its potential risks.

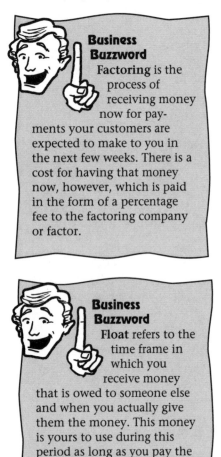

Business Buzzword

Factoring is the process of receiving money now for payments your customers are expected to make to you in the next few weeks. There is a cost for having that money now, however, which is paid in the form of a percentage fee to the factoring company or factor.

Business Buzzword

Float refers to the time frame in which you receive money that is owed to someone else and when you actually give them the money. This money is yours to use during this period as long as you pay the intended person when required.

Factoring, Credit Terms, Loans, and "Float"

Here you are, all dressed up to go to the dance with a hot date and no cash to pay for the cab. Now what do you do? You go to someone and borrow money against your next paycheck or income tax refund. Well, the same thing can be done with a business, and it's called *factoring*. With factoring, a company gives you a percentage of what customers owe you, sort of like a short-term loan.

You can also improve your cash situation by providing your customers with an incentive for paying their bills early (or even on time) and extending payments to your own vendors with whom you have credit. This improves your cash position by improving the *float* between when you receive money and when you must pay your bills.

Finally, you can get a short-term loan that is secured by your receivables from a bank or other funding source. This technique is less expensive than factoring and provides greater stability, along with other benefits.

Factoring Receivables

If you need cash now to cover business expenses, there are companies out there who will provide you with cash for your receivables in exchange for a fee. Here's how factoring, or discounting, of receivable notes works:

1. You close the deal and the customer agrees to pay you for your product or service.

2. The company that plans to factor your receivables issues an invoice to the customer (usually on your letterhead), which the customer is to pay.

3. The factoring company immediately gives you cash worth between 80 and 95 percent of the receivable value.

4. The factoring company then gives back a portion of the fee (usually up to 10 percent of the initial 5 to 20 percent discount) if the customer repays within the specified time frame.

For example, assume that a client contracts from you $10,000 worth of your product or service. You can realistically expect to receive that money within 45 to 60 days, which can put you in a bind depending on your company's cash situation. You could factor the note using the previously outlined procedure and have the numbers work out as follows:

1. You close the deal for $10,000.

2. The factoring company issues an invoice to your customer for $10,000 and indicates the terms in which the payment should be made to the factoring company.

3. The factoring company writes you a check for between $8,000 and $9,500.

4. If the customer pays within the allowed 30 days, then the factoring company writes you another check for around 10 percent (or $1,000) when payment is received. (The longer it takes for your customer to pay the factor, the less of a rebate you get back.)

Assuming that you receive an 85 percent factoring rate with a 10 percent rebate for payment received within 30 days, you see $8,500 immediately and $1,000 within 30 days. You give up 5 percent, or $500, to get your money up front instead of later and for pushing the collections issue over to the factoring company. Collection becomes their problem, not yours.

If you are in a cash crunch, factoring can save your hide. However, here are the down sides, and they are not trivial. If you factor on a regular basis at 5 percent per month, then you are paying 5 percent × 12 = 60 percent annual interest on your money. Wow! That's big bucks for the convenience of having your cash earlier instead of later. On the other hand, if you need it, you need it.

You can minimize the sour taste that factoring percentages can create by performing your own factoring services. If you have substantial personal resources, you can use them to replace the need for factoring. You can buy the receivables from your company with your personal funds and provide the same terms as a factoring company. At least, the interest is going into your favorite account (yours!) instead of some other company's.

Unfortunately, you can only factor up to the limit allowed by your personal resources. You then must look for other options.

Using Credit Terms to Enhance Your Cash Position

Timing is the secret to success, and that is particularly true when working with money. The time that money is in your hands, or in someone else's, either makes you money or costs you money. You must make every possible effort to turn your sales into cash as quickly as possible, paying as little as possible to get your money faster, such as by factoring or offering fast payment discounts.

You have an excellent opportunity to improve your cash flow by simply changing the way you pay your bills and collect receivables from your clients. If you must pay in 30 days and your clients must pay in 60 days, you have a problem. On the other hand, if they pay in 10 days and you pay in 45 days, you are in excellent shape. You accomplish this by simply offering your customers a discount (such as 2 percent of what they owe you) for payment within 10 days. Many companies will jump at the chance to save the 2 percent, and it's certainly cheaper for you to offer this discount than to pay a factoring service 5 to 15 percent for the same result!

Think about it. Plot out on a piece of paper the timing of payments made and received. Assume a $10,000 sale is made today. Mark on a calendar when you expect to provide the products or services, when you plan to receive the payment made under your credit terms, and when you have to pay your vendors and employees. Notice that the arrows for money going out and money coming in have a delay between them that usually doesn't work in your favor. You must pay the suppliers before you receive payment. Now mark where payment would be received with a 2 percent per 10-day incentive. Isn't life easier when the cash is in your hands, instead of in your customer's account?

Don't tell the IRS that I told you this, but you can improve your cash position for a two-week period, if needed, by holding your monthly payroll taxes until the middle of the month. You have to pay them on time, or you pay dearly for your transgression, but you can keep the cash in your account up to the last minute to cover other debts. Sometimes, providence will shine on you when that big check you've been expecting arrives just in time. This keeps you from having to factor at all, but it can keep you up nights worrying about the big check. By the way, this is a very last resort action because delinquent payroll taxes can land you in big trouble that has serious legal consequences. (See Chapter 18, "The Tax Files: Payroll Taxes," for more information on payroll taxes.)

Buying on Credit

Your grandmother may have always told you to stay debt free because a person in debt is a person in trouble. Well, that might be true for certain people, but credit is the lifeblood of a growing company. Credit in itself is not bad. It is how you use this credit that can either save your hide or hang it out to dry.

Try this technique for increasing your cash situation. Instead of paying $25,000 in cash for that bunch of computer equipment you intend to buy, why not go to your bank and have them give you a loan secured by the equipment? The bank will probably want 20 percent ($5,000) down and the rest financed over 24 to 36 months at the going interest rate. Notice that your monthly expenses go up, but you have $20,000 cash in your bank account to handle unexpected cash shortfalls.

How much debt is too much? This is often determined by ratio analysis, which is discussed in Chapter 11, "Making Sure That You're Making It." Keeping the applicable ratios under the danger levels for your industry should allow you to use credit to your benefit and increase your cash situation. By the way, you can also use ratio analysis to monitor when you have too much or too little cash on hand.

Even your grandmother would agree that paying your bills while having cash on hand is a healthy state of financial being.

Taking Out a Loan

You can imagine that every business has exactly the same problems in turning its receivables into cash. It should not surprise you that people, even banks, provide loans designed to cover exactly this short-term timing situation. It is essentially a line of credit secured by the receivables, and you are expected to pay it down as quickly as possible. (See Chapter 11 for information on this type of loan.) The interest rate is around 9 to 13 percent annually, instead of 60 percent, and you establish a credit history with your bank. That always pays off in the long run because the bank can become an integral partner as your success requires higher and higher borrowing levels.

Equity Funding

One reason to incorporate (see Chapter 6, "The Implications of Corporations") is to be able to sell stock for funding purposes. Notice that a stock sale makes the shareholders owners of the corporation and you do not need to repay their stock investment. They are taking a risk with their investment and get a say in the company operation in exchange. Taking out a loan still keeps the company 100 percent under your ownership and control, but you have to repay the debt. These shareholders now own a portion of the company. This is called *equity financing* or *equity funding*.

Equity funding is obtained through three basic means: selling shares of stock to private investors, selling shares of stock to professional investors such as venture capitalists, and "going public," which involves selling shares to the general public on one of the stock exchanges.

Business Buzzword
When someone gives you money in return for owning a portion of your company, they are providing **equity financing** or **equity funding**. You are giving up equity in the business in return for capital. You don't pay back equity financing. Investors get their money back by selling their shares to someone else. The other kind of financing is **debt financing**, in which you get a loan that you must pay back later.

Pick Your Investors Well

Selling shares of stock looks pretty good on the surface: You sell a portion of the company in exchange for some cash. All you give up is a little ownership in the company to get the cash you need. What is the down side? As usual, it comes down to whom you choose as your investors.

Business Tip
Other forms of funding that apply to non-corporations include loans and "buying in" investments where partners pay to become a member of the partnership.

The more sophisticated the investor, the better an ally she will make down the road. A professional investor knows the pitfalls associated with running a business and can guide you through potential minefields. However, professional investors also tend to be demanding and relatively heartless when you do not perform as expected. From their perspective, not living up to your plan indicates a lack of business control. A professional investor will take you to task if needed because she has a vested interest in your success.

Your Uncle Billy, on the other hand, might not need monthly reports from you on your progress and might purchase your company's stock on his faith in your ability alone. This makes getting your initial funding easier but might hurt you down the road. Suppose that the company has a rough quarter, for reasons that are outside of your control, such as flood or war. Billy might not understand why that dividend check you promised didn't arrive. He might not understand why you need more money due to the unforeseen circumstances. In fact, Billy might not have deep enough pockets to fund the next round of investing.

Be forewarned that many family conflicts have erupted over investments made in businesses that ultimately went under. Do you really want to be responsible for risking your Uncle Billy's retirement fund?

Professional investors also bring a wide array of business expertise and contacts to the table. This broadens the business resources available to you as the founder while also opening potential new marketing opportunities. In short, if you can get a trustworthy professional on your side, that is a better route than Uncle Billy.

In fact, the optimal investor might be another company with services or products that complement your offering. This other company might buy a certain percentage of your company's shares to provide a legal link between their organization and yours. This not only provides you with cash but also allows you to partner with them on a tighter basis when approaching the marketplace.

Some companies specialize in marrying one company's offerings with another company's in such a way that everyone wins. Naturally, they get a portion of the deal as payment for their matchmaking services, but without them, you might not have found the proper business mate.

Never knowingly involve someone in your business that you do not trust. You will be busy enough worrying about expanding your business; you do not need someone questioning your every move and undermining what you do. Stall, work harder, cut expenses, and play with cash float before getting involved with an investor who might be a potential headache.

Ultimately, it is your job to increase the value of the shareholders' investments. This is done by improving the company's sales while decreasing the cost of making those sales. In short, your job is to make the company more profitable from one year to the next. If the profit that the investors see is not substantially greater than what they could get from other investments such as the stock market or bonds, then why should they invest with you? Your job is to give them a better return on their investment than they could have with traditional methods.

The Stock Exchange

The likelihood of selling stock in a successful public offering is slim to none in the first few years of operation. The reason? You have no track record for an investor to evaluate. In general, you should not consider making a public offering until your company has seen at least four to eight quarters of profitable operation, with profits growing in each quarter. The first time you sell shares to the public is an *initial public offering* (IPO) and an excellent means for new companies to raise large amounts of capital for expansion.

A company needs $5 to 10 million in sales to make an IPO worthwhile because the $250,000 to $500,000 cost to handle the offering makes it almost impossible for smaller companies. Those expenses include legal and filing fees, public accounting fees, document printing (not a trivial item), and underwriter fees.

The *underwriter* is critical to the success of the offering and receives a hefty fee for that assistance (around 9 to 12 percent of the offering). Start looking for an underwriter today if you plan to go public in the next few years. An underwriter will advise you when and how to go public so you get the most money for your stock sale. Ask other companies that had successful IPOs who they recommend.

The basic procedure for a public offering is

➤ Have at least four profitable quarters with sales of at least $5 million a year.

➤ Find an underwriter who sees your company vision and believes in what you have to offer.

➤ The underwriter prepares an investment *prospectus* (a formal legal document detailing the pros

Business Buzzword

The first time you sell shares of your stock to the public is an **initial public offering** (IPO).

An **underwriter** is a company that handles all the paperwork and filings associated with marketing your stock. Underwriters must be licensed to sell stock, so they are usually affiliated with an investment firm or brokerage.

Business Buzzword

A **prospectus** is a formal legal document detailing the pros and cons of investing in a company. It is prepared by an underwriter.

and cons of investing in your company) and SEC registration statement, while coordinating accounting and legal activities.

➤ The underwriter then handles the marketing and sale of the stock. He gets 1 to 2 percent of the initial offering amount and another 7 to 10 percent of the total value of the actual stock offering.

As the business owner of a public company, you must do the following:

➤ File quarterly and annual reports with the SEC, along with annual certified financial audits.

➤ Create quarterly *proxy statements* (forms through which shareholders can vote on important issues) for new shareholders and annual financial reports.

➤ Announce and hold shareholder meetings.

➤ Send out dividend statements, checks, and tax reports.

➤ Complete special paperwork for the stock exchanges themselves.

In short, going public requires a lot of additional paperwork and staff. Consider these costs before deciding to go public.

The four basic public exchanges used in North America are the New York Stock Exchange (NYSE), the American Stock Exchange (AMEX), the NASDAQ, and the Canadian Stock Exchange. The New York Stock Exchange is usually for more established companies; the American Stock Exchange is another alternative for medium to large companies. The NASDAQ is where most new companies find a stock-trading home. The Canadian Stock Exchange is becoming a viable alternate funding avenue for firms based in the United States. Stocks are often priced at low investment amounts (under $1.00), and the restrictions are less stringent than those of NYSE, AMEX, or NASDAQ. Your underwriter is your guide into this world.

The Least You Need to Know

➤ Cash is the lifeblood, or air supply, of an organization. Without cash to pay employees or vendors, you are out of business.

➤ Cash will become scarce at some point in your business growth; of that you can be certain. Set up credit lines today that will help you when it happens.

➤ Factoring is a convenient, yet expensive, way of turning receivables into cash.

➤ Banks will give you short-term lines of credit secured by receivables, but the amount of credit will vary from month to month.

➤ Don't be afraid of credit. Purchasing capital equipment items with credit instead of cash shifts the purchase from a large cash outlay to smaller monthly payments, which improves your cash position as long as you don't go overboard.

➤ A private stock placement is possible, but unlikely, in the early stages of your company. If you need a lot of money, look toward an initial public offering (IPO), which requires one or two years of profitable operation and an experienced underwriter. It is most appropriate for companies generating $5 million or more in annual sales.

Chapter 14

Taking Charge:
Credit Card Sales

In This Chapter

➤ Comparing standard terms with credit card sales

➤ How much do credit sales cost you?

➤ Protecting yourself from fraud

➤ Telephone sales versus in-person credit card sales

➤ Determining the right credit card setup for you

Jamie was pumped up! Sales were going through the roof and things appeared to be financially on track. Why did his accountant want to talk with him? What could possibly be wrong? His trusty accountant, Raymond, was smiling but also shaking his head.

"Jamie, how would you feel about having another $1,000 in your pocket this month without lifting a finger?" asked Raymond. He knew Jamie well enough to already know the answer.

"Sure, and what's your cut for bringing this opportunity to me?" asked Jamie.

"Not a nickel. This one is on the house. Do you remember those two large training contracts you signed last month? The one for $17,000 and the other for $15,000? Well, guess what? The clients decided to charge the sales to their American Express card, and American Express charged

you 4.5 percent for processing those charges! These clients both have great credit records and probably would have jumped on the 2 percent discount we offer for payment within 10 days. In short, you gave up at least 2.5 percent of the sale price because your salespeople wanted to get credit for the sale before the end of the quarter!"

"Hmmm," Jamie thought. "2.5 percent of $32,000 is around $800, and 4.5 percent of $32,000 is worth close to $1,500. The sales reps just cost me enough to pay for a trip to Hawaii! What do you suggest?" asked Jamie.

"Let your salespeople know that credit card sales cost the company extra money because the credit card company charges a processing fee. Cards should be used only for sales under a certain dollar level and limited to specific situations, such as new customers without a solid credit history with our company. If you don't set some limitations on credit card sales, you give money away to credit card companies when you can have the cash in your pocket. Credit cards are an excellent way to avoid collections problems with new customers, but they get expensive with customers who you know will pay."

"Thanks for the feedback and information, Raymond," said Jamie as he walked out the door. "Let's make sure I don't give up another trip to Hawaii."

Credit cards are becoming the new form of legal tender. I know people who carry credit cards, a checkbook, and an ATM card but little-to-no cash. It is important to consider whether offering your clients the opportunity to pay using a credit card, instead of cash or a check, is a good thing. This chapter shows you how to make that decision.

How Do Credit Cards Work?

If you plan to go into a retail business, you have no choice. You must offer credit cards as a payment option or you risk losing sales. Period. However, if you'll be selling consulting services costing tens of thousands of dollars, then a credit card is probably not be the best way to get paid. Instead, request a credit application and check.

A person obtains a credit card from a bank, which provides a line of credit to the person whose name is on the card.

The credit card is issued as a Visa, MasterCard, Discover, or some other brand name. (American Express produces its own card, which requires payment in full each month, and provides its own credit processing operations, which I discuss in more detail later.)

You, as a business owner, set up your own account so that you can have credit card sales deposited in this account. You are issued a *merchant number* by your credit card processing company that helps them identify exactly who you are and where your money should be deposited.

The line of credit is generally *unsecured*, meaning the bank has nothing that it can take and sell to repay the person's debt if the person defaults on payments. The only recourse is to cancel the card, destroy the person's credit record, and bother him until he pays. Fortunately for you, the business owner, you get paid whether your customer pays his or her bill or not. That's what you pay the credit card companies for.

When a person purchases something from you and pays using a credit card, he is using his line of credit from the bank. The bank is essentially agreeing to pay the person's obligation to your company and takes the responsibility for obtaining payment from the person whose name appears on the card. In short, the bank is giving the person a loan that he uses to buy a product or service from you. In return for taking responsibility for collecting payment from the cardholder, the bank charges you a fee. Of course, you still get paid even if the credit card company doesn't.

You can generally think of a buyer who uses a credit card as someone with a line of credit from a bank. The company whose name appears on the card, such as Citibank or Chase, handles the cardholder credit application and marketing of the card. You process a customer's purchase using the credit card and signed receipt. In return, the bank deposits the amount of the purchase (minus the fees) into your bank account. The company that processes and clears your company's credit card transactions, debiting the charged amount from the proper credit card and then crediting your bank account, is called the *card processing company.*

Business Buzzword
A **merchant number** is a number given to your company that is used to identify which account should be credited when a customer makes a purchase. It also verifies that you're allowed to accept credit cards in payment. When you call your credit card processor for authorization to charge a customer's credit card, she asks for your merchant number, the customer's card number and expiration date, and the amount of the purchase before giving approval.

Business Buzzword
An **unsecured** line of credit is a line of credit that is not backed by some form of collateral.

Business Buzzword
A **card processing company** is one that processes and clears your company's credit card transactions. Card processing companies are independent businesses, not affiliated with any credit card issuer.

Business Tip
PaymenTech (800-866-9113) is one credit card processing company you might want to contact.

Bankruptcy Alert
Trying to avoid hassles by not going electronic will probably cost you money. Everyone is better protected with electronic processing because you lessen the chances of mistakes and omissions, and you should probably just take the electronic plunge from the start or expect to pay higher discount and transaction fees.

Business Buzzword
A credit card transaction processing company acts as a liaison between your company and the credit card processing network.

They can be independent businesses just like yours and may not be affiliated with the credit card issuer. On the other hand, some banks now have their own credit card processing units.

The Costs of Credit

Sounds pretty simple, doesn't it? Run the card through the credit card machine, punch in the purchase amount, and press Enter. You've just gotten paid. Too cool! Too easy! What's the catch?

The catch is that there's a cost to this great service. Take a look at who gets a piece of that simple transaction.

For the purposes of this discussion, I assume you are processing the transaction electronically as opposed to manually. With a manual system, you have to call and request authorization by voice, rather than let the credit card machine dial automatically by modem. The processing company also typically charges a higher fee for manual processing. Electronically is truly the way to go unless you only process a few credit transactions per month.

Terminal Fees

First is the cost of the equipment used for processing the cards. It is sometimes called a swipe machine because you can either type in the numbers on the keypad or swipe the card through the slot on the top of the unit. It comes from a *credit card transaction processing company*, a company that is often a bank or a bank's sales representative who acts as a liaison between your company and the credit card processing network. The machine is essentially a small computer terminal that connects you directly to your credit card processing company.

The credit card processing company typically charges you an application fee ($65–$100) and a programming and installation fee ($35–$50). For these fees, you can accept payment by Visa, MasterCard, and probably Diner's Club and Carte Blanche, but not American Express or Discover.

American Express has its own processing network called the Electronic Draft Capture (EDC) network. This is AmEx's way of processing customer purchases made using its card. Call 800-847-8848 for American Express EDC processing and setup procedures.

Once American Express receives and completes your request, you must contact your terminal provider (the folks who are renting you the credit card processing machine) and make sure that they program your machine to process American Express transactions.

American Express charges you a fee for the privilege of being set up on its network, usually $65 to $100. It also sends you a box full of supplies, including an imprinting machine (the box you use to imprint a person's name and number onto a sales slip) and sales and credit receipts. Of the organizations I worked with in setting up my accounts, American Express was by far the easiest to work with.

Of course, nowadays, credit card companies provide all-in-one units that automatically print out a computerized receipt after the card is swiped; no imprinting is done anymore except on manual systems.

But wait; there's more! The Discover Card also has its own network and requires the same actions. Call Discover at 800-347-2000 to start the process and get the electronic terminal.

Should you simply buy your own terminal instead of renting one? Good question, and the answer depends on your volume, monthly rental fee, and current cash situation. Rent for a few months and see how it goes. If after six months you start to resent the monthly charges, you should either go back to a hand processing system (in which you manually call each charge for verification) or buy your own electronic terminal. Typical costs for such terminals is $250 to $300.

Here you are with your credit card terminal and some receipts, ready to sell your product or service using credit cards. You thought the analysis was over, but it is really just beginning. In addition to the setup charges and terminal costs, the credit card companies also want a percentage of the transaction amount and often a per-transaction fee as their compensation for guaranteeing the charge. Read on to find out how much you have to pay for this privilege.

Business Tip
American Express has been, and probably still is, the preferred credit card for business-related expenses. American Express claims that more than 70 percent of Fortune 500 companies use its card and that many companies require that all business expenses be placed on the American Express Corporate Card. Be aware, however, that American Express frequently charges higher fees than the other credit card companies.

Business Tip
Find a company that provides access to Visa, MasterCard, Discover, and American Express as a single service. If your company doesn't want to do this, at least find out how to set up your machine so that it processes all the different credit cards.

Monthly Fees

First, you pay a monthly fee for the electronic terminal ($25–$40) that is automatically deducted from your bank account by the service company. You are also going to pay a monthly service fee ($5–$10) for the reporting of your account activity during the month. This is also automatically taken from your company checking account.

The credit card company then charges your company a percentage of the transaction amount for each purchase. This fee varies between service providers, credit card companies, the type of transaction involved, the size and frequency of the transaction, and whether the transaction is processed electronically or manually. The bank charges you a transaction fee for each deposit made to your account. Table 14.1 shows typical discount and transaction fees for the various credit card types.

Table 14.1 Typical Discount and Transaction Fees

Credit Card Type	Discount Rate (Percent of Purchase Amount)	Transaction Fee (Cost to Deposit in Bank Account)
Visa	1.8–3.0%	20 cents
MasterCard	1.8–3.0%	20 cents
American Express	4.0–4.5%	Varies
Discover	1.8–3.0%	20 cents

Keep in mind that home-based businesses may be charged higher fees by the processing companies—often starting at 3 percent.

Here is what you get for the fee and how the process works when you have an electronic system:

1. You run the card through the credit card machine (called swiping the card). The terminal reads the card number and card type off the black magnetic strip on the back of the card.

2. The credit card terminal requests the transaction amount and expiration date of the card. You type both when requested and tell it to process the transaction.

3. The terminal dials the card processing company and sends the information to the computer, which then confirms the card isn't stolen and the cardholder has enough money available on the card to process the charge.

4. If everything is okay, the computer responds with an approval code that you write on the sales receipt. If your machine is connected directly to a printer, the receipt prints automatically when the transaction is approved, just as you see in most restaurants and high volume retail stores these days.

5. The credit card processing company deducts the proper percentage from the purchase amount and deposits the rest in your business checking account. You essentially get the money right away instead of waiting for 30 days and taking the risk the customer won't pay. Make sure that your bookkeeping system is set up to track these charges.

6. Most banks also charge businesses a transaction fee for each deposit you make, so you are also charged for credit card deposits.

7. The processing company sends you a summary statement every month that outlines all transaction dates, sale amounts, credits applied (product returns), discount rates applied, and net deposits. This statement is handy for reconciling your bank deposits, invoices, and receivables when you have customers paying by different methods. Your bookkeeper definitely needs this statement, so don't throw it away.

Covering Your Legal Bases

We are always happy to sell our products or services and receive payment, but what happens if the client later contests the charge and refuses to pay? What if the person using the card isn't supposed to be using it? You could be stuck with a huge bad debt that takes a large number of healthy sales to correct. Table 14.2 lists a few things you can do to minimize the chance of those situations occurring.

Bankruptcy Alert
Beware of how discount and transaction fees affect your profits. Accepting American Express for a $10,000 charge from a solid account customer, for example, becomes $450 to 500 in American Express's pocket instead of yours. In that case, you might be better off persuading the customer to pay by other means. Using American Express instead of net 30-day payment terms with solid credit customers can cost you thousands in unnecessary credit protection expenses.

Some small businesses do not accept American Express or other credit cards because it costs so much. Review what slow or no payments are costing you each year, then decide whether you should accept credit cards.

Table 14.2 Credit Card Sales Protection Procedures

When Someone Charges Something in Person	Actions and Reasons
Check the expiration date and make sure it is still valid.	Look at the Valid From and Good Through dates on the card and check that it is embossed, not printed.
Look for a hologram or other security mark.	These emblems are difficult to duplicate. If you can't find one, you might be holding a fake card.

continues

Table 14.2 Continued

When Someone Charges Something in Person	Actions and Reasons
Disclose the terms of the sale and get a signature, if possible.	The more that's in writing and signed by the customer, the harder it is for him to contest the charge. Make sure terms and conditions are easily spelled out on the receipt.
Run the card through an imprint machine, fill out the sales draft completely, and get a signature.	Take the customer's card and run it through an imprint machine using the proper sales receipt. Make sure it is legible and completed with all pertinant information included. Verify that the signature on the card matches that provided by the customer on the sales form.
Get an authorization number for each transaction.	Run the card, amount, and expiration date through the electronic terminal to receive a sales authorization from the service company. Write the authorization number on the sales draft.

The preceding information is taken from the December 1992 issue of the Agency Inc. Newsletter, Volume 3, Number 12. This publication is dedicated to servicing the SABRE-related travel agencies and is available for subscription by calling Source Publications at 918-491-9088.

If you plan to take orders over the telephone without seeing the customer and getting his signature, you can still take a few steps to better protect yourself. Because the chances of getting burned over the phone or by mail are much higher than in person, the credit card companies will probably charge you a higher discount rate for this type of transaction.

When processing a telephone transaction, follow these steps:

1. Get all credit card information and repeat all numbers, dates, and names.
2. Verify that the person making the purchase is the person to whom the card was issued.
3. Always get an authorization number and write it on the sales receipt.
4. Verify the person's billing address before he hangs up.
5. Get him to come by to pick up the merchandise. Have him sign the sales form at that time.

If you are processing a credit card sale by phone, if at all possible, fax the customer a copy of the invoice including all credit card information. Request that he sign the invoice and return it to you by fax for a rough "signature on file" agreement. A signature on file agreement means the customer agrees to pay you for all future charges against that credit card by the same customer. A formal signature on a file card includes the agreement duration of effectiveness, the names and sample signatures of all persons authorized to charge against this credit card, an imprint of the credit card, credit card expiration date, termination stipulations, and change-related conditions.

What to Do If a Charge Is Contested

Unfortunately, even if you have a credit card payment approved, you can still run into problems. There is a lot of credit card fraud floating around these days, and certain people take advantage of situations if given the chance. Your established customers are not usually the problem. New customers or those you will never see again can leave you with a bad bill or a contested charge that can cost you money.

Taking the steps outlined here might seem like a hassle, but you will have a fighting chance with the credit card company if the charge is ever contested or disputed by the customer. If the customer signed the sales draft, saw the terms and conditions, and clearly knew what was being purchased and the proper amount, you have an excellent case in your favor. The more of the transaction that was handled in writing, the better the chance you have of keeping the money. Caution and procedures make the solution to this possible trouble area. Define credit terms, stick with them, and fight for your money when the time comes.

Responding immediately to any inquiries from your credit card companies is essential to maintaining your merchant status. For many retailers, losing merchant status would be disastrous. Don't test the system. Answer their questions, provide any information requested, and enjoy the additional sales you're earning because you are able to accept credit cards.

The Least You Need to Know

➤ You probably have to accept credit cards in one form or another or risk losing customers, especially if you run a restaurant or retail store.

➤ Electronic processing is the least expensive, easiest way to process credit card transactions.

➤ The various credit card companies charge between 2 and 5 percent of the transaction amount in exchange for their guarantee of payment. This can be very expensive when applied across the board to all transactions, so you might want to limit situations in which you accept credit cards.

➤ Treat each sale as a legal agreement. Get signatures and transaction details to back up any fraudulent claims made by the customer at a later date.

➤ Telephone and mail-order credit card sales are more expensive due to their higher likelihood of fraud. You are billed higher fees for the increased risk. You might also have greater difficulty finding a card processing company to work with.

➤ Get an authorization number from the credit card company for each transaction.

Chapter 15

Collections: When Customers Don't Pay

"What do you mean we are out of cash?" shouted Judy. "Our books clearly show sales of about $60,000 for last month, so how can we be out of cash?"

"We have this problem with a few of our major accounts that make up around $35,000 of our monthly sales. They have recently started paying us in 60 days instead of 30, which affects our cash flow," remarked Judy's accountant. "We didn't authorize the change and also didn't notice customers were taking longer to pay before it was too late."

"Where do we stand in the cash department?" asked Judy.

"We owe payroll and our vendors, and our annual licensing fees are due. Those total around $45,000, and we only have $30,000 on hand. How are we going to make up the $15,000 shortage?"

"I guess I will give the company a short-term loan of $15,000 and not take a salary for this month," answered Judy. "Remember, I can't keep doing this, or I will be out of business and we all will be out of jobs. Get those receivables on track, and get me involved personally if this doesn't start to improve immediately."

Billing customers for products and services you've sold is only part of the process of getting paid. Staying on top of payment due dates is also critical to ensure you're paid promptly. This chapter will teach you strategies for collecting from customers, as well as tips for dealing with customers who don't pay as promised.

Collection Problems Come with the Territory

It is an unfortunate fact of business life that some people do not pay their bills on time. For the most part, they are not trying to avoid their obligations but simply think that spending the money on something else is more important than paying you.

This doesn't do you much good and provides no consolation when you are writing checks from your own checking account to cover their delayed payment.

Even worse, some people simply are deceitful and intended from the beginning to use your products or services without paying. These people can cost you a lot of time and money trying to recover the agreed-upon payments. In addition, you rarely get the total amount due because collection fees, court fees, and a lot of your time are often required to make it happen.

The major problem with delayed payments is the impact it has on your cash situation. You have to pay your employees and vendors on time, which means that you need to collect payments from customers, or you are quickly out of business. This means that you are writing checks to cover the *float* provided to your customers, which is the time lag between when you have to pay your bills and when your customers pay their bills. Repeatedly being forced to pay your own bills on time while everyone else takes more time can lead you into serious financial problems. If you're growing quickly, you might be affected even more by slow-paying customers.

Plan from the start to have an effective credit and collections policy, and stick to it. Prevention is the best protection from collection problems. Not handling credit and collection properly can put you out of business, even though your sales exceed expectations.

Avoidance Is the Best Remedy

Just as avoiding saturated fats is a great way to minimize the likelihood of a heart attack from clogged arteries, avoiding deadbeat clients is the best way to avoid business problems from depleted cash reserves.

Implement policies from the beginning that address the need for credit. Ensure that you stick to the policy, that your employees understand the policy, and that you do not make exceptions to the policy without good reason to back it up. Every time you extend credit, you are giving someone a loan. Make sure they are worthy of the trust you are giving them.

Avoid giving credit to new customers without first having them complete a credit report. Many times, you can get a customer to pay for the order with a credit card if the amounts are relatively small (under $1,000). Over that, you can always ship products Cash On Delivery (COD) or only after you receive a check or money order, although you will find these methods difficult to implement in non-consumer sales environments.

Retail sales environments have a pretty simple credit policy. People pay cash or charge their purchases on a credit card and are there to personally sign the receipt. You receive the money at the time of purchase.

Some companies set up credit approval arrangements with finance companies so that consumers can easily purchase high-ticket items on credit. This approach is common with companies that sell appliances or furniture. The buyer completes a credit application at the store, which is sent to the finance company for approval. Once approved, the consumer receives a loan to purchase the items in question, the retailer receives money from the finance company, and the consumer goes home with the purchase. Everyone wins.

One way to avoid payment problems with customers is maintaining close contact to be sure that they are happy with what you provided them, whether it was a product or service. Don't just deliver the goods and send out the invoice. Follow up with a phone call to let your customers know that you care that they were happy with their purchase. This way, if you find out there was some problem or they are not satisfied, you have the chance to fix the problem. Once your customer is happy, your chances of being paid rise significantly.

It is common in service contracts to stage payments based on job completion levels. In this way, you have gradual payment for services provided and also have checkpoint milestones where you can gauge the customer's satisfaction level. It's better to find problems halfway through the project than to complete it and find out they don't want to pay.

Another important step is timely follow-up after you've sent out the invoice. Be friendly but firm as soon as the payment is due. You don't want to ruin your relationship with your customer by screaming and shouting over a late payment if there is a reasonable explanation why it is overdue. Always give customers the benefit of the doubt if they have a history of purchases from you and have paid promptly in the past. Also be firm in asking for a date when you can expect payment, and follow up on that date. By being friendly with customers but getting across the point that payment is expected, you increase the chances of keeping that customer, rather than losing him over some angry words. However, if you've spoken with a customer two or three times and a promised payment has still not arrived, it's time to get tougher.

You do not want to provide a service or sell a product to a customer only to find out that the customer cannot pay. If you run the financial numbers, you will find you must sell three or more of what you originally sold to recover the profits you would have received from the deadbeat order. However, you can never really make up for a sale a customer never pays for.

Bankruptcy Alert

If your business is growing quickly, your expenses are also growing quickly, giving you even more reasons to pay closer attention to your collections. If you aren't receiving customer payments in a timely fashion, you may soon be bankrupt.

Business Buzzword

Money already spent that cannot be recovered is called the **sunk cost**. Sunk cost does not take into account opportunity cost or how else the money could have been spent.

For example, at a 50 percent profit margin, a $20 sale costs $10 to produce; you make a $10 profit on the sale. When that client does not pay, you lose not only the profit but also the initial cost of the product, or $20. To recover that $20, you must sell two more items that make you $10 each in profit to recover the initially lost $20 sale, and at this point, you still haven't made any money. Add to this cost the collection fees, court costs, employee expenses, and interest expense on the loan you took out to cover the delinquency, and you can easily see that nonpaying clients are an expensive problem you need to avoid. The moral of the story is that no matter how hard you work, you can't make up for lost profits or cost of goods sold.

Some people treat the first deadbeat sale as a *sunk cost* and only look at recovering the $10 cost to produce the product as what they need to break even. I prefer to consider the cost of the entire lost opportunity, which makes me more respectful of the value of good customers and more leery of offering credit to companies or people I don't know.

Products Versus Services

In no way would I want to jeopardize your friendship by turning you into a lawyer, but a few legal issues are nice to understand before you start offering products or services to your customers.

All product sales transactions are covered by the Uniform Commercial Code (UCC), which are laws developed in the 1940s to ensure uniform sale transaction laws across the country. Although UCC rules are complicated, I try to simplify them for you here.

A thorough understanding of contract law is critical to understanding business because you are really selling an agreement, or contract, to perform a service or sell a product. In its simplest form, the customers agree to buy what you agree to sell, with all of the mutually agreed upon contingencies attached. The contract usually only comes into play when something has gone wrong and the parties involved cannot work out their differences among themselves.

The UCC only covers the sale of products ("goods" in UCC terms) and does not cover the sale of services. According to the Statute of Frauds section of the UCC, if you are selling goods with a sale price of $500 or more, then you must have a written contract before you can go after someone for a breach of contract. Under $500, a verbal agreement is enforceable, but it is still a good idea to get it in writing. After all, if a customer is afraid to commit to the sale in writing, what makes you think that they won't hedge on paying you later? If a client is serious, he will sign an agreement that outlines what is to be provided. If you think about it, the agreement protects both sides and helps prevent the possibility of a misunderstanding.

To have an enforceable agreement or contract, you must at least have

1. The seller and buyer specifics, such as name, address, and phone number.

2. The specifics regarding the products in question, such as quantity, price, and description.

3. Specific delivery and payment terms.

This might sound like a lot, but if you think about it, you couldn't really provide the product unless you knew this information anyway. Most importantly, both parties must sign the agreement.

If you plan to provide services, then you should have some type of written agreement between the client and you that outlines the services to be provided, the amount of up-front expense involved, the total amount of the service contract, when services are to be performed, and when payment is expected. Once again, if a customer hedges on signing a simple agreement with this basic information, then he will probably hassle you when it comes time to pay.

Getting some type of nonrefundable deposit up front (somewhere between 25 and 50 percent) is also a good idea as an indication of the client's seriousness and might help minimize the possibility of his changing his mind after you have already started the project. It is also a good idea to have clear, objective completion milestones that trigger partial payments.

For example, assume that you are an architect designing a house for a client. You might request 25 percent payment upon signing of the agreement, 25 percent upon completion of the first artist renderings, 25 percent upon completion of the final drawings, and the final 25 percent upon acceptance of the plans by the local building authorities. Notice that each of these steps provides the customer with a clear picture of the overall project, you get paid for the work done to date, and you built in quality checks to make sure that everyone is happy. Happy customers pay. Unhappy customers gripe, complain, take up time and energy, and often don't pay.

Cash First—Credit Later

Possession is nine tenths of the law, and this is particularly true when it comes to cash. Whoever has the cash is in the catbird seat, and more cash is almost always better than a lot of receivables from customers who can choose to pay at their discretion.

There are various ways to receive cash instead of dealing with credit of any kind. Cash comes in its standard green form (which is almost never used in nonretail businesses), personal or company check, bank draft, cashier's check, or letter of credit (which is typically used when dealing with international shipments).

Bank drafts and cashier checks are like cash because the issuing financial institution took money from the customer or an account before issuing the draft or check. There is a warm fuzzy feeling that you get deep in your pocketbook when you get a check that you know will go into default only if the issuing bank goes out of business.

When accepting a personal check, make sure it is signed by the person giving you the check and that the signatures match and get two forms of identification, such as a driver's license (for identity) and a major credit card (which indicates acceptable credit). Make sure it is not postdated or written in two different colors of ink.

If you are burnt by a bum check, start a list that shows the bad checks received and from whom. Some companies post the bad checks for public display. This is not necessarily legal, but peer pressure is often a strong motivator. Make sure all your employees know the procedures for accepting checks.

When shipping products, you can request COD, usually provided by United Parcel Service (UPS), which means that the customer must write a check to the delivering driver before the product is left. There is a COD processing fee of around $4.50 for the service. UPS then sends you the customer's check for you to cash.

Letters of credit are used frequently for international transactions. The customer's bank issues the letter of credit, which ensures that the funds in question are available for transfer once the company receives the desired products or services it ordered. The funds are then transferred from the issuing bank to your bank, and everyone is happy. (See Chapter 16, "Doing Business Internationally," for additional information on international credit.)

Credit cards come in all shapes, colors, and sizes. The most common are Visa, MasterCard, American Express, and Discover. Make sure the name on the card matches the name of the person making the purchase transaction and that the signatures match between the card and the credit receipt, and then run the card through the approval process. At that point, the funds should be transferred to your bank account and only lost if the charge is disputed by the customer. (See Chapter 14, "Taking Charge: Credit Card Sales," for more information about credit card sales.)

There is some disagreement on whether you should prefer credit card or check transactions. A check is a legal binding agreement between the issuing company (person) and your company. If the check is bad, you have a strong case for collecting on the check through the courts (assuming that you can even find the person who wrote the check). Credit card sales that have been approved are credited immediately to your account but can still be contested by the customer later. In those cases, you end up arguing with Visa or MasterCard about the charge. If there is a question about how you processed the sale, you could find yourself on the losing end of that battle. There are also credit card percentage fees paid.

Selling products or services using credit terms (such as net 30 days) is at the bottom of the credit ladder when dealing with consumers. Most larger commercial transactions are handled on a credit basis, meaning the customer has a specified time frame within which he can pay, which is usually 30 days. After 30 days, the account is considered delinquent, and collection procedures are started. (See "Know Your Rights When It Comes to Collections" later in this chapter for more about collecting from delinquent accounts.) Attaching a late payment penalty and interest for late payment helps keep commercial accounts current, although in some states, it might affect your collection position should the company become insolvent and declare bankruptcy. Check this out for your state before making this decision.

You probably need to offer credit terms to your standard customers, just as you want credit terms from your regular vendors. It is just a part of doing business that most people accept as a standard requirement. Here are some suggestions for handling credit transactions:

➤ Set an amount above which you require a credit application and credit background check before extending the credit.

Sample credit applications are available at most office supply stores. Make sure that you ask for at least three credit references as part of the application, and then call the references to verify the prospective customer's credit standing.

➤ Do the background check before you issue the credit or risk being disappointed later. Customers understand your need to protect yourself.

Some of the bigger credit information agencies include EquiFax Credit Information Services and Trans Union Credit. A credit report costs a few dollars but can save thousands if it keeps you from making a poor credit extension decision.

Business Tip
You can reach EquiFax at 800-223-2203 and Trans Union Credit at 800-544-5602.

➤ Offer customers early payment benefits, such as a 2 percent discount for payment within 10 days of invoice receipt. I know of one business that always takes advantage of these 2 percent terms; the owner claims that they save a lot of money doing that.

➤ For example, if you pay $20,000 each month to vendors and each offers the 2 percent early payment discount option, you can save $.02 \times \$20,000 = \$400$ monthly, which could be the monthly payment for another piece of equipment.

➤ Separate the sales process from the credit decision. If the salesperson is paid commission on sales revenue and not on paid accounts, then there is an incentive for the salesperson to provide a liberal credit policy because it makes it easier to sell. She gets her commission and you get a possible bad debt. Avoid this conflict of interest by separating the credit and sales decisions, unless you plan to do both yourself.

➤ Make sure that you run a credit check on your larger companies, and perform your credit checks every 12 months or so because company situations change. You are always looking to verify the "three Cs" of credit: character, collateral, and cash. If you know that company to be one of integrity, they pass the character test. Collateral and cash tell you about the company's current ability to pay the debt it is incurring. You can often verify the cash situation by calling their bank and verifying that they have enough cash to cover the credit they are requesting.

Financial Reports and Their Limitations

The industry standard for business information reporting is Dun and Bradstreet (D&B) at http://www.dnb.com. A D&B report on a company contains payment history, business officer names, addresses, phone numbers, revenues, number of employees, high and low credit balances, payment histories, and other pertinent financial information.

To receive these reports, you need to be a regular subscriber to the service, which involves a yearly contract fee along with a per-report cost. The overall cost is often too high for a small business to justify because you might only need a few reports each year.

A new possibility is to run a credit check through some of the available online services such as CompuServe or America Online. For a fee, you can request a credit report on a single company without paying for an annual contract. Of course, that fee is much higher than what you pay if you subscribe to the credit check service on an annual basis, but if you just need to run a check once in a while, using an online service might save you some money and give you some valuable information without a long-term commitment.

Of course, as you're reviewing some of the credit reports, keep in mind that a lot of the data is self-reported, so don't use any one report as your sole source of information. You might also want to make some phone calls to colleagues to see what they know about your new customer or scan some newspaper clippings on the company (your local library probably collects them). Using additional information sources improves your knowledge of your prospect so you can make a better informed decision about giving credit.

No credit reporting agency or technique is perfect, and you want to take as many precautions as are reasonable before lending money to a new client. After all, extending credit to a company is the equivalent of lending them money.

Collection Letters

Okay, you've decided that offering credit to your customers is a good thing. What can you do to best ensure they pay as agreed?

First, make sure your clients understand the credit policy when they initiate the transaction. This means being clear about when payment is due, what the interest rate is for late payments, and whether there are any additional fees or penalties for late payments.

Do not hide the specifics because this only contributes to later misunderstandings. You are extending the credit, so you get to specify the terms you can live with. They can either accept the terms or negotiate new ones. Try not to do custom terms too often or it gets confusing to administer.

Second, give them an incentive to pay early. Offer a small discount (2 to 5 percent) for payment within 10 days. This gets the cash into your hands more quickly and provides them with a financial incentive to pay earlier instead of later.

Third, call them 3 to 5 days before the 30-day point (or whatever payment due date you've set) to verify billing information and to remind them the payment is due in a few days. It is also a good idea to ask if there will be any problems with timely payment. If they say yes, this gives you a chance to be informed earlier so you can take proper actions.

Finally, once the account goes past the payment due date, it is time to begin the collection process. Your customer has broken his agreement and should be handled as a delinquent account. If you are prompt with the follow-up, he will probably pay more promptly in the future to avoid the embarrassment.

A standard accounting report, called an *accounts receivable aging report*, shows you the customers who currently have credit, the total amount they owe you, and the number of days (I hope it's not months) the account is past due. Most computerized accounting packages can easily provide an aging report that you can use as your trigger for focusing on trouble accounts. Run the aging report at least every two weeks, and make sure the collection follow-up is prompt, consistent, and professional, yet firm. Collecting outstanding debts is an interesting balancing act as you keep your customers on track with their payments without offending them.

If you are not currently using a computer software package to handle your accounting, you should seriously consider it. You'll find it much faster and easier to print reports regarding your customers' payment records. By the way, you need this receivables aging report if you decide to apply to your bank for a loan secured by your receivables. Refer to Chapter 13, "Cash Is King," for information on this type of loan and Chapter 20, "Get Automated," for more information on automating your business.

Business Tip
For sample collection letters you can use to pursue the money you're owed, take a look at *The Complete Idiot's Almanac of Business Letters and Memos*.

Business Tip
Send a card to your customers' accounts payable department once or twice a year thanking them for prompt payment. Acknowledgment works well on all types of people.

Bad-Debt Ratio: Counting on the Deadbeats

Each industry has its own standard *bad-debt ratio* (the ratio of the uncollectable funds divided by total sales, expressed as a percent). This information is generally provided by Standard Industrial Code (SIC) and is available from Dun and Bradstreet or through the *Almanac of Business and Industrial Financial Ratios* (Prentice Hall).

In general, your bad-debt ratio should be under 1 percent of your sales, but certain industries might see bad debts as high as 2.5 percent. Mail-order businesses can have bad-debt ratios that are much higher than businesses who deal with customers directly. Companies with high bad-debt ratios must take this into account each year or they will face a rude awakening when the bills come due and they are out of cash.

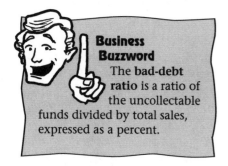

Business Buzzword
The **bad-debt ratio** is a ratio of the uncollectable funds divided by total sales, expressed as a percent.

You need to create a policy that dictates when an account is treated as a bad debt. Talk with your accountant to determine when this should happen. No matter what your situation, develop a tracking ratio that allows you to monitor changes in the situation closely.

Everything outlined so far can be handled by in-house personnel. However, there may come a point where you need the assistance of a dedicated group of professionals who know how to get people to pay. See the section "Working with Collection Agencies" later in this chapter, which covers dealing with collection agencies.

Know Your Rights When It Comes to Collections

The unfortunate has happened and a person is clearly not going to pay you. This should not happen very often, but when it does, you need to decide if pursuing the deadbeat customer is worth the time and effort. Make every effort to resolve the disputed amount before pushing things into court. Once the legal gavel falls, the conversation becomes stilted and often nonproductive. Get all agreements in writing to build your case if you ever have to take legal actions.

Small claims court is provided for resolving smaller dollar disputes in the $500 to $5,000 range, depending on the state you're in. (The filing fee ranges from $5 to $100. If you want to sue for under a few hundred dollars, the small claims process might not be worth it.) Small claims court is designed for nonlawyer types, and the rules are a lot less strict than seen on Perry Mason. Larger dollar disputes are handled in other courts and usually require the assistance of an attorney.

You will need two trips, minimum, to file a small claim: one to file the claim and the other to appear in court. You have to file in the county where the events occurred or where the deadbeat is resident. If you are suing a company, you need to file suit in the county in which the company is doing business. Unfortunately, it is much easier to win a judgment in small claims court than it is to collect the money. The judgment in your favor is a necessary first step and might be ego gratifying, but it is the cash that will bring you satisfaction.

Just because you won doesn't mean that you will be paid! It is your responsibility to collect the money involved, not the court's. Your basic collection options are

➤ Wage garnishment, where the employer is instructed to remove a specific amount of money from the deadbeat's paycheck.

➤ Nonwage garnishments, where the money involved is deducted from a company bank account.

➤ Property attachments, in which physical property is confiscated to pay the debt.

➤ Attaching the bank account, which means the company has to pay you first before paying any other bills. This might work if you are suing a business and know the company's bank account number.

Of course, none of these are options unless and until you have a judgment in your hands.

You can also file a lien against property owned by the nonpaying party. This lien is recorded at the courthouse and secures the debt with the prescribed property. The property cannot be sold until all liens are removed.

Numerous books on the market deal with the detailed intricacies of collections in general and the small claims process in particular. The best medicine for bad debts is to avoid them if at all possible using some of the techniques covered earlier in this chapter.

Working with Collection Agencies

When all else fails and you still want to pursue a deadbeat customer, then you should consider a collection agency. Whether the agency is national or local in coverage depends on your specific situation. Both kinds of agencies are listed in the Yellow Pages of your phone book. No matter where you find the agency, you should get a few references from their existing clients before you let them represent your company to your clients (even if they are deadbeat clients).

A collection agency charges a fee for their service, usually between 25 and 33 percent of the amount they collect for you. Higher fees might be charged for specialty accounts that require more extensive involvement by the agency.

Get a written contract from the agency and check their references before proceeding. They could do you more harm than good by threatening customers in an inappropriate way or by getting your initial money and alienating customers through the use of threatening practices. The contract should have specific performance objectives on the part of the agency, and if those objectives are not met, you should be able to terminate the contract. The collection agency should provide reports on a regular, mutually agreed to, basis for you to evaluate their performance.

In addition, make sure they conform to collection procedures outlined in the Fair Debt Collection Practices Act. These practices were designed to regulate collection agency activities, but companies performing their own collections should consider adhering to the same principles.

In general, the act states that threats to property, persons, or reputations are not allowed; obscene language and telephone badgering are not allowed; publicly humiliating the person by a printed list or other public statements is not allowed; and sending documents on misleading letterhead or threatening legal actions is not permitted, along with numerous other practices.

Collections is a tough business and one full of frustration. As a collection agency manager friend of mine puts it, "I don't like to talk on the phone. I think it comes from all those years of being lied to over the telephone."

The Tax Man Never Rests

Beware of the tax man when assessing the impact of bad debts. If you are using an accrual basis of accounting, then you are taxed on the outstanding receivables until they are declared as bad debts. This is because the receivable was recorded as income when the work or sale was completed. Consequently, you could be paying taxes on bad debts. Unfortunately, you have the burden of proving the debt is uncollectable, or bad, should the IRS call you on the expense deduction. Discuss your bad debts with your accountant before taking the deduction.

If you are on a cash basis of accounting, then the tax man only appears when the cash is received. Because you only record a sale as income when you actually get paid, there is no such thing as "bad debt" from the IRS's perspective. Of course, you want to pursue the money that's owed to you, but you only pay taxes on the sale when you actually receive the money.

The Least You Need to Know

➤ Customer credit should be earned, not treated as a right. Make the customer prove he can repay the debts he plans to incur.

➤ You have to sell multiples of your product to make up for the lost cost and profit associated with the one not paid for. Make sure you get paid the first time.

➤ Avoid credit problems by using a credit application and evaluation procedure before extending credit to ensure you will receive the payment when agreed.

➤ Just because you win a small claims court judgment doesn't mean you will collect. You still have to go after the customer for the funds.

➤ Be polite yet firm when first requesting an overdue payment. Anyone can overlook a payment. Few people resent being reminded of their commitments; most people resent being called a thief.

Doing Business Internationally

"Hey, boss! Check this out," cried Gary as he ran into the room. "We just got an order for 15,000 units from a guy in Singapore. He found us on the Internet and obviously likes what we do."

Brenda looked up from her desk. She was busy getting ready to leave town for a well-deserved vacation and only had a few hours before she and her family caught a flight to Florida.

"How many units?" gasped Brenda. "15,000? That is more than we have seen from a single buyer all year. Let me see that," she said as she reached for the fax. She didn't even know that they spoke English in Singapore.

Sure enough, here was an order for 15,000 units from a company she had never heard of before. She certainly wanted the revenue generated by this sale, but Singapore seemed a long way away. Why now? Why at the last minute just before she left town on vacation? Well, this might be business that paid the rent for next month. She took a deep breath and sighed to herself.

"What do you want me to do with this?" asked Gary. "Do you think that it's legit?"

"Hey. What do I know about Singapore other than it has great Chinese food? All I know is that 15,000 units is a lot of product for us to commit to provide unless this is a real order. Give me a few minutes to do some homework," was her reply.

As Gary left the room, Brenda hit the speed dial button for her banker. "Hi, Jim? Brenda. Listen. I just got an order from Singapore and have no idea how to handle it. Can you and the bank help me out with this?"

"Well, hello to you, too, Brenda. It looks like the world has discovered your little gold mine. Let me take a few minutes and talk to you about letters of credit," was Jim's reply.

History and literature are full of stories of entrepreneurs who weathered the high seas and foreign cultures to create business empires for themselves. These stories make international business sound like the last bastion of "wild west" entrepreneurship. In fact, international business is nowhere near as perilous as the stories might have you believe.

Is doing business internationally more complicated than simply selling domestically in your home country? Yes. Are the risks associated with international business higher? Yes. Are there opportunities that exist on the international market that just do not exist in your country? Yes. Can you turn those opportunities into financial rewards for you, your company, and family? Absolutely, but you need to be smart about how you take advantage of them. This chapter shows you how.

This chapter is not designed to teach you how to create an international business. That topic is far too complicated to cover adequately in a single chapter, and Appendix B, "Resources," lists several books that provide an excellent starting point. My intent is to explain the realities of international business transactions so that when you start getting marketing interest or orders from international customers, you are prepared with enough information to transact the business in a credible way.

International Business and the Internet

You might not have any intention of selling internationally and receive orders anyway if you have a presence on the Internet. (See Chapter 10, "Cybermarket: Using the Internet.") Remember that when dealing with the Internet, a person in Hong Kong is just as close to you as a person in Chicago. Assuming that the Hong Kong person can read your site—which is possible because English is a primary language in Hong Kong—then that person might want to order what you advertise on your site. Don't forget about all the other English-speaking countries around the world such as Australia, New Zealand, South Africa, England, Canada, and others.

In short, as soon as you present a site on the Internet, you open yourself to international orders. Is this good? I believe orders in most any denomination are good, as long as the customer gets what he expected when he ordered and you get paid as you expected. Read the rest of this chapter to familiarize yourself with the basics of taking an international order, shipping the product, and receiving payment. Take the fear out of doing business with the enormous international community by setting a few procedures based on these simple rules.

Taking and Processing Orders

I remember when my company got its first international order request. First we were excited, but as we walked through the many details associated with filling the request, we started to panic.

Use your international customer as a resource with respect to determining the best way to ship from your country to theirs. Ask them about the methods that have worked best for them, use their advice and then protect your financial interests. In this way you can save a lot of leg work, get your customer the products and delivery schedule they want, and minimize your financial exposure. Commununcation is always important, but it is particularly important when dealing across cultures.

Giving Product Information

For starters, look at the information request itself. Remember that the person at the other end of the request might not speak English as a primary language, and you should make this process as simple for her as possible.

If you received a request for information by a posted letter, fax, or e-mail message, responding with a lot of words is generally not a sound approach. Responding with product number, prices, and pictures is better. Keep your message short, polite, and clear, and you stand a better chance of your response being well-received.

Bankruptcy Alert
Faxing is great in that it transcends all time zone barriers, but beware the cost of sending faxes internationally because these costs can mount quickly. Using the Internet and e-mail for international communication is much cheaper.

Shipping and Handling

Both you and your customer should understand that products take a longer period of time to ship. When you ship internationally within shorter periods of time, the costs increase substantially.

Your customer is responsible for paying the shipping and insurance costs associated with the order. Let her tell you how the order should be processed so that it passes through her country's customs service with the least amount of headache and unnecessary expense.

If you incur the shipping charges because they are billed against your account, then make sure that you have a guaranteed method of payment with either a letter of credit or credit card (as discussed later in this chapter). If possible, use one of their designated shipping accounts so that you can avoid as much of the risk associated with international shipping as possible.

Let's face it; boats sink. Planes crash. Countries go to war and economies falter. You don't want to be in a position where you ship $15,000 worth of products to a country that just began a civil war and find out that you cannot get paid.

Pricing and Exchange Rates

Pricing is in terms of your home economy denominations, such as U.S. dollars. Designate this by including "USD" after all prices or by stating on the invoice that all amounts are in U.S. dollars. In this way, your customer inherits the *exchange rate liability* because you are paid in your home country currency.

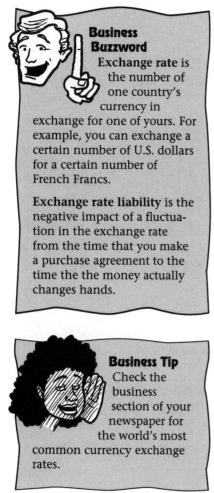

Business Buzzword

Exchange rate is the number of one country's currency in exchange for one of yours. For example, you can exchange a certain number of U.S. dollars for a certain number of French Francs.

Exchange rate liability is the negative impact of a fluctuation in the exchange rate from the time that you make a purchase agreement to the time the the money actually changes hands.

Business Tip

Check the business section of your newspaper for the world's most common currency exchange rates.

If you keep up with international exchange rate trends, it is possible to make money off of the exchange rate variations between countries by quoting prices in the currency of your customer's country or by specifying an exchange rate that is used for the transaction. (Assume that there are no exchange fees to simplify the discussion.) There is money to be made here, but it will take diligence on your part. And I suggest that you get your international business up and running before you worry about optimizing exchange rate financial opportunities.

For example, assume that your product sells for $10 USD, and the German Mark (DM) is trading for 1.79 DM per dollar. This means that a person buying your product must pay you 17.9 DM (1.79 × 10) to buy the product. You then convert that 17.9 DM into $10 US (17.9/1.79 = 10). Simple so far. Yes? This example is simple because it assumes that the exchange rate does not change between the time that you agree on a price and the time that you receive the payment and convert it into your home country's currency. Now, look at the same example and see what happens when the exchange rate fluctuates.

For the day in question, you quote a price of 17.9 DM. Assume that the exchange rate on the day that you convert the DM payment into USD is 1.60. When you convert your 17.9 DM into dollars, you now receive 17.9/1.6 = 11.19, or 1.19 more than the price in USD. Why? Simply because the international exchange rate changed enough, and in your favor, to allow you to squeak an extra $1.19 out of the transaction.

Could the exchange rate have just as easily gone the other way and cost you money instead? Absolutely. Prove it to yourself by using an exchange rate of 1.85 DM per USD and show that this type of fluctuation would have cost you money.

Making Sure That You Get Paid

Collecting from deadbeat customers in your home country is bad enough. Now try collecting from a deadbeat who lives 10,000 miles away. Not a chance! Extending credit for international shipments is very risky business indeed and should only be considered once you have an excellent working relationship with the client and you understand the legal safeguards on both sides for the specific country in question.

When getting paid, cash is always king, but few people are going to send cash internationally in exchange for goods unless your company is well known to them and they perceive that the transaction has minimum risk. You can start out with your terms being "Shipment upon receipt of payment in full in USD as a cashier check for products and shipping" and see how this is received. If it works, great. If not, then try some of the other approaches.

Credit cards are another excellent way of ensuring that you get paid for internationally shipped products. The credit card transaction is basically the same throughout the world, and most people are familiar with the process of paying for something over the phone with a credit card.

For smaller dollar amounts and working with smaller companies, I have found this to be the best approach. You perform a standard credit card verification, just as you do with a domestic shipment (see Chapter 14, "Taking Charge: Credit Card Sales"), except make absolutely sure that you get a fax of the order signed by the cardholder with his or her printed name and date next to it before shipping your products. You don't want an international order going into dispute. As the dollar amounts and companies become larger, you must use other payment methods.

Business Tip
Making money off of the exchange rate fluctuations might sound like a slick way to make easy money, but you are better off quoting prices in your home county currency until you understand how these fluctuations and their exchange rates affect your profits.

Bankruptcy Alert
Don't assume that the laws of your customer's home country match those of yours. Even in the U.S., laws vary between states. Assuming a law to be true is simply setting yourself up for a disappointment at best, and a disaster at worst. Check with a specialist on your target country or make sure that you are financially covered before committing yourself. You can find a specialist through your country's embassy that is based in the target country or by trying SCORE for referrals.

Business Tip

It is not uncommon to request payment in advance for a percentage of a large order. For example, if the order is for $50,000 in products, you can reasonably request 25 percent ($12,500) in advance to defray manufacturing costs. This is a good-faith gesture on the customer's part and it provides you with some protection later if the customer is slow to pay. (By the way, this rule holds equally true for domestic orders.)

Business Buzzword

An **irrevocable** L/C is one in which customer who issued the L/C cannot change the L/C terms.

A **confirmed** L/C obligates your bank to make payment on the L/C to you upon presentation of the proper paperwork. This means that your customer's bank is extending the customer enough credit to cover the purchase.

A **documentary L/C** is a financial arrangement set up between your bank and your international customer's bank. The banks act as third parties that verify receipt of product and transfer the funds. It is a bank-to-bank handshake confirmation that protects everyone's interests.

The most common form of international financial transaction for sale of products or services is a *documentary letter of credit* (L/C). With this type of payment, your bank deals with your customer's bank and both banks act as intermediaries to ensure that the transaction happens as agreed. This provides protection to both of you. The following steps outline a standard *irrevocable L/C* transaction between your customer (suppose she's in India) and your company in the U.S.

1. You and the customer agree upon the terms of the sale. Typical items agreed upon during this stage are price, quantity, time frame, shipping dates and method, payment terms, revocability of the L/C (discussed later), the banks involved on both the buyer and seller sides, whether partial shipments are allowed, when the letter is opened and when it expires, and how the letter is to be transmitted between the parties. Notice that the banks are not involved in any of these terms; you and your customer must work them out.

2. The customer goes to her bank, in India, and establishes the L/C.

3. The customer's bank opens an irrevocable L/C naming your company as the recipient, which includes all the terms and conditions that you and your customer agreed upon.

4. The customer's bank sends the L/C to your bank, requesting confirmation of its receipt.

5. Your bank then faxes to you a copy of the L/C along with a confirmation letter.

6. You review the L/C and confirmation letter for proper terms and conditions. At this time, it is a good idea to verify with your freight forwarder that it can meet the delivery deadlines specified. If not, then you should contact the customer to change the L/C terms to reflect the proper dates. The banks then re-issue the documentation.

7. You arrange with your freight forwarder to ship the product as indicated in the L/C.

8. When the forwarder has the products ready for shipment, they prepare all the needed documentation including the *bill of lading* which lists products included in this shipment.

9. The freight forwarder sends a copy of the paperwork, including the bill of lading, to your company.

10. Your present the documentation to your bank, indicating that the shipment is on its way.

11. Your bank usually airmails the documentation to your customer's bank, which then reviews the paperwork and sends it to your customer.

12. Your customer uses the paperwork to claim the goods when they arrive in India.

13. Your bank then honors the L/C payment terms and deposits the proper amount in your account. The timing of this deposit is based on the terms agreed upon at the beginning of the procedure.

Business Buzzword
A bill of lading is a document that accompanies shipments and contains information about the origin, destination, shipping means, and items included in the shipment.

Business Tip
Notice how important your bank is to the L/C process. Once again, you see that it is important to have a solid working relationship with your bank and banker.

Notice that the documentation is critical to proper execution of an L/C transaction. If the documentation is not executed properly, and consistently, it is very likely that your product shipment and payment receipt can be held up for a long time.

Here are some things to check when executing an L/C:

Business Buzzword
Shrinkage refers to breakage or loss of products during shipping or from theft.

➤ Make sure that you have an irrevocable statement that states that the L/C is confirmed by the designated bank.

➤ Verify the spelling of the name and address of both the customer and your company. It must be consistent across the board.

➤ Make sure that the L/C amount is enough to cover not only the product involved, but also the shipping, insurance, and other fees associated with the shipment.

➤ Beware of shipping or other documentation dated outside of the date range defined on the L/C.

➤ Watch for extraneous markings on the invoice that are different from those found on other documentation.

Business Tip
UPS, Federal Express, Airborne, and other major shipping companies have people who will help you complete the proper paperwork and act as your forwarder. They are happy to help so that they get your shipping business.

Business Tip
When you become more experienced, you might decide to perform the freight-forwarder function yourself.

Business Buzzword
A **freight forwarder** is a company that manages the shipping of products from your country to others. Freight forwarders handle all the paperwork required to legally ship your product to the desired customer country.

➤ Make sure you allow for breakage or loss during shipment, called *shrinkage*. To accommodate this situation, include the term "approximately" or "about" before the L/C amount. This provides a 10 percent variance allowance.

➤ Watch for inconsistent pricing, quantities, product descriptions, or other terms of sale.

Is this starting to look like a lot of paperwork? It can be, but it is better than not getting paid. Notice that this bank-to-bank handshake confirmation provides protection for both the seller and the buyer.

Are you going to handle all of this paperwork yourself? Probably not in the early days. Instead, you want to work with a *freight forwarder* who can walk you through the paperwork maze. A freight forwarder is a company that manages the shipping of products from your country to others.

Find a forwarder who works with your target countries by looking in the Yellow Pages under Freight Forwarding. Try this procedure for selecting a freight forwarder: Pick a typical shipping scenario regarding country, products, and so on that applies to your company and have several forwarders bid on the cost of their services for handling this shipment for you. Compare the services and costs and then make the decision that is right for you.

There are various types of L/Cs; talk with your banker to determine the one that is right for your particular situation. The first few times you go through this letter of credit process, you might wonder why you ever got involved, but once you see the checks appearing in your bank account, you will wonder why you waited so long.

Going International—All the Way

Assume that you have been bitten by the international bug and want to make that a primary focus of your business. I admire your fortitude and sense of adventure, but I want to caution you on the complexity of your intended venture.

It is difficult enough to run a successful business within your own country. Those difficulties increase exponentially (that is, a lot!) when you decide to cross cultural, language, economic, and geographic boundaries. Unless you have a specific country, market niche, and maybe even a product in mind for your international venture, then I suggest you test it at home first before moving overseas.

Most people I know who go into import/export do so to feed their travel lust. In this way, their business travel becomes an expense and they can travel abroad more often. This sounds good on paper, but you have to eventually make some money or you will be out of business.

Opening up foreign markets takes time and money. Most small businesses have limited amounts of both. To address this situation, they look for established outlets in their target countries and allow these outlets to sell and distribute their products for them. You get ready market exposure, and the distributor gets products that might otherwise be unavailable. Once you find the right outlet in your target country, follow their advice on how to present the product for best acceptance.

Pick your countries carefully or you can find yourself spread all over the globe and not making money anywhere, including at home. Most people I know choose countries where they once lived or where they have relatives. Speaking the local language is also a plus that is hard to over-emphasize.

Also, don't underestimate the overall complexity of selling a product or service internationally. You must comply with legal and governmental regulations, or you can incur the wrath of your government, the target country's government, or both. Check with your country's consulate office in the target country for advice on how to break into the local market. They often employ people who are dedicated to fostering economic relationships between the two countries. These people can save you hours of struggle and introduce you to people who can provide the services you need.

Can it be great if it works? You bet. Can it be overwhelming as it ramps up? Yes again. I suggest that you take your international orders when they come and follow the letter of credit procedures outlined in this chapter. As your experience in other countries increases, you will find the natural migration path for taking your company and offerings international.

The Least You Need to Know

➤ Expect that your Internet site will generate international interest.

➤ When you transact international business, work with credit cards and letters of credit to ensure that you are paid.

➤ Use freight forwarders to handle your international sales.

➤ Don't go international until you have a revenue stream at home or deep enough pockets to fund the slower startup.

➤ Target countries that you know, and work with local channels to increase your likelihood of success.

Part 5
Growing Your Business

You probably hope to deal with a business that's quickly growing. Everyone who starts his own business hopes that: What am I going to do if I get too many orders for my product today? Trust me, this is a good problem. Eventually, you will probably find that you need to hire employees to keep the business going and growing.

The majority of businesses in the U.S. are one-person shops with no employees. If you hire someone, you're bigger than most businesses—so congratulate yourself when you get to that point.

In this part, you'll learn how to find employees, calculate how much in taxes to take out of their paycheck, and use other automated systems to make your life much easier. The production chapter forces you to consider all the little details you must think about if you plan to build your dream widget. Then when you get really, really successful, the last chapter of the book helps keep your feet on the ground.

Chapter 17

Help Wanted: Adding Employees

In This Chapter

➤ Why adding people to your organization is a good thing

➤ The value, and risk, of a personnel manual

➤ Effective and legal interviewing procedures

➤ When a contractor is really an employee

➤ Dealing with employee benefits

"Tell me this again," said Julie. "Didn't you smell it when you went by her desk?"

"Sure I did," said Bill, the company lawyer. "But so what? There's nothing in your company procedures manual that covers drinking on the job."

"Because of that, I can't fire her?" asked Julie. "She carries a bottle in her purse. She takes a nip in the bathroom on a regular basis. I have even accidentally picked up one of her coffee cups to find that she was drinking Irish coffee. She's drunk on the job, and I want her gone!"

"That is understandable but not legal. Has her drinking affected her job performance in any way? Can you definitely point to business lost because of her drinking? Has it disrupted the normal flow of business in such a way that has cost the company money?"

"I know that it must have happened, but I can't point to a specific instance," said Julie. "So you're telling me that I'm stuck with her because firing her would open us up to a wrongful termination suit based on our not having a no-drinking policy in our manual."

"Pretty much. You need to watch her closely and look for signs of poor performance that can then be documented. Then you can let her go for poor performance. In the interim, you should never

mention the drinking problem to her and act as though nothing is wrong. Otherwise, you play right into her attorney's hands when you finally let her go. Sorry."

Adding employees represents a great leap for your business; there is so much demand for your product or service that you need to expand your staff. Yet managing other people brings with it a number of issues that you don't have to deal with when you work alone. In this chapter, I'll show you how to manage and lead your employees—successfully.

When You're Successful, You'll Need Help

If you follow all the great advice I'm giving you, you will probably become so successful you just won't be able to do it alone. At that point, you need to add employees to your organization. It might be only a clerical person who handles billing and answers the telephone or a complete staff of people who handle all those new projects you just brought in as a result of your incredible marketing skills.

In either case, you need to address the new challenges associated with running an organization that now has staff members. There are lots of ways to find employees, but before I jump into how to find the right employees, how to manage them, and all that detailed stuff, let me present a few bigger issues for you to consider:

1. You have been on your own, and possibly working alone, since you started your company. Make sure that you actually need an employee for functional reasons, not simply because you want someone around the office for business companionship. Have you gotten to the point that you are losing business because you don't have enough help?

2. Employees cost money and must pay for themselves either today or in the near future. Once you hire an employee, you assume the responsibility for paying him regularly, no matter what the business's financial condition is. Even if you have a really poor month, you still have to sign those paychecks to your employees. Are you ready to absorb that expense or would it be smarter to push yourself a little more for a short while and build up a nest egg?

3. When you add people to your organization, you inherit a responsibility for their financial support. If you aren't making enough money to support yourself, you probably can't afford to support someone else.

4. You become the last employee to be paid if the company has cash flow problems. Are you ready to accept not getting a paycheck for a week or two (or three or four) without resenting the other employees who have gotten paychecks?

5. Employees take up space, use telephones, and make decisions; you must expand your business operations to include them. They need to take responsibilities from you to help the company grow. Are you ready to let go enough to use them effectively?

6. Have you ever managed people before? Are you familiar with the challenges of encouraging and leading employees? Do you need to take some classes in effective

supervision before taking the plunge? Even if you have managed workers before, a refresher is probably a good idea.

7. Know that a small business is different from a large corporation in that one employee out of a total of two makes up 50 percent of the personnel. If that person has troubles, 50 percent of the company operations are in trouble. Be aware of the large effect one person can have on your business, your customers, and your earnings.

8. If you are in a service business, make sure that your employees reflect the proper attitude and image you have worked hard to establish. A few weeks of poor telephone attitude toward your customers can unravel years of consistent service on your part. If you are really lucky, one of your established clients will tell you about the problem first, but few customers ever complain; they just leave! Teach your employees early about the level of service they are expected to provide.

9. Your customers will need to adapt to working with someone on your staff. Make sure that the new employee maintains the same level of concern and dedication to customer satisfaction. The best thing that could happen for your business is for your customers to like working with your employee as much or more than they liked working with you. Now you can focus on other business issues besides customer satisfaction.

10. Don't forget that employees can always (and probably eventually will) find another job. This is your business and you will be around long after they are gone, unless you are very lucky and find the right long-term fit with an employee. If an employee leaves, you inherit her decisions. This means that commitments made by an employee can obligate you long after that employee is gone. You, on the other hand, can't just leave and find another job because this is your job. Period.

11. There are legal issues related to having employees that you could ignore when it was only you working at the company. Some form of a personnel policies manual would help you avoid situations such as Julie has in the introductory scenario. On the other hand, personnel policies that are too elaborate can get you into unnecessary trouble.

I have had both excellent employees and poor employees work with me over the years and have found that poor performers have a much bigger impact in smaller

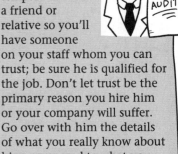

Bankruptcy Alert
You might be tempted to hire a friend or relative so you'll have someone on your staff whom you can trust; be sure he is qualified for the job. Don't let trust be the primary reason you hire him or your company will suffer. Go over with him the details of what you really know about him, compared to what you have simply assumed or heard since you first met. The last thing you want is a surprise that causes you to fire a friend or relative, which disrupts the business, ends a friendship, and makes holidays even more stressful than they already are.

Bankruptcy Alert

If the company only makes money when you are there, then a vacation becomes much more costly than the trip itself. You're really paying for: the actual vacation expenses, lost company revenues as a result of not being at work, and the time needed to get back up to speed once you return to the office and find you are very be-hind in your work. The solution? Set up your pricing so that the times you work cover the times that you are off. This is why consultants charge larger fees for work that could be performed by an employee at a lower rate. You could also define your operations flow so that the business makes money even when you are not there. This solution involves out-sourcing of routine operational components or hiring employees.

companies than they do in huge corporations. Larger companies can afford the luxury of one or two poor performers; smaller companies cannot. If you find employees with performance problems such as employees who can't seem to do the work right, or at a reasonable pace, let them go quickly before they do serious damage to your business.

Unfortunately, the tendency in small businesses is to take care of employees as if they were members of your family. Keep in mind that the best thing you can do for a person who doesn't have a work credibility with you is to get her off your payroll and out looking right away for her perfect job; obviously, the one you had to offer wasn't it, so why hold her up?

Don't ever forget that you started this business. It is yours, not your employees'. Try to let go of the daily decisions so that they can carve a place for themselves in the operation of the business, or you will wind up with morale problems down the road. Remember, however: You sign the checks, co-sign all company debts, and ultimately make the big decisions. They might also need to be reminded of this as you give them increasing responsibilities and they naturally take more initiative. How you do this is a matter of style; don't be too heavy handed because an overbearing boss can easily drive away a good employee (besides, they obviously know that you own the company). It is an interesting balancing act to promote employee initiative while also making sure that the employee doesn't get you into financial trouble.

Mentor

I tend to set dollar thresholds under which employees can make decisions within their business area before they have to contact me. For example, I might let an office manager make any decision under $250 on his own, up to a total of $1,000 in a month. I then review the purchases with him at the end of the month. In this way, I let him know what I expect of him and teach him how to make decisions that I would have made on my own.

This is beneficial to the employees in that they get to work with some autonomy, and it is better for me because I don't get bothered about each expense. If money is tight, I drop the thresholds. Or I start the employees at $100 per purchase and $400 per month, and increase the limits as I become more comfortable with their decision-making ability.

Once employees take on more responsibility for the company's activities, you might wonder how you ever did everything yourself. There isn't a more satisfying business experience than to find a series of orders, invoices, projects, and bank deposits that your employees created without your involvement. To call in from a well-deserved vacation and find thousands of dollars worth of revenues and profits coming into the company while you are gone is the essence of small business success.

Your business needs to be able to create revenue without your involvement or it will never grow beyond your own abilities. That can only happen when employees get involved and have the freedom to act on their own, within certain guidelines you set.

Keep an eye on your strategic goals (check out Chapter 3, "Plan to Win the War"). Do you want the company to become bigger than you or simply support you and your family? If you want to keep it small, then you might never need another employee, other than an occasional relative or temporary helper to handle clerical stuff. If you want to grow so the company works on a relatively independent basis, then you need employees. Accept that as a reality and plan for it in advance. That way, you can be on the lookout for the right person and snatch her up when the timing is right.

Good Help Isn't Hard to Find

Depending on your personnel needs, there are a few avenues you can take when you begin seriously looking for employees. First, you can try out potential employees through a part-time employment arrangement before making a full-time hiring commitment. You can also hire candidates for a specific project, as *independent contractors*, and see how they work out. Finally, temporary help agencies can serve as excellent sources of candidates who have already been screened for your particular job opening.

Other sources include college and university co-op programs where students learn on the job through structured programs that help them apply what they've learned in their course work, as well as high school programs that match interested students with part-time employers. Many colleges and high schools also encourage students to apply for "internships" during summer and winter vacations, where they work for an employer full-time during those breaks from school. Although internships are generally shorter term than co-op programs, you can have a student help on some important projects during a summer vacation. All these options are excellent ways to give students a chance to gain real-world experience while benefiting from their efforts at your company.

As your operation becomes more stable, you will want full-time employees on your staff so that you are not constantly having to train new hires that may only be around for a few months. Take your time finding the right people.

Start out the hiring process by first getting a clear picture of what you want this person to do. In essence, create a job description. Then picture the personality type you want in that job. Ask other business owners about personnel that they have worked with that might be right for your job opening. Place ads in the paper and prepare yourself for hours, or days, of reading resumes and interviewing applicants.

Work study programs at many universities provide an excellent way to test drive a new employee, without exposing yourself to any legal liability. There is someone out there who is right for your job opening. You just need to find them.

Temporary Agencies

Temporary agencies provide a wide array of personnel talents, from clerical (secretarial or typist) to industrial (heavy lifting or construction) to professional (CPAs or consultants). Turn to a temporary employment agency if you need someone on relatively little notice or for a short period of time. These people are also great for seasonal work, such as during the holiday rush, or for periodic work, such as end-of-month inventory taking.

There is rarely any long-term commitment for a specific temporary person, so when you decide to stop using him, make a phone call and he is gone. You can bring in temporary help almost on a moment's notice and use his services only for the amount of time you need them, but you do pay a price for this convenience.

Expect to pay at least $12 per hour for a worker through a temporary agency with minimal computer and clerical skills. The price goes up from there and varies based on geography. (You tell the agency the skill set you need and they give you an hourly rate that they charge for that person.) You do not pay that person's payroll taxes, medical, or other benefits, and she is never an employee of your business; she is employed by the temporary agency.

The level of professionalism associated with temporary agencies has improved significantly over the years. Most agencies have a satisfaction guaranteed policy, where you must be satisfied with the person's work or they either replace the person or do not bill you for their time. The more specific you are about the skills you need, the better they can fit your needs.

The down side of working with temporary agencies is that you can waste a lot of time in interviewing and evaluating different candidates sent over by temporary agencies for your consideration. If you aren't clear up front about the skills you need, you might also find yourself training new people on a regular basis.

The up side is that you can evaluate different job candidates quickly through a temporary agency, which handles a lot of the first-round screening and qualifying for you, and then hire the "temp" as a permanent employee later, if she works out. Typically, temporary agencies make you sign an agreement to pay them a fee if you hire one of their employees during a set time period (such as three or four months), but in most cases, it won't break the bank. Just think about how much easier the agency made your life by providing this employee. Don't they deserve that fee?

Independent Contractors

Independent contractors come in all shapes and sizes (literally). As with temporary agencies, you hire a contractor for a particular job and you let her go when you are done. Contractors expect to be let go at some point, so the parting is rarely accompanied by hard feelings. Typically, the length of a project is specified in a contract when a contractor is brought in, so there are no surprises about what happens when the work is done. (She leaves unless you want to hire her to work on a different project.)

Generally, these folks have an area of expertise such as accounting, computer graphics training, or specific business skills you know your company needs. You must qualify a contractor on your own and decide whether that person is the best for your specific project. The working relationship is between your company and the contractor directly, but she works as a consultant to your firm, not as an employee. You have no ongoing obligations to the contractor.

One of the major differences between working with a contract employee and a temporary employee is that the contractor has been hired directly by your company to do a specific task, but a temporary employee is actually an employee of the temporary agency that is "renting" her to you for a fee. With independent contractors, you spell out up front exactly how long they are asked to work, on what project, to do what specific types of activities, and at what cost. It is also a good idea to spell out the risks that you expect the contractor to assume, such as liability insurance and all associated payroll taxes.

Business Buzzword
An independent contractor is a temporary worker hired on a per-project basis. Often the contractor will sign a contract specifying the length of the project, the work that needs to be done, and the payment for that work.

Temporary employees, on the other hand, really don't have any part in setting the terms of their work with you; their employer discusses those with you and then provides the individual best suited to help you out. In many cases, temporary employment contracts are open-ended so you can end it whenever you want. With an independent contractor, you work out the specific end date of the project up front.

Expect to pay more for the contractor than a temp. One reason is that the contractor is operating as a business owner, too, and must cover all his business costs with each project. Typical price ranges for writing services start at $15 to $20 per hour, document layout and design contractor fees range between $20 to $45 per hour, and professional services such as attorneys range from $65 to $150 per hour. The beauty of working with a contractor is that the person comes in with well-developed skills that are immediately applied to your problem with little or no training needed. You get the desired results quickly and efficiently.

I generally learn a lot from working with a professional independent contractor. The good ones know their stuff and put it to work quickly. Finding a good one is a lot like finding a prince: You have to kiss a number of toads before you find the right one. When you find the right one, he appreciates working for you on a regular basis, and you are relieved to have someone you trust.

Fellow business owners are a tremendous referral source for specific contractors who do their jobs well. Start asking for referrals even before you have a need to use their services so when the need arises, you have a list of qualified contractors from which to choose. You will probably need these people when some type of emergency arises, so it helps to have the relationships already established before the crisis.

When hiring an independent contractor, remember that the IRS has specific criteria that determine whether a person is a contractor or an employee. If you hire someone as an independent contractor but the IRS decides later that she was really an employee of your company, you might be liable for past payroll taxes, Social Security payments, and penalties. Be clear up front about how the IRS would characterize your relationship before taking chances with an independent contractor. See the "When an Employee Is Really an Employee" section later in this chapter for a detailed listing of criteria.

At-Home Help

Here is an idea for you: Tap into the huge reservoir of people who have professional experience but who no longer work outside the home. This includes housewives and househusbands who now take care of their children during the day. It also includes retired men and women who might want to earn some extra money. Frequently, these workers bring substantial expertise to their work and present few personnel headaches.

In exchange for these talents, these employees require that you be pretty flexible on their work hours. People taking care of their kids need to work around school schedules, and the retired don't want work to cut too deeply into their free time. I have found these groups easy to work with and a great personnel financial investment as part-time workers. Check with the local PTA for people who are active with the schools and ask around. You might just be surprised who you find.

Take Your Employee for a Test Drive

Just as you can date for a while before deciding to get married, you can test potential job candidates before making a long-term commitment. There are several intermediate steps you can try before taking the plunge.

Because everyone is always on his best behavior during job interviews, it is very difficult to determine whether a person is a good fit for your company in that setting. You need to observe the job candidate in other situations before deciding whether to hire him.

Part-time employment is a great "try-and-buy" approach where you get to test the water with the prospective employee. Use the employee 20 to 30 hours per week, and see how you work together. If it works, you have someone who comes on full-time with a lot of background and who would otherwise need training at full-time rates. If it doesn't work, you can count your blessings and let him go.

Similarly, you can "try before you buy" with temporary employees. Why not leave the hassles of advertising for employees, interviewing them, and qualifying them to temporary employment agencies who specialize in that kind of thing? All you have to do is tell them what kinds of skills you need; they send over their best candidates for you to check out. After you select a temp and work with her for awhile, you can decide whether to try a new employee when her initial contract is up, or you can hire her permanently, which generally means simply paying the temp agency a small fee for all its work.

Checking out college and high school students through co-op programs where the student works for you a set number of hours per week for a semester or during a summer vacation is another option for testing potential full-time employees. After working with a student for several months, you can decide whether to offer her a full-time job when she graduates.

At a minimum, you should establish a 90-day *probationary period* that every new employee must endure. A probationary period is a time for both you and your new employee to decide whether this is the best job for him. Before the 90 days is up, you must let this person go or he automatically becomes a full-fledged employee, which means he is now entitled to any of the benefits you give your other employees. In other words, on day 91, this person automatically becomes an employee.

There's no reason to rush right into hiring full-time employees if you feel more comfortable taking it slowly. Try some of these approaches to checking your potential employees before making a big commitment to them.

Business Buzzword
A **probationary period** is a length of time (usually 90 days) during which both you and a new employee have a chance to see whether the employee is right for the position and vice versa. Before the 90 days are up, the employee is either let go or hired on an official basis.

When an Employee Is Really an Employee

It is incredible how complicated it becomes to determine whether a person is an independent contractor or an employee. The same person performing the same work under slightly different circumstances can be considered an employee, costing you much more financially than an independent contractor.

The IRS tends to lean on the side of finding workers as employees, not independent contractors, because it means they get more in employment taxes from you, the employer. Be sure you're clear on whether you have an employee or independent contractor working for you.

The basic test to determine whether someone is an employee is whether you control the person's daily activities or whether she makes those decisions herself. A person is an independent contractor if she is held responsible only for results and if her methods, hours of work, location at which the work is performed, and tools are under her control and not dictated by you.

Does the person perform services for more than one company? Is she responsible for her own profit and loss and is she used for specific expertise applied to specific projects instead of just showing up during specific time frames? The more restrictions that you apply to a contractor relationship, the more likely that contractor is considered an employee.

The IRS has a set of criteria that they consider when defining an employee's status. Use these criteria to substantiate your claim that a person is a contractor instead of an employee. Check out the IRS Web site for more information (http://www.irs.ustreas.gov).

Business Tip
Call the IRS office in your city and request its Publication 937 on independent contractors to determine whether you have employees or contractors or call 800-TAX-FORM.

Make sure you have a written subcontractor agreement with the person that clearly spells out the separate liability relationship. This is your best protection should the subcontractor status be questioned. These subcontractor agreements are a standard part of software packages (such as It's Legal) and are available from fellow business owners and from the library. Make sure that the contractor provides his own liability insurance and worker compensation insurance or you might find yourself the recipient of a nasty legal suit if the contractor gets hurt on the job.

More Employees, More Restrictions

All companies are not created equal. Depending on the state where you are doing business and how many employees you have, you will be affected by different rules and regulations. One way to deal with these various state and federal government regulations is to develop a *company policy manual*, or employee manual, for everyone's reference.

Business Buzzword
A company policy manual spells out what the company expects of its employees and what they can expect in terms of benefits and other topics related to employment. New employees are given a copy of the policy manual and are made aware that they will be held responsible for adhering to these policies.

A company policy manual spells out what the company expects of its employees and what they can expect in terms of benefits and other topics related to employment. New employees receive a copy of the policy manual and are responsible for adhering to these policies. A well-defined policy manual clears up employee confusion because everyone is given the same information. It also helps specify who should be contacted with follow-up questions. For smaller companies, the policy manual becomes the personnel policy manual. Know the laws of your individual state and create the proper policy manual to address those state laws.

A few personnel issues apply to all companies, independent of the number of employees. You should clearly spell out the number of company holidays provided to employees each year and the amount of vacation and sick time a person is eligible to take during the year. If you have other company policies that employees need to know, state them in the policy manual.

Drafting your own handbook is cheaper than having an attorney write it, but a legal review is essential to make sure you haven't made significant errors.

State and federal laws kick in at different company-size levels:

➤ If you have fewer than four employees (depending upon the state), you are the master of your domain and can hire, fire, and reward pretty much as you see fit.

➤ If you have fewer than 15 employees, you still have a lot of personal discretion on how you work with your employees. For example, race and sex discrimination laws do not apply to businesses of fewer than 15 employees, except as defined by specific states. However, some state employment laws do kick in, based on the state in which you do business.

➤ If you have between 15 and 49 employees, you have to worry about a wide array of federal laws that address discrimination and other important personnel-related issues.

➤ If you have 50 or more employees, you need the same level of policy manual as IBM or General Motors. It must include policies on family and medical leave, harassment, drug-related issues, discrimination, and virtually any other workplace-related issue such as smoking.

My recommendation regarding your personnel policy is this: Until you need a comprehensive manual as outlined in the previous paragraphs, simply include those items that you absolutely want and intend to absolutely enforce. A few of these might be no drinking on the job, no smoking in the workplace, excessive tardiness or absenteeism as grounds for dismissal, no sexual harassment, no discrimination in the workplace, and other rules that you know will be enforced.

Make sure that new employees get a copy of the personnel policies manual as part of the hiring process and that you expect strict adherence to these policies. In this way, if someone is caught drinking on the job,

Bankruptcy Alert
If you write a policy manual, make sure that you comply with the written policies. It is a good idea to leave out statements regarding policies that don't apply to your company yet because of its size. Whatever you state as a policy, you must be prepared to follow.

Business Tip
Smaller companies are exempt from many employment laws. For example, hiring relatives or friends over others is, by definition, discriminatory. This would make most small businesses in violation of federal and state laws. Call your local department of labor or your local chamber of commerce for guidelines when you begin preparing your policy manual.

you can let him go for being in violation of the company polices, even if his performance has not suffered. (Thus you can avoid Julie's position as outlined in the chapter opening.)

Beware the "policies in a can" approach which uses a standard software package or standard forms to define your personnel manual. They are probably overkill for your small organization and could open you to unnecessary exposure.

Medical Insurance

Wasn't life grand? As the business owner, you have always had your medical insurance paid by the company. Now you have an employee. Does this person get company-paid insurance just like you? What is the law?

To start with, the law covering medical and life insurance benefits is the Employee Retirement Income Security Act (ERISA) that was passed by Congress in 1974. This act does not require employers to provide medical, retirement, or any other benefits of any kind. It only regulates how these benefits must be handled if they are provided. Employers typically offer benefits as a way to attract employees to their company and as a way of improving everyone's own quality of life.

The snag comes in when you offer benefits to certain employees (such as you and members of your family) and don't offer the same benefits to other employees. In general, it is better for business and morale to offer the same benefits to everyone. The safest way to avoid this situation is to verify benefit offerings with an attorney or a benefits specialist.

The policy manual helps keep misunderstandings regarding employment benefits to a minimum, which will help you avoid possible litigation later due to unfulfilled expectations on the part of employees.

Determining the right medical insurance plan for you and your employees is a potentially confusing and time-consuming process. For starters, you generally must have at least two employees (you and one other) before you qualify for most group plans. The coverage may apply to local incidents, but not cover incidents that occur out of town. Does the plan allow you to choose your doctor or must you use doctors who are members of the plan you choose? The world of medical insurance is interesting and complicated. I suggest that you ask a few other business owners how they worked out their medical insurance situation, and you might save yourself a lot of legwork.

Do your homework and don't jump at the first plan you see, or you might find yourself changing plans on a regular basis.

> **Mentor**
>
> At one time, I (on and off) had only one other employee in my company. This meant that I was regularly having to go on and off of the group policy due to the two person minimum. (I guess one person doesn't comprise a group.) My agent let me know that I could set up a policy for myself, and then allow my employees to join my policy and set their own coverage levels. I upped their salaries enough to cover the employee's insurance premiums and insulated myself from having to define a blanket plan that applied to everyone or changed when I was back to running a solo operation.

Sexual Harassment

Picture this: Your company is sued for sexual harassment. You know nothing happened, but you are in front of the judge, who asks about your internal policy regarding sexual harassment. He wants to see it in writing. Oops. It has been verbally expressed to all employees but never in writing. He and the jury decide in favor of the person filing the suit on the grounds that if you really meant it, you would have put it in writing. If you did not specifically state that sexual harassment is prohibited, then the opposite must be true; you must condone sexual harassment.

If you do not put such important policies in writing, you are in potential trouble. If you are a small company not currently bound by the sexual harassment laws because of your size and you have a statement in writing, then it can also be used against you. Be safe, rather than sorry, and discuss the information provided in your handbook with an attorney to be sure you are not opening a can of worms with certain statements. It's always a good idea to discuss your sexual harassment policy with your attorney as a preventive measure.

Is there a lighter side to all of this? I have looked for it and can't find it. It is unfortunate that working with employees has become so dangerous, but it appears to be the nature of the beast. The best prevention for a nasty lawsuit is to avoid it in the first place. Treat all employees as people who perform a function for you. Mentally neuter them (and yourself) when you are on the job and treat them as company assets who perform a function. Nothing more.

Avoid the temptation to become friends with your employees. Keep the proper amount of professional distance between them and you (while never being unfriendly). They work for you. You sign their checks. No matter what, you are never going to be one of the guys or girls. It will become difficult to handle personnel situations with authority if you spend every evening socializing with your employees.

I've talked to several business owners, both male and female, who think of employees as nuns and priests as a way of attaching no gender at all to their employees. In all conversations, they relate as though they were talking to a member of the clergy so that no inappropriate remarks are made. This might seem a little extreme, but it seems to work for them.

You might not have to think of your business as a monastery, but don't ever forget that the primary reason for having employees is for them to perform a job function that makes money for them, the company, and you. Anything more than that might be misinterpreted and should be treated with caution.

Solicitation and Competition

How could these former employees do this? You spent three years building up that account, and they stole it away within 90 days of leaving your company. Their overhead isn't as high as yours so they undercut your price by 30 percent. What could you have done to prevent this? A *noncompete clause* might have been one way to go. A noncompete clause is an agreement that your employees sign, saying that they won't steal your business ideas or methods and go to work for a competitor or become competitors by starting their own firm.

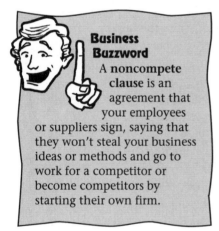

Business Buzzword

A **noncompete clause** is an agreement that your employees or suppliers sign, saying that they won't steal your business ideas or methods and go to work for a competitor or become competitors by starting their own firm.

Although noncompete clauses are treated differently from state to state, you should definitely look into them as one way to protect yourself and your company from ex-employees stealing your ideas and opening a business across town. When an employee signs a noncompete agreement, essentially he is agreeing not to compete with you in a specific geographic area (such as in a particular city or region of the country) for a specified period of time (such as one to two years) by performing the same function for another company as he did for you.

The theory says that your director of sales couldn't quit and go work for your competitor right away in a sales-related position. The reality of an employee noncompete is that it cannot keep a person from making a living in his chosen field. In other words, you really cannot keep a person from taking a job as a sales manager or design engineer with a competing firm. You can, on the other hand, keep that person from using any privileged, confidential, or proprietary system information in his new job because this information is proprietary to your company. A salesman can still sell; he just can't use your customer list. An engineer can design; she just can't use design procedures that are proprietary to your company.

Enforcing an employee noncompete that keeps a person from being able to earn a living in their selected field is a difficult, and usually fruitless, endeavor. You are better served making sure that people know that contact lists obtained at your company stay at your company and are not to be removed when the person leaves. Company confidential documents, which you should make sure are marked as such, cannot be removed from the company premises. Diligence on your part during hiring and while protecting sensitive information is the best defense you have against an employee using your information against you.

Think of an employee noncompete as a mechanism for keeping honest people honest.

Some states treat signed employee noncompete agreements very seriously and prevent a former employee from taking a job at a competing company if you file suit to that effect. Other states take the view that noncompete agreements limit where a person can work and don't uphold them. Check with an attorney who specializes in employment law to find out whether your state supports noncompete agreements. If it does, work with an attorney to write an agreement that protects you rather than do it on your own. You might just create more headaches for yourself down the road if you handle this stuff yourself.

You cannot keep someone from making a living in his home town. A noncompete clause signed as part of the employment process with your company essentially says that a person cannot earn a living in the same town as your business because he agreed to not compete with your company when he joined on, but few courts in the country will uphold a company's rights to keep a person from making a living.

Business Buzzword
A *nonsolicitation clause* is an agreement that your employees sign, saying that if they leave your company they will not pursue your existing customers for business that is related to your company.

They will, however, uphold a company's rights to retain its customers without worrying about a former employee stealing those customers away. This is called a *nonsolicitation clause*, which says that the employee agrees to not pursue your existing customers for business that is related to your company. This agreement lasts for a specific period of time, usually one to two years. Former employees are restricted from using the customer contacts acquired while working with your company to aid another company, including their own.

The best way for you to cover yourself in this situation is to have the employee sign a noncompete agreement as part of his employment. This is particularly true for an employee who has regular customer contact. It makes you seem a little paranoid, but it might also save thousands of dollars of business from walking out your front door. When a customer starts to wave cash in front of a former employee, her loyalty to you will be severely tested. Without the noncompete agreement, you might end up with a personal disappointment and a financial loss without legal recourse.

By the way, if a newly hired employee starts sharing confidential information about his last employer even though he signed a confidentiality agreement with that employer, then you should reasonably assume that he will do the same with your information when he goes to his next job.

Interviewing Techniques

There are some questions that should never be asked of anyone because they are either inappropriate, illegal, or both. You would probably never ask your best friend why she ever married that louse of a husband, or you risk losing a friend. Similarly, you should never ask certain taboo questions when interviewing people for a job.

Why? Simple. If you ask an illegal question and the person you were interviewing does not get the job, he can use the fact that you asked the question as grounds for a discrimination suit—even if the question was asked purely as a conversation starter, such as "Did your children enjoy the Christmas holidays?" or "How old are they now?" The problem is that the topic should never have come up, and now you need to show that you don't have discriminatory hiring practices.

Some people try to determine information from secondary questions. For example, asking why a person moved to your city might indicate that he came with a spouse who was transferred. Asking if working on Sundays is a problem might raise information about the person's religious activities.

You should avoid using secondary questions to solicit the disclosure of information that could be considered prejudicial. The purpose of an interview is to determine the employee's ability to do the job—nothing else. Don't trifle with potentially discriminatory questions; nothing the interviewee reveals is worth the cost of defending an employment discrimination lawsuit!

Start any job search with a clear definition of what you want in the ideal person for the job. Create a job description that includes areas of knowledge the person must have to perform the job. Education and former experience must be clearly defined; develop objective criteria by which candidates can be screened. The more clearly you know what job you want them to perform and the kind of expertise you need, the more likely you are to find the right person to fill the open position. Be specific in your requirements if you want to minimize the amount of training this employee will require. For example, "must know Word for Windows styles operation" is specific where "computer operation required" is general. If you are willing to train the employee, then you can make the requirements more general which broadens the candidate field.

Business Buzzword
A **job description** is a detailed listing of the duties to be performed by the person filling the job, also including the required skills, education and certification levels, and other criteria directly related to the job.

In reality, and in the eyes of the law, you are trying to find the right person for the job, regardless of race, sex, marital status, or other criteria. The suggested interview procedures help ensure that you find the information you need without jeopardizing your company in the process.

Never bring up the following topics while conducting the interview:

➤ Marital status

➤ Veteran status

➤ Race

➤ Religion

➤ Nationality

➤ Children

➤ The interviewee's age

➤ Sex and sexual orientation

You need to know answers to many of these questions after the person is hired because emergency and medical information might pertain to children and spouses, but do not include them as part of the interview. In addition, make sure that you provide no verbal agreements about the length of employment or reasons for future possible dismissal. These might later be construed as commitments by the person being hired. These verbal commitments might be used against you later if problems arise with this person's performance that cause you to let him go.

Here are several "do's" as taken from *The Personnel Policy Handbook for Growing Companies*:

➤ Give the applicant a copy of the job description and ask if there are problems performing any of the stated functions.

➤ Make written notes about the interviewee and how this person meets the criteria outlined in the job description.

➤ Get the applicant to discuss recent, prior work situations.

➤ Outline the positive and negative sides of your company.

➤ Explain the company policy on smoking and such.

➤ Tell the applicant all the great things about the company.

➤ Don't ask the applicant about his or her personal situation, such as marital status, parental status, religion, sexual orientation, race, or disabilities.

➤ Don't make notes on the application or resume about irrelevant information that could be construed as discriminatory such as hair color, weight, height, and clothing.

➤ Don't tell the applicant that you are looking for people with limited experience.

➤ Don't tell some applicants the positive parts of the job while telling others the negative aspects. Be consistent in how you describe the position.

➤ Don't ask about child care arrangements.

➤ Don't lie about or cover up any bad news about the company.

Present the most positive aspects of the company in the most consistent manner. Your final intent is to find the best person to fill the job opening—period. If you mislead them about company-related problems, you can find an employee making a substantial career change under false pretense, which can only lead to management troubles and a possible lawsuit.

The Least You Need to Know

➤ No man or woman is an island when it comes to succeeding in business. You must have the assistance of others if you want the company to grow beyond your capabilities.

➤ Create an environment where employees can grow professionally and financially. Allow them to feel like a part of the process, and you will reap the rewards associated with having a successful business that operates without you.

➤ Give potential employees a tryout before making a permanent commitment. Use probationary periods or temporary assignments to find out how they fit with your operations.

➤ An ineffective employee in a large organization can be disruptive, but in a small company, he can be disastrous because of the effect he has on others and on customers.

➤ State and federal laws kick in at different company size levels, based on the number of employees.

➤ Set up your minimum personnel policies to cover you on the "must adhere to" issues and add others later as needed.

➤ Make sure you conduct interviews in a legal and effective manner.

Chapter 18

The Tax Files: Payroll Taxes

In This Chapter

➤ An overview of payroll procedures

➤ Deposits and reporting deadlines

➤ When to consider an outside payroll service

➤ Unemployment tax payment and reporting deadlines

I'm a professional engineer, thought Kevin. I should be able to understand something as basic as payroll taxes. After 15 years of working and receiving paychecks, it was hard to imagine that it could be this complicated.

Okay. Deductions are made from the employee's paycheck based on earnings and several tax types. What is this FICA thing? And then there's unemployment. This is for both the state and federal taxes. I can handle that. The deposits are made quarterly for the state and annually for the federal. Or was that the reporting procedures?

Forget about that for now. Let's get this company portion of the payroll deductions under control. Hey. Wait a minute. These numbers are exactly the same as the employee ones. Did I make a mistake, or are they supposed to be equal? Maybe the company pays it all? No, that can't be.

Wow. Now I know what a dog feels like when it chases its tail. Time to take Jill up on her offer to explain this stuff to me. It's clear that it's really unclear, and I just don't have the time to figure it out on my own.

"Hi, Jill? This is Kevin. Have I got a deal for you. What are you doing for lunch today, and were you serious about explaining payroll tax procedures to me?"

Your business won't grow without employees, but adding employees adds responsibilities such as managing payroll tax deposits. More than one company has gone under due to improper management of payroll taxes and figuring this maze out for yourself can be costly and legally compromising. This chapter introduces the payroll process and outlines the IRS guidelines for making tax deposits. Learn this well and save yourself money and grief.

Payroll Taxes: You Can't Avoid Them, So Learn How to Deal with Them

Unless you intend to be a sole practitioner all your life, at some point, you will have employees. With employees come payroll taxes. No one I know thinks payroll taxes are fun or interesting, but as a business owner, you need to have a basic grasp of the legal requirements. Otherwise, you can get tangled up in bureaucratic red tape and headaches that make asking for a loan sound pleasant by comparison. You don't have to be a rocket scientist to calculate payroll taxes, but you do have to pay attention to the details.

As you read through this chapter the first time, you might feel kind of overwhelmed. Don't worry. Over time, this feeling will pass as you become more familiar with all the rules. Eventually, it will make perfect sense.

Here's one of my favorite business secrets: Just because you have employees doesn't mean that you have to do the accounting for your payroll. That's what staff (and service bureaus and accounting software) is for! Read on for an introduction to the regimented, deadline-filled world of payroll tax accounting—so that at least you can find out what you'll be delegating to someone else.

Payroll Tax Overview

Ever talk to someone from the IRS? To picture a typical payroll tax auditor, imagine that IRS representative without a sense of humor, and you're likely to be pretty close to the mark. The first thing you need to know is that all taxing jurisdictions (federal, state, and local) have their own requirements and filing deadlines that they take very seriously indeed. If you file all the right forms on time, most likely you won't have many problems.

That leads to the next question: How do you figure out which forms to file and when to file them? The three basic types of payroll taxes are income taxes (which you withhold from wages), Social Security and Medicare (you pay half, the employee pays half), and unemployment (you pay it all).

➤ States and some cities have income taxes, as does the federal government, so you need to consult both the federal guidelines and relevant state and local guidelines to determine how much to withhold and when to pay it over to the taxing authority.

➤ Social Security and Medicare are easier to figure out because they are federal taxes and subject only to the federal rules.

➤ Unemployment is subject to both state and federal rules, with potentially complex interactions between the rules requiring even more detailed record keeping.

To find the federal rules, contact the Internal Revenue Service (IRS), which has a package of tax rules and guidelines for businesses, including Publication 937, *Employer's Tax Guide*. It's not the most fascinating reading in the world, I'll admit, but it's something you need to know about if you have employees and handle your own payroll tax accounting.

For the state rules that apply to you, contact your state department of revenue (for income tax withholding information), department of labor (for unemployment tax information), or secretary of state (in case you can't find the right bureau to answer your question). Look in the blue pages (governmental section) of your phone book under Federal or State government to find out where to get the information.

Your employees will give you information about their tax status, number of dependents, and withholding allowances on a federal form W-4, and you can use that information to look up the right withholding amount in the tax tables or apply the right percentages for your state's formula. Some states have their own version of the Form W-4, which might contain different information from the federal form. In fact, some states don't have any personal state income tax at all. You must check the rules for your particular state and proceed accordingly.

However, just because you figure it out once, don't think you're done for the year. If your employee's pay rate, marital status, dependent status, or address changes, the withholding amounts may also change, and you also have to be aware of the relevant ceilings for Social Security taxes and unemployment taxes. Detailed, repetitive calculations are what payroll tax reporting is all about, together with weekly, monthly, quarterly, and annual reporting requirements. If you like this sort of stuff, you will be in heaven. I, on the other hand, use a software package to keep me out of trouble.

You've filled out the forms and followed the instructions; now you just drop them in the mail and relax, right? Wrong! Federal taxes and some state taxes are subject to depository requirements, and you can't just mail a check with your return. In essence, you deposit the taxes at your local bank using either a payroll tax coupon with your *employer identification number* (EIN) on it or paying electronically. The depository schedule

Business Buzzword
Your **employer identification number (EIN)** is a number given to any company that has employees, whether it is a corporation or a sole proprietorship. If you have employees, you must have an EIN to ensure all your tax payments are credited to the correct account, which is indicated by your unique EIN. Call the IRS to get your EIN (free!) and Federal Tax Deposit Coupon book (IRS Form 8109). You need a bank through which you make these deposits.

might not be the same as the reporting schedule (this depends on a whole bunch of factors), so read the regulations carefully.

Table 18.1 Breakdown of Payroll Tax Payments

Tax Type	Employee Portion	Company Portion	Total	Threshold
Federal Income Tax	As determined from the W-4 form.	None.	15%, 28%, 31%, 36%, or 39.6%, depending on salary level.	Depends on filing status.
State Income Tax	As determined from the W-4 form.	None.	Determined on a state by state basis.	Depends on filing status.
Social Security	6.2%	6.2%	12.4%	$60,600
Medicare	1.45%	1.45%	2.9%	Unlimited
Federal Unemployment	0%	6.2%	6.2% less the state percent payment.	$7,000
State Unemployment	0%	Depends on the state.	Depends on the state.	Depends on the state.

Fudge on these taxes, and you will pay big time and without mercy. It is one thing to be late on a payment to a creditor. It is another to be late on payroll deposit payments to the IRS because you are essentially playing with the employee income deductions. It is the IRS's money that you are administering for them. The IRS will eat you alive in late payment fees and interest if you delay, so make sure that you read the next section and file on time.

Filing and Paying Payroll Taxes

You have performed the calculations, made the payroll deductions, and paid the employees their well-earned paychecks, but there is still more for you to do. You now need to report the deductions to the IRS and make a bank deposit or electronic deposit to ensure that the IRS gets the money you've so carefully deducted from everyone's paycheck.

Tax Deposits and IRS Form 941, Employer's Quarterly Federal Tax Return

Make your payroll tax deposit with a company check at your local bank along with the Federal Tax Deposit Coupon that tells the IRS which company is making its deposit. The coupon should have the deposit amount filled in, along with the box associated with the quarter to which the deposit is to be applied and the type of tax based on the particular IRS form number (941, First Quarter). The bank will give you a standard deposit receipt in return.

You deposit the federal payroll taxes on either a monthly or semiweekly basis, depending on the size of your payroll. If your total tax deposits exceeded $50,000 in the prior four quarters, then you probably have to deposit semiweekly. If not, you can deposit on a monthly basis on or before the 15th of the month. The IRS will let you know, but you are ultimately responsible even if the notice was not received. It is a good idea to keep tabs on the amount of tax you pay. In general, you deposit taxes on a monthly basis for your first year.

> **Business Tip**
> Depository banks don't have to accept checks on other banks for payroll tax deposits, so when you are choosing your business bank, make sure that it can accept payroll tax deposits.

The IRS has moved into the 20th century and set up the Electronic Federal Tax Payment System (EFTPS). The plan basically dictates that employers who must make deposits semiweekly must make those deposits electronically. As might be expected from the government, they had problems with the implementation and extended the deadline for compliance to July 1, 1998. Once again, the IRS will notify you if you must comply with the electronic filing requirements, but you probably shouldn't trust them on this one either. You must complete and return to the IRS an enrollment form at least ten weeks before you plan to make your first electronic deposit.

Make sure that you get your payment into the bank before the end of the banking day. There is a time difference between the end of the banking day and the time the bank closes. Be sure you know when the banking day ends. For example, the banking day might end at 2:00 p.m. even though the bank closes at 4:00 p.m. The deposit must be in the bank by 2:00 p.m. in this situation.

If no wage payments are made in a month, no deposits are needed. If the 15th falls on a holiday or weekend, you can deposit on the following business day and still be on time.

> **Business Tip**
> The semi-weekly and monthly deposit designations have nothing to do with when you pay your employees. The IRS expects to receive payroll deposits monthly or semiweekly (depending on the size of your payroll).

Semiweekly depositors must stay on top of things. If you pay your employees on a Wednesday, Thursday, or Friday, then your tax deposit must be made by Wednesday of the following week. If payday falls on Saturday, Sunday, Monday, or Tuesday, then deposits are due at the bank on Friday of that week. There is a special three-day rule that adds a day to the deposit deadline for each day that a holiday falls between the payday and deposit date.

You report all the deductions you've taken from the payroll to the IRS for a given calendar quarter on IRS Form 941, Employer's Quarterly Federal Tax Return. This is for payroll tax information only. The form must be in the mail, and postmarked, by the last day of the month following each quarter. For example, for the first quarter (January through March), you must complete and mail the 941 form by the last day of April.

The following table summarizes the payroll filing procedures for you.

Payroll Deductions Made	When Payroll Checks Are Written
Federal bank deposits required.	Either semiweekly or monthly, depending on deposit levels. Deposits are made with IRS coupon form 8109 or electronically.
Payroll deduction form 941 completed and postmarked.	On a quarterly basis on the last day of the month following each quarter.
State unemployment reporting and payment.	Usually quarterly, but the last day of the month following each quarter.
Federal unemployment reporting and payment.	Annually, using IRS form 940 and deposit coupon form 8109.

Payroll tax calculations, deposits, and reporting are initially confusing and become a routine part of operation in a short period of time. Ignore them, and you will pay stiff penalties, so step up to the table and do it right from the start.

State and Federal Unemployment Taxes

This part gets easier. You have been accruing unemployment payments with each payroll period. The states make you complete a reporting form and deposit the required funds on a quarterly basis by the last day of the month following each quarter. The federal reporting is done on the IRS form 940, which you must complete annually by the end of January of the year following the reporting period and mail along with a check for the proper amount.

Business Tip
Your unemployment tax rate fluctuates, depending on how many employees have ever filed for unemployment. If former employees file for unemployment benefits, you see your unemployment rate increase, unfortunately.

The state tells you what rate you must pay for unemployment, based on past unemployment benefits paid to past employees. This unemployment rate indicates their assessment of the amount of risk your company poses to the unemployment fund. If a number of your employees leave your company and file for unemployment compensation, you see your unemployment tax rate increase. Tax rates reflect expected costs for your industry but are adjusted based on your specific experience. If no one leaves your company and files for unemployment, after a few years, your rates might even decrease.

Rules to Live (and Save Taxes) By

Here are a few rules that I learned the hard way. I relay them here with embarrassment and with the hope that I can save you from the same mistakes:

1. Report your payroll taxes—yes, all of them on all of the nice little forms—when the reports are due. That's right—on time!

2. Make sure that your deposits are accurate and on time. Only an act of God can save you from IRS penalties and fines if they are levied against you or your company.

3. Use a payroll software package such as QuickBooks, which includes a payroll module to ease the payroll process. Get to know the payroll features to save yourself a ton of time and uncertainty. I have consistently used QuickBooks' payroll features and been very pleased with its accuracy and ease of use because you can get the needed numbers from the system relatively painlessly.

4. Find someone who understands the payroll tax calculation and reporting process. Have them show you their completed forms and walk you through the process.

5. Stay on top of things, and always include the additional payroll tax expenses when considering an employee raise. Perhaps you should offer your employee additional benefits, instead of a raise because a raise has the additional payroll taxes attached, and certain types of benefits do not incur the incremental taxes.

The payroll tax reporting and deposit procedures will eventually become second nature to you, but it is definitely confusing when you first start out. I had a tough time finding all of this information in one spot and made some serious blunders that cost me thousands of dollars. Don't make the same mistake. Get the right advice early in the process and follow it. The late fees are tough to swallow.

As a final note, don't fiddle with these taxes. If you look at where the money comes from, you can see that you are holding your employees' money until deposited. If you are delinquent in making these deposits for any length of time at all, it might be viewed as theft and you can get yourself into real trouble that you really don't want. Don't take chances with payroll tax liabilities. If your company goes under, you still owe these taxes, so pay these guys before you pay everyone else.

Using a Payroll Accounting Service

You always have the option of giving this task to someone else. Your accountant will generally do payroll tracking for you as part of a standard service offering. Outside payroll services specialize in nothing but payroll accounting. This might be too much for what you need at this time, but you might ask your fellow business owners about how they handle their own payroll. After all, the payroll tax process is an important concern for all business owners independent of size and age; experience is a good guide in this area.

The Least You Need to Know

➤ Employee-paid payroll taxes include Social Security, Medicare, and federal and state withholding. The company and the employee pay equal amounts of Social Security and Medicare. The company pays all the federal and state unemployment tax.

➤ Payroll tax deposits are made either semiweekly, monthly, or electronically, depending on the size of your company's payroll.

➤ Federal payroll taxes are reported on a quarterly basis using the IRS 941 form. Similar forms are necessary for state payroll tax reporting.

➤ Federal unemployment taxes are paid quarterly if the unpaid liability exceeds $100. Otherwise, they are reported and paid annually using the IRS 940 form.

➤ Don't be late on reporting or deposit deadlines because the penalty fees are huge!

Working at Home or Away

In This Chapter

➤ The benefits and pitfalls of working at home

➤ IRS considerations for home offices

➤ Choosing the right location for your business

➤ When to rent, lease, and buy

"How's it going in your corner office?" Mary called to ask.

"Great! Instead of getting up at 6:00 a.m. to drag myself downtown by 8:30, now I can leave my bedroom at 8:29 and be at work 30 seconds early," Jim explained.

"Sounds wonderful. What do you do with all your free time now?" Mary asked.

"I work! One of the drawbacks of having a corner office in the basement is that it's just too easy to keep working long after all the downtown workers have left for home. And, while I see more of my children than I used to, they can be a distraction, especially when I'm on the phone."

"So, are you ready to come back to work with the big boys?"

"Not on your life!" came the reply. "I can handle the distractions, and running my own business from a convenient location is one of the most rewarding things I've ever done. Why, some days, the only reason I leave my home office is to make a deposit at the bank."

Who hasn't sat in rush-hour traffic and fantasized about working from home? What? Give up soot, smog, rude drivers, and several hours of my day to work from a spare room at home? Why do that? Simple: It sounds great. And it can be if you have the discipline to make it work.

Home Office: Pros and Cons

Take a look at some of the good and not-so-good points associated with a home-based business in Table 19.1.

Table 19.1 The Pros and Cons of a Home Office

Advantages	Discussion
A 30-second commute from the kitchen to the spare bedroom	You save 1–2 hours per day in commuting time, which provides more time for business. You can also work at night, after others have gone to sleep.
Save money	You already pay the rent or mortgage. Save the money you would spend on office space and put it back into your business.
Tax advantages	You should be able to deduct expenses associated with the office section of your house, which otherwise are not deductible. You might actually make money off the deal. (More on this later in the chapter.)
Family benefits	You are closer to the family, which allows for meals at home. You might be able to rope family members into helping, on occasion.
Risk-free trial run	You can test the water regarding your business idea without incurring a lot of outside financial costs and obligations. If your idea takes off, you can always move to a regular office.

Disadvantages	Discussion
Motivational liability	You can get sidetracked into personal stuff such as cleaning the kitchen. Personal phone calls can take up a lot of your day when people know you are at home. After all, "you're not at work" in their mind. You're at home. You need to set them straight on this one.

Disadvantages	Discussion
No commute	On the days when you don't want to work, the commute helps to separate your home life from business. When you work at home, you might spend that extra hour on the couch that otherwise would have been productive.
Lack of peer contact	You are relatively isolated in your home office, whereas a regular office provides contact with other business owners. They are not only colleagues, but also sources of leads, business, and guidance.

Starting your business from home is a relatively painless way to begin either a service business (such as consulting, accounting, massage, and so on) or a small product-oriented business such as mail order or light manufacturing. You are already paying for the house and utilities. It makes sense to use these prepaid expenses to your best benefit, but be cautious of the potential pitfalls associated with running a business out of your home.

This section deals with the financial and personal aspects of working from your home. You'll also find a section on determining the right time for moving out and whether you should lease, rent, or buy your office space.

Watch Your Overhead

As we said when I was in the Army: Uncle Sam can't make you do anything. He can only make you really sorry that you didn't! Working out of your home is financially attractive in the early days, but you need to follow the proper steps to ensure that the IRS allows your desired business and personal deductions.

It is tempting, and reasonable, to assume that expenses associated with the business section of your house are tax deductible as a business expense. They might be, but you have to be careful how you present it on your taxes and back up the claim with paperwork.

Bankruptcy Alert
Don't underestimate the impact of working alone. You might really start to miss those impromptu talks around the water cooler or having someone just down the hall to join for lunch. Some people set up office in an executive suite or office building simply so that they have other people around. More than one person has closed his own business to work for someone else due to the isolation.

Business Tip
You can deduct the expense of your home office even if you are employed by someone else, but the office still must be used solely for work and not as a part-time playroom for the kids.

Bankruptcy Alert
Local zoning, building, or landlord ordinances might keep you from starting a business in your home. If your business requires customer parking, increases street traffic, or causes wear and tear on your property, you might find it difficult to start a home-based business. Check with the city and your landlord for approval before investing too much money and time into working out of your home.

Business Tip
Keep in mind, however, that the home office deduction is not available to every company that wants to operate out of the president's spare bedroom. Corporations are not permitted to take the home office deduction, so if you've incorporated you need to factor in the loss of that tax advantage to your location equation. Maybe working from home doesn't have as many advantages for your business as you had originally thought.

As the judge says, "He who has the most paperwork wins!" Documentation of expenses is critical in making your case for home-office business deductions to the IRS.

Here is the key: The business section of your house must be used "regularly and exclusively" for business purposes. This means that your home office must be your principal place of business operation, such as where you actually do your work for clients. You must regularly meet with clients, patients, and suppliers in your home office as a part of your business operation. These meetings must occur in your home office and not in other locations within the house.

You must really use your home office as an office, not as a shortcut for some desirable tax deductions. The IRS is getting tighter on these restrictions instead of looser, and you must take the proper steps up front to back up your case for a home-office deduction.

The percentage of your home expenses that is allocated to your office is calculated on either a square-footage or number-of-rooms basis. For example, assume that you have a five-room house of 1,500 square feet. One room comprises one-fifth of your house if all rooms are about the same size. Take one-fifth of all housing expenses and allocate them to the business as expenses. You just saved money on your personal bills but gave up one-fifth of your house to the business in the process.

You can also use the square-footage approach if the one room is much larger than the others. For example, assume that the room is 500 square feet of the 1,500 square foot house, or one-third. You can still take the one-third deduction, but you should make the case that this particular room was the best candidate for the office and is exclusively used for that purpose.

Beware of your home computer. It is not both a home and business toy when speaking with the IRS, no matter how you really use it. By the way, you probably need to keep detailed track of usage hours or you might find yourself pushing Uncle Sam uphill, which is a tough one. If you plan to use it for business, then use it for business. (You really don't want your kids playing with important business files, anyway. Can you imagine the mayhem that would occur in your house if your five-year-old son accidentally erased all your accounting records and you did not have a backup?) Keep yourself, your clients, and your family out of this minefield and keep your business and personal computers separate.

See IRS publication 587 for details on home-office deductions. There are also numerous tax guides available at most bookstores (such as the store where you bought this great book) that provide detailed information on setting up your home office from a tax standpoint. The laws are changing on this hot area every year, and getting timely information is your best way to avoid trouble.

Don't Get Distracted

I mentioned this earlier, but it's worth saying again: When you work at home, you are tempted to start a little later, quit a little earlier, and maybe hang around at the swimming pool instead of making that business phone call. It's tough to leave the backyard on a beautiful summer day and walk into an office full of paperwork and stuff to do. However, if you don't walk into that office and start working, you will not keep that beautiful backyard for very long, if you know what I mean. It takes a lot of discipline to work at home and keep yourself on a work schedule. Your family also has to support you or you're already behind the eight ball.

Bankruptcy Alert
This tax-avoidance strategy gets complicated very quickly, so see a tax professional to help you, or you can trick yourself into a lot of hassles and minimal savings and become a potential IRS audit candidate.

Business Tip
It might cost more, but it makes life easier to have separate business and personal checking accounts and telephone lines. This allows you to clearly define business and personal expenses along with telephone charges. Otherwise, you really need to log every telephone call made. Ugh!

Mentor

I find that if I impose client deadlines on myself, I can make myself work on those days that I feel distracted. Just as a deadline set by a boss in a normal company can prompt you to work beyond your normal hours, so can a deadline commitment to your current boss, the client to whom you made the commitment.

Business Tip
The IRS is forever updating and modifying its guidelines for taking the home-office deduction. If this is a tax move you are considering making this year, check out the most up-to-date information on the IRS's Web site. Request a copy of their form on taking the home office deduction at http://www.irs.ustreas.gov/prod/forms_pubs/index.html.

It is tough to discuss a complicated $10,000 project with a client when little Jennifer walks into the room wearing a full pint of chocolate ice cream on her face. How do you get her out of the room while closing this client on the project? Get the picture? Put yourself and your family on a schedule and stick with it. Don't take personal calls at home. You probably wouldn't take them at your company office, so why take them at home?

Business is business, no matter where you transact it. Otherwise, it's a hobby. You wouldn't have made it this far in the book if you only wanted a new hobby. Stick to business, even if it occurs in the second bedroom of your house. One essential piece of equipment for the home office is a door! Make sure your can close your door to shut out the distractions of home and family life.

Make Your Office a Home

Now, here is the good news. If it really is a business office, then you should spend the money to make it work. Get a comfortable chair. Get the desk and table combinations you need to be productive. Spend the money needed for telephone and computer equipment. You might even want to pop the cash for a stereo just for the office. You'll be spending a lot of time in your office, so make it work for you. By the way, these all become business deductions because they are related to the business. Make your office into a home within your home to ensure that you want to go there and are productive once you arrive.

Business Tip
Renting furniture is a low-cash way to outfit your office. Rent-to-own plans allow you to make your furniture rental payments apply toward the purchase price. In general, if you rent for more than 12 months, you might as well have bought the furniture.

When Is It Time to Move Out?

You have been working diligently in your office for awhile now, and things appear to be stabilizing. Clients expect you to remain in business and start providing you with repeat business. The delivery people know that your business exists and don't freak out when they deliver a business-related package to a residence. Things appear to be going along well. Why would you consider moving out of the house and into a new location? Simple. To either make your life easier or to make more money...or both.

Typical indicators that it's time to consider a move include some of the following:

➤ When the office gets too small for the equipment and number of people you need to run your business.

➤ When the level of business activity at the house gets so high that it disrupts the daily routine.

➤ When your clients begin to wonder about your commitment because you don't have a "real" office.

➤ When your clients appear uncomfortable coming to your home for business meetings, and you start feeling uncomfortable having them walk through your house to get to the office.

➤ When you can't get temporary help because the agency won't let its people work in a private residence due to insurance reasons.

In short, you should move out when you have made it and when the problems associated with the business become operational and not financial.

Bankruptcy Alert
Letterhead, envelopes, business cards, and telephone listings must be changed when you move offices. These hassles and expenses are not trivial, and you might decide to get a separate office from the beginning to avoid the confusion and expense at a later date when you have to move out of the house.

Location, Location, Location

Locating your new, "real" office is a lot of fun, but it's time-consuming. Just like buying a house for your family, you are setting up an important part of your lifestyle. A long commute means you are away from home more, but this might place you closer to your clients and prospects. A more expensive space might present the desired image and bring in more money but with a higher up-front cost on your part. Consider all these factors when moving to an office that is not in your home.

Try these points on for size when looking at a new location:

1. If you provide a service, does it make sense to be centrally located near your clients and prospects? Probably. Is the potentially longer commute worth it on your part?

2. Are you moving to please yourself or to improve business operations? Either is fine, but understand your motivations.

3. Will you make up the commute time by being more productive while in the office, as compared to working out of your home? You might spend extra time with the commute but find that your day ends earlier because you are more productive while at work without distractions from home.

4. Is there a competitor in the area of your new office? If so, does this hurt you or help you? Sometimes, people want to " shop around" and look for locations where competing companies are easily accessible. This applies to retail and many professional services. Will this competitor cause you to lose existing clients or make it difficult to gain new ones? If so, should you move far enough away from the

established competitor so that you have a geographic advantage in your new location?

5. If you have a manufacturing type of business, does the new location make much difference to the operation? Probably not, because you ship to your clients and you can do that from just about anywhere. Once again, move to improve business operations, not to stroke your ego due to your newfound success.

6. Is moving going to cost you customers? People do not like change unless it benefits them. How will this change benefit, or cost you, your existing clients?

7. How much more business do you have to create from the new location to justify the additional expense? (Not sales revenue, but actual profits after all marginal costs are taken out.) Is this number reasonable and can you achieve it within the needed time frame?

8. What if you don't move? What would happen? Is there an external reason forcing the move that takes the "if" completely out of your hands and turns it into a where, when, and how?

9. Locate your permanent office in an area that allows you to keep the same phone number as the one you had at your house. In this way, you do not have to ask your clients to call you at a new number.

I'm sorry that I can't give you standard answers to these and the myriad other questions that no doubt will arise. The answers are heavily dependent on your particular situation, but here are a few rules that might help to narrow the field of confusion:

➤ Manufacturing business locations are chosen most often based on shipping, receiving, parking, space, and other operationally oriented criteria. If you primarily ship, mail, or work over the phone, it really doesn't matter where you locate your office as long as it supports the daily operation.

➤ Service businesses that require the clients to come to you are heavily location-dependent. Why would clients go out of their way to come to your place when your competition is just down the road from their office? Get geographically close to your clients, and they will come.

➤ A nicer location might present a better image but might not necessarily generate more revenue. Don't confuse appearance with profits; they are not always equal. (Read the opposite argument next.)

➤ Basing your service business in a well-recognized location or building might increase name recognition with your clients. You are associated with this respected office location, which should reflect well on you and increase trust. Trust is a necessary ingredient for any successful service business. Does the new location instill that trust without placing your company in financial jeopardy?

➤ Retail requires high-visibility frontage. Period. If your customers can't find you, they will not buy. They might not even know that you exist. Traffic is needed and encouraged in a high-visibility location such as a mall, craft and service fairs, downtown areas, and busy streets. F. W. Woolworth learned this with his first store and ended up closing after only a few months. After that, he never underestimated the value of location, location, and location.

Mentor

I know of one retail store that started out in a funky warehouse district. It provided high-quality products at a great price and developed a cult following with its clients. People would send friends to this store for both the " good deal" and the experience of the novelty of the situation. The store thrived and grew to the point that the owner decided to move to a high-visibility frontage that was substantially more expensive but offered the allure of more traffic.

The store moved and increased its overhead due to the increased rental costs but never saw the anticipated increase in sales. It was no longer funky and the novelty was gone. In addition, a new competitor moved in across the street when it moved. Which caused the decrease in sales? The owners are really not sure; it was probably a combination of both.

A possible moral to the story is to realize what has made you successful in the past, and don't fiddle too much with it. You have to make the tough calls, and this is one of them. By the way, this company is doing just fine and altered its operations to accommodate the new sales and cost situation. Small companies that survive do so only by responding to the changes in the market and their business operation.

Look at what your existing and potentially new competition is doing. Ask your customers about their reactions to your possible move. Get as much information as possible before taking the plunge. It would be a shame to take an operation that is working well from your home with its associated low overhead and place it in jeopardy due to an unnecessary office move.

Here is just a quick reminder to consider things such as lighted and adequate parking for your clients. Our training center's female clients like to use the covered, lighted parking area at night. Make sure that the building is in compliance with the Americans with Disabilities Act (ADA), which requires providing easy access for disabled persons. Check for wheelchair ramps, doorways that are wide enough to accommodate a wheelchair, and rest-rooms that are designed for wheelchair access. Signs should be posted in Braille for those who are visually impaired.

Ask your potential clients about the things that are important to them; I never expected that rest-room design would be as important to our female clients as it turned out to be. I worked with the building management to get our women's rest-rooms upgraded before those on other floors or the men's. It paid off, and we got higher evaluation marks for our improved facilities and more business from our female clients. Your clients know best what they are looking for. If you provide it, they will come.

Lease, Rent, or Buy?

Should you lease, rent, or buy? This one is simple. Which one works out to be the financially most attractive? Leasing ties you into the same location for a longer period of time but provides you with lease-rate stability. Renting provides you with the monthly option of moving elsewhere, but your rent can fluctuate at any time, and the landlord has the option of asking you to vacate. Buying provides tremendous stability but with a large financial commitment on your part.

I suggest that you consider this progression for a service business:

1. Start out at home until your business warrants moving out.

2. Look into renting space in an executive suite of offices. Here you get the clerical support needed to operate without incurring a huge financial commitment. You can also generate contacts with other suite members. Another option is to explore business incubators, which provide the same level of service as executive office suites, but often with more camaraderie and coaching.

3. Lease your own space when the restrictions of the executive suite begin to cost you time, money, or both.

4. Buy your own building when you have a successful track record under your belt. Many companies use the SBA for funding of this type of business-related building purchase.

If you have a manufacturing business, try this approach:

1. Work out of your house for as long as possible. You might be able to do this by using production houses for the actual production aspects while using your home for office-related functions.

2. See if you can partner with another company that already exists. Use their surplus capacity as an interim step.

3. Lease your own space when you're confident about future business, such as when you have ongoing contracts or automatic stocking-level agreements.

4. Buy when you are ready. Once again, look to the SBA for help in financing the purchase of a building.

The Least You Need to Know

➤ Office location is important for both you and your clients. Consider your business location from your client's perspective; consider the finances from your perspective to find the optimal blend of location and expense.

➤ Just because you run your business from your home doesn't mean that the expenses are tax deductible. Follow the IRS rules, and stay out of trouble.

➤ When you work at home, treat it just like a job. Go to work at regular hours and discipline yourself to stay on the job even though you are only in the basement.

➤ Location is critical to most service and retail operations. Don't overlook this very important aspect of your business.

➤ Product and manufacturing businesses are less location-dependent. Their location can be based on price, space, and access to transportation.

➤ Minimize your commitments and expenses in the early days of your business. Gradually work your way up to leases and purchases after you have a successful track record.

Chapter 20

Get Automated

In This Chapter

➤ Using technology for your benefit

➤ Automating your business

➤ Applying computer and telephone technology

➤ An overview of computerized accounting

➤ An introduction to online services

"So why hasn't the newsletter gone out?" asked Frank. "We intend to do this on a regular basis, and it shouldn't be such a big deal."

Todd, the marketing director, looked frustrated at the question and did his best to give a diplomatic answer. "The database of names is in an old format, and we do the mail merge for the labels in our word processing software package. Making the two work with each other is a headache. Why didn't we just stick with the package we started with?"

Frank thought back. He had taken all of his customer contact information to a typing service that entered it into a computer program. Then they gave him a disk and told him the name of the software package they used, so he bought it to make things simple. His now ex-brother-in-law had upgraded the database to a "fully relational" one, whatever that meant. Now, Frank couldn't even print out mailing labels. He wondered if he would ever be able to create a telephone list using the new package. It just shouldn't be this hard.

"I guess the latest and greatest is just not so great for us, is it? Let's call a temporary agency and see if we can get someone in here who understands how all of this stuff works. Maybe we should send one of us to a training class to learn how mail merging operates. One day in a class would certainly pay for itself if we could avoid a situation like this again," said Frank.

"Maybe we can get some training on that fax program, too," said Todd. "We mail out 1,000 pieces per month at around 50 cents each to our local customers. That is $500 per month in postage and printing that would be completely saved by using fax distribution instead of the mail. I know how much you like to save money. What about giving me some time and money to get trained on that, too?"

"Five hundred bucks a month? Not bad! I wonder how else this computer equipment can save us money and time."

Automate from the Start

Computers and other pieces of equipment are an essential part of business life. The sooner that you include them in the operation of your business, the easier it is to grow and make money. In many cases, equipment and technology can make it easier or faster to accomplish routine tasks, making it possible for you to get more done.

One type of equipment you definitely need is a computer, so you might as well start on the right foot.

The major reason to invest in a computer right off the bat is that over time, you will set up certain ways of performing office procedures. Many companies start by doing certain tasks by hand because it is cheaper than buying equipment. However, it's much more difficult to change procedures that were originally done by hand than it is to improve procedures that were set up on the computer from the start.

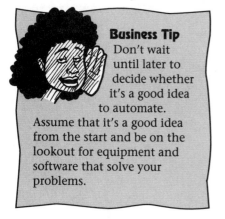

Business Tip
Don't wait until later to decide whether it's a good idea to automate. Assume that it's a good idea from the start and be on the lookout for equipment and software that solve your problems.

Automate the Routine and Savor the Creative

Picture this: You are moving a little screw from the left side of your desk to the right side of your desk and then back again. Repeat. Now, repeat again. Again. And again. Get the picture? Boring!

If you like this type of work, you are probably not cut out for the crazy world of entrepreneurship. Most entrepreneurs I know hate routine stuff such as paperwork, filling out expense reports, doing the bookkeeping, and completing tax forms. For this reason, paperwork, expense reports, bookkeeping, and tax forms are often done late or not done at all. It's a big problem that doesn't have to happen.

Computer programs already exist that can handle most of this boring stuff for you, and many of them cost under $200! Cheap once you own a computer.

You can find a software package to automate most routine office tasks such as word processing, making payroll and tax deductions, keeping spreadsheets, maintaining customer contact information, and more.

As mentioned in previous chapters, you can buy software to set up your company's corporation articles and bylaws and even create a policy manual. Check out the handy table at the end of this chapter that summarizes all these software packages; this should save you some legwork.

Setting up similar systems by hand requires a lot of paper, printed spreadsheets and charts, bound reference material, a calculator or adding machine, note cards, and a lot of pens and pencils. The down side is that all your manual record-keeping is not as accurate as a computerized system. Consider the amount of money you would have spent on supplies and add that to the extra time it takes to track simple customer and financial information by hand; then use that as a rough budget for your computer purchase. I'm sure you can see by now that buying a computer makes a lot of sense.

The weeks (yes, weeks!) you would have spent setting up these operations on your own are instantly eliminated for a small investment! Play your cards right and automate from the beginning.

Business Buzzword
Routine tasks are things you do that are pretty much the same every time you do them. Printing out monthly invoices or counting inventory are two routine tasks that don't take much brain power but that have to be done.

Business Tip
When a computer prints a bunch of numbers, people seem to think they must be true. This can get you into trouble if you make mistakes. Every now and then, spot check your entries to make sure things are accurate.

Typical Automation Strategies

Everyone has his or her own opinions about automation, computer systems, and software. Because it's always useful to hear others' opinions on important subjects, here are my recommendations for automating your business. It might turn out later that my suggestions are not perfect for your particular situation, but they should work well enough to get you started:

1. Look for the routine areas of your business operation that don't require any creativity; doing the same task over and over again is a sure sign of a routine activity. Typical areas include, but are not limited to, generating invoices, sending mass mailings to clients, generating proposals, pricing calculations, tracking customers,

sorting employee performance evaluations, and handling payroll tax-related clerical tasks, accounting, and bookkeeping.

2. Ask other business owners how they handle these areas for themselves. Guess what? They have the same problem. Why not learn from their experience?

3. To handle tasks such as invoicing, bookkeeping, financial report generation, payroll check generation, and tax reporting, look at accounting and payroll packages, such as QuickBooks, QuickPay, M.Y.O.B, and DacEasy, that are compatible with each other and with other software packages you put on your computer.

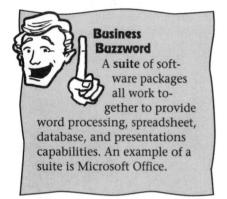

Business Buzzword

A **suite** of software packages all work together to provide word processing, spreadsheet, database, and presentations capabilities. An example of a suite is Microsoft Office.

Bankruptcy Alert

It's good practice to make two backups of your files: one for the office and another that is kept somewhere else in your building, such as in a safe deposit box. If an accident happens or someone steals your equipment, you might lose your software and your backup. The second backup is a safety net and one worth having when the time comes.

4. Pick a *suite* of computer software packages that all work with each other to provide word processing, spreadsheet, database, and presentation capabilities. A suite package combines several different software packages in one, rather than having you buy them separately, which typically costs much more. The most popular suite product sold today is Microsoft Office, which includes Word for Windows (word processing), Excel (spreadsheet), Outlook (database), and PowerPoint (presentation graphics). Claris Works Office works on both PC and Mac operating systems.

5. Take a training class on the software packages. Every day you spend in class will probably save you two to five days of working on your own. Trust me on this one; I see it all the time. The only exception applies to people who already know the packages in question; they stand a chance of making them work without a class.

6. Organize the various working files you create on the computer into meaningful directories, and use meaningful file names to identify them, just as you organize information in a filing cabinet. If you are not the person who creates and maintains this information, make sure you understand the filing system your assistant creates on the computer. Avoid embarrassing situations because your right-hand person has called in sick or decided to quit without notice.

7. Make a *backup* of that data on a daily basis, if possible. Computer hard disk drives fail. When they do, you end up losing your data or paying a lot of money to someone who will probably only recover a small portion of it. Look into backup programs that handle this for you automatically. They're not expensive and will help safeguard all your valuable files.

8. Keep it simple, Simon, is the KISS principle. (Okay, so it wasn't Simon the last time you heard this one. You caught me!) Anyway, keeping it simple is a good thing. You don't want to become a computer geek, spending hours and hours on your computer. You simply want to get your invoices and letters out as easily as possible. Create form letters, standard invoices, and credit letters. Try not to customize everything, and you'll save a lot of time with standard letters and packages.

9. Resist the temptation to apply new technology before someone else has tried it first. Keep away from the leading (or bleeding) edge of technology unless you specifically have the expertise to know what you are getting yourself into. A simple technology snafu can cost you tons of time, money, and aggravation. Let someone else work out the technical bugs.

10. Always invest in printers or copy machines that create high-quality results. The printed page is what your customers see and provides the impression you leave. A laser printer is almost a mandatory investment in today's business world.

Get Connected: Computers and Phones

Marketing and sales will make or break your business. Sales efforts involve keeping customer information, answering telephones, and responding to the mail. The more people you contact in a professional, timely manner, the more likely you are to increase your sales and the closer you are to retiring early. Computers and telephones are part of doing business, and you should take steps to use them to their full capacity.

Computer User

I am going to make this simple. Buy a computer! Take the plunge. You need a computer. Over 75 percent of the computers in use today are Intel-based, IBM PC-compatible types such as IBM, Compaq, Dell, Gateway, and others.

Another kind of computer is the Apple Macintosh brand, which is popular for people who work in graphic arts, layout, design, and multimedia. You'll frequently find Apple computers in advertising agencies, commercial printers, and other creative businesses. Although there are certainly Apple supporters still out there, the fact is that they've lost some ground to *IBM clones* (computers that work exactly like IBMs but are manufactured by different companies). With the Apple PowerMac model, you can now get a combination of Macintosh and Windows-based computers for a little more money. On these, you can use most software programs for either Windows-based or Macintosh systems. People who want the best of both computers often invest in PowerMacs.

Business Buzzword
An **IBM clone** is a computer that works like an IBM but is manufactured by a different company.

Fortunately, most software programs are getting better at recognizing the various programs that are out there, so that it is rarely that you will be unable to convert a file from Windows to Macintosh or vice versa.

If you don't have thousands of bucks to invest in a new computer right now, then maybe you should consider leasing. You pay a regular monthly fee for the use of a computer for a particular period of time, and at the end, you give the computer back or buy it for a small fee. Computer leases work a lot like car leases.

In addition to getting around spending a big chunk of cash all at once, leases also give you time to check out different computers to help decide which is best for you and your business. Of course, this is really only an advantage if you get a relatively short lease to test run the computer. If you sign up for a lease of many months, or years, you're effectively locking yourself in to using that type of computer. You are still able to switch to something else at the end of the lease, but several months down the road, you have all your files set up and know a lot of the programs for that kind of computer. At that point, you're probably not going to want to start over from scratch.

My suggestion is this: Try both a Macintosh and a Windows computer for a couple of days each to see which is easier for you to use and understand. Then, after trying both kinds, decide which one you want to own long term. Signing up for a lease is one way to finance that big investment.

My personal preference is an IBM PC or clone. Make it at least a 233 MHz processor with 32 megabytes of RAM and a 3.2 gigabyte hard disk drive. Also consider getting a CD-ROM drive because most software is sold on CD now (not diskette), a mouse, and 56 Kbps data and fax modem. If these numbers mean absolutely nothing to you, just bring this book to a computer store and have them show you the different models that meet these criteria.

With the computer you should also consider buying a high-quality 15-inch color monitor (because you will spend a lot of time staring at it) and a laser printer for business correspondence. Color inkjet printers have come down in price considerably in recent years to the point where you can buy one for under $200. If you have a little extra money to invest in your computer system, a color printer will certainly help you make a good impression with color presentation overheads and proposal covers.

Now go buy a fancy mouse pad, a computer workstation, and a comfortable chair. You will spend a lot of time using this beast. You might as well save the wear-and-tear on your body from the beginning and get the right stuff to make the boss comfortable. It is easier on you and everyone else!

Reach Out and Touch Someone by Phone

As for telephones, you can use your personal line for business calls, but you'll quickly discover this approach is inconvenient for your customers, your family, and your business. Naturally, your local telephone company charges you for the privilege of adding a telephone line, so economics plays a part in how many separate phone lines you can afford.

It makes sense to set up a separate business phone line right away. One reason is so that customers can find you in the Yellow Pages or through directory assistance. If you're operating from a home office, you have the option of installing another personal line, but don't. The reason is that no one will be able to get your business phone number from the phone book or directory assistance if you use a personal line. You lose business opportunities while only saving a few dollars each month.

Another reason for a separate line is so you can separate your business and personal life. If you have young children, it is imperative that they not speak with customers. You appear very unprofessional if your children answer calls or can be heard screaming in the background. So have a separate line installed.

You will find that one- and two-line phones are common and inexpensive. Make the first line your primary telephone line that is listed in the phone book and have it roll over to the second line when the first is busy. This means that calls to the first line ring on line one if the line is free but ring on line two if line one is busy with a call. You might also want to consider installing a separate phone line to handle your faxes. You will need to send and receive faxes at all hours, and you save yourself hassles by simply dedicating a separate line to fax transmissions.

When you need more than two incoming lines and are still operating from a home office, you need special wiring and have to shell out some money. The capabilities are greater, but the added expense can be substantial if you are not careful.

Voice mail is pretty common these days, having become a mandatory business tool. There will always be a continuing debate about whether a live person answering the phone is better than electronic voice mail, but there are advantages to each. You need to decide what works for you based on your workload and number of phone calls.

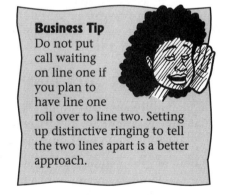

Business Tip
Do not put call waiting on line one if you plan to have line one roll over to line two. Setting up distinctive ringing to tell the two lines apart is a better approach.

I lean toward the electronic approach because the messages are usually more accurate and the cost is less. People who call me and find that I can't answer the phone can simply leave a message with a specific question or answer. Without a receptionist running interference, there is little chance of miscommunication or misunderstanding. However, many people just hate talking to a machine and hang up, even though they would leave a message with a person. I guess the best approach is to have both a live receptionist and the option to leave a message in someone's voice mailbox. That way, it is the caller's decision about what to do.

I suggest that you start with a live person answering your main phone line and monitor the number of messages left. Then compare that average number of messages with the number you receive with an answering machine or voice mail system. If you normally receive 30 calls, and only find five messages on the machine on the days you are out of the office, then you are losing 25 caller contacts during those times. That usually means lost revenue. Experimentation is the key.

To ensure that you rarely lose any calls, consider getting a cellular phone with voice mail as one of the calling features. Use today's technology to keep in touch with your clients and suppliers. Forward your business line to your cellular phone when you are not in the office. When your cellular phone is on, you receive calls without the caller knowing the difference. When your cellular phone is off, callers are forwarded to your voice mail system where they can leave you a message. Cellular technology is so developed now that you can have calls automatically forwarded to you even if you are in another city. The advantage is freedom, but the disadvantage is that it is harder to get away from clients.

For people who want to respond immediately to calls, you can also add a pager to the list of communication tools. Pagers can be set up to buzz or beep when a message is left in your voice mailbox so that you know to check it right away. You can then use your cellular phone to return the call.

Each new phone line and feature costs money, but the telephone is not a place to skimp financially. One lost call can mean a lost customer. How much is one sale worth to your company? How many new customers are needed to pay for this investment in technology? If the number is small (one or two in a month), then it is probably a good investment. If it is too large, look for another solution.

Electronic Mail and Faxing

In the past, electronic mail (e-mail) was used solely by major corporations with internal computer networks. However, the electronic world has expanded, and e-mail is now available to just about everyone at little expense.

You can also install electronic mail as a part of the computer network at your company. Assume that you have a few computers in your offices. You can connect them to each other using some type of local area network (LAN) product, and your employees can share printers and files. This is an improvement on the "sneaker-net" system that many companies have, in which you copy the file to a disk and run down the hall in your sneakers to print it on another person's machine. However, if you have just a handful of employees, an internal electronic mail network might be overdoing it a bit. It might be easier just to yell over the partition.

Electronic mail allows you to send a message (such as an electronic letter) to another person who also has an electronic mailbox. You can also send whole files from computer to computer. In this way, you can share information with others without using paper or overnight delivery services. The process is much faster and often less expensive. In writing this book, the authors e-mailed chapters back and forth with each other and with the publisher, which helped speed the process along.

Commercial services, such as CompuServe, Prodigy, and America Online, provide you with an electronic mail you can use to contact people (if you know their Internet addresses). More on online services later in this chapter.

A great way to maintain contact with your local clients and save money is through effective use of facsimile, or fax, technology. It costs you at least 32 cents, plus printing costs, to mail something via the U.S. Postal Service to your local clients. It costs you nothing, zero, zip, to fax to them, assuming you have unlimited local phone service. The only cost is for the fax paper, which they pay for. Instead of 100 customer contacts costing you $32 or more, it is now free! This is one of my favorite words.

When choosing to lease or purchase a fax machine, consider the convenience versus cost factors carefully. You want to be able to read what comes through the fax. Plain-paper fax machines are really the way to go so that you avoid photocopying faxes that come in on thermal paper. If you go with a thermal fax machine, make sure that it has a paper cutter and takes a long (98 foot) length paper roll, or you will drive yourself, or someone else, crazy cutting the fax pages and changing paper.

Business Tip
Don't expect your computer fax card to replace a fax machine. You will have paper documents to send, such as those requiring a signature or corrected with a pen. You need a regular fax machine in these cases.

Software packages on the market such as Procomm automate the fax procedures. You create the documents that you want to fax and decide who should receive them. Start the program and go home while the documents are faxed to everyone. The fax program also sends documents overnight while you sleep. The following morning, your clients receive this new information from your company and you got a good night's sleep… for free if you have unlimited local service! Yes, this is definitely worth investigating.

Of course, you should definitely check out your state's "junk" fax laws before deciding to send unsolicited information by fax. Some laws in place prohibit you from sending information by fax that someone has not

Bankruptcy Alert
Avoid fax overload. Your clients are happy to hear from you when you have something to say, but don't annoy them by wasting their time and paper. Use fax technology properly, and you can save money while maintaining better contact.

requested. Although companies can send junk mail through the U.S. Postal Service, they generally can't do the same by fax.

Automating Your Sales Procedures

Contact management software is to sales management what the word processor was to the typewriter. You can completely automate your sales contact procedures using one of the many contact management software packages currently on the market. Two popular packages are ACT! from Symantec and Lotus Organizer. Both are available at almost any computer software store.

These packages allow you to keep a complete record of customer addresses, telephone numbers, fax numbers, and e-mail addresses. In addition, you can keep all contact information in one file. For example, you note when you last spoke with a customer, what you talked about, and when you are supposed to make your next contact. This is all done automatically once you enter the information. Keeping such detailed notes helps you stay on top of valuable customer relationships.

My marketing manager came to me the other day with an ACT! success story. She had received a return call from a lady and couldn't remember why she had called her in the first place. She entered the lady's name quickly into ACT!, saw the reason for the call, and closed a sale that otherwise might have been lost. For $150, this program has already paid for itself.

Automating the Payroll

As I mentioned in Chapter 18, "The Tax Files: Payroll Taxes," you shouldn't even think about trying to become a payroll specialist. You don't have the time and probably don't have the expertise to do all the bookkeeping properly. Computer programs already exist that can do this for you in a simple and accurate way. Automated accounting is the way to go if you don't plan to hire an outside company to perform this service.

When evaluating bookkeeping, payroll tax, and accounting packages, be sure they include, as a minimum, the following features:

➤ A flexible chart of accounts that you can set up and modify at a later date to fit your business requirements.

➤ Easy-to-use reporting features (income statement and balance sheet preparation as bare minimums). You might benefit from budget versus actual reporting, or cash flow reports, so don't choose a software package that limits your reporting options too much.

➤ Options that meet your business needs. If you manage payroll or inventory accounting, for example, you need software that can handle those requirements.

This tax stuff is easy and painless, once the initial Social Security, unemployment, and state tax rates are set. Get help in the beginning to set up your accounts properly, and then use the program to track your financial success. You can also run financial statements from these financial packages, so there is no reason for you not to know the state of your company finances.

Other Useful Software

As I mentioned in Chapter 6, "The Implications of Corporations," there are software packages available to help you create legal corporate documents, such as employee policy manuals, corporation articles, and bylaws that you need when starting your business. I mention a couple here that I'm familiar with, but there are other packages. As always, be sure that the documentation you generate has been reviewed by professionals from a legal standpoint:

➤ You can use It's Legal (Parson Technology) for generating your corporation articles and bylaws. It's Legal also provides a standard subcontractor agreement, along with tons of other legal forms.

➤ Try Employee Manual Maker (JIAN Tools) for generating employee policy manuals and business planning documentation.

Planning for Obsolescence

Technology is great stuff. That is the good news. It is also expensive and constantly changing. That is the bad news. Whatever you buy today will probably be a boat anchor in three years. That's right! Three years.

For example, I bought a laptop computer from a factory outlet store in 1991 for $2,200. The same computer had been sold for $4,300 just 90 days earlier. The buyer changed his mind and I got it for 50 percent off the retail price because it was considered used equipment. I sold that same laptop in July of 1994, just three years later, for $650—$1,550 less than what I paid for it. As computer equipment improves and changes, older equipment drops in value very quickly.

This situation is not unusual when dealing with computer equipment. You typically see a major technological advancement every two years and software upgrades every 12 months, which means that you might find yourself constantly investing in newer, better equipment just to keep up.

Buy what you need for today because you need it now. Accept that it will decrease in value and get the most use out of it today. Never buy cutting-edge technology unless you need it. Use the old stuff until it slows down your business's efficiency and bottom line. Then upgrade. You can't guess what new features will be available even months from now; computer technology just changes too fast.

Online Services

CompuServe, Prodigy, and America Online are powerful computer services that can boost your business.

The most commercially available network is America Online (AOL), which recently acquired CompuServe. AOL has more than ten million members. Prodigy also has several million users, although it is more family-focused. All three services provide a software package that you use with your modem to access business discussions and news. You've probably already received a few America Online disks in the mail offering you free usage of the service for several hours.

As I mentioned in Chapter 10, "Cybermarket: Using the Internet," the Internet is an even wider network of communications activities than the commercial online services can offer. However, you can gain access to the Internet through commercial services as well.

CompuServe

How's this for being an entrepreneur? It's 1972. You and your dad are sitting around the house and come up with an idea. People cannot afford their own mainframe (computer-ese for huge) computers but still need to process information. What if you offered a service that allowed them access to a mainframe but on a sharing basis? If you got enough people to sign up, you could divide the cost of operation over a bunch of people and pay for the equipment and make some money. Well, someone and his dad did this, and it worked better than expected.

In 1972, this father-and-son team decided to tap into the massive amounts of processing power available on mainframes that were not being used in the evening and on weekends. Most businesses shut down during those times, but their computers were left running. They sold the processing time for around $5 per connection hour and charged a small connection fee for the service. The rest is history. What started out as MicroNet is now CompuServe and has more than six million subscribers.

CompuServe has tons of special interest groups (SIGs) called *forums*. These are great places to find information from other people who might be in a similar technical, personal, or business situation. Simply double-click the Forums icon on your computer screen and follow your nose to your desired forum.

Business Buzzword
A *forum* is a site on a computer service in which people with similar interests can post and read messages.

A CompuServe subscription costs $19.95 per month and allows unlimited use of the service, including up to 60 e-mail messages per month and a number of general information services. You can also choose to pay an hourly rate of $9.95. CompuServe can be accessed from just about anywhere in the country. To get the details, call 800-848-8990.

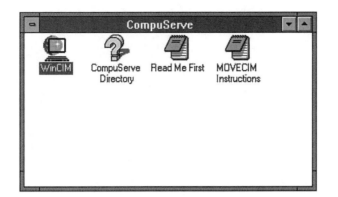

The CompuServe Information Manager (CIM) screen.

The Internet: The New Interstate

Internet-this, Internet-that. Everyone's talking about the Internet, but does anyone really know what the heck this thing is? Well, it's like a huge version of some of the commercial online services such as America Online and CompuServe. You can send messages to anyone else in the world who also has an electronic mail address, and you can do research and participate in discussions on just about any topic imaginable.

The Internet has become such a hot spot that virtually all the other commercial online services I've talked about here now also give you access to the Internet. You only have to join one online service and you can check out all that's happening out in *cyberspace*.

You might find it less frustrating to start with a commercial service that makes things as simple as possible for its subscribers and then graduate to the Internet down the road.

See Chapter 10 for more information about the Internet and World Wide Web.

> **Business Buzzword**
> The electronic world of online services is known as **cyberspace**. You can work from home, your hotel, or a cabin in the woods with equal effectiveness. Does this present incredible possibilities, or what?

America Online

America Online is an excellent place to begin your online adventures. America Online has been around since 1985 and has created one of the friendliest systems on the market. In fact, it bought CompuServe in 1997 after several years of explosive growth.

You can find a subscription to America Online in just about any magazine, new computer purchase information packet, or mail promotion. AOL is rapidly building the number of subscribers to its system and is sending free trial offers to everyone and his brother. You can also call 800-827-6364 to sign up. If you are not ready for CompuServe, give America Online a call. It's a great place to start.

America Online.

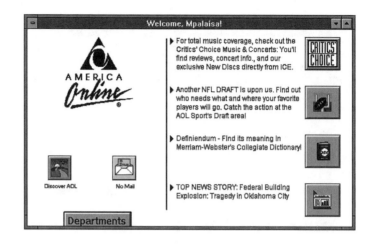

In a Nutshell

Just to keep all this software information in one place for you, I created a handy table (see Table 20.1) that summarizes all the packages I talked about and provided some phone numbers and price ranges to get your automation investigation on the right track.

Table 20.1   Business Planning Related Software Products

Product	Company	Cost	What It Does	Phone
Employee Manual Maker	JIAN Tools	$139	Personnel manuals	800-346-5426
Descriptions Now!	KnowledgePoint	$95	Employee job descriptions	Contact your local retailer.
Policies Now!	KnowledgePoint	$95	Custom policies	Contact your local retailer.
Biz Plan Builder	JIAN Tools	$129	Business plan development assistance	800-346-5426
Marketing Builder	JIAN Tools	$45	Marketing campaign assistance	800-346-5426
Cashmere Business Plan Software	PlanTec	$55	Business plan development assistant	Contact your local retailer.
QuickBooks	Intuit	$129	Business accounting	800-4INTUIT
PeachTree Complete Accounting+	PeachTree	$129	Business accounting	Contact your local retailer.

Product	Company	Cost	What It Does	Phone
ACT!	Symantec	$190	Contact management	Contact your local retailer.
GoldMine management	GoldMine Software	$190		Contact your local retailer.
WinFax	Symantec	$99	Fax management	Contact your local retailer.
FrontPage	Microsoft	$99	Web site development	Contact your local retailer.

The Least You Need to Know

➤ Automate from the start.

➤ Only use technology that is proven. Don't invest big bucks in the latest and greatest untested product.

➤ Automated accounting makes bookkeeping relatively easy to perform, as long as your accounts and procedures are set up properly from the beginning.

➤ Expect that your computer technology purchases will become obsolete in three years, which means you'll need to upgrade your current computer or buy a new one.

➤ Sign up for one of the online services, such as CompuServe or America Online, to gain access to a world of business contacts.

Chapter 21

Defining Your Production Plans

In This Chapter

➤ The importance of your production plan

➤ Production considerations for product and service companies

➤ Production personnel issues

➤ The importance of automation

➤ Setting expectations

Vickie was properly impressed by the activity level on the production floor. Tony, her friend and business owner, had taken his company from the idea stage and turned it into a full-blown production house.

"Wow," she said. "You really have something going on here. Stuff is stacked everywhere, and you literally have people climbing the walls to get at your products. This sure looks good!"

"Well, looks can be deceiving," replied Tony with a somber look in his eye. "The reason those people are climbing the walls is because I did not allocate enough space for inventory storage of finished products. We had to put a shelving system in place so that we stack our finished inventory along walls instead of in an inventory storage area as I initially wanted."

"Why are the wall storage areas color coded?"

"The red areas are for products that have not passed in-process inspection. The blue areas are for finished products that did not initially pass final inspection, have been reworked, and are now awaiting re-inspection. The green areas are for finished products that are ready for sale and shipment," explained Tony.

He paused for a moment and then continued. "Not properly planning and realistically estimating the square footage I needed forced me to hire three people who do nothing but shuttle things from the walls to the production floor and back again."

"It is pretty crowded in here," was Vickie's comment. "And the activity level is pretty intense. Why not just move to another facility?"

"I got a great lease rate by signing up for a three-year minimum. I have 12 more months on the lease that I would have to pay even if we moved to another facility. The money analysis just doesn't justify the move. So here we are: one busy, big, bustling, occasionally irate family waiting for our lease to expire. This is a mistake I will never make again."

No matter what you plan to do, whether it is produce products or provide services, there is some type of process that will be involved. The more efficiently that you plan and manage this process, the more easily you will be able to grow as your sales grow and the lower your costs of production will be.

If you plan to sell gizmos, then whoever funds your project must be convinced that you can build the gizmo you plan to sell. As a result, it is important to understand the production aspects of your business because if you can't produce, you won't get paid.

Production in Product and Service Environments

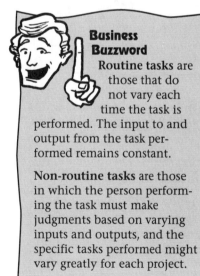

Business Buzzword

Routine tasks are those that do not vary each time the task is performed. The input to and output from the task performed remains constant.

Non-routine tasks are those in which the person performing the task must make judgments based on varying inputs and outputs, and the specific tasks performed might vary greatly for each project.

Think of production as the process of combining raw materials, labor, and manufacturing equipment into a finished good that can be sold.

For example, if you are building music CDs, you have a few components that add up to your finished product: the CD itself, the jewel case in which the CD is shipped, the paper inserts, and a plastic wrapper. You must combine all these pieces so that the final product can be sold in a music store. The process does not vary from one CD to the next. As a result, you can look for ways to streamline the assembly process and develop processes that make the assembly process as efficient as possible.

This type of production involves *routine tasks* that do not vary from one CD to the next. The more CDs that are produced, the better the assembly people become with the process and the more efficient the production process becomes. This increased efficiency translates into decreased manufacturing costs, which provide higher profits if you can keep your prices constant.

This process seems pretty straightforward for a product-based business, but what happens when you provide services, which is what most small business owners start out doing? The equation shifts: Materials become a very small portion of the process and the expertise and labor portion becomes dominant.

Product businesses are based on a process that is relatively independent of the people performing the tasks; service businesses often get their work because the client wants a specific person performing the task. The process and ingredients are different, but some similarities make the analysis of the production process easier to handle.

Service businesses rely heavily on the expertise of the personnel. The jobs typically performed by service personnel are non-routine in nature, meaning that each job is potentially different from the next. This doesn't mean that there aren't similarities, but to use the CD-packaging analogy presented earlier, the jewel case might be a different color, the CD a slightly different shape, and the cover literature might need to be edited for each CD. The overall process of putting it together is the same, but the specific steps required in making it all fit will likely involve tweaking for each CD.

The similarity in developing product and service processes is that you always want to find the common tasks involved in each process. This commonality presents an opportunity for applying automated, money-saving strategies to this stage of the process. Of one thing you can be sure: You will never reach high production volumes if everything you produce is a custom act of creation.

Mentor

If you look at a doctor's office, you see a blending of routine and non-routine tasks and how they are delegated to the proper personnel. For example, taking temperature, blood pressure, weight and performing other routine tasks are handled by a nurse, whereas the non-routine tasks— the examination and evaluation of each patient—are performed by the doctor. The patient might be in the office for an hour, but the doctor might only be with the patient for 15 minutes. In this way, the doctor can see four patients in an hour instead of only one, which would be the case if she performed all the routine tasks on her own.

You might have seen consulting companies that promote their design or assessment methodology. For example, the companies might produce standardized forms that are completed by each client and prescribed actions that are associated with the way those forms are completed. Notice that this is a move on the company's part to move a non-routine environment into a more routine environment by applying a specific methodology every time the overall tasks are performed. This methodology removes a lot of the uncertainty related to a project and allows less skilled personnel to perform many of the tasks.

Here are some key points to remember when defining your production process:

➤ The more times you do something, the more efficient you become at doing it.

➤ Increased efficiency usually translates into reduced costs and can mean increased profits.

➤ The more routine (repetitive) the task, the less skilled the personnel must be to perform it.

➤ The more tasks vary each time performed, the higher the personnel skill level required.

➤ Production in product-based businesses tends to be more routine where mass volume efficiencies are the goal.

➤ Service-based businesses tend to be more time-dependent because the overall project variations can fluctuate from one time a task is performed to the next.

➤ Service-based businesses should look for a methodology that make the non-routine tasks more routine, allowing less skilled personnel to perform the tasks without compromising quality.

➤ Personal customer contact is critical to a service business (would you go to doctor you don't like?), whereas product quality is critical in a product business. (Have you ever met the designer of your Sony Walkman?)

Are You a Mass Producer or a Job Shop?

It's time to add another level to the analysis process. Hang in there with me because this evaluation procedure becomes second nature after a short while. The more you understand your operation, the more likely you are to make it as reliable, efficient, and profitable as possible without sacrificing the overall quality of your offering.

This section compares *mass producer* to *job shop* environments. If you are continually producing the same thing, you are a mass producer. For example, a company that produces candles is a mass producer in that once set up to make candles, the process might make thousands, or even millions, in the single run. Can you imagine how good you get at something once you have done it a few million times?

Job shop environments require more customization to complete each job. This doesn't mean that the same underlying technologies are not used. It only means that they are used in a different way for each job. For example, creating a custom software package is a job shop environment in that the software is developed once for a specific customer. You are not going to take the same software and resell it to others since few other people will need EXACTLY what you developed for earlier customers. You might still perform the software programming operations using a specific programming language, but the software application itself is custom for each customer. Now, if you create the software and then package it for sale on retail shelves, the software creation process is non-routine, but the process of packaging the software and shipping it to Wal-Mart is routine for each software box shipped.

Business Buzzword

Mass producers continually produce the same products. **Job shop** operations require more customization to produce each product.

Mentor

Preparing tax returns is a good example of a service that is strongly routine in nature. Each of our incomes and expenses might be different in dollar amounts, but the overall return for the average person looks pretty much the same in terms of the types of income and deductions allowed. A tax preparation service might train its people to ask certain questions and then decide the level of preparer needed for the tax case in question. In this case, a methodology is developed to route the return to the proper expertise level, with the bulk of the returns completed by minimally trained personnel because the bulk of returns are not that complicated.

Certain parts of your company's operation will be routine, but others will be non-routine. You need to match the right people with the right tasks and "routinize" tasks wherever possible to take best advantage of the highly skilled personnel needed for the non-routine tasks. Performing this blend properly is one critical aspect of successful operations management. Notice that it affects your hiring decisions, personnel requirements, and the overall confidence you have in the quality of your offering.

> **Mentor**
>
> I have some friends who run a small business that specializes in custom injection plastic molding of very large parts. Once the process is set up, they might produce only one, two, or three parts for a customer. This is clearly not a mass production environment, but they have a unique process methodology that allows them to create the required parts in a reliable fashion. If they based their pricing model on mass production economies, they would be out of business. They realize that their offering is unique and charge the premiums needed to ensure that the customer does not get gouged, yet they cover the costs associated with a job-shop environment.

Linking Purchasing, Production, and Marketing Forecasts

Get ready; here comes another automation speech. If you have ever worked in a product manufacturing environment that did everything by hand, you understand the importance of automating your purchasing and inventory processes.

This can get pretty complicated, but it is really important, so bear with me. You need to order parts from your vendors before you can build your product. This means that you must have quantity projections about the products to be built. In addition, each of the components that you include in your product has some delivery lead time requirement from your vendors. This lead time can be as short as overnight for a standard part, such as a screw, or as long as several months for a custom casting part, such as the frame of a bicycle. This means that before the components can be purchased, you must know how many you plan to build, which means that you must know how many your sales and marketing people plan to sell.

The service equivalent is finding a person with the proper skill set to address your customer needs. You must either hire this person with the required skills, hire a person and train her to have the required skills, or train one of your internal personnel to have the proper skills. In any case, you have a lead time involved. You even have a lead time involved if you already have an employee with the proper skills on staff. Why? Because if you are operating profitably, that person is already busy on another project and might have to finish it before he can start on the new one.

Oh, by the way, you also need to ensure that you have the financial means to purchase the components (or hire the personnel) because there will be some manufacturing lead time on your side before the product gets out the door and into customer hands and you receive the payment. Before you flip out, go back to Chapter 13, "Cash Is King," and

Chapter 14, "Taking Charge: Credit Card Sales," and reaffirm to yourself that cash is king, credit is queen, and luck is the joker.

Most of the accounting software packages that I have seen, such as QuickBooks, allow you to track purchasing, inventories, and sales but don't integrate forecasting. Most of the canned sales support packages I have seen, such as ACT!, allow you to track contacts but really don't allow you to track forecasts.

How can you manage the critical gap between your sales forecast and your production and purchasing requirements? You either need to handle this gap in a rigorous, yet manual, manner at first, pay someone to develop custom software, or scour the industry for a software package that addresses your specific company needs. These packages are out there, but you might pay thousands of dollars finding the package that is right for you. They are generally referred to as *manufacturing requirement packages (MRP)*.

Is an MRP package worth the initial investment? It depends on how large you plan to grow and how substantial your initial funding is. Paying a lot for the right production control software package could deplete your cash reserves to the point that you jeopardize the company. Clearly not a good idea.

In keeping with my "automate from the beginning" philosophy, I suggest that you either buy the package if possible or train yourself to think of your company as a process from sales, through purchasing, through production, through shipping, to receipt of the product by the customer, to receipt of the payment check from the customer, to the final cashing of the check.

Business Buzzword
Software packages that link sales forecasts to production and purchasing requirements are generally referred to as **manufacturing requirement packages** (MRP).

Begin Mentor

With all of this automation, make sure that you don't lose the human touch. No computer will ever know your business as well as you do. Make sure that you spot check your MRP reports to ensure that the numbers flowing from sales to productions to purchasing make business sense based on your experience. The longer you are in business, the more accurately you will be able to estimate your sales forecasts, which better ensures proper production goal setting.

Create a Production Flow Chart

You don't have to become a process engineer to build many products, but you should have an idea of how the process flow works and what sections need special attention. This involves a big sheet of paper, or the use of a software package such as CorelFLOW, Microsoft Project, or other flow charting and project management software packages.

Map out the entire process on a piece of paper, and note which steps are routine or non-routine. Also map out the weak links, or *gating items*, in the process. These are the items that restrict your ability to produce in higher volumes (mass production) or produce in less time (job shop). Making these gating items more efficient always pays huge dividends later and you need to watch them like a hawk, for these are the items that can also put you out of business.

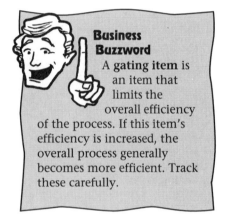

Business Buzzword
A **gating item** is an item that limits the overall efficiency of the process. If this item's efficiency is increased, the overall process generally becomes more efficient. Track these carefully.

For example, a large airplane manufacturer recently went through a huge sales growth spurt where its sales and marketing people sold many new planes to several foreign governments. Good news? Not for this company. They couldn't get many of their critical parts from their vendors in time to meet the production schedules. They had to shut down their plant for a few weeks in 1997 while they waited for the gating item parts to arrive. Here is a company with a stellar sales record and a black eye simply because it outsold its production capability due to gating item parts.

Finally, look at your process map, and determine the amount of space needed for each stage of production. Don't forget that the raw inventory parts that you receive from your vendors need storage space along with the finished products. In addition, products that go through many stages of production need interim storage space along with those products rejected during the production process. If you don't take a detailed look at the space requirements early, you might end up like our friend in the opening story who had employees literally climbing the walls.

Mentor

Another small business owner I know created a product for holding snow skis while people traveled from their home to a ski resort. It was a hard plastic shell with end caps. He had an outside company build the products for him from parts that he got from other sources. The problem was that once the products were completed and ready to sell, he had no place to put the large number of them because each one took up a lot of space. He ended up dedicating a room in his house to finished goods storage which pleased his wife to no end. It kept his overhead down but wasn't helpful for domestic relations, if you know what I mean.

Successful Project Management

I am not going to go into the details of project management in this chapter, other than to point you in the direction of understanding basic project charts and tools. By the way, another book in this series called *The Complete Idiot's Guide to Project Management* is an excellent introduction to project management. I suggest using it to add meat to the skeleton outline provided in this section.

A *Gantt chart* shows you the relationship between the various project components and their required orders of completion (see the following figure). I create my Gantt charts on a spreadsheet package with the tracked items listed in the left column and the column headings labeled as the weeks, or days, on which each stage of the project is to be completed.

The *critical path analysis* allows you to determine the process bottlenecks so that you can keep an eye on them. Project management software packages perform this critical path analysis for you. You don't have to go overboard on all this stuff in the beginning, but if you don't get a realistic picture of your space and time requirements, you can be seriously hit later when you get into actual production.

To quote Hannibal on the A-Team, "I love it when a plan comes together." There are few better feelings in the world than creating a process flow on paper and then seeing it work in action, just as you planned it. Do it once, and you might be hooked. I was.

By the way, the more detail you have in your planning, the more likely you are to get money from your investors. The details show them that you have thought through the steps and understand what you are doing. Without the details, you are winging it with their money. Think about it. Would you rather give money to someone who has spent the time thinking about the details or to someone who says, "Trust me; it will be okay"?

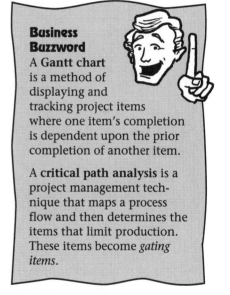

Business Buzzword

A **Gantt chart** is a method of displaying and tracking project items where one item's completion is dependent upon the prior completion of another item.

A **critical path analysis** is a project management technique that maps a process flow and then determines the items that limit production. These items become *gating items*.

Maintaining Quality

Nothing will put you out of business faster than being a new company that gets a reputation for bad quality. Happy customer referrals are critical to the success of your business, and if you let the quality suffer, your referrals will become negative instead of positive. Ouch, then bye-bye!

CIG to Starting Your Own Business, First Edition
Project writing schedule - Gantt Chart
cigtimng.xls

Milestones		12/23	12/27	12/29	1/2	1/5	1/9	1/12	1/16	1/19	1/23	1/26	2/2	2/6	2/9	2/13	2/16	2/19	2/22	2/25
	25% Completion				MM															
	50% Completion										MM									
	100% Completion																MM			
	Author Review																	XX	---	XX
Chapter No.	Introduction																	XX		
1	So, why go into business....		▓																	
2	Preparing the business plan	▓																		
3	Strategic vs. tactical planning			▓																
4	Which business form to choose							▓												
5	Additional corporation considerations								▓											
6	Effective marketing makes selling easier									XX										
7	Dealing with competition										XX									
8	Without sales, nothing happens										XX									
9	Making sure that you are making money						▓													
10	Working with banks...										XX									
11	Cash is more important than you mother											XX								
12	Setting up for credit card sales					SS	▓													
13	What to do if they don't pay				▓															
14	Complicating life by adding employees												XX							
15	Simplifying payroll....													XX						
16	Other stuff...													XX						
17	Using automation															XX				
18	Dealing with success															XX				
Appendix A	An actual business plan									XX										
Appendix B	Glossary																		XX	
Legend:	Milestone	MM																		
	Proposed Completion Date	XX																		
	Duration of Completion	XX	---	XX																
	Completed Item	▓																		

A sample Gantt Chart.

I recently gave a speech to a group of quality professionals on the importance of instilling quality in small business environments. It forced me to formalize some of my thoughts on the topic. The talk was well received, so here is a synopsis of the high points for your consideration and specific application to your company environment:

➤ Know what you sell and what your customers buy. Make sure that the critical qualities that your customers expect from your product or service are inspected by you or someone who knows your standards before your customers see your offering. This applies to both product and service companies. If your company offers massage services, every now and then get a massage by each of your massage personnel to ensure that it meets your standards.

➤ Don't ever let your customers become your final product inspection team. Make sure your product or service meets your expectations before you let them see it. They won't ever forget that you sold them deficient goods.

➤ *Under-promise* and *over-deliver.* This is where I see many small business owners suffer. Because you are small, you might feel that you have to over-promise to compete with a larger company. You know that you are over-promising when your evenings and weekends are tied up doing extra stuff for a customer, and you are cursing yourself for having promised things that are not part of what you normally offer. If what you promised must be there as part of the standard offering, then make the proper production changes and set up for it. If not, do not over-promise unless you have a lot of free time.

➤ Never *over-promise* and *under-deliver.* You can deliver exactly what all of your brochures promote and still have an unhappy customer if the customer was promised additional items that were not delivered. This is an easy problem to fix. Only promise what you can deliver or know that you and the company will continually be jumping through hoops complying with "loose lips" promises.

➤ Personally spot-check the products or services before they leave your business, and let everyone know that you do it. This tends to keep employees on their toes and ensures that your toes don't get stepped on.

➤ Work with customers up front to set their expectations. This is particularly true for service agreements, or you can find yourself working for a client forever, with the best of intentions, not getting paid for it, and still having an unsatisfied customer even though you delivered what you thought they wanted. For example: "My Company agrees to supply Your Company with a draft of the document, circulate the draft to the client for comments, and then incorporate those comments into the final draft." Notice how only one level of revision is included in this agreement; this means you do not waste time and resources endlessly revising your work.

Business Buzzword
When you **over-promise**, you make a commitment to a customer that exceeds what your company is set up to deliver. When you **under-deliver**, you deliver less than what was promised. This behavior is almost guaranteed to generate a nasty phone call and possibly a poor recommendation from your customer.

Savvy business owners may **under-promise**—that is, promise to deliver less to the customer than they actually intend to deliver. Nobody ever gets mad when they receive more than they expected for the same price.

➤ Define concrete expectations, and do not leave them general. (General: "To deliver a product or service to the customer's satisfaction." Concrete: "To deliver a product that meets the specifications as outlined on product specification sheet 01-A, dated 9/27/98.")

The Least You Need to Know

➤ You must understand how your company creates and delivers its offerings and then ensure that the quality that makes you successful is an integral part of the process.

➤ Understand the routine and non-routine aspects of your business, and assign personnel accordingly.

➤ Automate as much as possible from the beginning (again!).

➤ Map out your production process and understand the personnel, raw materials, space, and equipment needed at each step of the process.

➤ Under-promise and over-deliver.

➤ Know what you offer and what your customers buy.

➤ Spot-check quality yourself and never let your customers do your final quality inspection.

Chapter 22

The Secrets of Your Success

In This Chapter

➤ The personal aspects of success

➤ The financial pitfalls of success

➤ Separating reality from your public image

➤ When to pass the baton

"Rick does seem a little disoriented lately," said Emily to her husband. She started working for Rick five years ago and had never seen him like this. "It's weird. He shows up late for meetings, signs checks weeks after they are written by the accountant, and just doesn't seem to care. I hope that he's okay."

Jack, her husband, shook his head. "He just sounds bored to me."

"How could he be bored?" cried Emily. "We're doing more business than ever. Our clients are happier than ever, and we just can't seem to do anything wrong. The word around town is that our rocket is the right one to be affiliated with, and Rick made all of this happen. How could he be bored?"

"I'm sure that Rick likes all the activity and the money," said Jack. "I'm talking about the daily routine. He has never struck me as a 9 to 5 sort of person, and now he has to show up to make sure things get done. Sometimes, he even has to wear a tie; you know how he feels about them! He has essentially become an administrator. That's like putting a racehorse in a petting zoo. Maybe Rick needs to run again."

"What do you suggest?" asked Emily. She felt Jack was onto something here, but she was too close to the situation to clearly see the next step.

"Take him out for a cup of coffee and tell him what you think. He might be waiting for you to come forward as his replacement," said Jack. "You are the natural successor, and I'd be amazed if Rick was against giving you even more decision-making power at this point. Maybe he just needs you to give him a nudge, to let him know you are ready to take on more authority."

Emily smiled. She remembered Rick's energy during the early years of the company, as they succeeded in growing 200 percent a year. She wanted to see that energy and enthusiasm return. Maybe Rick could focus on the new publishing side of the business, leaving her to manage the training side that had become the company's bread and butter. That would be a win for all concerned. But how would Rick react?

Do you remember in the beginning I promised you one of the most exciting rides of your life? Well, here you are, and I hope that this book has contributed to your successful journey. Keep your professional perspective while basking in your success. You earned it!

Your fears and joys have found you. You are still in business and exceeding your wildest expectations. In short, you and your business are a success. Too cool!

Bask in the glory of your new situation, but know that success has its own sets of traps that can undo all your hard work and achievements. This chapter is designed to introduce you to life after success and to help you decide what comes next in your business venture.

Business Tip
Find a quiet, peaceful place and ask yourself this question: "If I don't go out of business, then what will I do?" Watch the flood of insight that occurs when you stop focusing on just making it. Where should you head next?

Dealing with the Personal Aspects of Success

As you built your business, you undoubtedly put in long hours, suffered through numerous trials, and dug deeper into your soul than you ever thought possible. Otherwise, you would not be where you are now. As a business owner, you recognize all the hard work and commitment it takes to keep a business going. Business life is different for you now, and your new insight is well-earned.

They All Love You When You Are Successful

Who helped you when you first started out? Think about it. Were there many colleagues and advisers or just a few? Were they old friends or new acquaintances who saw that what you were trying to achieve had merit? Many people who know you today probably did not know you back when things were tough.

Nothing breeds business interest faster than the smell of money. Your business success makes you a desirable business partner, dinner date, speaker, and financial planning client. You will soon appear on everybody's mailing list. You will be invited to parties and other social functions. You might even be the guest of honor. (Can you believe it?) These acknowledgments are well-deserved, and I encourage you to enjoy them while they last. I also encourage you to remember that you can become an unknown again as quickly as you became a success.

People who helped you along the way might need help themselves from time to time. Supporting competent people who stood by you in the past almost always pays positive dividends. Remember: Unless you are extremely lucky, you and your business will have a wide array of ups and downs. Business, family, and personal friends are the people who will get you through the dark times and allow you to prosper when it is light again.

Success breeds success, but it also brings out opportunists who try to benefit from all your hard work and offer nothing in return. Determine early in your business relationships whether someone is trying to offer help, take help, or use you—and respond accordingly.

Watch Your Ego and Your Pocketbook

Have you ever known someone whose emotional state was linked to his credit cards? The better his mood, the more money he spent. Now multiply that effect several times over and you have the potentially dangerous situation of a successful business owner whose ego is linked with the financial success of the company.

Mentor

I have seen people, including myself, start to pay for events, dinners, and other nonessential items simply as a way of expressing their business ego. I was essentially saying that the business was doing so well that I didn't need to worry about petty little things like a few hundred dollars for dinner. In reality, frivolously spending that money drove me nuts, but I still did it. I just needed to stroke my ego with my charge card. That's very dangerous.

Bankruptcy Alert
You might be tempted to look at your company's profits as a means for you to enjoy yourself. This is a scary situation. Before you spend, ask yourself this: "If this were other people's money and I were the president of their company, would I still spend the money this way?"

Bankruptcy Alert
If your business is structured as a corporation, the money that comes into the business cannot be spent for your personal use unless you take it as income, dividends, or a stock sale. It belongs to the company separately. However, if you run a sole proprietorship, taking money out of the business is fine from a tax standpoint because you and the business are really one entity. However, you shouldn't be spending company funds on yourself.

Once the business gets to a certain point, you will be tempted to dip into the till and spend for personal gratification instead of for business. Sure, it is your business; nobody doubts that. The issue revolves around your need to spend company resources for personal gratification. Several thousand dollars is a lot to an individual, but a nominal amount to a business. Beware when you start to spend business money for items the business doesn't really need. You can spend your company right out of business if you're not careful and put yourself, the company, and the employees in the same spot they were in a few years ago when first starting up. You owe them and yourself more than that.

Pat yourself on your back for your successes, but leave the business checkbook at work. Even the United States constitution requires a separation of powers. You should do the same, even if only in your mind. Don't treat your business as your personal checkbook.

Instinct Is Good, but Planning Makes It Work

Thinking on your feet is a great characteristic for boxers and business people. Here is the potential problem: How do you maintain the quick decision-making techniques that got you through the early times while still moving in a smart direction today? I have seen successful business people violate their own plans because they thought a new direction was better than the one previously evaluated. Don't move too quickly to change company direction or switch strategy just for the sake of change.

Now that the company is really doing well, avoid the tendency to think that you are always right. Your instincts obviously are good, but rely on input from your staff regularly to ensure you don't miss opportunities. In many cases, your employees might have excellent suggestions and strategies to propose that could be better than your initial plans. Don't leave them out of the decision-making process. Get others involved so that the company can grow and prosper.

Even When It's Going Great, You Still Feel Like Throwing Up!

Old habits die hard, and this is one of those tough situations for people who survive hard times. When you become used to difficult times, it is hard to adjust to good times. It might become so stressful that you wonder, "When will the situation go back to normal—back to those hard times?"

I don't think you ever let go of the fear that things can go back to how they were in the slow, old days. I remember days in a row when my phone did not ring. My training lab often felt more like a tomb than a thriving business. In the very early days of the company, during the late 80s, economic times in Austin were tough, few people knew who we were, and our product mix was untested. Marketing efforts were underway, but it just took time for them to work. Things were slow. When I thought we might go under, I was physically ill.

Things are better today. Much better! (Whew!) But I still have this nagging fear that activity will suddenly drop off for no reason and we will be back where we were. I use this fear to keep me moving forward with new ideas, marketing approaches, and business concepts.

Business Tip
Know that slow times happen as part of the start-up phase, and don't let them get you down. Use these times to invest in more marketing, developing new products and services, training to improve your skills, and planning for the future. Once things get rolling, you will probably have less time for these activities.

Take a Reality Check

Keep people around who can act as a sounding board. Sometimes you need to make important decisions and your employees cannot give you the feedback you need. In many cases, you need to consider whether to invest more of your personal funds to grow the company or how to improve your personal life without damaging the business. Only you can make some of these decisions, and other business owners are often the best advisers to consult for those issues.

I have a team of fellow business people who know me, know my business, and bring tremendous business expertise to the table. They act as my reality check when I make major decisions. I encourage you to keep out a sharp eye for such people so you can form your own personal network of business advisors. They are invaluable resources as rapid growth and its associated opportunities arise. Setting up an informal business advisory or discussion group can be an invaluable way of getting regular feedback from trusted colleagues.

Business Tip
You invest your own money in a way that promotes the company's success and your own personal goals. You have to invest in your business to keep it going; just do it wisely.

> ### Mentor
>
> One of my employees wants me to invest in another training lab. She contends that we are losing money by not having the additional space and wants me to make the investment. For her, it is a matter of where she spends her time. For me, it is a three-year commitment to making that lab work. She can get another job, but I can't think of working for someone else unless the company goes under and I'm forced.
>
> I gave her the three estimates for the additional training lab (all were over $100,000) and asked her if she knew enough about the business opportunity to happily invest at least $100,000 of her own money. She looked serious for a moment as she realized the decision that I had faced. She is now working on a financial and capacity utilization report to justify the additional expense.

Dealing with the Financial Aspects of Success

It eventually comes down to money. You must be making money or you would be out of business. Congratulations! Now that you have all that cash floating around, take a look at some potential pitfalls associated with the financial aspects of success.

When Small Expenses Turn into Big Bucks

> ### Bankruptcy Alert
> Spending $200 here, $300 there, and another $700 on a new piece of equipment adds up to $1,200. Would you have spent $1,200 on that particular combination of items? If so, the money was well spent. If not, then you need to start considering all expenses above a certain dollar amount in terms of their total impact on the company and not as separate, unrelated purchases.

I have several coffee cans at my house that are filled with pennies, nickels, dimes, and quarters. A friend recently visited and noted that there was probably a lot of money in those cans. Funny how all of those little coins add up to some major savings.

Likewise, in your business, little expenses here and there can add up to big cash drains. This is particularly true when you allow your employees to order products, inventory, and office supplies without your approval. You have to let go of many tasks for the company to grow, which includes some purchasing functions. However, a surprise bill for thousands of dollars is never fun. Set up procedures for tracking or approving expenses over a certain threshold (for example, $200). Review your accounting on a monthly basis and always review your financial statements to ensure that your expenses aren't way out of line. It is your job to keep the company financially healthy. If you can't do that job, you should find someone such as an accountant or bookkeeper who can.

Watch Your Overhead

Overhead is a revenue-eating shark. Every month it requires the same, if not more, cash feeding than the month before. This is the nature of overhead items. They occur every month, and you must pay them or you are out of business. Generally, these include office rent, utilities, phones, and employees. If sales drop off, you still have to pay these. It is scary to write checks for each of these expenses during months when sales are low. If the situation continues for long, you need to take steps to correct it, which often means reducing overhead through layoffs and downsizing the operation. These are tough decisions for any business manager.

Avoid the situation by only adding to overhead when absolutely necessary. Avoid spontaneously adding people, space, or equipment unless you know that the expense is justified for the long-term. (Refer to my lab expansion example in the earlier in the chapter.)

By keeping your overhead low and your relationships with contractors and temporary agencies in good standing, you have the ability to provide your clients with the services they need. That is your secret weapon when competing against the big guys: You are nimble enough to adapt to a client's particular situation and can charge less because of lower overhead expenses. The big guys have a lot of inertia and overhead, which can seriously get in the way of change. By the time they realize that they should change, you have already won some of their customers.

Justifying New Employees

When you are lean and hungry, your tendency is to watch where every penny goes and squeeze as much performance out of your personnel as possible. When things start to go better and you feel a little more comfortable, you might be tempted to hire that additional person or two that will take some of the load off you or your staff.

This might be a solid business decision, or it might be a decision driven by your personal desire for a little less pressure. If you aren't careful, you can end up increasing your salary costs to the point that your currently solvent business becomes top-heavy. It is sometimes ego-gratifying to have a large number of employees, but all of that gratification goes away in a second when you can't pay your bills.

Make your hiring decisions based on sound financial judgment. If the numbers work out, then you have an employee who can pay for himself. If not, and you still hire this person, then you know it is a speculative arrangement that eventually might have to end if business takes a downturn. After all, non-essential personnel are the first to go. Right?

Follow this procedure to determine whether you need another employee:

1. Determine the salary range of a person with the needed skills. Ask what other business owners pay for people performing the same work to get a benchmark.

2. Add between 15 and 30 percent to that number to account for payroll taxes and other benefits such as vacation and sick time.

Business Tip

Make sure that you perform the incremental revenue analysis based on gross margin, after the cost of goods sold (COGS) are taken out, or you might find yourself caught on the lean side of the money equation. If the person creates $100 in new revenue, and your COGS is 30 percent, then the amount of gross margin that can be applied to operating expenses, including the new salary, is only $60. If you use $100, you are inflating this person's worth. Use the $60 and play it safe.

Bankruptcy Alert

It is a good idea to perform periodic, spontaneous spot audits of the money flow in your company. This becomes more important the further you get away from the daily operational action. Also, make sure that multiple people must handle the receipt and deposit of cash or checks received by the company. This ensures that at least two people must cooperate in skimming cash or checks.

3. Outline the current costs that the business incurs, which are associated with the tasks that this new person would perform.

4. Add to that additional revenues that the company would gain as a result of freeing up the current personnel or the actions of this particular person. This is especially important in the case of a sales or marketing person.

5. Subtract the new employee cost from the sum of the new revenues and anticipated cost savings. If the difference is positive, then this is a reasonable personnel slot. If not, then you might either expand this new person's duties or hold off for awhile.

You might find your own variations on this evaluation procedure, but the net result must come up the same. You cannot hire people who do not pay for themselves either by reducing costs (such as hiring a person full-time instead of using more expensive contractors) or by generating adequate new revenues so that the gross margin pays their employment costs.

Handing Over the Checkbook

Afraid to hand over the checkbook to your most trusted assistant? You should be! It is a big deal and you should treat it as such. Once you turn it over, it is tough to take it back without hard feelings.

You can stall passing the checkbook by taking a few steps to get you out of daily activities while still maintaining some control:

1. Set up credit accounts with your suppliers and let your assistant be the one who approves purchases while running them past you at the end of the month.

2. Start to involve your assistant in your financially related business decisions. Show him how you analyze different purchases and situations so he knows how you would handle a situation. This doesn't mean he must give up his own perspective, but he must understand that it is your money he is spending.

3. Be sure this is the right time to let go; you might be going through a semipersonal crisis that will pass. If so, you might be back to normal in a short period of time. If not, and you are ready to remove yourself from the day-to-day operation of the business, then it's time to pick a successor and begin the training program.

Mentor

I separated several stages of the financial flow process to protect myself and the company's funds. The same person creates invoices and makes check deposits after first making a photocopy of the check and the invoice stub. The photocopy is given to the bookkeeper, who makes the appropriate accounting entries. I am also given a copy of the receivable aging report and other financial statements at the same time. I sign all checks written against the company checkbook. Notice from this flow that the accountant and the employee must work with each other to ensure that I can't figure out if some form of theft is occurring. To be even safer, I can have another person make the deposits, but I choose not to carry it that far and I have never been burned... that I know of.

Reporting and budgeting becomes critical when you hand over the checkbook. Set up the financial reports and budgeting process so you can closely track the company's overall financial performance at least monthly. Otherwise, things can get out of hand without your knowledge. Look at all the celebrities who lost their shirts when they turned over their financial dealings to another person. You are right to be cautious in this regard. Don't rush this decision, but make it if you think it's the right move for the company.

Dealing with Ups and Downs

This section covers a tough topic. Every business goes through its high and low points. When the highs are more frequent than the lows, everyone is happy. When the lows hang on for awhile, interesting personnel dynamics start to happen.

You are going to see good and bad times. This is especially true if you are in a seasonal business, such as retail or sprinkler system installations in New England. You have to plan the rest of the year to accommodate these lows or you won't be able to start business when your high season starts again—and it will start again! You have to believe that or you should find another career.

I have seen a few different reactions to down times and they seem to mostly depend on the personality type of the person involved:

1. Some managers deny that anything is wrong and keep going with business as usual, even when critical depletion of company funds is happening. This ostrich approach to management is rarely a good idea.

2. The over-reaction managers see two days of low income as a terminal illness. These people often turn the organization upside down for the simple reason that they weren't patient enough to let things turn around on their own. This approach causes mayhem, depletes employee morale, and drains company resources in paying for the changes.

3. Some people see that something is wrong and believe that it will turn around, so they keep hocking their heart and soul to keep the dying business alive. When this kind of business finally dies, it is really a heart breaker.

4. Some people see a few months of downturn and close up shop. Take the money and run. These people suffer the next time they start a business because their clients from the previous company know that they have minimal staying power.

Which is the right approach? You will only know the answer to this question in retrospect. You, as the manager, get paid to decide the proper course for the company. I suggest that you take a combined approach from the preceding types, and look at things this way:

➤ Know how much you are willing to risk before closing up shop.

➤ Talk to your customers and find out why things are slow. They might be in a special budget cycle that will clear itself up in 60 days, and they already have money budgeted for your company's offerings.

➤ Ask employees if they want to take some time off either without pay or to use up vacation. Either way you win.

➤ Protect yourself by never allowing reserve cash to drop below the point where you can still pay your bills, salaries, and payroll taxes and get out with your skin. It is painful enough to close a business. It is even more painful to close a business and pay off its debts for the next few years.

➤ Talk to other business owners to determine whether they are seeing the same downturn. (However, beware of talking to competitors because they will always tell you things are great, especially if they think that you are having problems.)

➤ Make whatever decisions you make for your own reasons. Be fair to your employees, customers, and yourself, and you will either weather the storm or close up shop with your reputation intact for your next round.

Unless you are in a business segment that has become obsolete, such as the steel manufacturing business, any downturn you see is probably only temporary. Whoever has the deepest financial pockets wins in this situation. You can't stop selling and you have to keep on doing what you do best while you walk through what might seem like a tunnel. Know that it will turn around eventually, and have preset safety limits to ensure that you don't bankrupt yourself in the process of waiting for the turn around.

Use the high periods to stash three to six months of liquid assets so that you can weather the lows. When things slow down, she who has the most cash wins.

Don't Believe Your Own Hype

You really have three faces when your company is small: the face your company presents to the outside world of prospects and customers, the face you present to your staff and other company personnel, and the face you present to confidants and family. The one you present to the outside world is essentially your "advertising" face and should not be confused with reality.

You would never advertise that your company is struggling with a particular issue or problem. This doesn't mean the problem doesn't exist, just that you are dealing with it quietly and internally. You might advertise that your services are the best in town, but if customer feedback indicates satisfaction problems, you need to address them or you are out of business. If you believe your advertising, you might think things are fine when they are really in trouble

Keep your ego out of the way and monitor company performance with a keen eye on reality. Make your external promotions as positive, upbeat, and benefit-oriented as possible, but don't deceive yourself or your staff in the process. There are always internal struggles that you must handle for your company to continue to be successful.

When Is It Time for You to Step Aside?

This section covers a tough question. When is it time to let go and turn the reins over to someone else? Every situation is different, but here are a few points to consider:

1. Are you doing what you want to do? Just because you started the business doesn't mean that you must still like it. Would you rather be doing something else on a daily basis?

2. Would you serve the company better in another capacity? Perhaps the temperament that served the company in start-up mode no longer applies to a maturing business. Should you turn over the day-to-day operations to your more consistent associate who likes the daily grind?

3. Should you merge the company with another so that the joint skills and marketing capabilities together can be more powerful? The president of the other company could become president of the new company. This takes care of your people, clients, and you.

4. Do your employees want to own the company? Perhaps you should sell the company to them, freeing yourself for other entrepreneurial ventures.

You will know when the time is right to get out of the way. If you have a corporation with a board of directors, they will probably let you know when you become more of a liability to the company than an asset. This isn't a personal insult, just a recognition that different skills might now be needed to grow the company. Your business is now at the point where professional management needs to take over and the entrepreneur needs to look for new business and growth opportunities.

Instead of treating opportunities for change and transition as a negative, I encourage you to view them as an opportunity and look for the right combination of talents and positions. You were successful before, and you will be successful again. Sharing that success is a treat rarely experienced; consider yourself lucky to have the opportunity.

The Least You Need to Know

➤ Beware of turning over the company checkbook to others without safeguards in place.

➤ Adjust your thinking to accept that fact that others might now see you as the big guy that they need to compete against.

➤ Don't always believe what other people say about you. Don't pretend that there aren't any problems when there really are; just deal with them quietly.

➤ Don't mix your personal interests with those of the company. Your decisions must make good business sense for the company, or you can cause more harm than good.

➤ Step aside when the time is right. Treat your obsolescence as a sign of your success instead of as a threat to your survival. You might be able to better serve the company in other ways while letting other managers deal with the routine, daily issues.

The Kwik Chek Auto Evaluation Business Plan

Recommendations for Using This Business Plan

What follows is an actual business plan I wrote back in the late 1980s for a used car evaluation service business called Kwik Chek. When I wrote this business plan I was trying to determine whether the idea would fly as an independent investment with national franchise potential or whether I should go back to the drawing board and find a new idea.

The plan showed that the idea wasn't right for me since I did not want to be doing the work on the cars myself, and the analysis shows that owner/operator management was the way to go. Notice that the plan did what was expected of it. It told me that this idea did not fit my criteria for a business venture that I wanted to sink my time and money into. For the right person who is willing to do the work required, this plan could easily be modified for presentation to investors or could be self-funded. (Make sure that you update the numbers for the 1998 marketplace and verify that it still makes money before taking the plunge.)

I encourage you to review this plan as a road map for the development of your own plan and don't take the specific plan content too literally. You might notice that the exact section titles and flow do not exactly match those shown on the tear card or within Chapter 4, "Preparing Your Business Plan." Don't let this throw you. A plan should address the questions of the intended readers which means that sections can be added or deleted as needed. Your plan should always include an executive summary along with the business description, competition, marketing plan, organization, operations, funding requirements, and financial statements sections. The industry analysis, market analysis, and conclusion section contents will vary based on the market familiarity of the intended readers.

This point is very important. The appendix should support the overall plan contents and the overall plan contents should support the conclusions drawn in the executive summary. Write the executive summary after you have completed the plan to avoid writing something that meets your picture of how things should be as opposed to how they really are.

This Kwik Chek plan should serve as a model as you prepare your own business plan but it will probably not become your business plan. Your levels of detail, section flows and writing style will probably differ from that presented in the Kwik Chek plan. That is okay. It is YOUR plan for YOUR company. No single plan can do justice to the numerous business opportunities and entrepreneur styles that exist. Read this plan as a guide, and make your plan your own. Good luck and start writing.

Executive Summary

This plan presents the Kwik Chek used automobile inspection service to determine whether it is a profitable business venture to pursue. The report begins with a brief description of the service concept and then proceeds with an in-depth look at the services proposed, an in-depth look at the used car market for purchasing characteristics, an operational analysis of the requirements for providing the service, and a financial analysis of the cash flows expected over the first three years of operation.

The results of the study show that Kwik Chek, when treated as an absentee owner investment only, requires over $100,000 in cash to accommodate negative cash flows in the first year of operation and doesn't show a positive return on investment until Year 3 of operation.

Further analysis shows that Kwik Chek, when treated as an owner/operator business, still requires $70,000+ in cash, but it shows a positive return on investment in only two years instead of in three and shows a substantial positive cash flow in Year 3 and beyond. The return on investment time period is reduced by one year.

There is already competition in the used automobile inspection area, but there is substantial market share to be had by each entrant. The Kwik Chek analysis assumes that only 20 percent market penetration is achieved by Kwik Chek to achieve the goals outlined.

Because the owner/operator scenario requires less initial investment, shows a positive return in two years instead of three, and also provides increased cash flow in Year 3 and beyond, Kwik Chek should be offered to mechanic/investor groups who want to own and operate the business while establishing themselves for the long term as a service to the used car industry. The number of used car customers will continue to grow as the number of licensed drivers continues to grow, and the expected life of automobiles continues to be extended through higher quality manufacturing.

It is not recommended that Kwik Chek be pursued as strictly an investment by an absentee owner because the return on investment period is over three years and the longer term cash flows are nominal. It is, however, recommended as an investment for an owner/operator who can serve as both owner and inspection technician with another family member working as dispatcher.

Table of Contents

Exhibit XI: Summary Financial Analysis for Kwik Chek in Austin

Exhibit XII: Owner/Mechanic Summary Financial Analysis for Kwik Chek in Austin

Legal Considerations

Market Need Definition

The automobile marketplace has been in a state of transition since the beginning of the 1980s. There has been a trend in recent years away from purchasing new automobiles and toward purchasing an automobile on the used car market.

It has recently become common knowledge to the general public that a new car purchased from a dealer loses a tremendous amount of its resale value almost immediately. This amount of initial loss is generally financed and paid for by the owner over a three- to five-year period and consequently does not get amortized as quickly as the car loses its money. A used car, on the other hand, does not lose value as quickly after purchase because the bulk of the "new car" depreciation has already occurred by the time of purchase.

Data from the 1988 Motor Vehicle Manufacturers Association Facts and Figures as shown in Table A.1 shows that the total number of registered vehicles on the road today has increased steadily from 1980 to 1988, and the mean and median ages have also increased.

Table A.1   Registrations and Vehicle Ages

	1980	1988
Registered vehicles	150 million	180 million
Mean age of vehicles	6.6 years	7.6 years
Median age of vehicles	6.0 years	6.8 years

There are many possible reasons for this recent trend. The increased need for fuel-efficient cars, combined with difficult financial times for the public at large, have made people more cautious about how they spend their money. They are tending to treat an automobile purchase as an investment decision, rather than an impulse buy.

The major problem with a used automobile is that the buyer generally purchases the vehicle in "as-is" condition. The buyer is typically unaware of the mechanical condition of the vehicle and consequently purchases the vehicle on faith that it does not have major mechanical or electrical problems that will substantially increase the overall cost of ownership.

The current alternative to buying on faith is to take the car to a mechanic for a complete mechanical review. This action takes time and money on the part of the buyer, and the scheduling of the mechanical inspection is typically done during the day when the buyer is at work. In essence, it is a hassle. Consequently, even though everyone agrees that an independent inspection is a good idea, few people actually have the inspection done.

From the seller's perspective, it is valuable to have an independent inspection report of the mechanical condition of the vehicle to assure potential buyers that there are no hidden defects in the vehicle.

This procedure is similar to that done when a person buys a house and arranges an inspection of the physical condition of the house. In some states, it is a legal requirement to have a house inspection before the house can be sold. Because a house and a car are the typically the two largest purchases the average person makes in a lifetime, it stands to reason that they should both be treated with the same level of care.

It makes intuitive sense that a service that offers reliable mechanical inspection of vehicles in a convenient way and for a reasonable price would be well received by the public.

An analysis of the business potential of such an offering is the subject of this report. The proposed company name is Kwik Chek, and the company would initially be based in Austin, Texas. The business will be analyzed from a marketing, operations, and financial perspective to determine whether it is viable in Austin only and whether it has potential for being nationally franchised.

A Description of the Kwik Chek Service Proposed

The customer calls a local number and schedules an appointment to have an inspection performed on an automobile he or she is considering buying. The inspection is performed at the car's location, and a complete report of the mechanical and electrical condition of the car is provided.

The next section contains a listing of the inspections performed during a Kwik Chek inspection.

In total, approximately 90 points are inspected. The customer can be assured that the major components will be inspected and that any major defects will surface during the inspection.

The inspection time takes around 40 minutes once the mechanic is set up. Each Kwik Chek technician is an experienced mechanic. The equipment in the Kwik Chek van is designed to streamline the inspection process as much as possible. (See Exhibit X for a detailed listing of van equipment.)

The primary benefit being purchased by the user is the peace of mind associated with an objective, informed third-party opinion of the purchase. Most people want to know what they are buying and not be surprised by major defects later when the vehicle is theirs. The Kwik Chek information can also be used as a negotiating tool to achieve a more equitable price for the vehicle.

A major benefit of using Kwik Chek over the existing method of inspection (that is, bringing the car to a mechanic) is the convenience of having the car inspected without borrowing the car or interrupting the customer's day to have the car inspected.

In essence, the benefits associated with the Kwik Chek service are peace of mind and convenience. The major questions are how many people are willing to pay for the service, and at what price? The next section addresses these marketing-related issues.

Kwik Chek Tests Performed

Engine Diagnostics

Compression

Rotor

Cap

Capacitor (as required)

Points (as required)

Electronic ignition

Oil leakage

Spark plug fouling

Spark plug wires

Belts

Exhaust for age and leaks

Oil consumption/burning

Suspension and Steering

Tire wear

Shock absorbers

Alignment (from tire wear in front)

Torsion bars tightness

Cracked leaf springs

Spare tire condition

Brakes

Check pads/shoes for wear

Check one rotor/drum for wear

Check for pulling when breaking

Check emergency brake

Accessories

AM/FM radio/cassette

Power windows

Power locks

Power seats

Air conditioning

Heater and fan speeds

Gauges

Speedometer/odometers

Cigarette lighter

Windshield washer

Windshield wiper operation and blade condition

Transmission

All speeds

Clutch slip and adjust (manual)

Reverse

Lights

Headlights (low/high)

Turn signals

Hazard lights

Backup lights

License plate lights

Dome lights

Instrument cluster lights

Outside lights

Fluid Levels and Condition

Oil

Transmission

Differential

Clutch

Brake

Coolant plus hoses for leaks

Battery

Washer fluid

Steering

Hydrometer test of coolant for anti-freeze

Electrical

Alternator charging

Battery load test

Slow leak test

Body

Undercoating

Accident repairs

Rust

Fading/peeling paint

Proper closure of doors and windows

Mirrors (inside and out)

Trailer hitch hook-up residuals

The Market and Industry Revenue Potential Analysis

The Scarborough Report on Austin Automobile Purchases for 1988 shows that 31 percent of all adults in Austin are planning to purchase an automobile, and 47 percent of those are planning a used car purchase. This implies that 14 percent of all adults in Austin are planning a used car purchase. (See Exhibit I.)

It is assumed that the Kwik Chek service proposed would be most applicable to used car purchases because new car purchases come with a warranty. This report will concentrate on the used car market as the potential opportunity for Kwik Chek.

There are 569,000 adults in the Austin SMSA. Fourteen percent of this number indicates that it can be expected for 81,190 used cars to be purchased each year. (See Exhibit I.)

On a national basis, 23,386,400 used cars were purchased in 1988. Of these, 7,607,172 (33 percent) were purchased from dealers. It is then assumed that the remaining 15,779,228 (67 percent) were purchased on the open market. (See Exhibit I.)

For purposes of analysis, it is assumed that the 33 percent dealer/67 percent open market ratio outlined in the previous paragraph of used car purchases is indicative of the entire nation, including Austin, in determining the number of used cars purchased from dealers or on the open market.

Referring to Exhibit II, it can be seen that Austin should be purchasing more used automobiles than indicated in Exhibit I because the total purchases divided by the total registrations indicates a holding period of 4.6 years per purchased vehicle. This is more than the 3–4 years indicated by the *Medical Economics Journal*, February 6, 1989, page 174.

The estimated new car purchases are assumed accurate because they comes from manufacturer data. An increase in the total number of used cars purchased would decrease the holding period for vehicles and indicate a larger turnover than estimated for this analysis. A larger turnover would decrease the holding period and make it closer to the 3–4 years estimated. Consequently, it is assumed that this analysis is conservative and reflects a slightly pessimistic case for analysis.

Pricing of Kwik Chek Inspections

Exhibit III reflects the price demand curve for the Kwik Chek service at different prices. The curve is derived from data obtained from a survey of prospective purchasers of the service. They indicated that only 70 percent would use the service at any price and that with a service price of more than $110, none would use the service. The curve is most flat in the $40–60 range, with most people saying that $49 sounded "about right." It should also be noted that some mentioned a tendency to price the evaluation service at a percentage of the purchase price of the vehicle in question.

Verification of the $49 price came from the Credit Union National Association *Guide to Buying and Selling a Used Car*. The guide indicates that "If you think this is a car you want, hire a mechanic or car care center to evaluate the car. You can usually do so for $40 or less."

Based on the added convenience of performing the evaluation on site, a $49.95 price seems reasonable and justifiable. Exhibit III also indicates that with a price of $49.95, the available market of potential users of the Kwik Chek service becomes 37.5 percent of the total number of used car purchasers.

It should also be noted that purchases are seasonal in nature, as indicated in Exhibit IV. The peak buying season appears to be March (9.6 percent of purchases) through August, with the end of the year and the beginning of the year relatively slow (with 6.98 percent of purchases according to Exhibit V). It is recommended that Kwik Chek be introduced to the buying public in January to allow familiarity with the concept in time for the March–August buying peak.

As mentioned previously, 33 percent of all used cars are purchased from dealers. Kwik Chek can provide a similar service to the dealers as it intends to provide on the open market. The dealers will probably want a discount off the retail price of 20 to 25 percent, based upon past experience. This discount can be justified by Kwik Chek because of the ease of inspection of many vehicles in the same location, instead of many locations all over the city.

It is assumed that there will be two classes of service: 1) the dealer service at $39 per inspection and 2) the open market at $49.95 per inspection.

Market Sales Potential

Exhibit V indicates that at the $49.95 price, and with 37.5 percent of the used car buyers as potential customers, the total U.S. revenue potential is $438M and that a 20 percent national penetration of the potential market will generate $87.6M in sales for Kwik Chek. It is assumed that Kwik Chek cannot obtain more than 20 percent penetration due to competition.

Exhibit VI indicates that the Austin Market alone has a total potential market of $1.5M at the $49.95 price and that a 20 percent penetration of that market will generate $304,000 in annual revenues.

Exhibit VII indicates that the national potential revenues with 20 percent penetration of both the dealer and open markets is $81M, slightly down from the previous estimate but still a substantial number.

Exhibit VIII outlines the same breakdown as mentioned in the previous paragraph, but for the Austin area. It is seen that Austin can be expected to generate $282,000 in revenues and perform 6,090 inspections per year with 20 percent potential market penetration.

Competition

Kwik Chek already has two competitors in the Austin Area: Auto Chek and No Lemons. In addition, a potential competitor named CheckOut may be about to launch a national franchise.

Auto Chek

Auto Chek has been in business for almost one year. The president is a successful entrepreneur who recently sold another company, and he started Auto Chek a short time afterward.

The president has every intention of making Auto Chek a national franchise and has already sold the franchise rights to an organization in Dallas and San Antonio.

Auto Chek wants an initial franchise fee of $25,000 and an 8 percent royalty on sales. It has advertised a great deal in Austin, but an informal survey of people regarding the service showed that there is awareness of the service but not the name of the company. There is a potential free rider opportunity available to Kwik Chek.

Auto Chek charges $49.50 for its services and checks 90 points on each car.

No Lemons

No Lemons has come onto the market in the last month. It charges $59.50 for its service and claims to inspect 120 points, but it inflates the number a little (by treating each tire as an inspection point, wipers as two inspection points instead of one, and so on).

Rumor around town is that many dealers are shying away from doing business with No Lemons. It is definitely in the market and already out there with a van and providing the service. No Lemons is planning to franchise nationally. Fees and royalty information was not available.

CheckOut

CheckOut is an inspection company in New Jersey that has been providing services for over five years but is confined primarily to the New Jersey/New York area. It charges $59 for its service and checks around 90 points.

CheckOut is rumored to have started a national franchise, but to date, I haven't found evidence of that.

The Management Team

John Doe is the author of this plan and the proposed president of the new company. He has worked as a mechanic for over ten years and has experience repairing both domestic and import automobiles. He has served as the shop foreman for the local Ford dealership for the last two years. His foreman duties also include profit and loss projections for the service segment of the local dealerships operation. Mr. Doe would be the initial test technician with others hired as business grows.

His wife, Judy, intends to work as the secretary/dispatcher to make the initial Austin, Texas operation a success and to improve their income from the business. She has experience as both a switchboard operator for a large corporation and as an executive secretary.

Mr. Doe has a wide network of mechanic colleagues who are interested in working with Kwik Chek once the idea proves successful.

Operations Plan

Exhibit IX outlines the logistical analysis used to determine the total number of vans that would be required to address Austin at the 20 percent penetration rate. Twenty percent was used to determine the state of the company when working at its peak efficiency.

It is assumed that inspections are provided 11 hours per day, 7 days per week. Dealer inspections will occur during the week, and open market inspection will occur on the weekends and evenings.

It is assumed that a dealer inspection will constitute 33 percent of inspections. Using the estimated 40 minute inspection time per vehicle, dealer inspections are expected to take .67 hours. The open market inspections cannot be scheduled closer than 1.5 hours (90 minute) intervals due to travel times and other unforeseen circumstances.

Based on these assumptions and the 33 percent dealer/67 percent open market split mentioned previously, a maximum of 272 inspections can be performed by one van.

The chart indicates that at the 20 percent penetration rate, an average of 1.9 vans will be needed to meet demand in Austin.

It is recommended to start out with one van with Mr. Doe performing the inspections and then add a technician along with progression to a second van when the number of inspections warrants the addition. (See Exhibit XI.)

Marketing and Sales Strategy

The most powerful tool for promoting Kwik Chek's success is positive word of mouth where one satisfied user tells several friends about the value received from using the service. This applies equally well for the dealer and open market segments. The most difficult initial problem is increasing the public's awareness about the service availability and benefits. A special referral reward system should be established where a person can earn a free inspection for recommending ten people for the service. Vouchers can be used to track the referrals.

Monthly marketing expense of $2,500 is assumed and it should be spent in the following areas:

Monthly Yellow Pages advertising	1/2 page ad at $1,200 per month = $1,200
Direct mail pieces to dealers	200 pieces at $1 each = $200
Direct mail pieces to households	$400 as an insert in a bulk mailing pack
Commissions for part-time sales	$700 per month at 10 percent of partial revenues

It is also assumed that around $10,000 will be spent during the first few months on radio and newspaper advertising. In addition, special promotions should be set up with the dealers around town in conjunction with radio simulcasts where free used car inspections are provided if you bring your car in for inspection while the radio station is present.

Financial Analysis

This section presents a detailed financial analysis of the Kwik Chek business idea. It first looks at the variable and fixed costs associated with the business operation. This section includes a profit analysis for each van, determines the break-even number of inspections needed to support the van and its driver, and then ties the pieces together into a complete profit and loss analysis over a three-year period.

Fixed and Variable Cost Analysis

Exhibit X outlines the fixed and variable costs associated with the operation of Kwik Chek.

It can be seen that the van with its equipment has a cost of $24,140. If financed over a three-year period, this becomes a payment of $779 per month. It is also assumed that a technician/mechanic is dedicated to the van with a salary of $1,800 per month, which is initially paid to Mr. Doe. Adding in paging, service, and maintenance, the costs associated with operating a van are expected to be $2,925 per month.

The general overhead cost is outlined in Exhibit X to be $7,191 per month. This number assumes that most equipment such as computers, copiers, and so on is financed over a three-year period at 10 percent. It also assumes a secretary who doubles as an appointment scheduler and earns $1,500 per month and $2,500 in monthly marketing expenses. The General Overhead number also includes a $417 monthly amortization of a franchise fee of $15,000 that is equally divided over 36 months. All appointments for inspection are scheduled through the main office dispatcher.

Exhibit X also shows that the variable costs associated with dealer inspection is $10, and it is $11 for the open market inspection because gas mileage is involved. Included in this cost is a $5 incentive to the mechanic for each inspection performed and paid for by the customer. This is to keep the drivers motivated to complete as many inspections as possible while assuring quality work.

It can be seen from Exhibit X that total contribution to overhead for operations when at 20 percent (and working with 2 vans) is $16,475 per month. The total overhead is expected to be $13,040, which leaves the net profit before taxes at $3,435. Up to this point, there has not been any allowance for owner income other than the income earned by Mr. Doe as the test technician. At this point, it appears that the maximum before-tax income to the owner of the Austin Kwik Chek franchise would be $3,435 per month or $41,220 per year. If the franchise were owned as a subchapter S corporation, the owner would still need to pay taxes on this amount.

It is also seen from Exhibit X that the inspection break-even for the entire operation with 2 vans is 402 inspections and that the incremental costs associated with another van are covered with 90 inspections.

Overall Financial Analysis

Exhibit XI shows the financial results expected from Kwik Chek operation when the owner is not involved with the inspections. Exhibit XII shows the expected financial results when the owner actually performs inspections from one of the vans. The owner/operator actually makes the $20,000 allocated to the van operator and retains whatever profits are left over at the end of the year.

It is assumed that Kwik Chek acquires 1 percent additional market share for each month it is in operation. At the end of the second year, Kwik Chek is assumed to be at the 20 percent penetration target.

The chart also indicates that there is a substantial negative cumulative cash flow during the first year. The peak negative value is $102,026 for absentee owners and $72,000 for the owner operator. The profits derived by the second year of operation begin to erode the negative cumulative cash situation. Kwik Chek is still in a negative cumulative cash flow situation by the end of Year 3 for the absentee investors but shows a positive turn for owner/operators. Absentee owner/investors begin to show a return on their investment beginning in Year 4.

The chart shows that the company operates with a negative net operating income over the first year of existence for absentee investors and turns slightly positive for the owner/operator and turns positive for both scenarios in Year 2. The owner/operator stands to make substantial money after the first year should business plan projections be accurate.

An additional van is required during the second year to meet market demands. When included in the expenses of the second and ongoing years, Kwik Chek can be expected to yield a net profit before tax of $41,208 for absentee owners and $89,808 for owner/operators.

Anyone who invests in a Kwik Chek franchise must be willing to risk between $70,000 and $100,000 in cash and wait between 2 and 4 years for a positive return on that investment.

Conclusion

It can be seen from the previous discussion that the investment potential of a Kwik Chek franchise is not a viable option for a person who treats it exclusively as an investment.

Exhibit XII shows what happens to the financials of the project if the owner is also the mechanic for the first van. This creates a saving on two counts: 1) The $5 incentive per inspection is not needed to motivate the mechanic because the mechanic is the owner, and 2) there is a $18,000 savings per year in the salary paid the mechanic.

It can be seen from Exhibit XII that there is still a substantial negative cumulative cash flow for the first year, but the cash flow drain reverses direction in Month 11 as opposed to early in Year 2. We see that the project becomes a positive cumulative cash flow project by the end of Year 2 and becomes a generator of substantial cumulative cash ($107,841) in Year 3.

It still requires $75,000 (plus living expenses) to assure minimum cash reserves for the business. If the marketing penetration ramp-up is greater than expected, then the business will generate cash faster.

Kwik Chek is not a viable investment for someone who does not intend to operate the business and perform inspections in one of the vans. It does not generate a positive return on investment until Year 3 and requires over $100,000 in cash reserves to start.

If a person wants to invest his own time in the project and operates one of the vans, then there is substantial future revenue-earning potential after Year 3. There is still over $75,000 in cash required to fund the business, but the long-term prospects for return are much improved over treating the project as only an investment.

Kwik Chek should be started in Austin by a mechanic who wants to start his or her own business. If it begins to show the returns expected, then the project should be set up for national franchising to mechanic/investor groups who want to provide the service. At that time, additional funding can be obtained based upon the company's successful track record.

Exhibits

Exhibit I: Scarborough Report on Automobile Purchases

From the Scarborough Report on Austin automobile purchases (1988)

Percent of adults planning to purchase a car:	31%
(This fact implies that people change cars every 3.2 years)	
Percent of adults planning a used car purchase:	14%
Total number of Austin SMSA Adults:	569,355
Percent of woman adults buying used cars:	69%
Total number of planned used car purchases:	81,190
Women planning to buy a used car:	56,021
Men planning to buy a used car:	25,169

Notes:
1) The median price range for women's purchases is $6,900
2) The median price range for men's purchases is $10,300
3) The bulk of those buying used cars have median incomes of $27,000
4) The total number of licensed drivers in the U.S.=   164,000,000

There are	Number of male drivers=	85,000,000
	Number of female drivers=	79,000,000

Assuming the Austin ratios for adults purchasing used cars is valid for the the entire U.S., then we can assume that the total number of used car in a year are:

Total number of drivers:	164,000,000	
Percent buying used cars:	14%	
Percent buying new cars:	16%	
Total used car purchases:	23,386,400	
Cars purchased by women:	16,136,616	
Cars purchased by men:	7,249,784	
Cars purchased from dealers:	7,607,172	[from Wards, p. 166]
Cars purchased on open market:	15,779,228	

Exhibit II: Validation of Conservative Estimates

To determine whether Austin is representative of the U.S. in general, we can compare the new car purchases nationally to those expected in Austin. Austin is expecting new car percentage purchases of 15.5%.

New car information:

1988 new vehicle purchases:	15,245,843
Percent of licensed drivers:	9%

This information indicates that the national average of used car purchases may actually be higher than that seen in Austin.

Total new car purchases:	15,245,843
Used car purchases:	23,386,400
Total annual purchases:	38,632,243
Total registered vehicles:	179,000,000
Percent purchases to registration:	22%
Average holding period:	5

The national average for holding a car is 3-4 years. These numbers indicate that the numbers used for analysis are conservative and that more used cars are probably sold annually than predicted.

Sources:
Motor Vehicles Manufacturers Association Facts and Figures (1988)
Wards Automotive Yearbook, 1989

Exhibit III: Price Demand Curve

Price ($)	Demand	Tot Rev ($)
0	100	0
20	70	1,400
40	50	2,000
50	38	1,875
60	25	1,500
110	0	0

Exhibit IV: Seasonality of Buyer Purchasing Habits (1988/1988)

Month	1987	% of total	Cumulative %	1988	% of total	Cumulative %
1	1,001,879	5.99%	5.99%	1,211,704	6.98%	6.98%
2	1,249,911	7.48%	13.47%	1,412,058	8.14%	15.12%
3	1,527,827	9.14%	22.62%	1,667,601	9.61%	24.73%
4	1,554,248	9.30%	31.92%	1,493,641	8.61%	33.34%
5	1,464,754	8.76%	40.68%	1,629,931	9.39%	42.74%
6	1,584,114	9.48%	50.16%	1,634,603	9.42%	52.16%
7	1,478,519	8.85%	59.01%	1,426,720	8.22%	60.38%
8	1,522,813	9.11%	68.12%	1,446,218	8.34%	68.72%
9	1,413,512	8.46%	76.58%	1,339,803	7.72%	76.44%
10	1,330,895	7.96%	84.54%	1,381,685	7.96%	84.40%
11	1,231,478	7.37%	91.91%	1,313,526	7.57%	91.97%
12	1,352,231	8.09%	100.00%	1,392,945	8.03%	100.00%
	16,712,181			17,350,435		

Exhibit V: National Potential Sales in Units and Dollars at 5, 10 & 20% Penetration

Month	1988 Percent	Used Car Sales (Units)	Total KwikChek Market @ $49.95 (Units)	Total KwikChek Revenues @ $49.95 (Dollars)	At a 5% Penetration of Total Market (Units)	At a 5% Penetration of Total Market (Dollars)	At a 10% Penetration of Total Market (Units)	At a 10% Penetration of Total Market (Dollars)	At a 20% Penetration of Total Market (Units)	At a 20% Penetration of Total Market (Dollars)
January	6.98%	1,633,238	612,464	$30,592,594	30,623	$1,529,630	61,246	$3,059,259	122,493	$6,118,519
February	8.14%	1,903,293	713,735	$35,651,048	35,687	$1,782,552	71,373	$3,565,105	142,747	$7,130,210
March	9.61%	2,247,735	842,901	$42,102,891	42,145	$2,105,145	84,290	$4,210,289	168,580	$8,420,578
April	8.61%	2,013,257	754,971	$37,710,821	37,749	$1,885,541	75,497	$3,771,082	150,994	$7,542,164
May	9.39%	2,196,960	823,860	$41,151,814	41,193	$2,057,591	82,386	$4,115,181	164,772	$8,230,363
June	9.42%	2,203,258	826,222	$41,269,771	41,311	$2,063,489	82,622	$4,126,977	165,244	$8,253,954
July	8.22%	1,923,055	721,146	$36,021,228	36,057	$1,801,061	72,115	$3,602,123	144,229	$7,204,246
August	8.34%	1,949,336	731,001	$36,513,505	36,550	$1,825,675	73,100	$3,651,351	146,200	$7,302,701
September	7.72%	1,805,901	677,213	$33,826,784	33,861	$1,691,339	67,721	$3,382,678	135,443	$6,765,357
October	7.96%	1,862,353	698,382	$34,884,203	34,919	$1,744,210	69,838	$3,488,420	139,676	$6,976,841
November	7.57%	1,770,483	663,931	$33,163,353	33,197	$1,658,168	66,393	$3,316,335	132,786	$6,632,671
December	8.03%	1,877,530	704,074	$35,168,491	35,204	$1,758,425	70,407	$3,516,849	140,815	$7,033,698
		23,386,400	8,769,900	$438,056,505	438,495	$21,902,825	876,990	$43,805,651	1,753,980	$87,611,301

Notes:
1) 1988 percentages taken from Exhibit IV: Seasonality of Buying Chart
2) Used car sales derived from data in Exhibit II for total National used car purchases
3) Total Kwik chek market derived from Exhibit III. 37.5% demand expected at $50 pricing
4) 20% penetration is the maximum expected due to future entrants and other competition

Exhibit VI: Austin Potential Sales in Units and Dollars at 5, 10 & 20% Penetration

Month	1988 Percent	Used Car Sales (Units)	Total KwikChek Market @ $49.95 (Units)	Total KwikChek Revenues @ $49.95 (Dollars)	At a 5% Penetration of Total Market (Units)	At a 5% Penetration of Total Market (Dollars)	At a 10% Penetration of Total Market (Units)	At a 10% Penetration of Total Market (Dollars)	At a 20% Penetration of Total Market (Units)	At a 20% Penetration of Total Market (Dollars)
January	6.98%	5,670	2,126	$106,208	106	$5,310	213	$10,621	425	$21,242
February	8.14%	6,608	2,478	$123,769	124	$6,188	248	$12,377	496	$24,754
March	9.61%	7,803	2,926	$146,168	146	$7,308	293	$14,617	585	$29,234
April	8.61%	6,989	2,621	$130,920	131	$6,546	262	$13,092	524	$26,184
May	9.39%	7,627	2,860	$142,866	143	$7,143	286	$14,287	572	$28,573
June	9.42%	7,649	2,868	$143,275	143	$7,164	287	$14,328	574	$28,655
July	8.22%	6,676	2,504	$125,054	125	$6,253	250	$12,505	501	$25,011
August	8.34%	6,767	2,538	$126,763	127	$6,338	254	$12,676	508	$25,353
September	7.72%	6,270	2,351	$117,436	118	$5,872	235	$11,744	470	$23,487
October	7.96%	6,465	2,425	$121,107	121	$6,055	242	$12,111	485	$24,221
November	7.57%	6,147	2,305	$115,132	115	$5,757	230	$11,513	461	$23,026
December	8.03%	6,518	2,444	$122,094	122	$6,105	244	$12,209	489	$24,419
		81,190	30,446	$1,520,790	1,522	$76,040	3,045	$152,079	6,089	$304,158

Notes:
1) 1988 percentages taken from Exhibit IV: Seasonality of Buying Chart
2) Used car sales derived from data in Exhibit I for total Austin used car purchases
3) Total Kwik chek market derived from Exhibit III. 37.5% demand expected at $50 pricing
4) 20% penetration is the maximum expected due to future entrants and other competition

Exhibit VII: National Dealer/Open Market Potential Sales in Units and Dollars at 10 & 20% Penetration

Dealer Percentage: 33%
Open market Percentage: 67%

Month	1988 Percent	Used Car Sales (Units)	Total KwikChek Market @ 37.5% (Units)	Potential Dealer Sales @ 33% (Units)	Dealer Revenues @ 10% Penetrat. of Dealer Potential & $39 price (Dollars)	Dealer Revenues @ 20% Penetrat. of Dealer Potential & $39 price (Dollars)	Potential Open Market Sales @ 67% (Units)	Open Market Revenues @ 10% penetrat. of Open Mrkt. Potential & $49 price (Dollars)	Open Market Revenues @ 20% penetrat. of Open Mrkt. Potential & $49 price (Dollars)
January	8.14%	1,903,293	713,735	232,165	$905,443	$1,810,887	481,570	$2,405,441	$4,810,882
February	9.61%	2,247,735	842,901	274,180	$1,069,303	$2,138,607	568,720	$2,840,758	$5,681,517
March	8.61%	2,013,257	754,971	245,579	$957,756	$1,915,512	509,393	$2,544,417	$5,088,835
April	9.39%	2,196,960	823,860	267,987	$1,045,148	$2,090,297	555,873	$2,776,587	$5,553,175
May	9.42%	2,203,258	826,222	268,755	$1,048,144	$2,096,288	557,467	$2,784,546	$5,569,093
June	8.22%	1,923,055	721,146	234,576	$914,845	$1,829,690	486,570	$2,430,418	$4,860,835
July	8.34%	1,949,336	731,001	237,781	$927,348	$1,854,695	493,220	$2,463,632	$4,927,265
August	7.72%	1,805,901	677,213	220,285	$859,112	$1,718,224	456,928	$2,282,354	$4,564,709
September	7.96%	1,862,353	698,382	227,171	$885,967	$1,771,935	471,211	$2,353,700	$4,707,401
October	7.57%	1,770,483	663,931	215,965	$842,262	$1,684,525	447,966	$2,237,592	$4,475,183
November	8.03%	1,877,530	704,074	229,022	$893,188	$1,786,375	475,051	$2,372,882	$4,745,764
December		0	0	0	$0	$0	0	$0	$0
		23,386,400	8,157,436	2,653,466	$10,348,517	$20,697,034	5,503,970	$27,492,329	$54,984,657

Notes:
1) 1988 percentages taken from Exhibit IV: Seasonality of Buying Chart
2) Used car sales derived from data in Exhibit II for total National used car purchases
3) Total Kwik chek market derived from Exhibit III. 37.5% demand expected at $50 pricing
4) 20% penetration is the maximum expected due to future entrants and other competition
5) It is assumed that dealers will want a 20% discount off of retail to use the service
6) The breakdown of dealer to open market sales percentages is taken from Exhibit I.

Exhibit VIII: Austin Dealer/Open Market Potential Sales in Units and Dollars at 10 & 20% Penetration

Dealer Percentage: 33%
Open market Percentage: 67%

Month	1988 Percent	Used Car Sales (Units)	Total KwikChek Market @ 37.5% (Units)	Potential Dealer Sales @ 33% (Units)	Dealer Revenues @ 10% Penetrat. of Dealer Potential & $39 price (Dollars)	(Units)	Dealer Revenues @ 20% Penetrat. of Dealer Potential & $39 price (Dollars)	(Units)	Potential Open Market Sales @ 67% (Units)	10% penetrat. of Open Mrkt. Potential & $49 price (Dollars)	(Units)	Open Market Revenues @ 20% penetrat. of Open Mrkt. Potential & $49 price (Dollars)	(Units)
January	6.98%	5,670	2,126	692	$2,697	69	$5,395	138	1,435	$7,166	143	$14,332	287
February	8.14%	6,608	2,478	806	$3,143	81	$6,287	161	1,672	$8,351	167	$16,702	334
March	9.61%	7,803	2,926	952	$3,712	95	$7,425	190	1,974	$9,862	197	$19,724	395
April	8.61%	6,989	2,621	853	$3,325	85	$6,650	171	1,768	$8,833	177	$17,667	354
May	9.39%	7,627	2,860	930	$3,628	93	$7,257	186	1,930	$9,639	193	$19,279	386
June	9.42%	7,649	2,868	933	$3,639	93	$7,278	187	1,935	$9,667	194	$19,334	387
July	8.22%	6,676	2,504	814	$3,176	81	$6,352	163	1,689	$8,438	169	$16,875	338
August	8.34%	6,767	2,538	825	$3,219	83	$6,439	165	1,712	$8,553	171	$17,106	342
September	7.72%	6,270	2,351	765	$2,983	76	$5,965	153	1,586	$7,924	159	$15,847	317
October	7.96%	6,465	2,425	789	$3,076	79	$6,152	158	1,636	$8,171	164	$16,343	327
November	7.57%	6,147	2,305	750	$2,924	75	$5,848	150	1,555	$7,768	156	$15,536	311
December	8.03%	6,518	2,444	795	$3,101	80	$6,202	159	1,649	$8,238	165	$16,476	330
		81,190	30,446	9,904	$38,624	990	$77,248	1,981	20,543	$102,610	2,054	$205,221	4,109

Notes:
1) 1988 percentages taken from Exhibit IV: Seasonality of Buying Chart
2) Used car sales derived from data in Exhibit II for total National used car purchases
3) Total Kwik chek market derived from Exhibit III. 37.5% demand expected at $50 pricing
4) 20% penetration is the maximum expected due to future entrants and other competition
5) It is assumed that dealers will want a 20% discount off of retail to use the service
6) The breakdown of dealer to open market sales percentages is taken from Exhibit I.

Exhibit IX: Operations Breakdown for Austin to Determine the Number of Vans Required

Dealer Price:	$39.00
Open Market Price:	$49.95

Number of inspection hours per day:	11
Number of days per week:	7

Inspection hours per week:	77
Inspection hours per year:	4,004
Average inspection hours per month:	334
Maximum Inspections per van/month:	272
(Assuming 33%-67% dealer-open market split)	

Inspect time (Hrs.):	1.50 (Open market inspection time including 30 minutes travel)
Inspect time (Hrs.):	0.67 (Dealer inspection time of 40 minutes)

Month	20% Penetrat. of Dealer Potential & $39 price (Dollars)	(Units)	Inspection Hours Required	20% penetrat. of Open Mrkt. Potential & $49 price (Dollars)	(Units)	Inspection Hours Required	Total Num. Inspt.	Total Van Hours Needed	Total Vans Needed
January	$5,395	138	92	$14,332	287	430	425	523	1.6
February	$6,287	161	107	$16,702	334	502	496	609	1.8
March	$7,425	190	127	$19,724	395	592	585	719	2.2
April	$6,650	171	114	$17,667	354	531	524	644	1.9
May	$7,257	186	124	$19,279	386	579	572	703	2.1
June	$7,278	187	124	$19,334	387	581	574	705	2.1
July	$6,352	163	109	$16,875	338	507	501	615	1.8
August	$6,439	165	110	$17,106	342	514	508	624	1.9
September	$5,965	153	102	$15,847	317	476	470	578	1.7
October	$6,152	158	105	$16,343	327	491	485	596	1.8
November	$5,848	150	100	$15,536	311	467	461	567	1.7
December	$6,202	159	106	$16,476	330	495	489	601	1.8
	$77,248	1,981	1,320	$205,221	4,109	6,163	6,089	7,483	1.9

345

Exhibit X: Fixed and Variable Cost Breakdown per van and Inspection

Van Equipment		Cost
The Van		$15,000
Test Equipment:		$290
Compression	$50	
Calipers	$50	
DEpth Gauge	$50	
VOM	$125	
Hydrometer	$15	
Scope and Analyzers		$3,500
Portable Personal Computer		$3,000
Other Equipment:		$1,350
Generator	$200	
Hydraulic jack	$200	
Jack Stands	$150	
Scooter	$50	
Misc hand tools	$750	
Van Cusutomization		$1,000
Total Van Cost:		$24,140

Van Fixed costs:		$2,925	
Monthly payment		$779	(Finance over 3 years at 10%)
Technician Wages		$1,800	($20k per year + benefits)
Paging Service		$25	
Insurance		$220	
Maintenance (@ 5%)		$101	

General Overhead Costs:		$7,191	(Including 20% buffer for error)
Office rent		$450	
Postage		$150	
Marketing		$2,500	
Insurance/benefits		$500	
Franchise fee ($15K)		$417	(Divided over 36 months)
Telephone		$140	
Secretary/appointment		$1,500	(Includes appointment scheduling)
Office Equipment:		$336	(Finance over 3 years at 10%)
Computer	$5,000		
FAX	$900		
Copier	$1,500		
Furniture	$1,500		
Telephone	$500		
Misc	$1,000		
Total	$10,400		

continues

continued

Fixed cost per van Assuming Two Vans are in Operation: $6,520

Van Fixed Cost $2,925
Office Overhead (pro-rated) $3,595

Fixed Cost per Van-Hour of Operation (the scarce item): $20

Pro-rated cost per dealer inspection $13
pro-rated cost per Open Market Inspec $29

Variable costs per Inspection: $11

Gasoline $1   (Assume 10 miles/call @ 10mpg & $1/gal.)
Misc consumables $5
Incentive to tech $5

Profit Margin Analysis for Dealer and Open Market Inspections

	Open Market	Dealer
Revenue	$49.95	$39.00
7% Franchise fee	($3.50)	($2.73)
Variable cost	($11.00)	($10.00) (No gas for dealer insp.)
Contribution	$35.45	$26.27
Inspections per month:	342	165
Segment contribution:	$12,138	$4,336

Monthly Expected Total Contribution:	$16,475
Less: Total Fixed Cost	($13,040)
Net Total Profit Before Tax:	$3,435

Assuming a 33% Dealer/67% Open market breakdown in inspections:

Breakeven Monthly Inspections Quantity:		402
Total 2-van fixed cost:	$13,040	
Dealer inspections:	133	
Open market Inspections:	269	

Breakeven Quantity for Justifying Another Van Purchase:

Van Breakeven for 33%/67% split:		90
Van incremental fixed cost:	$2,925	

347

Exhibit XI: Summary Financial Analysis for Kwik Chek in Austin

	Start	Mo. 1	Mo. 2	Mo. 3	Mo. 4	Mo. 5
Market Share	0%	1%	2%	2%	3%	3%
Dealer Inspections	0	8	17	17	25	25
Open Market inspects	0	17	34	34	51	51
Total Inspections	0	25	51	51	76	76
Number of Vans needed	1	1	1	1	1	1
INCOME FROM PRODUCTION ACTIVITIES						
Dealer Sales ($)	0	322	644	644	966	966
Open Mkt Sales ($)	0	855	1,710	1,710	2,565	2,565
Less: Cost of Good Sold						
Variable Costs	0	(271)	(542)	(542)	(813)	(813)
Franchise Royalty	0	(82)	(165)	(165)	(247)	(247)
Gross margin	0	824	1,647	1,647	2,471	2,471
OPERATING EXPENSES						
General Fixed costs	(7,191)	(7,191)	(7,191)	(7,191)	(7,191)	(7,191)
Van fixed costs	(2,925)	(2,925)	(2,925)	(2,925)	(2,925)	(2,925)
Net Operating Income	(10,116)	(9,292)	(8,469)	(8,469)	(7,645)	(7,645)
ADDITIONAL EXPENSES						
Promotion cost	(10,000) [Initial advertising, public relations, etc.]					
Misc. Start-Up Cost	(5,000)					
Net Profit Before Tax	(25,116)	(9,292)	(8,469)	(8,469)	(7,645)	(7,645)
CUMULATIVE CASH FLOW	(25,116)	(34,408)	(42,877)	(51,345)	(58,990)	(66,635)

Assumptions:
1) There is a 33%/67% quantity split between dealers and open market inspections
2) Dealer inspections cost $39.00 and Open Market inspections cost $49.95
3) The maximum number of inspections per van is 272 per month.
4) Office fixed expenses can handle up to 4 vans without expansion.
5) Demand will never exceed 37.5% of all used car purchases.
6) Kwik Chek can achieve a 20% share of the demand within 2 years.
7) More than 20% share may not be possible due to competition.
8) Available market for Dealers and Open Market inspections in Units is:

        Dealers: 9,904 (From Exhibit VIII)
        Open Mkt: 20,543 (From Exhibit VIII)

Mo. 6	Mo. 7	Mo. 8	Mo. 9	Mo. 10	Mo. 11	Mo. 12	Year 2	Year 3
4%	4%	5%	6%	7%	8%	9%	20%	20%
33	33	41	50	58	66	74	1,981	1,981
68	68	86	103	120	137	154	4,109	4,109
101	101	127	152	178	203	228	6,089	6,089
1	1	1	1	1	1	1	2	2
1,288	1,288	1,609	1,931	2,253	2,575	2,897	77,251	77,251
3,420	3,420	4,276	5,131	5,986	6,841	7,696	205,225	205,225
(1,083)	(1,083)	(1,354)	(1,625)	(1,896)	(2,167)	(2,438)	(65,003)	(65,003)
(330)	(330)	(412)	(494)	(577)	(659)	(741)	(19,773)	(19,773)
3,295	3,295	4,119	4,942	5,766	6,590	7,414	197,700	197,700
(7,191)	(7,191)	(7,191)	(7,191)	(7,191)	(7,191)	(7,191)	(86,292)	(86,292)
(2,925)	(2,925)	(2,925)	(2,925)	(2,925)	(2,925)	(2,925)	(70,200)	(70,200)
(6,821)	(6,821)	(5,997)	(5,174)	(4,350)	(3,526)	(2,702)	41,208	41,208
(6,821)	(6,821)	(5,997)	(5,174)	(4,350)	(3,526)	(2,702)	41,208	41,208
(73,456)	(80,277)	(86,274)	(91,448)	(95,797)	(99,323)	(102,026)	(60,818)	(19,610)

Exhibit XII: Owner/Mechanic Summary Financial Analysis for Kwik Chek in Austin

	Start	Mo. 1	Mo. 2	Mo. 3	Mo. 4	Mo. 5
Market Share	0%	1%	2%	2%	3%	3%
Dealer Inspections	0	8	17	17	25	25
Open Market inspects	0	17	34	34	51	51
Total Inspections	0	25	51	51	76	76
Number of Vans needed	1	1	1	1	1	1
INCOME FROM PRODUCTION ACTIVITIES						
Dealer Sales ($)	0	322	644	644	966	966
Open Mkt Sales ($)	0	855	1,710	1,710	2,565	2,565
Less: Cost of Good Sold						
Variable Costs	0	(144)	(288)	(288)	(432)	(432)
Franchise Royalty	0	(82)	(165)	(165)	(247)	(247)
Gross margin	0	951	1,901	1,901	2,852	2,852
OPERATING EXPENSES						
General Fixed costs	(7,191)	(7,191)	(7,191)	(7,191)	(7,191)	(7,191)
Van fixed costs	(1,125)	(1,125)	(1,125)	(1,125)	(1,125)	(1,125)
Net Operating Income	(8,316)	(7,365)	(6,415)	(6,415)	(5,464)	(5,464)
ADDITIONAL EXPENSES						
Promotion cost	(10,000) [Initial advertising, public relations, etc.]					
Misc. Start-Up Cost	(5,000)					
Net Profit Before Tax	(23,316)	(7,365)	(6,415)	(6,415)	(5,464)	(5,464)
CUMULATIVE CASH FLOW	(23,316)	(30,681)	(37,096)	(43,511)	(48,975)	(54,439)

Assumptions:
1) There is a 33%/67% quantity split between dealers and open market inspections
2) Dealer inspections cost $39.00 and Open Market inspections cost $49.95
3) The maximum number of inspections per van is 272 per month.
4) Office fixed expenses can handle up to 4 vans without expansion.
5) Demand will never exceed 37.5% of all used car purchases.
6) Kwik Chek can achieve a 20% share of the demand within 2 years.
7) More than 20% share may not be possible due to competition.
8) Available market for Dealers and Open Market inspections in Units is:

    Dealers: 9,904 (From Exhibit VIII)

    Open Mkt: 20,543 (From Exhibit VIII)

Mo. 6	Mo. 7	Mo. 8	Mo. 9	Mo. 10	Mo. 11	Mo. 12	Year 2	Year 3
4%	4%	5%	6%	7%	8%	9%	20%	20%
33	33	41	50	58	66	74	1,981	1,981
68	68	86	103	120	137	154	4,109	4,109
101	101	127	152	178	203	228	6,089	6,089
1	1	1	1	1	1	1	2	2
1,288	1,288	1,609	1,931	2,253	2,575	2,897	77,251	77,251
3,420	3,420	4,276	5,131	5,986	6,841	7,696	205,225	205,225
(576)	(576)	(720)	(864)	(1,008)	(1,152)	(1,296)	(65,003)	(65,003)
(330)	(330)	(412)	(494)	(577)	(659)	(741)	(19,773)	(19,773)
3,802	3,802	4,753	5,704	6,654	7,605	8,556	197,700	197,700
(7,191)	(7,191)	(7,191)	(7,191)	(7,191)	(7,191)	(7,191)	(86,292)	(86,292)
(1,125)	(1,125)	(1,125)	(1,125)	(1,125)	(1,125)	(1,125)	(21,600)	(21,600)
(4,514)	(4,514)	(3,563)	(2,612)	(1,662)	(711)	240	89,808	89,808
(4,514)	(4,514)	(3,563)	(2,612)	(1,662)	(711)	240	89,808	89,808
(58,953)	(63,466)	(67,029)	(69,642)	(71,303)	(72,014)	(71,775)	18,033	107,841

Legal Considerations

The primary legal issues that should be considered in establishing Kwik Chek as a national franchise are 1) franchisor liability for franchisee actions and 2) termination of franchise agreement by either the franchisor or the franchisee.

The principle way that the franchisor can be held liable for the actions of a franchisee is if the franchisee represents itself as an agent of the parent company. To avoid this agency issue, all collateral literature published by the franchisor should indicate that all Kwik Chek operations are independently owned and operated. In this way, there can be no mistake on the part of the customer that the local franchisee is working their own business and on their own behalf.

A clear definition of the agency relationship will protect the franchisor from liability related to injury or accidents resulting from improper inspection and also from any financial liabilities that the franchisee may incur.

To address the termination of franchise agreement issue, it should be clearly delineated in the franchise agreement what the required payment procedures and time frames should be from the franchisee to the franchisor. In addition, the level of support that the franchisee can reasonably expect from the franchisor should also be clearly defined. In this way, there is less likelihood of misunderstanding by either party, and the franchisor is protected from having a franchisee who is not performing up to expectations bring down the rest of the organization.

In addition, if the franchisor has agreed to supply credit to the franchisee to start the business, then the franchisor should protect the investment by having strict reporting procedures as to the actions being taken by the franchisee to meet the required revenue goals.

Franchising agreements are being treated more as "relational contracts" that extend over a longer period of time than as individual contracts that have a clearly defined duration and outcome. Many courts are treating franchise agreements as a sort of marriage, and many of the precedents established for divorce law in community property states are being incorporated into termination of franchise agreements. The relationship is treated as a type of partnership, and the parties involved are compensated for their "expected" returns from the venture should it be terminated.

In this way, it should be clearly understood by the franchisee that should the franchisee lose the right to operate under the Kwik Chek name, the business is returned to the franchisor. An equitable settlement for the return can be established at the time of transfer.

Resources

The following list offers you extra resources on a variety of business and entrepreneurial subjects. I included Web site addresses where possible.

Small Business—General

American Chamber of Commerce Executives
4232 King Street
Alexandria, VA 22302
703-998-0072
Internet: http://www.acce.org

The American Institute for Small Business
Educational Materials for Small Business and Entrepreneurship
7515 Wayzata Blvd.
Minneapolis, MN 55426
800-328-2906

American Success Institute
Internet: http://www.success.org

Business Resource Center
Internet: http://www.morebusiness.com

CCH Business Owner's Toolkit
Internet: http://www.toolkit.cch.com

eWeb: Education for Entrepreneurship
Internet: http://www.slu.edu/eweb

Howard University Small Business Development Center (SBDC)
2600 Sixth Street NW, Room 125
Washington, DC 20059
202-806-1550
Internet: http://www.sbaonline.sba.gov/SBDC

The National Association for the Self-Employed
1023 15th Street NW, Suite 1200
Washington, DC 20005-2600
202-466-2100
Internet: http://www.nase.org

National Business Incubation Association
20 East Circle Drive, Suite 190
Athens, OH 45701
Internet: http://www.nbia.org

National Organization of Business Opportunity Seekers (NOBOSS)
8281 Northwind Way
Orangevale, CA 95662
916-723-0344
Internet: http://www.noboss.com

Service Core of Retired Executives (SCORE)
Internet: http://www.score.org

Small Business Development Center Research Network
Internet: http://www.smallbiz.suny.edu

U.S. Chamber of Commerce Small Business Institute
201 E. Dundee Rd.
Palatine, IL 60067
800-429-7724
Internet: http://www.usccsbi.com

U.S. Department of Commerce
14th & Constitution Avenue NW, Room 5053
Washington, DC 20230
202-482-5061
Internet: http://www.mbda.gov

U.S. Small Business Administration (SBA)
409 3rd Street, SW
Washington, DC 20416
202-205-7701
Internet: http://www.sba.gov

U.S. SBA/Business Information Center
1110 Vermont Ave. NW, 9th Floor
Washington, DC 20059
202-606-4000, ext. 279

Special Topics

The following are specialized resources that may be of use to you in your business.

Census Information

Here is an excellent place to obtain information regarding general population characteristics in your area of question.

U.S. Bureau of the Census
Public Information Office
Washington, DC 20233-8200
301-763-4040
Internet: http://www.census.gov

Financing

Here are several locations you can review for information on preparing for financing, or actually obtaining finance for your venture.

Business Loan Center
1301 N. Hamilton Street
Richmond, VA 23230
804-358-6454

Datamerge Financing Sources
800-580-1188
Internet: http://www.datamerge.com

FinanceNet
Internet: http://www.financenet.gov

National Financial Services Network
Internet: http://www.nfsn.com

Franchises

Don't buy a franchise before talking to these people to determine as much as possible about the parent company of your possible franchise purchase.

American Association of Franchisees & Dealers
PO Box 81887
San Diego, CA 92138-1887
800-733-9858
Internet: http://www.aafd.org

International Franchise Association
1350 New York Avenue NW, Suite 900
Washington, DC 20005-4709
202-628-8000
Internet: http://www.franchise.org

International Business

Business Network International
199 S. Monte Vista, Suite 6
San Dimas, CA 91773-3080
Internet: http://www.bni.com

International Chamber of Commerce
156 Fifth Avenue, Suite 308
New York, NY 10010
212-206-1150

International Small Business Consortium
2015 Martingale Dr.
Norman, OK 73072
Internet: http://www.isbc.com

International Trade Law Monitor
Internet: http://www.it.irv.uit.no/trade_law

U.S. Agency for International Development (USAID)
Public Inquiries
320 21st Street NW
Washington, DC 20523-0016
202-647-1850
Internet: http://www.usaid.gov

U.S. Council for International Business
Internet: http://www.uscib.org

Marketing

Marketing Resource Center
Concept Marketing Group, Inc.
115-B Mark Randy Pl.
Modesto, CA 95350
800-575-5369
Internet: http://www.marketingsource.com

Minorities in Business

National Minority Business Council
235 E. 42nd Street
New York, NY 10017
(212) 573-2385

National Minority Supplier Development Council
15 W. 39th Street, 9th Floor
New York, NY 10018
212-944-2430

SBA Office of Minority Enterprise and Development
Internet: http://www.sba.gov/MED

Patents

U.S. Patent and Trademark Office
Office of Public Affairs
2021 Jefferson Davis Highway
Arlington, VA 20209
703-557-4636
Internet: http://www.uspto.gov

Women in Business

American Society of Women Entrepreneurs
2121 Precinct Road, Suite 240
Hurst, TX 76054
888-669-2793
Internet: http://www.aswe.org

Interagency Committee on Women's Business Enterprise
National Economic Council
The White House
Washington, DC 20500
202-456-2174

National Association of Women Business Owners
1100 Wayne Avenue, Suite 830
Silver Spring, MD 20910
301-608-2590

National Foundation for Women Business Owners
1100 Wayne Avenue, Suite 830
Silver Spring, MD 20910-5603
Internet: http://www.nfwbo.org

U.S. Small Business Administration Office of Women's Business Ownership
409 Third Street SW
Washington, DC 20416
202-205-6673
Internet: http://www.sbaonline.sba.gov/womeninbusiness

Bibliography

Almanac of Business and Industrial Financial Ratios. Prentice Hall, 1992 Edition, ISBN: 0-13-038282-5.

The Best Home Businesses for the '90s. Paul and Sarah Edwards. Jeremy P. Tarcher/Putnam Books, 1994 Edition, ISBN: 0-87477-784-4.

The Complete Communications Handbook. Ed Paulson. Wordware Publishing, 1992, ISBN: 1-55622-238-6.

Creating the Successful Business Plan for New Ventures. LaRue Hosmer. McGraw-Hill, 1985, ISBN: 0-07-030452-1.

The Essence of Small Business. Colin Barrow. Prentice Hall, 1993, ISBN: 013285-362-0.

Getting Paid in Full. W. Kelsea Wilber. Sourcebooks Inc., 1994, ISBN: 0-942061-68-3.

The Internet Roadmap. Bennett Falk. Sybex, 1994, ISBN: 0-7821-1365-6.

Job and Career Building. Richard Germann and Peter Arnold. 10 Speed Press, 1980, ISBN: 0-89815-048-5.

"A Liability Shield for Entrepreneurs." Ripley Hotch. *Nation's Business*, August 1994.

The Little Online Book. Alfred Glossbrenner. Peachpit Press, 1995, ISBN: 1-566609-130-6.

Nobody Gets Rich Working for Somebody Else: An Entrepreneur's Guide. Roger Fritz. Dodd, Mead & Company, Inc., 1987, ISBN: 0-39608877-5.

The Personnel Policy Handbook for Growing Companies. Darien McWhirter. Bob Adams, Inc., 1994, ISBN: 1-55850-430-3.

Small Claims Court Without a Lawyer. W. Kelsea Wilber. Sourcebooks Inc., ISBN: 0-942061-32-2.

Additional Reading

The 7 Habits of Highly Effective People. Covey. Fireside/Simon & Schuster, 1989, ISBN: 0-671-70863-5.

1000 Things You Never Learned in Business School. Yeomans. Mentor, 1985, ISBN: 0-451-62810-1.

Beyond Entrepreneurship. Collins and Lazier. Prentice Hall, 1992, ISBN: 0-13-085366-6.

Business Owner's Guide to Accounting and Bookkeeping. Placencia, Welge, and Oliver. Oasis Press, 1991, ISBN: 1-55571-156-1.

The Complete Idiot's Guide to Business Management. Klopp. Macmillan, 1997, ISBN: 0-02-861744-4.

The Complete Idiot's Guide to Marketing Basics. White. Macmillan, 1997, ISBN: 0-02-861490-9.

The CompuServe Yellow Pages. Tidrow. New Riders Publishing, 1994, ISBN: 1-56205-396-5.

The Entrepreneur's Business Law Handbook. Melvin. Macmillan, 1997, ISBN: 0-02-861751-7.

Essentials of Media Planning. Barban, Cristol, and Kopec. NTC Business Books, 1989, ISBN: 0-8442-3018-9.

Exporting, Importing and Beyond. Tuller. Adams Media Corporation, 1994, ISBN: 1-55850-777-9.

Financing the Small Business. Tuller. Prentice Hall, 1991, ISBN: 0-13-322116-4.

Free Money for Small Businesses and Entrepreneurs. Blum. John Wiley, 1992, ISBN: 0-471-58122-4.

Home Based Mail Order. Bond. Liberty Press, 1990, ISBN: 0-8306-3045-7.

How to Advertise and Promote Your Small Business. McClung and Siegel. Wiley Press, 1978, ISBN: 0-471-04032-0.

How to Start a Service Business. Chant and Morgan. Avon, 1994, ISBN: 0-380-77-77-6.

How to Think Like an Entrepreneur. Shane. Bret Publishing, 1994, ISBN: 0-9640346-0-3.

Inc Yourself. McQuown. Harper Business, 1992, ISBN: 0-88730-611-X.

Insider's Guide to Growing a Small Business. Richman. Macmillan, 1997, ISBN: 0-02-861176-4.

The Internet Business Guide. Resnick and Taylor. Sams, 1994, ISBN: 0-672-30530-5.

Internet Yellow Pages. New Riders Publishing, 1997, ISBN: 1-56205-784-7.

One Minute for Myself. Spencer. Avon, 1985, ISBN: 0-380-70308-4.

Start, Run and Profit from Your Own Home-Based Business. Kishel. John Wiley, 1991, ISBN: 0-471-52587-1.

Starting an Import/Export Business. Entrepreneur Magazine Group. John Wiley and Sons, Inc., 1995, ISBN: 0-471-11059-0.

Starting Right in Your New Business. Tetreault and Clements. Addison-Wesley, 1988, ISBN: 0-201-07795-7.

Strategic Planning for the Small Business. Rice. Bob Adams, Inc., 1990, ISBN: 1-55850-858-9.

The Strategy Game. Hickman. McGraw-Hill, 1993, ISBN: 0-07-028725-2.

The Successful Business Plan. Abrams. Oasis Press, 1993, ISBN: 1-55571-194-4.

Tax Deductions for Small Business. Weltman. J.K. Lasser, 1997, ISBN: 0-02-860313-3.

Using CompuServe. Ellsworth. Que, 1994, ISBN: 1-56529-726-1.

West's Business Law. Clarkson, Miller, Jentz, and Cross. West Publishing Company, 1989, ISBN: 0-314-47214-2.

Your Income Tax. Lasser. Macmillan, 1998, ISBN: 0-02-861996-X.

Business Buzzword Glossary

accounting period   A period of time used to correlate revenues and expenses usually defined as a day, week, month, quarter, or year.

accrual basis of accounting   A method of accounting that relates revenues and expenses based on when the commitments are made as opposed to when the cash is spent or received.

action plans   The steps needed to achieve a specific goals.

advisory board   A group of business associates who act as advisors to your company on an informal basis. You can set regular meeting dates and times for the group to come together to discuss business issues, but you do not compensate advisors for their advice. You may want to pay for dinner, however, so they know you appreciate their time.

analysis statement   A statement provided by your bank that details the various deposits and charges associated with your business account. It is used to detail the bank account service fee amounts.

articles of incorporation   A set of documents that are filed with the secretary of state's office that formally establish your corporation in that state.

assets   Those items of value the company owns, such as cash in the checking account, accounts receivables, equipment, and property.

authorized shares   The total number of shares of stock the corporation is permitted to issue. For instance, if 1,000 shares of stock are authorized at the start of the corporation, only a total of 1,000 shares can ever be sold to shareholders—no more than that.

bad debt ratio   The amount of money you believe customers will never pay (also called uncollectible funds), divided by total sales and expressed as a percent.

balance sheet   One type of financial statement that you (or your accountant) create to show all the company's assets and all the liabilities and equity owned by investors. The value of your assets must equal the value of your liabilities and equity for the statement to balance, which is where the term came from.

banking day   The days of the week that banks are open for business. You must make deposits at the bank before a certain time of day, which is usually around 2:00 p.m., for the deposit to be credited on that same day. If you make the deposit after the 2:00 p.m. cutoff, the deposit is not credited to your account until the next banking day, which may be the next day. If you make a deposit near the end of the week, the next banking day may not be until Monday of the next week.

benefit   What the customer gains by using your product or service. For example, the benefit of the drill bit is that it makes holes.

board of accountancy   The group of accountants that make decisions regarding generally accepted accounting principles.

board of directors   A group of experienced business leaders who are asked or elected to serve as advisors to a company. In return for assuming responsibility for the long-term growth of the company, directors generally receive either cash compensation or shares of stock. In other cases, the largest shareholders may ask for or require a seat on the board of directors as a means of protecting their large stake in the company.

bookkeeping   A system for accurately tracking where your money is coming from and where it is going. You can hire a bookkeeper to manage your record-keeping or invest in a computer program to do much the same thing. Bookkeepers are not necessarily accountants, although they do help organize all your information for use by your accountant.

break-even analysis   An analysis technique used to determine the quantity of an item that must be produced and/or sold to cover the fixed expenses associated with the time period in question.

break-even point   The quantity point where the gross margin equals the fixed expenses for the period in question. Above the break-even point, the company makes money and below the break-even point, the company loses money.

browser   A software program that runs on a computer and allows Internet HTML pages to be properly viewed.

business inertia   The inability of a company to change its thinking or ways of doing business. Generally, larger, more bureaucratic companies have more inertia than smaller, leaner businesses that can respond quickly to changes in the marketplace.

business judgment rule   A concept that protects members of corporate boards of directors from lawsuits filed by shareholders, customers, or others if the decision that caused the lawsuit was made in the best interests of the corporation.

business plan   A document that outlines your overall business objectives, their viability, and the steps you intend to take to achieve those objectives. Can be for internal use, external use, or both.

bylaws   The overall rules for operation of a corporation. Bylaws are an integral part of the corporation filing procedure.

C corporation   The business structure used primarily by major corporations so they can sell shares of stock to the public. Other forms of a corporation have restrictions on the number of shareholders that can exist, but a C corporation does not.

calendar fiscal year   A company which has its financial year start on January 1 and end on December 31.

card processing company   A company that processes the credit card transactions for the retailers by verifying the account validity, credit amounts available, and the transfer of funds into your company checking account.

cash basis of accounting   A method of accounting where expenses and revenues are tracked based on when cash is received or actual checks are written.

cash flow analysis   A financial statement that shows how much money the company had at the beginning of the month, how much money came in through sales and payments, how much went out in the form of payments, and what was left at the end of the month. Successful entrepreneurs carefully watch the amount of money coming in and going out of a company (cash flow) so the business doesn't run out of cash.

chain style franchise   A franchise arrangement where the franchisee pays a fee for an established chain store outlet like Midas or McDonald's.

chart of accounts   A list of all the categories a business uses to organize its financial expenditures and sales.

class of stock   Corporations can issue different types of stock that each have different legal rights with regard to dividends, voting, and other rights. Each of these different stock categories is called a class of stock.

clipping services   Companies such as Bacon's and Luce Clipping Services that read thousands of newspapers and magazines on the lookout for articles about or references to specific companies. Many businesses hire clipping services to watch for articles about their company and the competition. Unless you have the time to read virtually every major business magazine and newspaper, you might want to hire some professionals to do it for you.

close   A request by the salesperson for a specific action on the customer's part. Asking for the order is the ultimate close, but there are smaller closes that occur at each stage of the selling process to gradually move the customer closer to the sale.

close corporation   A company where owners or shareholders are active in the daily management of the corporation, which has no public investors.

commodities   Products that have no distinguishing features or benefits, such as flour, salt, and pork bellies, so that there is little or no difference in pricing between competitive products.

company policy manual   A manual that outlines the overall company policies that apply to all employees.

consideration   Something of value, such as money or a right to do something, that is given usually at the signing of a contract.

content (Web site)   The information included in a Web site that is viewed by Internet visitors.

corporation   A legal entity that is created as an umbrella under which business operation can occur. Corporations are chartered with the state and come in various forms such as the S corporation and the Limited Liability Corporation (LLC).

cost of sales   The costs directly linked to the production or sale of a product or service, also called the Cost of Goods Sold (COGS). These generally include the cost of raw materials, the cost of labor to run the machine that produced the widget you sold, and other expenses that were required to sell the product or service.

cost plus profit pricing   Calculating your price using the cost to the company plus your desired profit margin. A widget that costs $1 to produce with a desired 50 percent profit margin would sell for $1 + ($1 \times .5) = $1.50

credit card transaction processing company   An organization that processes the typical credit card transaction and handles the transfer of funds from a credit card account into yours.

current assets   Company assets that are liquid or can be converted to cash in less than one year.

cyberspace   A term used to designate the networked computer world that continues to permeate business.

debt financing   A means of securing funding to start or expand your business by way of a loan of some sort. The business takes on debt, instead of investors, as a way of getting the money it needs now.

demographic profile   Usually refers to a specific set of demographic characteristics used by sales and marketing to target likely sales prospects. Sometimes called an ideal customer profile.

demographics   A set of objective characteristics that describe a group of people. Includes characteristics such as age, home ownership, number of children, marital status, residence location, job function, and other criteria.

depreciation   An accounting procedure that deducts a certain amount of an asset's worth for each year of its operation.

direct competitor   Anyone who can, and will, eat your lunch today if you let them. (These are companies that sell the same product or service your company does, going after the same customers.)

direct shareholder vote   A voting procedure where the shareholders personally cast their votes instead of voting by proxy.

distribution channel   However your product or service gets from your facilities into the hands of customers. Different ways of distributing your product include direct sales, employees selling your offerings, retail stores, mail order, and independent sales representatives or manufacturers' representatives.

distributor franchise   A franchise arrangement where the franchisee actually acts as a distributor for a major manufacturer's products, such as with a large auto dealership.

dividends   Money paid to shareholders out of the corporation's net income (after taxes are taken out). This is a form of compensation to the shareholders for having made the investment in the corporation by purchasing shares.

doing business as d/b/a   When you start a sole proprietorship that is named something other than your given name, you must complete some forms to officially use that name. The form you complete is a doing business as, or d/b/a, form. For instance, Jane Smith & Associates would need to file a d/b/a at the county clerk's office because the name is something other than just Jane Smith.

domain name   A unique name used to define an Internet location.

double taxation   Where the business pays tax on its annual profits and then passes the income to you, the majority shareholder, who again gets taxed at the personal level; thus, the same dollar is taxed twice.

Earned income   Income attributed to business operations during a specific period of time.

electronic mail   A method of sending mail from one location to another using an electronic delivery medium such as the Internet.

employee manual   A document prepared by the company and issued to all employees, indicating the company's policies and procedures.

employer identification number (EIN)   A number issued by the IRS to any company with employees.

Entrepreneur   Someone who is willing to take personal and financial risks to create a business out of a perceived opportunity. A cool person who bought this book and wants to make more money than the rest running the show.

equity financing   When someone gives you money in return for ownership of a portion of your company. You are giving up equity in the business in return for capital, which is equity financing. The other kind of financing is debt financing, which is when you get a loan that is paid back later. Equity financing does not get paid back. Investors get their money back by selling their shares to someone else.

exchange rate   The rate at which one form of currency is converted into another.

exchange rate liability   The uncertainty that comes from holding a purchase/sale agreement that is not in your home country's currency in an environment where exchange rates change.

factoring   The process of receiving money now for payments your customers are expected to make to you in the next few weeks. There is a cost to having that money now, which is paid in the form of a percentage fee to the factoring company or factor.

feature   The different characteristics of a product or service. For example, the features of a drill bit might include its size, length, and the type of material it is made of.

federal tax deposit coupon   Coupons issued by the IRS for collection of employee withholding taxes on a regular basis. Your employee identification number (EIN) and the amount due for the tax period are printed on the coupon. The coupon then accompanies your check made payable for the amount due.

fictitious name statement   See doing business as d/b/a.

fiscal year   The period of time over which you track your annual business accounting operations.

fixed expenses   Business expenses that do not vary each month based on the amount of sales, such as rent, equipment leases, and salaries. Payments for these expenses are essentially the same each month, whether you achieve $1 million or $1 in sales.

float   The time period during which you have to cover expenses that should have been paid out of money received from customers. During this time, you are essentially lending money to your customers.

forum   A site on a computer service in which people with similar interests can post and read messages.

franchisor   A company that has created a successful business operation and concept that offers to sell the rights to the operation and idea on a limited geographic or market basis. The buyer of the franchise rights is called the franchisee.

freelancer   An individual who works for several different companies at once, helping out on specific projects. Freelancers are like consultants; they are paid a set rate for their services and receive no benefits, no sick pay, and no vacation allowance. The advantage is that freelancers can usually set their own hours, earn a higher hourly rate than they would get from full-time employment, and work with more than one company at a time.

freight forwarder   A company that specializes in shipping, duties, customs, and other administrative complexities related to international commerce.

gating item   The section of a process that limits the overall process speed. Increase the gating item's throughput and you increase the overall process throughput.

Gantt chart   A method of tracking project items so that their order of completion, time frame, and status are easily monitored.

gross profit   The amount of money left after you cover the cost of sales. Out of gross profit, you pay your operational expenses. Gross profit = revenue – cost of sales.

Hypertext Markup Language (HTML)   The programming code embedded in a Web site's pages that is interpreted by a browser for display on the user's computer.

IBM clone   A personal computer that uses technology similar to that used for the IBM personal computers.

income   The amount of money left over after expenses are deducted from the sales revenue amount.

income statement   A type of financial statement that reflects all the income and expenses for a particular period of time, which is generally a year.

independent contractor   Another word that the IRS frequently uses for a freelancer. It means that the company you're doing work for is not your employer. You have the freedom to decide when, where, and how you will get the work done that your client has given you. You pay your own taxes and benefits, but you can also deduct expenses associated with getting your work done, such as a business phone line, travel, and supplies.

industrial espionage   The practice of collecting information about competitors through devious methods. Using public information sources that everyone has access to isn't considered espionage, but rummaging through corporate waste paper baskets after hours would be.

inertia   Indisposition to motion, exertion, or change; resistance to change.

initial public offering (IPO)   A stock trading event where the stock for a corporation is offered to the general public for the first time.

interests   Things that you enjoy doing, including the parts of your current job that you like the most, as well as what you do for fun in your spare time.

Internet   An electronically connected network of computers that spans the globe. Once you are connected to it, the usage is typically provided at a flat fee for unlimited usage.

Internet service provider (ISP)   A company that provides access to the Internet for users with a computer, modem, and the proper software.

job description   A detailed listing of the duties to be performed by the person filling the job in question; a listing of the required skills, education, certification levels, and other criteria directly related to the job.

job shop operation   A company which has a process flow that creates unique items at lower production volumes for each of its customers, as opposed to producing a standardized product in high volumes.

letter of credit (L/C)   A financial note that is set up through international banks by buyers and sellers who reside in different countries. Establishes a third party bank-to-bank handshake to ensure that both sides of the transaction are executed properly.

liabilities   Amounts that you owe. Typical liabilities include loans, credit cards, taxes owed, and other people to whom you owe money. Short-term liabilities, which are paid back within 12 months, are also called accounts payable. Long-term liabilities include mortgages and equipment loans.

life cycle   The four general phases that a product or service goes through between being introduced to the market and being discontinued or taken off the market.

limited liability company (LLC)   A new type of business structure available in almost every state that has many of the advantages of a partnership or subchapter S corporation but fewer of its disadvantages.

limited partnership   A special form of partnership in which a partner invests money and does not participate in the daily operation of the business. This partner is also only liable for the amount of money he has invested and no more.

link   A technological tool used to connecting one Internet site's pages with Web site pages either on the home site or on another. A simple click on a link takes the viewer to the next page location attached to the link.

liquid assets   Anything the company owns that can be quickly sold and turned into cash, such as accounts receivables, computer equipment, or stocks and bonds. Assets such as buildings or huge machinery would not be considered liquid because selling them would take a considerable amount of time.

logistics   The set of activities that deal with making the daily routine effective. The daily grind of answering the phone, mailing letters, and dealing with customers takes time. You will probably need clerical help once you become successful to offload the daily routine paperwork so you can have time for other activities.

long-term goals   Goals that extend beyond the next twelve months.

maintenance temperament   Someone who enjoys keeping established systems running like a well-oiled machine.

managerial accountants   People who help you use your financial information to make business decisions. Generally, these accountants are on staff at a company and are responsible for record-keeping and reporting.

manipulation   When customers feel that they are not in control of the sales process—that they will be encouraged and persuaded to purchase something they don't really need. Underlying this activity is the sense the salesperson really doesn't have the customer's needs and interests at heart.

manufacturing franchise   A franchise arrangement where the franchisees are licensed to manufacture a specific product such as Coca-Cola.

manufacturing requirement package (MRP)   A software package that integrates production forecasts with purchasing volumes to ensure that component parts needed to assemble final product are available to meet production schedules.

market maker   A company with the clout to create an entire market opportunity simply by its involvement. IBM and Microsoft are examples of market makers in the high technology area.

market niche   A segment of the market that has an existing need for a product or service that nobody currently offers.

market penetration   The percent of prospective users of your products and/or services who are already existing customers.

market positioning   Creating a positive image in the minds of potential and existing customers. The purpose of market positioning is to have potential customers perceive your product or service in a particular way that makes them more likely to want to buy from you.

market segmentation   Dividing the total available market (everyone who may ever buy) into smaller groups, or segments, by specific attributes such as age, sex, location, interests, industry, or other pertinent criteria.

market value   The value of a product or service as determined by what the market will pay for it. The market value of a used computer is much less than what a business probably paid for it because computer values decline quickly.

market-based pricing   Where offerings are priced at a level set by what everyone else is charging, rather than by costs. With this strategy, you can generally make more money, assuming your competition is charging reasonable rates and you can keep your costs down.

marketing   Selecting the right product, pricing strategy, promotional program, and distribution outlets for your particular audience or market.

marketing theme   The overall thought that pops into people's minds when they think of your company and its offerings. For example, Pepsi's theme is "youth." Its soda is the drink for people who feel, or really are, young—the "new" generation.

markup   The amount of money over and above the cost of producing a product or service that is added to pay for overhead expenses and profit.

mass producers   Companies that produce the same product(s) in very high volume as opposed to a large number of products with very small production runs.

merchant number   A number given to your company that is used to identify which account should be credited when a customer makes a credit card purchase. It also verifies that you're allowed to accept credit cards in payment.

mind share   The portion of a person's thinking processes that includes perceptions of your company's offerings. One hundred percent mind share means that any time he needs your type of offering, he thinks of your company.

mission statement   A simple statement that clearly defines the overall goals, or mission, of the company.

momemtum   Describes the direction in which things are naturally moving and implies the amount of work or energy that would be needed to change the natural course of the business as it is currently operating.

net income   Money left over after all company expenses have been paid out of revenues. Net income can be either positive or negative, depending on how good a year you had, but it can't stay negative for long or you'll be bankrupt.

noncompete clause   An agreement that employees or suppliers sign indicating they won't steal your ideas or business methods and go to work for a competitor or become competitors by starting their own firm. Generally, noncompete clauses are one section in a larger employment agreement.

non-solicitation clause   A statement included in most noncompete agreements that restricts former employees from contacting prior customers with the intention of soliciting business from that customer for the employee's current employer.

nuisance   Someone who takes up a lot of your time but really poses no threat to your lunch plans. (A weak competitor who has no clue.)

objectives   Goals that define the overall direction of an organization, which can be divided into a number of shorter range action items.

officers   Senior members of a management team or board of directors elected to serve as secretary, treasurer, president, and vice president of the corporation or board.

operational expenses   Those expenses associated with just running your business. No matter how much you sell this month, you will still have these expenses. These include your salary, your rent payment, the cost of the electricity in your office, and other similar costs of operating the company.

opportunity cost   The profit that would have been gained by pursuing another investment instead of the one currently in process. For example, if you go out on a date with one person, you lose the potentially good time you could have had with someone else. Sound familiar? That is opportunity cost.

outsourcing   Corporate-speak for hiring outside consultants, freelancers, or companies to provide services that in the past have been provided by employees.

over-promise   When you promise more to a customer than you actually deliver. It is never a good idea if you want to keep happy customers.

over-deliver   Delivering more to the customer than was agreed to, or more than the customer expected. It is usually a good idea if you can afford it.

owner's equity   What is left over when the liabilities are subtracted from the assets. Take what you have, subtract what you owe, and you are left with owner's equity. This is the number that you want to maximize because it reflects the value of your company. The initial value of your company stock and retained earnings are added together to calculate owner's equity.

partnership   When you and one or more people form a business marriage; your debts and assets are legally linked from the start. Any partner can make a commitment for the business, which also commits the other partners.

pending event   An future event with a specific date that forces business people to make decisions that they would otherwise put off until later.

perceived value   The overall value the customer places on a particular product or service. This includes much more than price and considers other features such as delivery lead time, quality of salesmanship, service, style, and other less tangible items than the price. Essentially, a perceived value pricing strategy means determining what people are willing to pay and charging that amount, assuming you can still cover all your costs.

percentage markup   The amount of money a business adds into a product's price, over and above the cost of the product, expressed as a percent. A piece of candy costing $.05 to produce that has a markup of $.10 (meaning that the price to the consumer is $.15) has a percentage markup of 200 percent. This is calculated by taking the original cost, dividing it into the amount of markup, and then multiplying the result times 100.

performance to plan   A measurement tool used by investors to determine how close an organization is to performing according to the initial business plan goals.

personal attributes   Things such as being patient, working with other people, taking initiative, and other intrinsic personality-related traits.

Potential sale revenue   A measurement of the total amount of money that can be made from a specific customer or event.

pretax profit   The amount of money left over after all the business expenses and costs of goods sold are subtracted from total sales, but before taxes have been subtracted and paid.

price erosion   When competitive sales present enough alternate product selections to your customers that you must drop your price to keep their business. This erodes both price and profit margins.

price war   When all competitors compete based on price and keep undercutting their competitors to get sales. As each company lowers its own price, others drop their prices to compete, resulting in profit margins in the industry as a whole falling to critically low levels.

probationary period   A time frame within which an employee is evaluated by the company, and vice versa. At the end of the probation period the employee and company can part ways with no negative implications or connotations.

product positioning   A conscious attempt on the part of your company to differentiate between your offering and those of your competitors. You position your product in people's minds by creating a perception of your product or service so that potential customers think of your products or services when they have a need.

professional corporation   A type of corporation, such as the subchapter S and subchapter C used by professionals such as attorneys and accountants. Such corporations have P.C. after the company name to indicate the company is a professional corporation.

pro-forma balance sheet   A balance sheet comprised of numbers that are calculated based on historical performance and known future events. Typically used to project future financial expectations.

prospectus   A formal legal document a company prepares before being able to sell shares of stock to the public. The prospectus details all the pros and cons of investing in that company, so the potential purchaser of the company's stock is fully informed of the potential risks up front.

proxy statement   A form distributed to shareholders who will not be attending the company's annual meeting so their votes regarding the election of the board of directors, or other issues, can be counted. If a shareholder cannot attend the company's annual meeting but wants to vote, he can submit a signed proxy statement turning over the right to vote a certain way to the board.

Publicity   Working with the media to have your company covered by the professional media such as magazine, newspaper, TV, and radio.

pull and push marketing strategy   A pull strategy convinces your potential customers to request your offering through their suppliers. In essence, the end user pulls your offering through the distribution channel by putting pressure on suppliers to carry it in their inventory. A push strategy sells your product to distributors, who then promote it to their customers. A pull strategy is driven by customers. A push strategy is driven by distributors.

registered agent   The official contact point for all legal matters. The registered agent is located at the registered office, which is the official address for corporate business.

retained earnings   Earnings from the company that are reinvested in operating the business. An item usually found on a company's balance sheet.

revenue   Money you receive from customers as payment for your services or the sale of your product. Some people also call it sales.

routine tasks   Things you do that are pretty much the same as the last time you did them, except for minor variations. Printing out monthly invoices or counting inventory are two routine tasks that don't take much brain power but that have to be done.

sales   Begins where marketing leaves off and involves all the steps you take to get the customer to buy your product or service.

sales revenue targets   The sales goals you set that affect all the other financial figures.

scattergun marketing   A scattergun sends buckshot in a wide pattern in the hopes of hitting something. Scattergun marketing sends marketing information everywhere in the hopes that someone will hear it and buy—the opposite of target marketing.

Securities and Exchange Commission (SEC)   A regulatory body that monitors and defines policy for the exchange of stock on the public markets.

scope of work   A highly recommended section of a proposal that defines the overall intent of the work to be performed. This can be detailed or simple, depending on the work to be performed.

search engine   Internet technology that allows a program to categorize Web site information in such a way that a search can be performed on the site based on specific key words.

secured line of credit   A line of credit that has some form of asset such as account receivable or equipment as collateral for the loan.

shareholders   Any individual or organization that owns shares of stock in a company.

short-term goals   Goals that occur within a short period of time and, ideally, lead to the completion of a long-term goal.

short-term loan   A loan that is to be paid off within one year.

shrinkage   The loss of product due any number of means including loss in shipment or theft.

skills   Acquired skills such as typing, speaking a foreign language, playing golf, and so on. Natural skills are inherent and less quantifiable such as speaking voice quality, physical appearance, running speed, etc.

sole proprietorship   You transact business without the legal "safety net" associated with a corporation. You are personally responsible for all the business's obligations, such as debt.

start-up temperament   Someone who thrives on new and exciting projects and challenges.

strategy   A careful plan or method; the art of devising or employing plans toward a goal.

S corporation   A type of corporation that has a limited number of shareholders, and the profits are passed directly through to the owner.

suite   A term used in relation to software where a number of different application programs are sold under the same name, so that purchasing a single product actually provides a variety, or suite, of other software packages.

sunk cost   Money already spent that you cannot recover. Does not take into account opportunity cost or how else you could have spent the money.

superstore   An organization that provides a little, or a lot, of everything as opposed to specializing in a specific area.

tactics   Relating to small-scale actions serving a larger purpose, such as a strategy.

target marketing   A marketing approach involving focusing your marketing efforts on those groups—those potential customers—most likely to buy your products or services.

tasks   Things that need to be completed as part of working toward goals.

tax accounting   A type of accounting concerned solely with how much money you will have to pay in taxes. Tax accountants can help you take steps to minimize your tax bill.

under-deliver   Delivering less to the customer than you promised. Guaranteed to create a disappointed customer.

under-promise   Promising less to a customer than you actually plan to deliver.

underwriter   A company responsible for marketing and selling shares of stock in a company to outside investors.

unearned income   Payments made by a customer for work that has not yet been performed that show up as income on the financial statements.

unqualified prospect   An individual who says he needs your product or service but who has not yet confirmed he is able to make the purchase decision.

unsecured line of credit   A line of credit such as a credit card that a company can turn to for cash and that is not backed by some form of collateral. Secured lines of credit are usually backed by some form of deposit, accounts receivable statement, or other company asset that the bank can use to pay off the debt if the company can't pay off the line of credit.

variable expenses   Those costs that vary according to how much of a product or service is produced. Just as things usually cost less when you buy them in bulk, producing a product in large quantities works the same way. The more you produce, generally the lower the cost per product. The cost of sales varies according to how much is produced.

wealth   Consistently having money left over after all your bills are paid.

World Wide Web (WWW)   The interconnection of many Internet locations, or sites. These sites consist of HTML-coded pages that are read by a user's browser. These sites also refer to each other through links so that users can easily move from one Internet site to another.

Index

Symbols

3 C's of credit policies, 230
90-day probationary periods for
  employees, 254-255

A

accounting
  accounting periods, 169, 363
  automated, 294-295
  bookkeeping, 184-186
  chart of accounts, 175
  financial statement types, 174
  Generally Accepted Accounting
    Principles (GAAP), 169
  income
    earned versus unearned,
      170-171
    statements, 175-176
  managerial accounting,
    184-186
  methods, cash basis versus
    accrual, 171-172
  payroll software, 288
  periods, 361
  personnel, selecting, 186
  purpose, 169
  services, payroll tax preparation,
    271
  software packages, 186
  tax accounting, 184-186
  types, 184-186
accounts payable, 178
accounts receivable
  aging reports, 231
  factoring process
    and cash flow, 204
    loan percentage, 204-205
accrual basis of accounting, 363
  advantages, 173
  defined, 171
  disadvantages, 173-174
  preference by large businesses,
    171-172
  reasons for use, 171-172
  scenario, 173
  tax complications, 173
  versus cash basis of accounting,
    171-172
acquiring business franchises, 80
Adobe PageMill, 160
advertising
  cooperative, 119
  infomercials, 120

mind share, 118
  on Internet, 120
  primary purpose, 118
  radio/TV, 119
  Yellow Pages, 119
advisory boards, 363
  versus board of directors, 94
*Almanac of Business and Industrial
  Financial Ratios* (Prentice Hall),
  232
alternatives to starting own
  business, 35
America Online (AOL), 156
  cost, 297
  subscription information, 297
American Association of Franchisees & Dealers Web site, 356
American Chamber of Commerce
  Executives Web site, 351
American Demographics, 26
  Web site, 108
American Express, credit card
  processing, terminal fees,
  216-217
American Society of Women
  Entrepreneurs Web site, 358
American Stock Exchange (AMEX),
  210
American Success Institute Web
  site, 353
Americans with Disabilities Act
  (ADA), 281
analysis, financial
  credit checks, 230
  financial statements, 184
  niche, superstore versus
    specialty store, 146-147
  pricing strategies, 111-112
analysis paralysis, 47-48
analysis statements, 363
articles of incorporation, 89, 361
  automated software packages,
    95-96
  elements
    board of directors, 93
    capital structure, 92
    company purpose, 92
    initial capitalization, 93
    legal address, 93
    name of corporation, 92
    name of incorporator, 94
    period of duration, 92
    registered agent, 93
assessing risks, 48-49
assets, 363
  bank sell-offs, 195
  book value, 178
  calculating, 177-179

defined, 178
  depreciation, 177
  fixed types, 178
  market value, 178
assigning priorities to tasks, 47
AT&T WorldNet (ISP), 156
authority, delegating, 42-44
authorized shares (corporations),
  92, 363
automated accounting, 294-295
automated software packages,
  business plans, 67-68
automation
  computers versus manual
    record-keeping, 286-287
  strategies
    accounting/payroll software,
      288
    data backups, 289
    high quality printers/copiers,
      289
    office suite software
      packages, 288
    routine tasks, 287
average price, calculating, 34-35

B

bad checks, displaying, 228
bad debts
  collecting, 231
  effect on profit margins, 226
  IRS tax implications, 234
  ratios, 364
    type of business, 232
balance sheets, 364
  account types, 179
  asset calculation, 177-181
  financial statement type, 174
  liabilities, 178
  net income, 178
  owner's equity, 178
  retained earnings, 178
banking days, 364
banks
  as source of monies, 190-191
  business failures of the 1980's,
    191
  conservative lending practices,
    193
  default scenario, 193
  loan officers, relationship
    development, 191-192
  loans
    equipment purchases,
      206-207

381

J - K

Java, Web site functions, 163
job descriptions, creating, 251-252, 262
job experience as selection factor in own business, 22-23
job shops versus mass producers, 304-306

Kwik Chek Auto (sample business plan)
competition, 334-335
conclusions, 338-339
executive summary, 326-327
fixed and variable cost analysis, 336-337
legal considerations, 352
management team, 335
market need definition, 328-329
marketing strategy, 336
operations analysis, 335-336
overall financial analysis, 337-338
overview, 325-326
pricing structure, 333
revenue potential analysis, 332-334
sales potential, 334
service identification, 329-332

L

large banks versus small banks, lending guidelines, 198-199
lawyers
appropriate situations, 82-83
selecting, 83
leasing
computers, 290
office space, 282
legal aspects of business
corporations, 73-78
advantages/disadvantages, 76-77
privately-held corporations, 77-78
professional corporations, 80
registering, 82
S corporations, 78
franchises, 80-82
acquisition process, 80
types, 81
lawyers
appropriate situations, 82-83
selecting, 83
limited liability companies (LLCs), 79-80
multistate businesses, 82

partnerships, 72-76
general partners, 75
limited liability partnerships (LLPs), 75
Uniform Partnership Act (UPA), 72
sole propietorships, 72
employer identification number (EIN), 75
advantages/disadvantages, 74
doing business as (d/b/a) forms, 74
employees, 75
lending monies, bank requirements, 190-191
letters of credit (L/C), 228, 370
confirmed, 240
documentary, 240
irrevocable, 240
processing, 240-242
types, 242
warnings, 241
liabilities, 370
long-term, 178
short-term, 178
Liberty Legal, corporation kits, 96
liens, filing, 233
life cycle (products)
embryonic (Stage 1), 112
market decline (Stage 4), 112
market growth (Stage 2), 112
maturity (Stage 3), 112
limited liability companies (LLCs), 79-80, 370
versus S corporations, 79
limited liability partnerships (LLPs), 75-76
limited partnerships, 370
linking production processes, 306-307
links to Web sites, 160-161
liquid assets, 178, 371
loans
bank discretion, public versus private, 192-199
conservative bank policies, 193
default scenario, 193
equipment purchases and cash flow, 206-207
factoring process, 204-205
five C's of lending, 195-196
float period, 204
large banks versus small banks, guidelines, 198-199
personal loan guarantees, 193-194
personal requirements, 195-199
repayment guarantees from SBA, 198
Small Business Administration (SBA)
atttractiveness to banks, 198
insurance fees, 198

small business versus corporations, risk levels, 192-194
types
short-term loans, 194
unsecured line of credit, 194
logistics, 43
"long distance" incorporation, 88
long-term earning potential, evaluating, 30-32
long-term planning, 39-40
LowDoc loan program, Small Business Administration (SBA), 197
Luce Press Clippings, 142
Lycos Web site, 162

M

MacWorld magazine, 83
magazines
Home Office Computing, 83
MacWorld, 83
PC Magazine, 83
PC World, 83
mail order products, 122
maintaining cash flow
credit terms, 206
equipment purchases with credit, 206-207
maintenance temperament, 371
managerial accounting, 184-186, 371
manipulative selling, 126
manual credit card processing versus electronic means, 216
manual record-keeping versus computer automation, 286-287
manufacturer's representatives, 136
manufacturing franchises, 81, 369
manufacturing requirement packages (MRP), 307, 371
markups on products, 121-122
market decline (Stage 4), product life cycle, 112
market growth (Stage 2), product life cycle, 112
market maker, 369
versus followers, 148
market needs as selection factor in own business, 26
market niches, 149, 371
market penetration, 371
market positioning, 371
market segmentation, 372
market value, 372
market-based pricing, 109-112, 372
marketing
business plan elements, 53
defined, 106
demographics, 107-108
infomercials, 120
messages, consistency, 114-115